The World of Deaf Infants

Perspectives on Deafness

Series Editors
Marc Marschark
Patricia Elizabeth Spencer

The World of Deaf Infants: A Longitudinal Study
Kathryn P. Meadow-Orlans, Patricia Elizabeth Spencer,
and Lynne Sanford Koester

The World of Deaf Infants

A Longitudinal Study

KATHRYN P. MEADOW-ORLANS
PATRICIA ELIZABETH SPENCER
LYNNE SANFORD KOESTER

OXFORD
UNIVERSITY PRESS
2004

OXFORD
UNIVERSITY PRESS

Oxford New York
Auckland Bangkok Buenos Aires Cape Town Chennai
Dar es Salaam Delhi Hong Kong Istanbul Karachi Kolkata
Kuala Lumpur Madrid Melbourne Mexico City Mumbai Nairobi
Sao Paulo Shanghai Taipei Tokyo Toronto

Published by Oxford University Press, Inc.
198 Madison Avenue, New York, New York 10016
www.oup.com

Illustrations by Liz Conces Spencer

Library of Congress Cataloging-in-Publication Data
Meadow-Orlans, Kathryn P.
The world of deaf infants : a longitudinal study /
Kathryn P. Meadow-Orlans, Patricia Elizabeth Spencer,
and Lynne Sanford Koester.
p. cm.—(Perspectives on deafness)
Includes bibliographical references and index.
ISBN 0-19-514790-1
1. Deaf children—Family relationships—Longitudinal studies.
2. Infants—Care—Longitudinal studies.
I. Spencer, Patricia Elizabeth.
II. Koester, Lynne Sanford.
III. Title. IV. Series.
HV 2391 .M4 2004 362.4′2′0832—dc22 2003018781

1 2 3 4 5 6 7 8 9

Printed in the United States of America
on acid-free paper

Foreword

Anyone who knows the research literature pertaining to deaf infants, parenting of children with special needs, or the development of deaf children is familiar with the work of Kathryn Meadow-Orlans, Patricia Spencer, and Lynne Koester. Kay Meadow-Orlans has been a pioneer in studying the development of deaf children, their social-emotional functioning, and links among communication, mother–child relations, and development. Similarly, Patricia Spencer's research on the role of deaf children's play in development and her work on mother–child attention and language interactions have made her "must" reading for anyone interested in language and social growth of deaf children. So, too, with Lynne Koester's investigations of *intuitive parenting,* the importance of touch and multisensory stimulation for deaf infants, and the relations of social-emotional development and mothers' behaviors toward their deaf babies. In short, working together and separately, these three investigators have largely defined the study of early development and parent–child relations involving deaf children, and their work has shaped research in a variety of allied fields.

Throughout their longitudinal study, Meadow-Orlans, Spencer, and Koester have welcomed research partners as colleagues, friends, and members of the laboratory "family" that grew up around the investigation. In what is surely the largest and most impressive long-term study in the field, this team has given us all a window to the world of deaf infants. Thanks largely to their efforts, we know what "works" and what does not work in early interactions of deaf infants and their parents; and we have an understanding of the interactions of social, cognitive, and language development that would not have been possible otherwise. As large and diverse as this body of literature has become, however, the study described here lies at the core of it all, providing guidance to both researchers and parents and to those students of development looking for what we know and what we still need to discover.

In the following chapters, the authors and their collaborators weave together two decades of research, the theoretical and practical considerations that led to them, and the many implications that flowed from both the core study and numerous follow-up investigations. Held together with previously unpublished work and the nuances and synergy provided by a skilled group of collaborators, the natural history of this project takes on the character of a biography, revealing much about the development of deaf infants and their interactions with the world.

The many unique aspects of this work make *The World of Deaf Infants* the perfect starting place for the new Oxford University Press *Perspectives on Deafness* series. Just as Meadow-Orlans, Spencer, and Koester had to develop new methods and integrate diverse findings in establishing an important new area of study, this series will bring together multidisciplinary perspectives in theory and research pertaining to adults and children who are deaf or hard of hearing. As with the investigation described in this book, *Perspectives on Deafness* necessarily will be broad, including language, learning, culture, and development across a variety of domains.

The authors of this volume offer an inside perspective on their groundbreaking research, presented in a way that is both comprehensive and intimate. I can think of no better way to recognize their achievements than by sharing that story with others who can take advantage of their work and build on it so as to illuminate further the world of deaf infants and to make it an even better place to live.

Marc Marschark

Acknowledgments

We are grateful, first and forever, to the eighty families who faithfully participated in the four separate data-collection sessions that made this book possible. We also acknowledge, with thanks, these funding sources: the Gallaudet Research Institute, Maternal and Child Health Research Program, Office of Special Education and Rehabilitation Research, and March of Dimes/Birth Defects Foundation. Oxford University Press editor Catherine Carlin and series co-editor Marc Marschark facilitated the editorial process in many ways, and six anonymous reviewers provided helpful feedback. Our co-authors, off-site collaborators, research assistants, and coders have been indispensable. Their names are sprinkled throughout the following pages. Our husbands—Otto Koester, Ron Outen, and Harold Orlans—each deserve a medal for distinguished service.

Bethesda, Maryland K.P.M.-O.
Bethesda, Maryland P.E.S.
Missoula, Montana L.S.K.

Contents

Contributors

LISA R. BROOKS
Department of Psychology
SUNY College at Buffalo
Buffalo, New York

BIRGIT DYSSEGAARD
Department of Education and Culture
County of Copenhagen
Denmark

CAROL J. ERTING
Department of Education
Gallaudet University
Washington, DC

ANDREA M. KARKOWSKI
Behavioral Sciences Department
Capital University
Columbus, Ohio

LYNNE SANFORD KOESTER
Department of Psychology
The University of Montana
Missoula, Montana

JENNIFER L. LUDWIG
Pine Rest Holland Clinic
Holland, Michigan

ROBERT H. MACTURK
Psychologist/Educator
Rockville, Maryland

KATHRYN P. MEADOW-ORLANS
Department of Educational Foundations and Research
Gallaudet University (Emerita)
Washington, DC

DONALD F. MOORES
Department of Education
Gallaudet University
Washington, DC

SYBIL SMITH-GRAY
Clinical Psychologist
Fort Washington, Maryland

PATRICIA ELIZABETH SPENCER
Department of Social Work
Gallaudet University
Washington, DC

ANNIE G. STEINBERG
Department of Child and Adolescent Psychiatry
University of Pennsylvania
Philadelphia, Pennsylvania

M. VIRGINIA SWISHER
Department of Instruction and Learning
University of Pittsburgh
Pittsburgh, Pennsylvania

MEG ANN TRACI
Rural Institute
The University of Montana
Missoula, Montana

ROBYN P. WAXMAN
Clinical Psychologist
Towson, Maryland

The World of Deaf Infants

1

Introduction

Kathryn P. Meadow-Orlans, Carol Erting,
and Donald F. Moores

This book reports research conducted during a 15-year period with deaf and hearing infants of hearing or deaf parents. Data were collected longitudinally when infants were 9, 12, 15, and 18 months old, with the goal of describing their social, cognitive, and communicative development, addressing broad questions about the impact of absent or diminished hearing on the babies and their parents. To evaluate and appreciate the research results, it is useful to know something of the place and time in which the work was done, as well as the backgrounds and perspectives of those involved: in short, the history of the Gallaudet Infancy Study.

Research was conducted in three phases: the pilot years (1984–87), data collection from deaf and hearing infants and their hearing parents (1987–91), and data collection from deaf and hearing infants with deaf parents (1992–95). Data analysis and report writing continued to 2003. Like any major research program, the roots of the work go much deeper than the years during which data were collected and analyzed. The research site, events in deaf education, changes in the identification of infant deafness and in the Deaf community all played a role.

Context of the Gallaudet Infancy Study (GIS)

Research Site—Gallaudet University

The Columbia Institution for the Deaf and Dumb was established in Washington, DC, in 1857 as a school for elementary and high school students. In 1864, President Lincoln signed a bill allowing the school to confer baccalaureate degrees, and college students were admitted to the collegiate branch, the National Deaf Mute College. The name was changed to Gallaudet College in 1894, in honor of Thomas Hopkins Gallaudet, a pioneer in deaf education. Congress changed the name to Gallaudet University in 1986 (Christiansen & Barnartt, 1995). Gallaudet also serves deaf preschool, elementary, and high school students at the Laurent Clerc National Deaf Education Center (formerly Kendall Demonstration Elementary School [KDES]) and Model Secondary School for the Deaf [MSSD]). The only liberal arts college in the world for deaf students, the university awards bachelor's degrees, has a variety of master's programs, and offers doctoral studies in education, psychology, and audiology. Over the years, most of the leaders of the national Deaf community have attended Gallaudet (Moores, 2001), and the institution plays an important role in Deaf culture (Padden & Humphries, 1988) not only in the United States but also throughout the world (Erting, Johnson, Smith, & Snider, 1994). This means that Gallaudet researchers are well placed to recruit participants for their projects and to benefit from the sign-language expertise of professional staff and graduate students. Conversely, because of wide perception that Gallaudet affiliates favor sign language and denigrate the use of oral communication, some potential hard-of-hearing or oral deaf participants may be less likely to participate in Gallaudet-sponsored studies. The Gallaudet Research Institute (GRI) provided generous support to this project until 1996, when shifts in administrative priorities led to the closing of most research centers, including the Center for Studies in Education and Human Development (CSEHD), which housed the infancy project.

The Times—Mid-1980s: Prevalence and Identification of Deaf Infants

By 1984, when planning for the project began, there were almost no published studies of deaf children younger than 2 years of age. There were two reasons for this lack: *(1)* the low incidence of early severe deafness and *(2)* the lag in identification time, especially for deaf infants with hearing parents, who usually had no reason to request early screening for hearing acuity.

With consensus on the importance of early intervention, and some indications that deaf infants were indeed being identified at earlier ages, the time seemed right to mount a study focusing on the beginnings of development for deaf children.

Early Team Members

One of the team leaders had written a Berkeley sociology dissertation on deafness (Meadow [-Orlans], 1967) focused on socialization practices and outcomes in hearing and deaf families with deaf children. Her focus on personality and social structure in graduate school was an important frame for future research. This was enriched through later collaboration with child psychiatrist Hilde Schlesinger at the University of California, San Francisco (UCSF) (Schlesinger & Meadow, 1972; Meadow, 1978), where the value of longitudinal data and an interdisciplinary team were demonstrated. Those were exciting times for research with deaf children and adults, and many pioneers in the field were beginning their work: William Stokoe in the Linguistics Research Laboratory at Gallaudet; Ursula Bellugi at the Salk Institute in San Diego; John Rainer and Kenneth Altshuler at the New York Psychiatric Institute; McCay Vernon and Eugene Mindel at Michael Reese Hospital in Chicago. However, federal funding became more and more difficult to obtain, and deafness was not a priority at UCSF. With support dwindling, Kay Meadow moved from California to Washington, DC, in 1976, accepting a position as Director of Research at Kendall Demonstration Elementary School on the Gallaudet campus.

Early in the California years, Meadow and Donald F. Moores met at an A. G. Bell convention where both were attending a keynote address by a specialist in language acquisition, Susan Ervin-Tripp, in which she suggested that the use of sign language might benefit some deaf children. Together, they watched in disbelief as the speaker scurried up an escape aisle with several protesting oral-only proponents in hot pursuit. As perhaps the only two audience members supporting Ervin-Tripp's position, Meadow and Moores established a relationship that led to joint workshop participation and writing projects before their Gallaudet collaboration began in 1979 when he was recruited to lead a research team at the college.

Moores had completed his dissertation at the University of Illinois on the assessment of psycholinguistic abilities of deaf adolescents (1967) after a master's degree in deaf education at Gallaudet College and a second master's at the California State University, Northridge Leadership Training Program in Deafness. At the University of Illinois, he was a research associate at the Institute for Research on Exceptional Children (IREC), working with Stephen Quigley on the first large-scale assessment of preschool programs for deaf children, and with Samuel Kirk, "the father of special education," on the standardization of the Illinois Test of Psycholinguistic Abilities. Kirk's emphasis on interdisciplinary research was to have a profound career-long effect. At the University of Minnesota, Moores was a professor of Psychoeducational Studies and director of the Research and Demonstration Center in Education of Handicapped Children, completing several research projects (Moores, 1970; Moores & Oden, 1978; Moores, Weiss, & Goodwin, 1978). He then headed the Department of Special Education at Pennsylvania State University, where he completed the first edition of what was to become a widely used text in deaf education, now in its fifth edition (Moores, 2001). In 1980, Moores was named director of the newly established Center for the Study of Education and Human Development (CSEHD) in the Gallaudet Research Institute. Meadow was appointed Senior Research Scientist in the center, joined by other members of the MSSD and KDES research units.

One of these was Carol Erting, recruited by Meadow in 1977 to work with her in the KDES research unit. She had previously taught preschool deaf children, studied the linguistics of American Sign Language (with William Stokoe) and cultural and social anthropology (at American University and the School of Oriental and African Studies in London). While a member of the KDES group, she completed a doctoral degree in anthropology (1982) at American University (Erting, 1994). Erting and Meadow's KDES research projects on attachment and the interactions of deaf toddlers with deaf and hearing mothers were important for the later design of the Gallaudet Infancy Study.

The Pilot Phase—1984 to 1987

In 1984, Meadow and Erting began to plan a major project to study deaf infants. There had been an enormous expansion of interest in and knowledge about infant development in the preceding years, particularly concerning infants' capacities to regulate social and affective interaction, to respond to environmental stimuli, and to affect the environment by those responses. Although little research had been done with deaf or hard of hearing infants, much had been done with other infants who had special needs: those born at-risk (Field, 1978, 1980); blind or multiply handicapped (Fraiberg, 1977; Tronick, & Brazelton, 1980; Als, 1982); with Down syndrome (Cicchetti & Sroufe, 1976; O. H. M. Jones, 1980), and with depressed mothers (Cohn & Tronick, 1982; Tronick & Field, 1986). Some of these investigators had demonstrated the unhappy effects of high risk or handicapping conditions on parents and/or infants. Others had reported the absence of reciprocity in dyads where infants were later found to have severe behavioral problems (Massie, 1982). Still others discovered that infants with disabilities engaged in behaviors adaptive for their particular condition, but that parents viewed these adaptive behaviors as dysfunctional because they were unlike expected responses (Roskies, 1972; Fraiberg, 1977).

The Gallaudet researchers were especially interested in research conducted by Tronick and his colleagues, investigating infants' efforts to regulate social interaction through alternating periods of looking at and looking away from a partner, usually the mother. The Still Face procedure had been developed as a way of creating mild stress for infants, providing researchers with a means of observing infants' strategies for dealing with a stressful situation (Tronick et al., 1978; Tronick, Ricks, & Cohn, 1982). The Still Face is an episode inserted in a sequence of normal mother–infant interactions during which the mother is instructed to remain motionless, noncommunicative, and without expression. This is also viewed as an analogue for the Strange Situation Procedure, developed to study attachment behavior in infants and toddlers (Ainsworth, Bell, & Stayton, 1974; Ainsworth, Blehar, Waters, & Wall, 1978), which had already been utilized with young deaf children (Greenberg & Marvin, 1979), and by the Gallaudet KDES researchers in collaboration with Mark Greenberg (Meadow, Greenberg, & Erting, 1983).

In the spring of 1984, Erting and Meadow approached Edward Tronick about receiving training in the use of the Still Face procedure as a first step in launching pilot studies of deaf infants. Tronick was receptive to the idea, and visited Gallaudet in October and December 1985 to help set up trial videotapes of mothers and infants.

The CSEHD was then housed in a newly completed KDES building, where facilities included a production-level television studio. Technical help was available with the equipment necessary for capturing mothers and infants on tape simultaneously in a split-screen format. After initial training in videotape procedures, one of Tronick's doctoral students, Andrew Gianino, made several visits over a 12-month period in 1986 to help with coding tapes using the time-intensive monadic phase system (Tronick, Als, & Brazelton, 1980).

The design for the pilot project called for the collection of mother–child interaction videotapes when infants were 3, 6, 9, and 12 months of age: deaf infants with deaf mothers (Dd), hearing infants with deaf mothers (Dh), and hearing infants with hearing mothers (Hh). Because of the early (3-month) starting point and expected delay in identification of deaf infants with hearing parents (Hd), this group was not included in the initial design.

Recruitment of Staff

The importance of an interdisciplinary team for an elaborate longitudinal study of deaf infants cannot be overstated. Specialists are needed in pediatric audiology, others fluent in American Sign Language (ASL) and Speech Supported Sign (Total Communication), developmental psychology, language and communication, research methodology, and statistics.

One of the first new staff members to be recruited was Carlene Thumann-Prezioso, a productive and valuable member of the group. She had strong interpersonal skills and was a native user of ASL. As a trained counselor, she organized a parent support group for deaf families participating in the research program, which focused on issues of child development and relationships of deaf parents with deaf or hearing children.

In late 1985, Patricia (Day) Spencer joined the group. Spencer had a master's degree in education (Boston University) and a PhD in communication disorders with a minor in child development (University of Texas at Dallas). Her background in language development and the speech sciences, including audiology, made her an ideal candidate. Early in 1986, Robert H. MacTurk accepted an appointment. His doctoral studies in developmental psychology and special education (Penn State University) led to a position in the Child and Family Research Section of the National Institute of Child Health and Human Development. This group, led by Leon Yarrow, was engaged in research on mastery motivation with Down syndrome children (see MacTurk et al., 1985).

David Deyo, a trained audiologist, contributed greatly to the project as a research associate. After his death in 1991, Victoria Trimm took his position. Visiting scientists during this period included Birgit Dyssegaard, on leave as Director of Special Education, County of Copenhagen, Denmark, and Mary Gutfreund, language specialist, from Bristol University in England. Annie Steinberg, pediatrician, child psychiatrist, and certified ASL interpreter from the University of Pennsylvania School of Medicine, participated in the project as a Robert Wood Johnson Clinical Scholar. Sybil Smith-Gray, Gallaudet graduate student in psychology, participated in several coding and analysis activities.

In 1987, Carol Erting formed her own research unit within the GRI, the Culture and Communication Studies Program. She and Carlene Thumann-Prezioso continued to be involved with the infancy work, conducting ethnographic home visits with some of the families involved with the larger project. To replace Erting on the CSEHD team, developmental psychologist Lynne Koester was recruited. After earning her PhD (University of Wisconsin), Koester taught at the University of North Carolina, Greensboro, before moving to Germany for several years. There, she worked with Hanuš and Mecthild Papoušek, who were developing their theories of intuitive parenting (Papoušek & Papoušek, 1987; see Chapter 2). When Koester accepted the CSEHD position, the team for the long-term project was essentially in place and remained intact until Koester left Gallaudet in 1993 to chair the Department of Psychology at the University of Montana.

Results of the Pilot Study

The goal of the pilot study was to observe and describe, through microanalytic techniques, the facial, tactile, and kinesthetic communication strategies used by deaf mothers with deaf or with hearing infants, and to compare these interactions with those of hearing mothers and their hearing or deaf infants. The format for the mother–infant videotaping called for the mother to sit facing her infant, who was belted in an infant seat that was (for safety) bolted to a table.[1] A Still Face episode was preceded and followed by periods of normal interaction. Several conference papers were presented, based on Monadic Phase analyses of nine infants at 3 and 6 months of age. Three infants were deaf with deaf parents (Dd), three were hearing with deaf parents (Dh), and three were hearing with hearing parents (Hh).

The results of the pilot data analyses can be summarized as follows: During the play episodes, the deaf mothers' time showing positive affect was twice that of the hearing mothers (73% vs. 37%). At 3 months all infant groups attended to mothers' faces (mean = 70%). At 6 months, Dd and Hh infants made the expected shift from attending to mothers' faces (mean = 31%) to attending to objects, whereas the Dh infants continued to focus on mothers' faces (64%) (Meadow-Orlans et al., 1987b). During the Still Face episode at 6 months, Dd and Hh infants were more likely to avert their gaze from mothers, while Dh infants were more likely to signal their mothers (MacTurk, [Spencer] Day, & Meadow-Orlans, 1986). Deaf mothers were observed to use more rhythmic, tactile, and kinesthetic interactions than were hearing mothers, interpreted as a substitute for the rhythmic vocal play that is characteristic of "motherese" and baby talk (Meadow-Orlans, Erting, Bridges-Cline, & Prezioso, 1985). Deaf mothers also were observed to modify the sign language they used, signing more slowly, shifting hand formations, simplifying grammar, and relating signs to the infant's directional gaze. Like mothers' baby talk, mothers' infant-directed sign was related to interactional context, baby's behavior, or mother's interpretation of the baby's feelings (Erting, Prezioso, & Hynes, 1990/1994).

Three deaf infants with hearing parents (Hd) were videotaped when they were between 10 and 12 months of age. Compared with three Hh infants, they were found to watch their mothers for longer time periods, to become more distressed during the Still Face segment, and to display more negative affect (Meadow-Orlans et al., 1987a). Another analysis of these data showed Hd mothers to be less responsive to their infants' object-gaze and more directive in their play interactions than Dd or Hh mothers (Spencer, Bodner-Johnson, & Gutfreund, 1992).

Research with Deaf and Hearing Infants with Hearing Parents—1987 to 1991

While pilot data were being collected and analyzed, plans also progressed for a larger, more ambitious project to study deaf and hearing infants with hearing parents. In addition to the early interaction data collected for the pilot study, the intent was to compare infants' social, cognitive, and linguistic development at several ages, and to investigate the influence of stress and support on their parents. This preparatory work included construction of a more appropriate laboratory/video studio designed specifically for infants and parents, approaches to experienced investigators/collaborators in other geographic areas, and a grant application to be submitted to a potential funding agency.

Construction of Appropriate Video Studio

Pilot project videotapes had been filmed in a studio that was not optimal for mother–infant research, so the GRI agreed to construct and equip a specially designed space within the CSEHD office area. This consisted of a 10-by-14 foot room equipped with sensitive overhead microphones and large one-way window/mirrors on two walls. Each of these adjoined a

5-by-10-foot observation room where powerful video cameras were attached to movable tripods. This arrangement enabled more flexible scheduling and more comfortable and unobtrusive videotaping of mothers and infants. It also demonstrated GRI commitment to the program.

Contacts with Potential Collaborators at Other Sites

Because of the expected difficulty of locating babies whose hearing loss had been identified before the age of 6 months, it was considered necessary to recruit in a wider area than metropolitan Washington, DC. Therefore, several developmental scientists were contacted; these individuals were known to be specialists either in infancy or in deafness and had access to laboratories equipped to collect the wide range of data envisioned for the project. Four qualified research groups agreed to collaborate as subcontractors to assist in the proposed collection of data, if funding were found. These included Lauren Adamson and Roger Bakeman at Georgia State University; Jeffrey Cohn at the University of Pittsburgh; Amy Lederberg, University of Texas, Dallas; and Edward Tronick, University of Massachusetts. Each senior investigator at Gallaudet served as liaison with one of these groups.

Proposal Submitted to Funding Agency

In April 1987, a detailed grant proposal was submitted to the Maternal and Child Health Research Program, Bureau of Maternal and Child Health and Resources Development (MCH), Public Health Service, Department of Health and Human Services, with Meadow-Orlans named as principal investigator. Although 12 months had been devoted to conceptualizing the research design and developing hypotheses and procedures, in addition to the pilot work described above, the group dared not hope that the project would be funded after the first submission. Therefore, we were both surprised and gratified when the 3-year funding award was announced.

In broad outline, the proposal called for the recruitment of twenty 6-month-old deaf or hard of hearing infants (four at each of the five sites), all with hearing parents. In addition, the Gallaudet team would recruit twenty 6-month-old hearing infants with hearing parents to serve as a control group. Infants were to be developing normally, with no identified cognitive or physical disabilities. Data were to be collected when infants were ages 6, 9, 12, 15, and 18 months old. Like Coates, Vietze, and Gray (1985), we believed that once the sample was recruited, it would become a "precious commodity," even more precious because participants were members of a high-risk, low-incidence population.

Several months into the project, research assistants had been identified at each of the five sites, and their training at Gallaudet had been completed. Pilot subjects were recruited at each site, and trial data sessions were completed and critiqued. Beginning in January 1988, each research group contacted hospitals, audiological clinics, and early intervention programs in their metropolitan area, requesting assistance in locating families of infants with hearing loss. In addition, notices were placed in several professional publications with national circulations, describing the project and asking for referrals. Despite this broad coverage, 2 years elapsed before the twenty infants with hearing loss were located and enrolled. Almost no deaf or hard-of-hearing 6-month-olds were located. Reluctantly, the MCH project officer was contacted, and a revised proposal submitted, amending the original one to begin data collection at 9 months rather than 6 months. With this modification, the project proceeded as planned.

Research with Deaf and Hearing Infants with Deaf Parents—1991 to 1994

With the completion of the report comparing deaf and hearing babies with hearing parents, the team geared up to write a proposal to collect comparable data from twenty deaf and twenty hearing babies with deaf parents. Meadow-Orlans took a long-delayed sabbatical leave and Moores agreed to coordinate the proposal effort and serve as principal investigator. This proposal, submitted to the Office of Special Education and Rehabilitation Services (OSERS) of the U. S. Department of Education, was funded for 3 years.

A persistent difficulty in research with members of the Deaf community is the scarcity of deaf researchers and researchers who are fluent in American Sign Language (ASL). As work progressed, we were fortunate to recruit several research assistants who had these qualifications. In addition to Carlene Thumann-Prezioso, they included Anne Marie Baer, Barbara Gleicher, Natalie Grindstaff, Arlene Kelly, Linda Stamper, and Louise Tetu. These team members recruited deaf families, supervised taping sessions, conducted videotaped interviews in sign language with deaf parents, and kept in touch with the Deaf community. Elaine Gale transcribed the sign language interviews. Chapman Hom's computer expertise contributed greatly to coding videotapes and analyzing data.

Data collection with infants and deaf parents was completed on schedule in 1994. In addition to the eighty core participant families (twenty in each group: Dd, Dh, Hd, Hh) data were collected from some children who were later excluded because of co-occurring physical or cognitive conditions not apparent at the time of recruitment, and from families who were unable to meet the strict scheduling requirements for laboratory visits (plus or minus 2 weeks of the 9-, 12-, 15-, and 18-month birth anniversaries).

Conclusion

This chapter has provided the background of the complex longitudinal study of the world of deaf infants with deaf or hearing parents as compared with hearing infants with hearing or deaf parents to which the book is devoted, with an abbreviated chronology of the research process, and description of the key staff members responsible for framing the research questions, collecting the data, and analyzing the results. Chapter 2 outlines domains that were investigated and some research relevant to those areas. Chapter 3 presents characteristics of participants and the procedures utilized to collect data; Chapters 4 through 13 are devoted to results, and Chapter 14 suggests some of the theoretical and practical implications of those results for parents, teachers, and other researchers.

Note

1. As an example of difficulties infrequently discussed in research reports, early in the pilot taping, staff members neglected to strap a baby into the infant seat. During the course of the taping, while the mother was turned away, between the initial play segment and the Still Face segment, the baby squirmed out of his seat and slipped to the floor. The (deaf) mother did not hear the baby's activity, and staff members were unable to get to the baby in time to catch him. Fortunately, he was unhurt, but parents and staff members were completely unnerved. This served as a valuable and unforgettable lesson for all.

2

Theoretical Rationale for the Longitudinal Study

Kathryn P. Meadow-Orlans, Lynne Sanford Koester,
Patricia E. Spencer, and Robert H. MacTurk

Infants are born into many different worlds that help determine the course their lives will take: the worlds of race, ethnicity, national origin, and culture, the worlds of poverty and privilege, of rural farmhouse, metropolitan apartment, and suburban condominium. Each has an impact on the immediate experience of the newborn, as well as the future opportunities and experiences that await the growing child. For infants who are deaf, another characteristic may outweigh all others: the hearing status of their parents. The world of a deaf infant may be shaped more profoundly by this feature than by several others combined.

This volume is concerned with many dimensions of the world of deaf infants. This chapter provides a general view of the different worlds of deaf and hearing infants born to hearing or to deaf parents, and a summary of the major variables investigated in our study. The chapter is organized to show the major tasks and achievements of infants during this period, the parental behaviors that facilitate development, and the *research questions* that framed the Gallaudet Infancy Study (GIS). These sections are followed by a description of the ordinary course of parent–infant relationships when infants are deaf and parents are hearing, and then by a description of the influence of Deaf culture on the relationships of deaf infants with deaf parents.

The First 18 Months of Life

All infants, deaf or hearing, have certain "irreducible needs" to "grow, learn, and flourish." As conceptualized by two developmental specialists, these include nurturing relationships, physical safety, developmentally appropriate experiences tailored to individual differences, limits and structure, and supportive communities with cultural continuity (Brazelton & Greenspan, 2000). Our focus is on the earliest period in the life cycle, from birth to 18 months, the period identified by Erikson as central to the individual's development of trust. For that trust to develop, a warm and nurturing relationship and a physically comfortable environment are posited as irreducible needs (Erikson, 1963; Schlesinger, 2000). A secure base is created by attachment to a stable caregiver (Cassidy, 1999) as the drive toward competence to master the environment is furthered (MacTurk & Morgan, 1995). Intuitive parenting is one useful model explaining the processes by which caregivers provide infants with these basic needs early in their lives (Koester, 1992).

Much early research on family processes was based on an assumption that parents are generally conscious of their own behaviors and thus able to report them. More recently, using microanalytic techniques to study the interactions of parents and infants, researchers have concluded that many parental behaviors promoting development of competence are unconscious or intuitive (Papoušek & Papoušek, 1987, 1997; Stern, 2002). Several studies demonstrate that parents respond to an infant's limited repertoire by adjusting their own levels of communication and their methods of eliciting and maintaining attention so that newly emerging skills receive the most supportive attention. (e.g., Fogel, 1977; Stern & Gibbon, 1979; Pine, 1994). Some parental behaviors occur with a high degree of regularity and are perhaps ways of conveying both meaning and enjoyment to infants. However, parents are not aware of these behaviors, cannot recall or report them when questioned, cannot predict how they would solve certain learning situations again, and are usually unaware of the competence of their infants in relevant domains (Papoušek & Papoušek, 1983; Stern, Hofer, Haft, & Dore, 1985). Furthermore, most parents have difficulty modifying these intuitive behaviors in response to experimenters' instructions. *An important research question, then, is the extent to which these intuitive behaviors are disrupted—or need to be modified—for hearing parents with deaf infants and deaf parents with hearing infants.*

Examples of Intuitive Parenting Behaviors: Parents as Dyadic Partners

Baby Talk. The earliest human social interchange begins with a compelling desire for dialogue on the part of the adult and the acceptance of any newborn response as satisfactory participation in that dialogue (Schaffer, 1979). Adjustments in vocalizations demonstrate how parental behaviors are precisely tuned to the needs and abilities of young infants (Papoušek, Papoušek, & Bornstein, 1985; M. Papoušek, 1989). Typically, "baby talk" is slowed and modified for intelligibility, with a restricted and concrete vocabulary, and with higher and more variable pitch. The melodic contours of parental vocalizations are tailored to the interactional context: falling contours are associated with attempts to soothe, and rising contours with efforts to activate or reward the infant (Ferrald, 1989; M. Papoušek, 1989; Cruttenden, 1994; Stern, 2002).

Visual Distance Regulation. Adults show a strong tendency to use two specific eye-to-eye distances with infants (Papoušek & Papoušek, 1984): one might be called an *observational distance*, as it corresponds to most adults' optimal reading distance of about 16 to 20 inches (40 to 50 cm) and is normally used when watching an infant who is not attending to the adult in return. More striking, however, is the *dialogue distance*—within 8 to 10 inches (20 to 25 cm)—corresponding to the young infant's range of visual acuity, and used as soon as the infant shows interest in communicative interaction (Schoetzau & Papoušek, 1977). When eye contact is achieved (i.e., when the infant turns toward the partner's face) the parent frequently rewards this behavior with a contingent greeting response: first, the head is retroflexed slightly, then the eyebrows are raised, the eyes opened widely, the mouth opened, and finally the infant is greeted verbally or with a smile (Haekel, 1985). These visual behaviors—reducing the distance to the infant's optimal range, incorporating movement and exaggerated facial expressions to capture the infant's attention, and reinforcing the infant's own responsiveness to the social partner—ensure that the caregiver is a salient feature of the infant's perceptual world.

Temporally Patterned Stimulation. The timing, repetitions, and rhythms of stimulation in all modalities may be especially important to a child in the early months, when most communication is nonverbal (Fogel, 1977; Tronick, Als, & Adamson, 1979; Koester, Papoušek, & Papoušek, 1985; Stern, 2002). Similarly, parental vocalizations do not typically occur in isolation, but are accompanied by a wide variety of tactile, kinesthetic, and visual stimulations of the infant. During this time when the infant is struggling to control its own internal conditions of arousal, affect, and attention, the effective caregiver must be sensitive to the infant's tolerance level and be ready to modify strategies and tempos accordingly (Stern & Gibbon, 1979). Parents can elicit and maintain their infant's attention and facilitate the infant's adaptive processes by modifying their own behaviors to match the baby's individual rhythms. The prevalence of simple repetitive patterns, essential for infant learning, is an inherent feature of the rhythmic stimulation so common during parent–infant interactions (Papoušek, 1977; Koester, 1986, 1988; Stern, 2002).

The Infant's Contributions

On the one hand, there is persuasive evidence, outlined above, of adults' intuitive or nonconscious mechanisms designed to facilitate infant development. On the other hand, there is evidence of the infant's propensities to orient, attend, process, and regulate information to contribute to developing integrative skills (Sameroff & Cavanaugh, 1979; Schaffer, 1979; Brazelton & Cramer, 1990). Thus, "With the birth of each child, a unique set of inborn characteristics begins its lifelong dance with an equally distinctive sequence of experiences" (Greenspan, 1997, p. 137). *To what extent does an infant's limited auditory contact with the environment change the expected response to parents and to objects?*

Reflexes and Senses. The newborn has reflexes and senses equipping her for developing competence, some of which promote physical survival, others that seem to invite social interaction: the Moro reflex causes a baby to reach out, then grasp the mother's body; the step or standing reflex is accompanied by a brightening of the face as she appears to try to participate. Response to visual stimuli and preference for a responsive adult's face is apparent even in the delivery room (Brazelton & Cramer, 1990).

Signals of States of Alertness. In many cases, the infant's behavioral state is all too clear to the caregiver, particularly when she resorts to the earliest form of communication, crying. At other times, the infant's level of arousal, attention, or readiness for interaction may not be so apparent. Several behaviors assist the caregiver in evaluating the newborn's state and determining the need for additional or reduced stimulation. The transition from waking to sleeping is characterized by a gradual decrease in muscle tone, dropping or extending the fingers, hands, and arms. These signals facilitate parental responses that help the infant make the transition from one state to another and may serve to protect the infant from too little or too much stimulation (Koester & Trimm, 1991; Koester, 1994). These early signals may be more transient and less clear to parents than those that the more mature infant learns to provide. As parents learn to read signals and respond appropriately, the stage is set for the synchronous dance of interaction that becomes more and more rewarding for both members of the dyad.

Temperament. *Temperament* is defined as an individual's unique characteristics that help to determine his or her responses to the physical and social environment. These include typical levels of qualities like energy, irritability, and flexibility that may be based on physical attributes but quickly, from birth onward, influence and intertwine with social interactions so that they become difficult to separate. This melding of physical and social attributes helps to explain the fierce debates about the nature of temperament as the term was often invoked in discussions of theoretical differences related to nature versus nurture in human development (J. E. Bates, 1987; Goldsmith et al., 1987; Calkins & Fox, 1992). For a long period of time, "temperament" was considered an outmoded topic, until Alexander Thomas and Stella Chess courageously reintroduced the concept in the 1950s (Kagan, 2001). Chess and Thomas have argued that constitutionally derived temperament is a powerful determinant of the responses of others to the human infant, and that it has a more powerful effect on the response to an infant with a disability than on other infants (1996). Temperament has been related to infants' self-regulatory abilities and to selective attention (Huffman et al., 1998) and to general level of activity, energy, and tempo (Buss & Plomin, 1984). "Easy" babies and "difficult" babies may experience their social worlds in very different ways (J. E. Bates, 1994). *Does a hearing loss influence these characteristics and/or a person's perception of an infant's temperament?*

Mastery Motivation

In several influential papers, Robert White (e.g., 1959, 1963) conceptualized an intrinsic drive to engage and control the environment: a motive that was not explained by traditional theories of motivation. His formulation of a drive toward competence, which he termed *Effectance Motivation,* sparked efforts to study the concept and to develop an appropriate methodology, beginning in the early 1970s. The results of these efforts, with normally developing hearing infants and developmentally delayed hearing infants, showed moderate relationships to standardized measures of competence (Messer et al., 1986; Hupp, 1995), and linked parental behaviors to infants' motivations to master the environment (Jennings et al., 1979; McCarthy & McQuiston, 1983; Busch-Rossnagel, Knauf-Jensen, & DesRosiers, 1995). Several researchers have also explored the social aspects of motivated behavior (Vondra & Jennings, 1990; Wachs & Combs, 1995). These investigations established the importance of the social domain and prompted further interest in the relationship of infants' socially oriented and object-related activities. *How might an infant's hearing level influence the tendency to master the object environment and make it more or less difficult to focus on an objective task?*

Language and Communication

Infants bring to interaction with others the capacity for language and the motivation to communicate with their social worlds. Language acquisition is built on an infant's developmental repertoire of prelinguistic vocal and visual-gestural behaviors for expressing communicative intent. Sophisticated babbling and conventionalized gestures predict the imminent onset of formal spoken language (Dore, 1974; Bates, 1979). Two additional factors influence the onset of language: provision of an adequate language model and semantic contingency between the adult's language and the infant's attention focus (Snow, 1984; Petitto, 1988; Pine, 1994; Richards, 1994). Communication mode is a major issue for hearing parents with a deaf child (and, to a lesser extent, for deaf parents with a hearing child. *How does the presence or absence of very early visual communication affect a deaf infant's later language acquisition?*

Parent–Child Reciprocity

The importance of a difference in infant and maternal temperament is either explicit or implied in much research on mother–infant interaction. An important theme in recent developmental research has been the degree to which parents and infants respond to and influence each other's behaviors, or ways in which behaviors of either member of the dyad contribute to their interaction (Belsky, Taylor, & Rovine, 1984a, 1984b; Isabella, Belsky & von Eye, 1989). This bi-directional influence has been documented in studies of normal mother-infant interaction (Brazelton, Koslowski, & Main, 1974; Tronick, Ricks, & Cohn, 1982), as well as in studies of infants with mothers who are depressed (Cohn, Matias, Campbell, & Hopkins, 1990). *Do mothers whose hearing status does not "match" that of their infant feel less competent as parents, and might that influence parent–child reciprocity?*

Attachment

Attachment has been defined as an enduring affectional tie binding two people together, and it is characterized by maintenance of close physical contact or frequent communication. The attached infant seeks and maintains proximity by approaching, following, clinging to the caregiver, or signaling through crying, smiling, or vocalizing to the adult (Bowlby, 1969; Ainsworth & Bell, 1970; Cassidy, 1999). The infant who has formed a healthy attachment to a caregiver will be able to use this bond to further explore the environment. Because moving out into the world involves risks, however, the securely attached infant uses the attachment figure for reassurance during times of distress or uncertainty. When reunited after a separation from a caregiver, the securely attached infant actively reestablishes proximity and comfort and is then able to resume play and exploration. In general, securely attached infants are able to explore an unfamiliar environment without the direct involvement of the attachment figure. *What are the implications of hearing loss for the attachment process?*

The World of Deaf Infants with Hearing Parents

Between the years 1971 and 1991, prevalence of deaf persons ages 3 to 17 in the United States remained stable, at slightly more than 2% of the population (Reis, 1994). (This included those with postlingual as well as prelingual hearing loss.) Prevalence is greater among males (53%) than among females (47%) (Moores, 2001). Analysis of data from the third

National Health and Nutrition Examination Survey (NHANES III), conducted in the years 1988 to 1994 among children ages 6 to 19 years, found 13% with at least a mild hearing loss (≥16 decibels [dB]). Prevalence data for those with a hearing loss in the high frequencies included more males than females (14.4% cf. 10.9%); more children ages 12 and older than those 11 and younger (13% cf. 12.2%); and more children from low-income than high-income families (16.3% cf. 7.9%) (Niskar et al., 1998). The children included in the GIS are "prelingually deaf" because they were deaf before the age of 3 years. The incidence of prelingually deaf children is generally estimated to be 1 in 1000 births. Profound deafness is estimated to occur in about 1 in 1000 children who are deaf from birth or before the age of 3 (Schein, 1996). The prevalence of mild to moderate losses (26 to 70 dB) is estimated at 16 per 1000 and that of lesser degrees of reduced hearing in one or both ears is reported to be about 50 per 1000 (Bess, 1985). A recent analysis of the hearing status of children ages 6 to 19 receiving special education shows that 96% either have two hearing or hard-of-hearing parents (Mitchell & Karchmer, in press, 2004).

Identification of Deafness. For many years, early identification and intervention with deaf infants has been widely accepted as important to later achievement (Moores, 1978). Early intervention can maximize a child's speech, language, cognitive, and psychosocial development (Mace, Wallace, Whan, & Stelmachowicz, 1991; Calderon & Naidu, 2000; Moeller, 2000; Yoshinaga-Itano, 2003). Although in earlier years identification of congenital deafness did not usually occur before the age of 3 years, there were indications when these studies began that identification procedures and standards were improving. The 1982 Position Statement by the Joint Committee on Infant Hearing recommended that identification be completed and intervention begun by age 6 months. Two research groups had reported median age of identification for children with profound hearing losses to be between 15 and 16 months (Elssmann, Matkin, & Sabo, 1987; Mace at al., 1991). This lag time was the primary reason for the absence of research with young deaf infants at the time our Gallaudet pilot project was begun in 1985. Then, Universal Newborn Hearing Screening (UNHS) was considered to be an unattainable dream. By 2001, almost half the states had legislation mandating screening at the time of birth, with a goal of confirming hearing loss before a child is 3 months old (Meadow-Orlans, 2001). By 2002, 65% of infants were screened for hearing loss at the time of birth (Meadow-Orlans, Mertens, & Sass-Lehrer, 2003). By 2003, forty-one states had passed UNHS legislation, and an additional five states mandated it without legislation (Yoshinaga-Itano, 2003).

Parental Response to Identification: Stress and Support. Most hearing parents have no experience with deafness, and they view their infant's condition as a tragic deficit. Their reactions to the diagnosis may encompass shock, grief, depression, guilt, and chronic sorrow (Meadow, 1968b; Schlesinger, 1987), although some families' bonds are strengthened by their response to the unexpected event (Koester & Meadow-Orlans, 1990). It has been proposed that stress related to the diagnosis of deafness is one reason for repeated research findings describing hearing mothers with deaf infants as less sensitive than comparable mothers with hearing children (Schlesinger & Meadow, 1972; Nienhuys, Horsborough, & Cross, 1985; Power, Wood, Wood, & MacDougall, 1990; Calderon & Greenberg, 2000). It has also been shown that counseling and social support have a positive effect on the sensitivity or responsiveness of these mothers (Greenberg, 1983). In addition to stress created by the diagnosis of deafness, stress for hearing parents may result from a sense that their usual (vocal/spoken) mode of communication is inadequate for the communication needs of a child who is deaf.

Another potential source of stress for hearing parents is the ongoing and ubiquitous controversy about the use of sign language. Moreover, the increasing use of cochlear implants with young children has introduced another heated controversy for parents to consider (Spencer, 2000, 2002). The field of deaf education continues to be plagued with conflict regarding many decisions that parents need to make (Meadow-Orlans, 2001; Moores, 2001). There is encouraging evidence that early identification and intervention may contribute to lesser degrees of stress among mothers of deaf and hard-of-hearing children, compared to mothers whose children are identified later (Pipp-Siegel, Sedey, & Yoshinaga-Itano, 2002; Yoshinaga-Itano, 2003), and lead mothers of early identified children to exhibit heightened sensitivity and emotional availability (Pressman, Pipp-Siegel, Yoshinaga-Itano, & Deas, 1999; Pressman et al., 2000; Lederberg & Golbach, 2002).

Facilitating Visual Attention. Sign language may or may not be the communication vehicle chosen by hearing families. However, even if the family opts to use spoken language only, deaf and hard-of-hearing children must become attentive to visual and environmental clues. They must also learn to divide their visual attention between the person communicating and the object being discussed (Wood, 1982; Wood, Wood, Griffiths, & Howarth, 1986). The ability to focus visually on the subject of another person's comment, or "sharing attention" with a conversational partner, is said to be a cornerstone in "the origins of regulation, of communicative intentions, and collective meanings" (Adamson & Bakeman, 1991, p. 31). This ability, important for hearing children, may be even more important for children who are deaf and cannot rely on audition to provide conversational focus (Erting, Prezioso, & Hynes, 1990/1994; Harris & Mohay, 1997).

Mastery Motivation in the Deaf Child. The rationale for previous investigations with atypical populations rested on the assumption that their motivation to interact with the environment and their ability to benefit from their attempts to gain mastery are depressed. Strong support for this assumption is found in reports by MacTurk and his colleagues (see MacTurk & Morgan, 1995; Hupp, 1995). Several studies of deaf school-age children have found them to lack achievement motivation and attributional sophistication, and to be overly impulsive (Stinson, 1974, 1978; R. I. Harris, 1978; Kusché, Garfield, & Greenberg, 1983; Calderon & Greenberg, 2003). Pilot studies with small subgroups of deaf infants suggested that their integration of social- and object-oriented activities serves either a different or a more potent function for them than for hearing infants (MacTurk & Trimm, 1989; MacTurk, 1990). One large-scale study (n = 200) utilizing paper-and-pencil instruments collected from hearing mothers of deaf children showed a significant relationship between children's expressive language and their mastery motivation (Pipp-Siegel, Sedey, VanLeeuwen, & Yoshinaga-Itano, 2003).

Attachment and Deaf Children. The degree to which attachment is affected by infant deafness is mediated by other variables such as communication proficiency. Greenberg and Marvin (1979) found that deaf preschoolers with poor communication skills were often insecurely attached, but those with good communication skills developed secure attachments. (They studied preschoolers and used a "goal-oriented" coding system rather than the usual Ainsworth classification code.) Lederberg and her colleague found no significant differences in the attachment classifications for deaf and hearing toddlers, and little effect of hearing status on their more global interaction ratings. Attachment was related to toddler behaviors primarily in the sense that secure children initiated more of the interactions and engaged in more shared affect with their mothers. The investigators concluded that "sensitive caregivers can adapt to a variety of special needs of their infants/toddlers in such a way as to make their children feel secure in their care" (Lederberg & Mobley, 1990, p. 1602).

A report of atypical attachment patterns in at-risk children warns of potential confounding of symptoms related to the atypical condition with coding of the Strange Situation (Atkinson et al., 1999). This caveat might also be applied to deaf children where the absence of the auditory sense can moderate expected responses to mother's presence or absence (Marschark, 1993a).

Language and the Deaf Infant with Hearing Parents. Other than the work to be reported in Chapter 10, systematic developmental studies of prelinguistic, intentional communication by deaf infants with hearing and with deaf parents are not available, but some small sample and case studies suggest that the process is different for the two groups (Wedell-Monnig & Lumley, 1980; Spencer & Gutfreund, 1990; Harris & Mohay, 1997). Oller and Eilers (1988) describe delayed metaphonological development in deaf infants compared to those with normal hearing. Hearing loss interferes with infants' reception of vocally produced language; hearing parents typically are not fluent in signed language systems, and some are less responsive in their interactions with deaf infants (Schlesinger & Meadow, 1972; Spencer & Gutfreund, 1990). There are indications that early intervention with hearing families of deaf infants has a positive influence on mother–child interaction and on language acquisition (Meadow-Orlans, 1987; Rodda & Grove, 1987; Yoshinaga-Itano, 2003). One research group reported that children whose hearing losses were identified before the age of 6 months showed significantly better language progress compared to those identified after the age of 6 months, regardless of the degree of loss. All children in the study received intervention services within 2 months of identification (Yoshinaga-Itano, Sedey, Coulter, & Mehl, 1998).

Mothers' Interactions with Deaf Children. Early studies of hearing mothers and deaf toddlers uniformly found heightened maternal intrusiveness and control compared to interactions of hearing mothers and hearing toddlers (Schlesinger & Meadow, 1972; Brinich, 1980; Greenberg, 1980; Nienhuys, Horsborough, & Cross, 1985). Later studies showed lesser quantities of interaction among hearing-deaf dyads (Lederberg & Mobley, 1990) and high levels of maternal control associated with lesser gains in language level (Musselman & Churchill, 1992), although this may not be the case across time and environments (Gallaway & Woll, 1994; Lederberg & Prezbindowski, 2000). Maternal sensitivity appears to be more important for language gain for deaf than for hearing children (Pressman, Pipp-Siegal, Yoshinaga-Itano, & Deas, 1999).

Temperament patterns of individual children can have either a positive or negative influence on the psychological outcomes of a child's development, regardless of whether a child has a disability. In either a "difficult" or an "easy" child, the attitudes and responses of adults toward these temperamental expressions will affect adult–child interaction. "The difficult child [with a disability] is at greatest risk for evoking aversion in others. . . . New situations, people, and routines evoke withdrawal and protest, and adaptation takes a long time. . . . [W]hen stresses occur, stormy interactions are all too likely" (Chess & Thomas, 1996, p. 175).

The World of Infants Born to Deaf Parents

Only about 3% of deaf children have two deaf parents, and 1% have one deaf parent (Mitchell & Karchmer, in press, 2004). Deaf individuals are more likely to marry deaf spouses, but most of their children will be hearing. One of the "irreducible needs" of infants is for a supportive community with cultural continuity. Infants born to deaf parents are members of such a community. The hallmark of this Deaf community[1] is fluency in American Sign Language (ASL), although manual English (contact sign) may also be used in everyday conversation (Woll & Ladd, 2003). Community membership also assumes a visual approach to life and the common experiences of disadvantage that accompany a generally stigmatized condition (Padden & Humphries, 1988; Meadow-Orlans & Erting, 2000). The lives of many members of the community are based in local Deaf clubs that sponsor social events and sports activities, amateur theater, mime, and dance groups (Wilcox, 1989; Stewart, 1991). Storytelling, jokes, puns, and riddles in ASL, nicknames or name signs, and folklore create a base that is incorporated into an ongoing history (Rutherford, 1989; Supalla, 1992). National and international organizations offer both cohesive bonds and advocacy campaigns (Erting, Johnson, Smith, & Snider, 1994). Like the general culture in the United States, cultural diversity and a wide range of interests and experiences are found within the Deaf community (Parasnis, 1996). Like the general culture, the Deaf community is constantly shifting and changing in response to contemporary events (Padden, 1996).

Deaf Children, Deaf Parents

Deaf parents are not likely to experience the diagnosis of a child's hearing loss as an unexpected or tragic event. In fact, some deaf parents feel more comfortable and competent with a deaf infant than with one who is hearing:

> We will become parents in June. I am very excited about becoming a father. I hope to have a deaf child. The doctor told us that we could never have a deaf son because my deafness is X-linked, through my mother. But maybe we can have a daughter. (Orlansky & Heward, 1981, p. 24)

Deaf parents have visual and tactile interactive techniques that substitute for auditory cues to facilitate the development of visual attention (Swisher, 1993; Waxman & Spencer, 1997; Erting, Thumann-Prezioso, & Benedict, 2000; Mohay, 2000; Loots & Devisé, 2003). Deaf mothers also have special discourse strategies and scaffolding behaviors to establish joint visual attention with their deaf children (Jamieson & Pedersen, 1993; Jamieson, 1994b). Koester (1992; Koester, Papoušek, & Smith-Gray, 2000) suggests that these strategies have been developed in response to the parents' own visual needs and have become adaptive over the course of their lives.

Several studies from the 1960s and 1970s reported academic performances of deaf children with deaf parents to be superior to those of deaf children with hearing parents. The same pattern was reported for social adjustment and self-image (Stuckless & Birch, 1966;

Meadow, 1968a, 1969, 1980; Vernon & Koh, 1970; Brasel & Quigley, 1977).

Hearing Infants, Deaf Parents

There is a paucity of research concerning hearing children with deaf parents, but the existing literature suggests no major developmental or linguistic problems in this population (Schiff-Myers, 1993; Preston, 1994; Meadow-Orlans, 2002). One study of language in matched and unmatched hearing status dyads with 2-year-olds reported hearing children with deaf mothers performed at the same level as hearing children with hearing mothers, and at a higher level than deaf children with deaf mothers who outperformed deaf children with hearing mothers (Bornstein et al., 1999).

Some narrative reports of the experiences of older hearing children of deaf parents suggest problems of role reversal related to children's interpreting for their parents and to their direct early involvement in family crises because of their role as interpreter (Rayson, 1987; Harvey, 1989; Preston, 1994). Positive aspects of this family situation are also reported. Many children of deaf adults (CODAs) report pride in their early independence and in their interpreting skills, as well as a deep appreciation of Deaf culture and the Deaf community (Hoffmeister, 1985). Almost no research has been reported on social interactions of hearing infants and deaf parents in the first 2 years of life. One early study of deaf mothers' interactive characteristics included both hearing- and deaf-infant dyads (Maestas y Moores, 1980). Another study reported interactions of eight deaf mother/hearing-infant pairs, where the only marked difference with eight hearing-mother/hearing-infant pairs was in the frequency and duration of maternal vocalizations (Rea, Bonvillian, & Richards, 1988). Because hearing children can process either vocal or visual communication, there should be no functional barriers to sign communication with deaf parents. It is typical for these parents to sign to hearing children and for the children to acquire ASL as their first language. Many deaf mothers also supplement signing with vocalization.

Although they vary greatly in their capacities to produce speech, all deaf people are functionally capable of vocalizing. Degree of residual hearing will determine their ability to monitor their vocalizations, but Rea and her colleagues (1988) found that deaf mothers did vocalize to their hearing infants, although less than half as frequently as the hearing mothers with whom they were compared. These findings suggest that many deaf mothers modify their habitual communication in order to accommodate the needs of hearing children. However, some women experience feelings of incompetence about parenting a hearing child, as illustrated by the reaction of a deaf mother who "tested" her 3-day-old infant by banging a spoon on a metal tray:

> Oh, my God, she's hearing! . . . What on earth am I going to do with her? . . . I don't even know how to talk to her. (Preston, 1994, p. 17)

This suggests that for some deaf mothers of hearing children, like many hearing mothers of deaf children, sensitive intuitive parenting might be blocked by feelings of incompetence stemming from parent–child difference—that is, unmatched hearing status—and from concerns about accommodating that difference.

Conclusion

Deaf infants have the same irreducible needs as do hearing infants for nurturance, safety, limits, structure, and supportive communities. Their first 18 months are focused on mastering the physical world, interacting with attachment figures, and searching for symbolic meaning. Their world is more reliant on vision than on sound, and their caregivers must facilitate that visual world. The ways in which hearing and deaf parents manage these developmental tasks is the focus of the research to be reported in the remaining chapters of this book.

Note

1. It is a common convention to capitalize "deaf" when referring to members of this "Deaf community" or "Deaf culture." In a lengthy document such as this, it becomes cumbersome. It is also difficult to distinguish between deaf people who do and do not consider themselves to be members of the community. For these reasons, we have opted to capitalize "deaf" only when referring specifically to the community or the culture.

3

Participant Characteristics and Research Procedures

Kathryn P. Meadow-Orlans

Readers accustomed to research on infants recruited from the general population may view the numbers on which our data are based to be small (eighty cases divided among four groups of twenty each). Several factors combine to expand the importance of this cohort of families, and its relative uniqueness. First is the low incidence of prelingual deafness, generally estimated to be 1 in 1000 births (Schein, 1996). Second is the likelihood of identification in the first year of life. In the years when these infants with hearing parents were recruited (1988–89), perhaps one-quarter would have been identified before the age of 9 months (Meadow-Orlans, Mertens, & Sass-Lehrer, 2003). Other researchers interested in the early development of deaf children have solved the difficulties of participant recruitment in a variety of ways. Some have relied on intensive study of a few cases (Schlesinger, 1972; Maestas y Moores, 1980; Petitto & Marentette, 1991). Others have added to a database over an extended period (Orlansky & Bonvillian, 1985; Bonvillian & Folven, 1993), or modified a research plan after failing to recruit infant participants (Schlesinger & Meadow, 1972).

Since 1999, when Congress passed the Newborn and Infant Hearing Screening Intervention Act (Marschark, Lang, & Albertini, 2002), many states instituted mandatory screening for newborns, and early identification became more likely. Even before the formal passage of this legislation, the state of Colorado screened the hearing of most newborns. As a result, one research group has been able to recruit more than 100 deaf or hard-of-hearing participants identified before the age of 6 months, and has published a number of important papers based on data from those children (e.g., Yoshinaga-Itano, Sedey, Coulter, & Mehl, 1998; Yoshinaga-Itano, 2003). Their studies have helped to underscore the importance of early identification of hearing loss through Universal Newborn Hearing Screening (UNHS). However, in that project, the characteristics of the cohort were less controlled and amount of data collected less extensive than in the Gallaudet study. When similar developmental issues are reported, group numbers decrease to the level of ours (Pressman, Pipp-Siegel, Yoshinaga-Itano, & Deas, 1999; Pipp-Siegel, Sedey, & Yoshinaga-Itano, 2002) or include no data for comparison groups of hearing children or children with deaf parents (Pipp-Siegel, Sedey, VanLeeuwen, & Yoshinaga-Itano, 2003).

The only other study to collect data on all four parent–child deaf-hearing groups was based on 2-year-olds and a cross-sectional design (Bornstein et al., 1999). Thus, the analyses presented here describe the only comprehensive data for deaf and hearing children with deaf and hearing parents for whom data were collected at ages 6, 9, 12, 15, and 18 months. This design and cohort provide a unique opportunity to investigate developmental processes relating to characteristics and behaviors of children with hearing loss and their parents.

Although the original protocol calling for initial data collection at age 6 months was modified to begin at 9 months, younger infants were included when possible and videotaped at age 6 months in face to face interaction with their mothers. Early data are available for fourteen Dd infants, six in group Hd, eleven in group Dh, and ten in group Hh. These data are reported in Chapter 4. It should be noted that although most Hd infants were not recruited for the project before 9 months, all but the two babies deafened by meningitis (one at 6 months, the other at 7 months), all GIS infants were identified with hearing loss before the age of 6 months. This means that they are, in this respect, comparable to infants identified more recently through Newborn Hearing Screening procedures.

In addition to the core group of eighty participants, seventy-seven others participated in one or more data-collection sessions but did not complete the protocol. Five Hd infants and one Dd infant were excluded from the central pool because of cognitive or motor disabilities. (The five Hd infants are described in Chapter 6.) Although these infants were excluded from major analyses, it should be noted that some disabilities such as attention disorders or emotional disturbances are not identified during infancy and might be found in some of these participants at older ages. Younger siblings of Dd infants were included when parents were prepared to participate again, with the idea that comparisons of siblings would be informative. (Resources to complete these analyses were not available.) Two Hd infants and four Hh infants were recruited as back-ups for some flawed or missing data (e.g., videos without sound) after the initial data reports were completed. Some infants were eliminated after their parents missed a data session because of the child's illness or a schedule conflict.

As described in Chapter 1, participants were recruited in two separate waves: *(1)* Between 1988 and 1991, sixty-five deaf and hearing infants were videotaped and their hearing parents videotaped and interviewed at research sites in Washington, DC; Amherst, Massachusetts;

Atlanta, Dallas, and Pittsburgh; *(2)* from 1991 to 1993, a total of ninety deaf and hearing infants with deaf parents were recruited and tested, all but one at Gallaudet University in Washington, DC.

With few exceptions, all data were complete for the group of eighty infants included as the final cohort. The recruitment of participants for studies of young children from low-incidence at-risk populations and the collection of data following a complex protocol over a time period encompassing four or five meetings with parents and infants is a demanding undertaking. Dedication of both families and staff members is required.

Characteristics of Participants

Family Background Characteristics

Parents in all four groups were generally in their early to mid-thirties and were well-educated. On average, both mothers and fathers had some training beyond high school, and the mean level for fathers of hearing infants was postcollege education. When education and occupation were combined to create a socioeconomic status index, one statistically significant difference was found: hearing fathers of hearing infants (Hh) had higher status levels than did deaf fathers of hearing infants (Dh) (Table 3-1).

Most families were intact in the traditional sense, although fathers were absent in four Dh families and one Hd family (deaf infants with hearing parents). Step siblings were present in the homes of one Hh and two Hd infants. All but two of the eighty parents were Caucasian, with European ancestors. Mothers' religious preferences across the four groups were similar: 70% reported their preference as either Catholic or Protestant, 15% Jewish, and 15% "none."

Characteristics of Infants

Infants did not differ significantly for sex or birth weight, although boys were somewhat overrepresented in groups Dd (deaf infants with deaf mothers) and Hh, and mean birth weight of Hd infants was somewhat below that of others. Babies were developing normally, according to their 18-month scores on the Alpern Boll Physical and Self-Help scales (Table 3-2). One Dh infant and two Hd infants were members of (different) twin sets. One of these had a triplet sibling who died soon after birth.

Degree of hearing loss for the two relevant groups is shown in Table 3-3. At the time these data were collected, the difficulty of determining the precise level and nature of hearing loss in a young infant was generally acknowledged: results can vary from one testing session to another. Most of the infants were assessed initially by means of an Auditory Brainstem Response test (ABR).

Table 3-1. Age, years of education, socioeconomic status. Mothers and fathers, by mother–infant hearing status

	Group			
	Dd	*Hd*	*Dh*	*Hh*
N	20	20	19	21
Age (years)				
Mothers (mean)	32.5	31.5	29.7	32.4
(SD)	(4.4)	(3.6)	(5.2)	(4.4)
Fathers (mean)	34.0	33.4	32.1	34.1
(SD)	(5.1)	(5.0)	(3.6)	(5.0)
Education (years)				
Mothers (mean)	16.2	15.8	15.9[a]	16.5
(SD)	(2.1)	(2.2)	(1.2)	(2.3)
Fathers (mean)	15.5	15.4	17.0[b]	17.7
(SD)	(2.1)	(2.6)	(5.5)	(2.1)
Socioeconomic Status (SES)*				
Mothers (mean)	28.3	28.8	31.2	25.0
(SD)	(10.8)	(11.8)	(11.5)	(10.8)
Fathers[c] (mean)	29.4	31.1	40.0	20.4
(SD)	(14.0)	(17.2)	(27.5)	(10.5)

[a]Missing data for one case.

[b]Missing data for three cases.

[c]F (3,76) = 3.89; p = .01; Group Dh > Group Hh.

N.B.: Higher SES scores reflect lower SES status levels. No other group differences are statistically significant.

*Hollinghead's Two Factor Index of Social Position.

> To record the ABR, surface electrodes are attached to the scalp, clicks of varying intensity are delivered through an earphone placed over the infant's ear, and recordings of brainwave activity are made during the first msec after stimulus onset. (Murray, 1988, p. 572)

If a hearing level can be reliably determined, it is reported in decibels (dB), usually as an average of frequencies for sounds within the speech range (500–1000–2000 Herz) of the better ear: profound = 91 dB and above; severe-profound = sloping 71 to 90 dB with a greater loss at the higher frequencies; severe = a flat loss of 71 to 90 dB (that is, the loss at each of the three speech frequencies is essentially the same, which means that hearing aids may be more useful than if the loss is characterized as "sloping"); moderately severe = 56 to 70 dB; moderate = 41 to 55 dB;

Table 3-2. Infants' sex, birth weight, and 18-month Alpern Boll scores, by mother–infant hearing status

	Group			
	Dd	*Hd*	*Dh*	*Hh*
Sex				
Boys	12	10	9	12
Girls	8	10	10	9
Birth Weight				
Mean (grams)	3477	3054	3478	3456
(SD)	(612)	(1031)	(672)	(507)
Alpern Boll Scores				
Physical scale (mean)	110.5	112.3	117.3[a]	108.2
(SD)	(11.2)	(9.7)	(9.7)	(14.8)
Self-help scale (mean)	119.0	115.4	121.2[a]	115.4
(SD)	(9.4)	(11.5)	(12.1)	(14.1)

[a]Two cases are missing.

Dd = Deaf parents, deaf infants

Hd = Hearing parents, deaf infants

Dh = Deaf parents, hearing infants

Hh = Hearing parents, hearing infants

mild = 26 to 40 dB. Generally, if a hearing loss is profound, speech cannot be amplified enough to be understandable, and the person would be considered to be "deaf." Those with less than profound losses might be classified as "hard-of-hearing," depending on the extent to which they benefit from a hearing aid for understanding speech sounds.

Table 3-3. Estimated hearing levels, deaf infants

	Hd	*Dd*
Profound	3	7
Severe to profound	10	5
Severe	3	1
Moderately severe	1	3
Moderate	2	1
Mild	1	1
Total	20	18
Not available	—	2

Hd = Hearing parents, deaf infants

Dd = Deaf parents, deaf infants

Behaviorally, these hearing levels have been summarized as follows:

> *Profound*: Maximally amplified speech is not understood by most persons; most will use total communication systems (a combination of speech with sign language).
> *Severe*: Conversational speech must be loud; child will experience difficulties with classroom discussions and telephone conversations; will need considerable support in acquiring speech. Some will understand strongly amplified speech but will have difficulty with consonants.
> *Moderate*: Child has difficulty with whispers and normal speech; understands conversational speech at 3 to 5 feet; needs auditory training, language training, and hearing aids. With sufficient training and no other impairments, child will function in regular classrooms with minimum support.
> *Mild*: Without awareness of hearing needs, problems in language and speech may emerge. (Fewell, 1983, p. 258)

The decibel levels of the two groups of infants with hearing loss in our study (those with deaf parents and those with hearing parents) were fairly similar, as shown in Table 3-3. One in each group had a "mild" hearing loss. According to her mother, that child with deaf parents was treated as if she were deaf (that is, parents signed to her without using their voices). The Hd infant with a mild hearing loss was excluded from analyses of language behavior and acquisition. Any level of hearing loss is a reason for the provision of special services to the child and the family, as well as for hearing parents' concerns about development.

Prenatal, Postnatal, and Diagnostic Events

Mothers' Prenatal Experiences

Target children were first live births for about three-quarters of Dh mothers and for about half of the mothers in each of the three other groups. Five Hd mothers reported "severe" problems during their pregnancies. In retrospect, only four mothers (20%) considered their pregnancies to be "normal," compared to two-thirds of mothers in the three other groups. All but four of eighty mothers attended childbirth classes either before the birth of this child, or before an earlier birth. Three of the four nonattendees (all in group Hd) either had premature deliveries or were on prescribed bed rest and unable to attend. Most mothers (85%) expressed satisfaction with support of husbands during their pregnancies.

Circumstances of Labor and Delivery

The four groups of mothers had fairly similar experiences during the labor and delivery of their infants, although hearing mothers had more problems than did deaf mothers. (Four of these mothers had elective C[cesarean]-sections.) Four additional Hd mothers and two additional Hh mothers experienced unexpected problems that led to unplanned C-sections.

All but five of the eighty fathers were present for at least part of their wives' predelivery labor (including one father substitute who served as coach). Infants of two absent fathers were delivered more quickly than anticipated, and fathers did not arrive in time. Another father fainted during his wife's labor, hit his head on the monitor, and was rushed to the hospital emergency room. Two mothers experienced severe difficulties, and their husbands were asked to remain outside the delivery room.

Postdelivery Problems

High proportions of mothers in three of the four groups reported some level of postpartum depression: Dd = 30%, Dh = 50%, Hh = 71%, Hd = 85% (chi-square = 14.53; $df = 3$; $p < .01$). The high incidence of depression among Hd mothers might well have been related to the neonatal difficulties of their infants. Infants of the depressed Hd mothers were more likely to have severe problems: five mothers listed three serious problems for their infants soon after birth, whereas only one infant in any other group had such serious difficulties (chi-square = 12.0; $df = 3$; $p < .01$). These babies included one who required immediate surgery, one with severe anoxia, and three who were premature. Their birth weights ranged from 1 pound 12 ounces to 2 pounds 7 ounces, and they spent an average of 79 days in hospital after birth.

Postdelivery problems included jaundice in one infant, so severe that it was the cause of deafness. Two babies were deafened by meningitis, one at age 6 months, and the other at age 7 months.

Diagnosis of Hearing Loss and Hearing Aid Use

The two groups of deaf infants (Hd and Dd) were very different in almost every circumstance related to hearing loss. Deaf parents were expecting that their infants might be deaf. Most welcomed that possibility and were certainly prepared to care appropriately and to communicate with a child who, like themselves, did not hear. All these parents tested their baby's hearing informally during the initial hospital stay, and 85% suspected the child's deafness at that time. All had professional hearing tests confirming deafness by the time the infant was 4 months old. Twelve Hd babies had been tested by the age of 2 months, sixteen by age 4 months, nineteen by age 6 months. The twentieth baby was identified with a hearing loss while he was hospitalized for meningitis. Only one family felt they had difficulty obtaining prompt testing or that their pediatrician dismissed their suspicions concerning auditory responsiveness.

Seven Hd parents requested auditory testing because their infants did not respond to sound. Some of these also noted that the child was unusually alert visually, that the baby's cry was unusually loud, that she was difficult to calm, or that her vocalizations were not as expected. Four babies received testing because an older sibling had a hearing loss, and one was tested because her father had a hearing loss.

Only four Dd infants were wearing hearing aids by the time of the final interview when they were 18 months old. In contrast, mean age for beginning hearing aid use for Hd infants was 6.95 months. Six were fitted with aids by age 5 months; all had received aids by age 9 months. Two children had objected vigorously to their hearing aids, and their mothers temporarily discontinued use of the device. At the 15-month interview, twelve Hd mothers reported that their children wore hearing aids "almost all day" or "all their waking hours."

Data Collection Procedures

Table 3-4 summarizes procedures employed with participants at ages 6, 9, 12, 15, and 18 months. Procedures involving infants and mothers were videotaped in a laboratory where two cameras were placed behind one-way mirrors on two sides of a room. One camera focused on the infant, the other on the mother. A special effects generator was used to produce a split-screen image. Interviews with hearing mothers were audio-recorded and transcribed. Interviews with deaf mothers were videotaped and transcribed.

Face-to-Face Interaction (6 and 9 Months)

For this segment of data collection, the baby was secured in an infant seat that was firmly attached to a table placed in front of a chair in which the mother sat, looking into the child's face. No objects were available. This procedure provided data for analyses of mothers' verbal, nonverbal, and tactile communications to their infants, and infants' affective and behavioral initiations and responses to mothers.

Episode 1—Normal Interaction. For 3 minutes, the mother was instructed to interact with her infant as she would normally at home. The first minute was considered to be "warm-up." The next 2 minutes were coded.

Turn Away. In order to mark the transition from episode 1 to episode 2, the mother was asked to turn 90 degrees in her chair for 30 seconds (not coded).

Episode 2—Still Face Procedure. For 2 minutes, the mother faced her infant again and looked at her, but was instructed not to touch, speak, smile, communicate in any way, or to respond.

Table 3-4. Procedures at infants' ages 6, 9, 12, 15, and 18 months

Groups	*Hd/Hh*	*Dd/Dh*
Six Months (laboratory) (for infants recruited early)		
1. Introduction to project, informed consent	X X	X X
2. Face-to-face mother–infant interaction (unstructured, Still Face, unstructured)	X X	X X
3. Interview with mother		
a. Pregnancy, delivery, postpartum experiences, demographics	X X	X X
b. Alpern Boll Physical and Self-Help scales	X X	X X
Nine Months (laboratory)		
1. Introduction to project, informed consent (for new participants)	X X	X X
2. Face to face mother–infant interaction (unstructured, Still Face, unstructured)	X X	X X
3. Mastery motivation: 4 toys (infant and examiner)	X X	X X
4. Mother–infant free play with toys: 15 minutes	X X	X X
5. Interview with mother		
a. Pregnancy, delivery, postpartum experiences, demographics	X X	X X
b. Alpern Boll Physical and Self-Help scales	X X	X X
6. Parenting Stress Index (mother and father complete at home and mail back)	X X	0 0
7. Stress of Life Events (mother and father complete at home and mail back)	X X	0 0
Twelve Months (laboratory)		
1. Mother–infant free play with toys: 15 minutes	X X	X X
2. Mastery motivation: 4 toys	X X	X X
3. Strange Situation Procedure	X X	X X
4. Interview with mother: Alpern Boll Physical and Self-Help scales	X X	X X
Fifteen Months (home visit)		
1. Interview with mother		
a. Family events	X X	X X
b. Impact of hearing loss on the family	X 0	0 0
2. Family Support Scale (mother and father complete and mail in)	X X	0 0
3. Parenting Events Inventory (mother and father complete and mail in)	X X	0 0
Eighteen Months (laboratory)		
1. Strange Situation Procedure	X X	X X
2. Mother–infant free play with toys: 20 minutes	X X	X X

(*continued*)

Table 3-4. (continued)

Groups	*Hd/Hh*	*Dd/Dh*
3. Refreshments	X X	X X
4. Self-identification task*	X X	X X
5. Teaching task*	X X	X X
6. Interview with mother		
a. Family events and Alpern Boll Physical and Self-Help scales	X X	X X
b. Child's communicative status	X X	X X

X = Procedure included.

0 = Procedure not included for this group.

*Data not utilized in this volume.

Episode 3—Normal Interaction. For the final 2 minutes, the mother resumed normal interaction, as in episode 1.

Mastery Motivation (9 and 12 Months)

During presentation of the toys, selected to arouse infants' interest, infants sat on their mother's lap at a feeding table with the examiner seated across from the mother and child. To initiate the sessions, infants were given a warm-up toy for approximately 1 minute. The warm-up toy was removed, and four toys were presented, one at a time in a standard order, each for 3 minutes. The examiner first demonstrated a toy. If the infant showed no interest during the first minute, the toy was demonstrated again. Otherwise, the examiner sat quietly while the child played with the toy except to reposition it or to keep it from falling off the table. Toys were designed to be progressively more "difficult." The two more difficult toys from the 9-month session were included in the 12-month session, plus two additional toys. (Toys are described in the appendix to Chapter 7.)

Free Play with Toys (9, 12, and 18 Months)

A set of toys was arranged randomly on a quilt placed on the floor of the laboratory. Toys included many of those recommended by McCune-Nicolich (rev. 1983): a baby doll with nursing bottle, boy and girl dolls, blocks in a wheeled cart, a ball, tool kit, child's sunglasses, tea set, picture book, toy telephone, sponge. These were supplemented with a seashell and a tongue depressor, used by Belsky and Most (1981) to increase opportunities for imaginative and symbolic play.

Mothers were told that we wanted to see how their infants played in an unstructured situation, what toys they preferred, how they played with them, and that we were observing infants' communicative behaviors. For 5 minutes, infants explored the toys alone while mothers sat and chatted with a member of the research team. Mothers were then instructed to sit on the floor with their child and to "play with (your baby) as you would when there is free time available at home—as naturally as possible."

This procedure provided data for analyses of mother–infant interactions and infants' language, visual attention, and play behaviors.

Strange Situation Procedure (12 and 18 Months)

This procedure was developed by Ainsworth and her colleagues (1978) to provide a measure of a child's attachment to the mother. It was designed to enable researchers to observe infants (typically either 12- or 18-month-olds) in a standardized laboratory situation that includes separations of the infant and mother. The reaction of the child to the separations and subsequent reunions is the basis for classifying the mother–child attachment relationship.

The procedure consists of the following 3-minute episodes: *(1)* mother and infant enter an unfamiliar playroom; *(2)* mother sits in a chair while the infant plays with some toys; *(3)* a stranger enters the room and sits beside the mother; *(4)* mother leaves the room while the stranger remains; *(5)* mother returns to her chair, stranger exits; *(6)* mother leaves the infant alone; *(7)* stranger returns, comforts infant if needed; *(8)* mother returns, stranger departs.

Refreshments (18 Months)

Juice and animal crackers were served to mothers and children, providing a bit of respite for mothers and a bit of nourishment for children. (Bathroom and diaper breaks were taken when necessary.)

Interviews (6, 9, 12, 15, 18 Months)

Interviews were conducted from structured schedules with a different form for mothers in each of the four groups. These were audiotaped by hearing team members with hearing mothers and videotaped by deaf team members with deaf mothers. Interview material was coded and entered on computer (Statistical Program for the Social Sciences—SPSS) for analysis.

During the initial contact (age 6 months or 9 months), family composition was determined, as well as detailed pregnancy, delivery, and postpartum histories, child's neonatal and current health status, parents' ages, and parents' educational histories. For mothers with deaf children, details of the diagnostic process were elicited, along with questions about the responses of parents and extended family members to the diagnosis. When children were 9 months old, family stress and support indicators were collected from all participants.

When the child reached age 12 months, recent family events were queried. At age 15 months, the interview was conducted during a home visit. Information was collected on family events since the 12-month meeting, in addition to the child's current height, weight, and health status; the parents' work schedules and childcare arrangements. Parents of deaf children were queried about hearing aids, intervention services, and communication used. At age 18 months, questions focused on child's communicative abilities, both spoken and signed.

At each of these contacts, age-appropriate items from the Developmental Profile II (Alpern, Boll, & Shearer, rev. 1980) Physical and Self-Help scales were included as part of the interview.

Developmental Profile II. This consists of five scales: Physical, Self-Help, Social, Academic, and Communication. The Physical and Self-Help scales were most appropriate for screening infants in this study. Each scale consists of three questions describing progress in respective domains at each 6-month age level (0–6 months, 7–12 months, etc.) from birth through 3½ years, and for each 12-month age level from 4 through 9 years of age. The instrument's developers conducted a standardization study involving more than 3000 subjects, with at least 200 subjects for each targeted age level. The report of these studies includes the information that agreement between mother's report of a child's skills and the child's actual skills, as demonstrated by a direct test, was 84% for the Physical scale and 85% for the Self-Help scale. For a measure of test-retest reliability, two interviewers procured scores several days apart from the same mothers of 11 children ages 11 months to 10 years of age. Mean score differences were 1.5 points for the Physical scale and 2.4 points for the Self-Help scale on score ranges of 8–59 points and 6–58 points, respectively.

Questionnaires (9 and 15 Months)

Questionnaires were distributed only to the two groups of hearing mothers (Hd and Hh). Written questionnaires can be especially onerous for deaf participants whose native language is ASL; the questionnaires are often ignored or answered carelessly. It was believed that to request the return of four lengthy questionnaires might jeopardize continuing participation in the project by Dd and Dh families. Two alternatives—the sign language translation of the material on videotape and individual administration by a signing interviewer—were dismissed as unmanageable because of the limitations of time and money.

For Hd and Hh parents, two copies of questionnaires were given to mothers at the close of the 9- and 15-month interviews: one for her, the other for her husband. After completion at home, the questionnaires were to be returned by mail. All forty mothers returned the four questionnaires. Responses to the 9-month questionnaires were received from thirty-four fathers; thirty-one fathers returned the 15-month questionnaires.

Parenting Stress Index (PSI). Distributed to parents after the 9-month interview, the PSI (Abidin, 1986) consists of 101 items divided into Child and Parent domains. The Child Domain (47 items) is divided into six subscales: Adaptability, Acceptability, Demandingness, Mood, Reinforces Parent, and Distractibility/Hyperactivity. The Parent Domain (54 items) has seven subscales: Depression, Attachment, Restrictions of Role, Sense of Competence, Social Isolation, Relationship with Spouse, and Parent Health. Alpha coefficients (a measure of the internal consistency of a scale) for Child, Parent, and Total scales are .89, .93, and .95, respectively (based on 534 subjects in Abidin's norming population). Questionnaires were completed by all forty mothers and by thirty-four fathers.

Stress of Life Events Scale (SLE). This was the second questionnaire completed by parents after the 9-month interview, and it was constructed specifically for this project. It is based on a research technique used frequently since the initial publication of the Social Readjustment Rating Scale (SRRS; Holmes & Rahe, 1967). One review showed that at least 1000 studies had utilized the approach (Thoits, 1983). The original SRRS included forty-three items reflecting either positive or negative life changes that might occur. The theory behind the technique was that change per se creates stress. Other researchers argued that respondents themselves should define the direction and the extent of the stress created by a life change (Dohrenwend, 1973; Dohrenwend, Krasnoff, Askenasy & Dohrenwend, 1978; Cleary, 1980). Each of these investigators proposed their own sets of events that might be expected to create stress. Our list of thirty events was constructed after consulting numerous sources. Among the events included were those known to be relevant for our population: "diagnosis of a handicapping condition," "pregnancy," "childbirth," "care of newborn." In addition to the thirty items listed, space was provided for respondents to write in two additional events that created stress for them. Respondents were asked to indicate whether they had or had not experienced each event, and the degree of stress, on a scale of one to five, for those they had experienced.

Family Support Scale (FSS). This scale consists of eighteen items. Parents are asked to report the degree to which individuals or groups have been helpful to them. In addition to a Total Support Score, scores are compiled for Family Support, Friends' Support, and Community Support. When the test was given to 139 subjects, the researchers found the alpha coefficient for the total score to be .77. Test-retest reliability (a month after first completion) was .75 for individual items and .91 for scale scores (Dunst, Jenkins, & Trivette, 1984).

Parenting Events Inventory (PEI). Crnic and his colleagues (1983) showed that mothers who reported high stress and low social support were less sensitive to infants' cues and less likely to behave in ways that reinforced infants' positive social-emotional development. From the evidence of these studies, it seemed that the measurement of stress and support in parents was particularly important for understanding the social, cognitive, and linguistic development of the deaf infants in this study. The Parenting Events Inventory, adapted from Crnic and Greenberg's (1985, 1990) instrument consists of a set of twenty statements designed to measure the level of stress associated with the "daily hassles" of child-rearing. This was completed by parents after the interview when infants were 15 months old.

Data Management

Coding schemes will be described as data are presented. Each team member was responsible for managing the coding and analysis of separate portions of the protocol, as reflected in the authorship of chapters to follow. Meadow-Orlans managed the interview and questionnaire data, plus the mother–child interaction data coded from the free-play sessions. Spencer was responsible for analyses of language, play, and visual attention, based on the free-play sessions and language questionnaire/interview data. Koester shepherded the 6- and 9-month mother–child face-to-face interaction data, and MacTurk managed the mastery motivation information. Koester and MacTurk collaborated on the collection and coding of attachment data for the two groups with hearing parents. MacTurk supervised the coding of attachment data for the two groups with deaf parents; Koester and Meadow-Orlans analyzed attachment data for the four groups.

Koester consulted with Hanuš Papoušek in developing codes for face-to-face interactions and worked with Sybil Smith-Gray to code the data. She received funding from the March of Dimes for some of this work. After moving to the University of Montana, Koester continued to analyze the face-to-face data with assistance from then-graduate students Lisa R. Brooks, Andrea M. Karkowski, and Meg Ann Traci (Chapter 4). Spencer consulted with Lauren Adamson for coding visual attention (Chapter 11) and with Lorraine McCune for coding play behaviors (Chapter 12). Spencer's work on play was supported by her grant from the Office of Special Education and Rehablitation Services. For some analyses of visual attention, she worked with Virginia Swisher and Robyn Waxman, whose dissertation was based on the Gallaudet data (Waxman, 1995).

MacTurk worked with Jennifer L. Ludwig (Chapter 7), who used the Gallaudet mastery data for a dissertation (Ludwig, 1999). Meadow-Orlans collaborated with Annie Steinberg in developing a code for the mother–child interaction data, and she was assisted by Steinberg, Carol Erting, Carrin Stika, and Sybil Smith-Gray in coding interaction (Chapter 8). Birgit Dyssegaard's expertise was essential for evaluating the group of children with cognitive and physical disabilities (Chapter 6).

Special Considerations in Research with Deaf Children and Families

Hearing researchers are often challenged: What right do they have to conduct research in a community where they are outsiders? What are their credentials for research on a population whose condition they have not experienced? These are legitimate questions and the answers are not simple:

> Studying in someone else's backyard is [not] easy. . . . When the researcher does not share the culture of those she or he studies, there is the danger that the research will be conceived, conducted, and reported within a world view that seriously distorts the experience of informants. Strategies . . . to enhance . . . collaboration, feedback, and empowerment of research informants may help both insider and outsider researchers reduce distortion of findings and discover the perspectives of those they study. (Foster 1993/1994, 9–10)

Every effort was made throughout the conduct of the project to be sensitive to the special needs of parent and child participants, and to ensure that they recognized our gratitude for their cooperation. One way of showing appreciation was to make copies of all videotapes for parents to keep as a permanent record of their child at these early ages. Another was to honor a commitment to make presentations and write papers for parent, teacher, and researcher audiences.

Ethical Concerns

Distinctive ethical concerns arise in research with special populations. In low-incidence groups, the same participants may be overtaxed, their privacy endangered, and they may lose the innocence often assumed by researchers. Informed consent is a special concern, especially in research where participants "have impairments that would limit understanding and/or communication" (American Psychological Association, 1982, p. 3). Psychologists should "identify situations in which particular . . . assessment techniques or norms may not be applicable or may require adjustment in administration or interpretation because of factors such as individuals' gender, age, race, ethnicity, national origin, religion, sexual orientation, disability, language, or socioeconomic status" (American Psychological Association, 1992, Standard 2.04c). Pollard (1992) proposed that researchers in the Deaf community use ethical guidelines developed for cross-cultural research, being sure to include community members in the research team and advisory board.

Confidentiality assumes additional importance in small communities or subcultures. Descriptors for individual cases should be modified or eliminated to assure anonymity. In her research with mothers of thalidomide children, Roskies (1972, p. ix) found it "both more important and harder than usual to keep the pledge of confidentiality." In populations where participants are difficult to find or to enlist, the inadvertent disclosure of identities can cost the trust of and future access to an entire community.

Videotaped data collection increases the need to guard confidentiality carefully, because there is no simple way to mask identity. For this project, potential participants were asked to sign a consent form to cover research participation, where only those on the research team would have access to their videotapes. If participants were willing to have tapes shown to broader audiences for educational purposes, a second clause to that effect required an additional signature. Even with this consent, an ethical issue arises in showing tapes as "negative examples." (There may also be a legal issue of guarding participants' reputations [Department of Health and Human Services, 1991].) Our practice, in showing videotapes for professional or parent–teacher–student groups, was never to show a videotape as a negative example. Only positive interactions or "successful" segments were to be viewed. Although there are some dangers of distorting research findings by showing too positive a view, this can be addressed in presentation of nonvideo data. We believed that showing parents or children and then criticizing them would have been a negation of the trust implied in their consent to participate.

Revised federal regulations for the protection of human subjects contain new provisions related to obtaining a child's assent. "In determining whether children are capable of assenting, the IRB (Institutional Review Board) shall take into account the ages, maturity, and psychological state of the children involved" (Department of Health and Human Services, 1991, p. 16). As in research with children (Thompson, 1990), it may be especially important to develop clear explanations of research procedures and sensitive debriefings for populations of adults with limited experience or sophistication.

Conclusion

The analyses presented in the following chapters are based on rare longitudinal data collected from deaf/hard-of-hearing infants with either hearing or deaf parents. This design offers a unique opportunity to investigate developmental processes important not only to those interested in deafness but also to those broadly concerned with child development. Chapters 1, 2, and 3 provided a view of the wide-ranging scope and effort required to collect and analyze the data in the remainder of this volume. A major contribution came from the eighty participating families whose dedication to the project made this book possible.

4

Mother–Infant Behaviors at 6 and 9 Months

A Microanalytic View

Lynne Sanford Koester, Meg Ann Traci, Lisa R. Brooks, Andrea M. Karkowski, and Sybil Smith-Gray

The infant's world is centered on caregivers—purveyors of the warmth, nourishment, and social experiences that provide physical comfort and emotional satisfaction from the earliest days and months of life. For deaf infants, the world is perceived primarily through vision (though tactile/kinesthetic experiences also play an important role), and it is important for their caregivers to adapt to this basic fact. For parents who can hear, especially those who decide to use sign language, many behaviors linked to vocal face-to-face communication will be modified to accommodate a visual-gestural language. New methods of eliciting and maintaining attention through other sensory channels will be incorporated into their communicative repertoire, sometimes unconsciously and intuitively but at other times requiring awareness and conscious practice (Swisher, 1984, 2000; Spencer, Bodner-Johnson, & Gutfreund, 1992; Spencer & Meadow-Orlans, 1996). For parents who are deaf, these visual skills are already in place but interaction with a hearing infant may produce in them a sense of discomfort similar to that of the hearing parent with a young deaf child.

In this chapter, our first window into the world of deaf infants, we examine the face-to-face interactions of mothers and infants. In most Western cultures, face-to-face encounters between parents and infants are frequent, commonplace occurrences. They provide opportunities to observe the mutual influences or reciprocal effects so important to continued parent–infant exchange. Behaviors typical of each partner, such as maintaining or breaking eye contact, "motherese" adaptations in language behavior, touching and comforting, infant cooing, babbling, or self-regulation, and expressions of joy or displeasure, are indices of mutual affective and dyadic synchrony (Brazelton, 1982; Stern, 1985; Papoušek

& Papoušek, 1987; Isabella & Belsky, 1991; Koester, 1995; Crandell, Fitzgerald, & Whipple, 1997).

Maternal responsiveness to the infant's behaviors was investigated because this is an important component of successful interactions and fosters the infant's emerging sense of self as a competent social partner (Traci & Koester, 2003). Hearing parents with deaf infants may rely heavily on vocal productions in response to the infant's signals. When an infant has a hearing loss, access to this prominent feature of most early interactions is limited. Although this might lead to some variations in the usual interactive patterns, it is possible that both partners will adapt and compensate successfully by relying more heavily on other communicative modalities. However, in the absence of concurrent or supplementary use of other modalities when reinforcing the infant's visual attention, responding to positive social bids, or comforting distress, otherwise appropriate vocal responses may be ineffective.

Parents may be motivated and perhaps even preadapted to accommodate an infant's needs. However, there may be factors that either facilitate or inhibit these modifications. For example, the infant plays a crucial role in eliciting interaction, signaling readiness or fatigue, and providing feedback and reinforcement to the caregiver (Brazelton, Koslowski, & Main, 1974; Field, 1978; Morales, Mundy, & Rojas, 1998; Tamis-LeMonda, Bornstein, & Baumwell, 2001). The infant's behaviors help to shape the responses of the adult partner, whose contingent responses in turn support the infant's developing awareness of self-efficacy.

The research strategy of incorporating a Still Face episode (in which the mother is instructed to be unresponsive for a short period of time) makes it possible to observe the infant's responses to mild stress, and to draw inferences about the infant's awareness of social expectancies (Tronick et al., 1978; Tronick, Ricks, & Cohn, 1982; Ellsworth, Muir & Hains, 1993; D'Entremont & Muir, 1997). This interruption of the expected sequence of social interchange elicits the infant's coping strategies, which may include increased efforts to reengage the mother, self-regulatory or comforting behaviors, and in many cases heightened negativity (Carter, Mayes, & Pajer, 1990). Researchers have found a predictable sequence of infant reactions, often beginning with a positive greeting, then a brief turning away, with periodic referencing of the mother's behavior, and gradually diminishing efforts to recruit her response or to "repair" the interaction (Murray & Trevarthen, 1985; Mayes & Carter, 1990; Stack & Muir, 1990; Stifter & Moyer, 1991; Weinberg & Tronick, 1991). Soon the infant stops smiling altogether and consistently looks away from the mother's face (Gusella, Muir, & Tronick, 1988; D'Entremont & Muir, 1997).

Over time, the infant develops increased competence for coping with such minor disruptions, gradually using more sophisticated and efficient means of communicating desires and responses to social partners. Repeated experiences with sensitive and responsive caregivers, who provide feedback that the infant's behaviors are effective, are essential to the infant's continued motivation and success as a social partner.

One adaptation necessary for a deaf child involves shifting visual attention from communicator to the object under discussion. Visual attention generally is an important skill for deaf children to master, and one to be investigated in our data. Conversely, mothers must wait for their infant to look back to them before signing or responding to the child's focus of attention. This ability to coordinate gaze patterns is of particular significance for a deaf child, who relies on vision for dual purposes: receptive language and exploration of the physical world (Waxman & Spencer, 1997).

By looking to deaf parents with deaf children, one can find models of intuitive parenting that may lead to important insights for hearing parents and for early intervention specialists. Even "oral" deaf parents not using any formal sign system appear to unconsciously facilitate the child's access to parental language input by incorporating gestures extensively when interacting with their deaf children (de Villiers, Bibeau, Helliwell, & Clare, 1989; Petitto, 2000). Deaf parents often incorporate strategies not typical among hearing parents; as a result, they appear to display responsive and contingent interaction patterns (Spencer, Bodner-Johnson, & Gutfreund, 1992).

This chapter reports results from a large number of analyses completed for 6- and 9-month-old infants during face-to-face interactions with their mothers. Interactive behaviors of both members of the dyads are described, including tactile, visual, and auditory modalities or sensory channels.

Methodology

Participants

Analyses of maternal and infant vocal and nonvocal behaviors are based on videotaped interactions between sixty-nine 9-month-old infants and their mothers: Dd = 14; Hd = 21; Dh = 14; Hh = 20. Thirty-six of these same infants were also observed during similar interactions at age 6 months: Dd = 10; Hd = 5; Dh = 11; Hh = 10. Analyses of maternal tactile behaviors were based on twenty-three mothers: Dd = 6; Hd = 5; Dh = 6; Hh = 6. Analyses of maternal responses to infants' gaze averts were based on forty mothers, evenly divided among the four groups. Videotapes were coded separately for mothers' and infants' vocal and nonvocal behaviors, using a microanalytic coding scheme adapted from the Monadic Phase system (Tronick, Als, & Brazelton, 1980). Separate coding systems were devised for tactile and eye-gaze behaviors.

Data Collection

Methods are described in Chapter 3. Briefly, they involve three episodes of mother–infant interaction: in episode 1, the mother is instructed to "play" with her baby for 3 minutes. In episode 2, she is instructed to sit without moving, with a "Still Face," for 2 minutes, returning to normal play in episode 3.

Coding

Infants' and mothers' vocal and nonvocal behaviors were coded separately. Infant vocal behaviors included *laugh*; *positive/non-fussy vocalizations* (e.g., cooing, babbling, "raspberries"[1]); *cry* (prolonged, rhythmic and spasmodic); and *quiet*. Nonvocal behaviors included *rhythmic activity* (e.g., cycling feet, kicking, waving arms, closing/opening fists); *positive/negative affect* (e.g., smile, grimace, frown); *neutral/observe*; *self-regulation* (e.g., suck thumb/fingers, rock, twirl hair); *signal-reach* (e.g., point, reach, lean or wave to mother); *look at mother*, *look away from mother* (toward self or surroundings).

Mothers' vocal behaviors included: *laugh*; *vocal play* (game routines like Pat-a-Cake, songs, nursery rhymes, tongue clicks, raspberries); *talk*

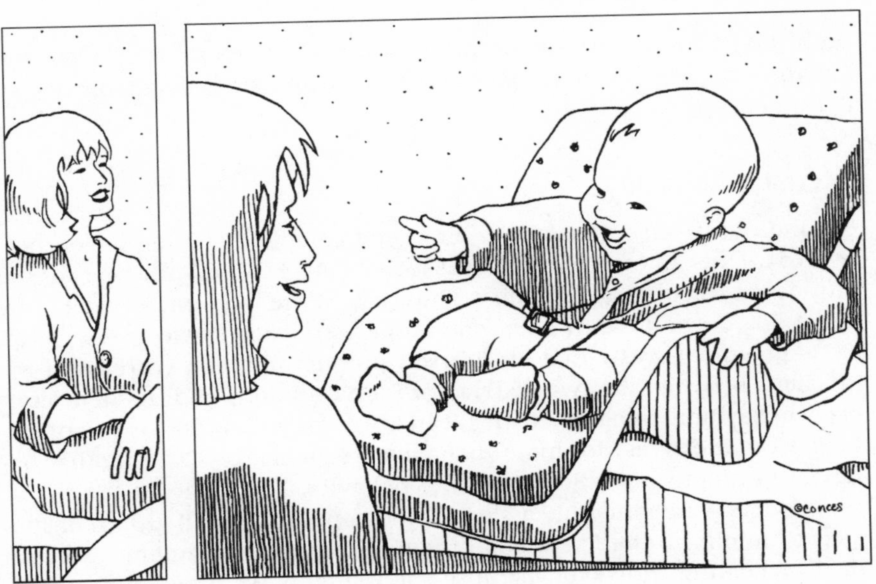

Figure 4-1. After 3 minutes of normal play, mothers were asked to sit without moving with a "Still Face" for 2 minutes. Some babies were eager to reengage with their mothers, like the one depicted here. The child was unable to maintain her composure and broke into a broad smile. (Illustration by Liz Conces Spencer)

to infant ("babytalk" or "motherese" register, questions or commentary about the infant's behavior or surroundings); and *imitation of baby's vocalizations*. Nonvocal maternal behaviors included *games* (such as peek-a-boo, tickling or nuzzling); *smile; exaggerated facial expression* (e.g., mock surprise or anger, raising or knitting eyebrows); *visual/gestural activities* (signing, finger play, finger spelling, shaking or nodding head, pointing); *look at baby;* and *waiting* (neutral/observe only—no other tactile or visual activity).

For a subset of mothers, two additional behaviors were coded (ten dyads from each group were chosen from those whose videotapes were of the best quality for positioning of mother and infant to allow for these analyses):

1. Tactile behaviors, including *passive contact* (point of contact does not change for at least 1 second, and mother is not moving any part of child); *active/moving* (tapping, stroking, or moving the point of contact on the child's body); *active/passive combination* (with one hand passive and the other active). Location, intensity, and duration of contact were also coded.
2. Mothers' reactions to their infants' gaze aversions, including *observing/waiting* (for at least 1 second); *vocal response; tactile/vibratory response; visual response* (e.g., gesture/sign within the child's visual field).

Both the frequency and the duration of these behaviors were recorded. For this chapter, however, the discussion will usually focus on one or the other.

Interrater Reliability

For the overall microanalytic coding, one complete episode for each of twelve infants and ten mothers was recoded by a second observer for the purpose of calculating reliability. Thus, 5% of the total infant video time and 6.5% of the total mother video time were coded twice.

Agreement was based on Pearson product-moment correlation coefficients between the two coders, for both durations and frequencies of each behavioral category, with mean correlations of .90 for infant behavior durations, .81 for infant behavior frequencies, .82 for mother behavior durations, and .80 for mother behavior frequencies.

Coders were randomly assigned videotapes from both groups of subjects to minimize the likelihood of identification of the infants as either deaf or hearing. However, because some infants were wearing hearing aids during the observations, and because some mothers were using sign communication, it was not always possible to mask the hearing status of the participants. (Reanalyses comparing a subgroup of infants whose hearing aids were visible to those without hearing aids revealed no significant differences.)

Statistical Analyses

For mother and infant vocal and nonvocal behaviors, multivariate analyses of variance (MANOVAs), followed by Tukey's Honestly Significant Difference (HSD) post hoc analyses, were performed, using a 4 (group)-by-3 (episode) repeated-measures design. For maternal tactile contact behaviors, repeated-measures analyses of variance (ANOVAs) were applied to explore age differences using a 4 (group)-by-2 (age) design, with data collapsed across the two interaction episodes.

Only behaviors with significant results either at 6 months or at 9 months are reported in the following tables, which have been simplified to make the data more accessible.

Results and Discussion

Infant Behaviors at Ages 6 and 9 Months

Previous Still Face studies have shown that infants typically exhibit behavioral changes across the three episodes (normal play, mother unresponsive, normal interaction resumed). More negative infant behaviors are expected when mothers are unresponsive, and these behaviors may continue when normal interaction resumes, especially if dyads have a history of interactive difficulties.

Similarities Across Groups of Infants. In our data, all four groups of infants, both at age 6 months and at 9 months, spent more time displaying negative affect and vocalizations during the Still Face episode than during the other episodes, as was expected. (See Table 4-1. Because groups did not differ, combined means of the four groups are shown in this table.) There was less smiling and more struggle/protest during that episode than in the others, although struggle/protest remained quite elevated in the final interaction episode. Self-regulation behaviors were somewhat higher in the Still Face episode at 6 months, but only at 9 months was self-regulation significantly different across episodes, increasing during Still Face and continuing during episode 3.

Changes in gaze behaviors (both looking at and away from mother) also differed across the three episodes in expected ways for all the groups. Frequency of looking away from mother increased for all four groups of children from 6 to 9 months, and this was especially true when mothers were nonresponsive during the Still Face episode (see Table 4-2).

Therefore, the four groups of infants reacted like infants reported in previous studies. They showed effects of stress during the Still Face procedure through increased negative vocalizations, struggle/protest behaviors, and decreased smiling. At 9 months, these behaviors were accompanied by increased attempts at self-comforting or self-regulation behaviors. Self-regulatory behaviors represent an effort to contain re-

Table 4-1. Infant behaviors at 6 and 9 months: Smile, struggle/protest, self-regulation. Episodes 1–3 (Normal Interaction, Still Face, Normal Interaction) (mean frequency or duration)[1]

	Episode 1	*Episode 2*	*Episode 3*
Age 6 Months, N = 36			
Smile[a*]	2.8	1.8	2.5
Struggle/Protest[b***]	4.0	24.8	24.3
Self-regulation[b]	10.8	15.5	9.3
Age 9 Months, N = 69			
Smile[a***]	4.3	2.3	3.0
Struggle/Protest[b***]	8.0	21.8	19.8
Self-regulation[b***]	6.8	10.8	12.5

[1]Because no significant group differences existed for these variables, values for the four groups were averaged.

[a]Frequency.

[b]Duration in seconds.

*$p \leq .05$.

***$p \leq .001$.

flexive or affective responses to stress, overstimulation, or displeasure (Lipsitt, 1983, 1990; Kochanska, Coy & Murray, 2001; Trevarthen & Aitken, 2001).

Some of these stress-related effects continued into the following interaction episode. In addition, infants showed a pattern of increasing changes in gaze with age, being less likely to look unwaveringly at their mothers than before. This tendency to look away and then briefly back at mother was especially evident during the Still Face episode when mothers were not actively interacting with the babies (see Table 4-2).

Group Differences: Gaze Behaviors. Despite these group similarities, the hearing status of the infants and their mothers was associated with significant behavioral differences. Visual fixation and following are among the most sophisticated of infant behaviors from the early months of life, "acts . . . that are both intentional and subject to [the child's] control," enabling him or her to construct "an on-off system that can easily modulate or eliminate external sensory input" (Robson, 1967, pp. 13–14).

Gaze behaviors differed across groups in some potentially important ways (see Table 4-2 above). At 6 months, both groups of infants with deaf parents (Dd, Dh) had more "looks to mother" and "looks at other" than did the two groups with hearing parents (Hh, Hd). This suggests that the first two groups were switching their gaze to and from mother

Table 4-2. Infant gaze behaviors, 6 months and 9 months: Look at mother, look at other: Episodes 1–3 (Normal Interaction, Still Face, Normal Interaction), four groups (mean frequency)

	Episode 1	*Episode 2*	*Episode 3*
Age 6 Months			
Look at mother^{G*E*}			
Dd	5.2	7.1	5.6
Hd	2.0	5.4	3.4
Dh	5.6	6.6	6.6
Hh	3.4	4.8	3.3
Look at other^{G*}			
Dd	4.3	6.0	5.0
Hd	1.6	3.8	3.4
Dh	4.9	5.7	5.2
Hh	3.1	3.9	3.6
Age 9 Months			
Look at mother^{G***E*}			
Dd	6.5	7.0	3.8
Hd	6.4	5.9	5.8
Dh	6.1	7.1	6.0
Hh	9.3	10.0	9.3
Look at other^{G***E***}			
Dd	4.4	6.5	3.6
Hd	6.6	5.5	4.9
Dh	4.3	5.8	4.8
Hh	8.0	9.2	7.1

^{G}Group.

^{E}Episode.

$^{*}p \leq .05$.

$^{***}p \leq .001$.

Dd = Deaf mother, deaf infant. N = 10 @ 6 mos., 14 @ 9 mos.

Hd = Hearing mother, deaf infant. N = 5 @ 6 months, 21 @ 9 mos.

Dh = Deaf mother, hearing infant. N = 11 @ 6 mos., 14 @ 9 mos.

Hh = Hearing mother, hearing infant. N = 10 @ 6 mos., 20 @ 9 mos.

more often than the latter two groups. At 9 months, a different pattern is seen, with Hh infants making more frequent looks to mother and to "other" compared to the three other groups. It is not clear why the patterns would diverge at these two ages, but it should be noted that the 9-month difference (between Hh and the three other groups) is greater than differences at 6 months. It is tempting to speculate that the lesser gaze shifting for the three groups of dyads with a deaf member reflects infants' increasing responsiveness to visual signals from their mothers.

Infants' Physical Activities. Other significant group differences are summarized in Table 4-3 where the data show that groups of infants differ significantly in the duration of their repetitive physical activities at age 6 months and also at 9 months. At 6 months, both groups of infants with hearing mothers (Hd and Hh) engaged in these activities more during the first interaction than during the Still Face (second) episode, whereas infants with deaf mothers increased these activities during the Still Face episode. At 6 months, infants in unmatched dyads (Hd and Dh) increased their time in rhythmic activity during the second interaction (episode 3), when those in the two other groups (Dd and Hh) decreased the time spent in repetitive physical activities. It is also notable that hearing infants with hearing mothers spent the least amount of time in these behaviors during all the episodes at 9 months.

Differences at 9 months are also seen in the frequency of signal/reach behaviors. These were most often produced by the Hh infants in all three episodes, with Dd infants next most likely to produce them during the first two episodes (although not during the third episode when interaction was resumed). This type of behavior is important because it is a clear and easily understood request for interaction and one that is difficult for adults to ignore.

Positive/Negative Vocalizations. Productions of positive and negative vocalizations also differed across groups (see Table 4-3). Although negative vocalizations were relatively rare at 6 months, the frequency of their production increased across the episodes for the Hd children, while there was a striking peak in production for Dh infants during the Still Face episode compared to the other episodes. A fairly flat profile is seen for the Dd and Hh infants, with a very low initial production of negative vocalizations maintained across episodes. At 9 months, the duration of positive vocalizations was longest for Dh children during all three episodes. Thus, the vocal productions of hearing (Dh) children did not seem to be limited by their mothers' hearing status.

Mothers' Behaviors

These infant behaviors were occurring in an interactive context and were intimately entwined with those of their mothers. Thus, maternal behaviors were expected to differ across groups not only because of differences in mothers' hearing status, but also because their interactive behaviors were likely to be modified for infants' needs and responses to varied signals, messages, and modalities. In fact, more differences were found across groups for mothers than for infants. However, similarities also existed for the mothers.

Similarities Across Groups of Mothers. No group differences were seen at either 6 or 9 months in mothers' productions of nonvocal game rou-

Table 4-3. Infant behaviors at 6 months and 9 months: Repetitive activity, signal/reach, positive vocalizations, negative vocalizations, episodes 1–3 (Normal Interaction, Still Face, Normal Interaction), four groups (mean frequency or duration)

	Episode 1	*Episode 2*	*Episode 3*
Repetitive Activity[b]			
Age 6 months[G×E*]			
Dd	44.4	65.3	58.5
Hd	79.9	42.2	52.1
Dh	60.2	72.8	75.2
Hh	70.5	60.7	54.1
Age 9 months[G*** E**]			
Dd	29.2	52.3	34.2
Hd	31.5	47.0	32.1
Dh	51.5	48.7	49.5
Hh	18.6	20.6	17.6
Signal/Reach[a]			
Age 9 months[G*** G×E**]			
Dd	6.4	5.4	4.2
Hd	4.3	3.9	4.7
Dh	3.7	4.6	4.5
Hh	7.9	10.3	9.0
Negative Vocalizations[a]			
Age 6 months[E* G×E*]			
Dd	.9	1.1	1.2
Hd	.5	1.5	2.3
Dh	.8	4.1	1.8
Hh	1.1	1.1	1.0
Positive Vocalizations[b]			
Age 9 months[G*]			
Dd	21.4	13.9	18.5
Hd	10.4	15.3	15.4
Dh	24.2	26.7	20.4
Hh	19.1	11.7	6.8

[a]Frequency.

[b]Duration in seconds.

[G]Group.

[E]Episode

[G×E]Group-by-Episode.

*$p \leq .05$.

**$p \leq .01$.

***$p \leq .001$.

See Table 4-2 for group definitions and Ns.

tines, laughter, or imitation of baby's vocalizations. At 6 months, mothers did not differ in the frequency of their smiles or the duration of their passive observations. At 9 months, mothers did not differ in production of exaggerated facial expressions. In addition, all groups of mothers increased moderate or high-intensity tactile contacts and touches of medium duration from the first to the second interaction episode at 6 months. They increased touch to arms or hands from first to second interaction episode at 9 months, perhaps as an additional form of reassurance or intuitively adding modalities to reinitiate interaction.

Group Differences: Mothers' Facial, Visual-Gestural, and Vocal Behaviors. As Table 4-4 indicates, mothers differed at 6 months in frequency of production of exaggerated facial expressions and in visual-gestural behaviors. In each case, not surprisingly, both groups of deaf mothers produced more of these behaviors than did hearing mothers. As expected, hearing mothers' durations of talk/narrate were longer than those of deaf mothers, but Dh mothers also produced significant amounts of this behavior. When vocal play was considered, the same pattern emerged.

When infants were 9 months old, hearing mothers produced more frequent smiles, longer durations of talk/narrate, longer durations of passively observing their infants, and more vocal play (by Hd mothers only) compared to deaf mothers. Deaf mothers of hearing infants also produced significant durations of vocal play and somewhat more talk/narrate than did Dd mothers. The frequency of visual-gestural behaviors was highest for Dd mothers, followed by Hd, Dh, and Hh mothers. This set of group differences underscores the effects of mothers' primary language modality, but also shows modifications in behaviors of both Dh and Hd mothers that accommodate their infants' communicative needs. Deaf mothers vocalize more to hearing than to deaf infants and, by age 9 months, hearing mothers use more visual-gestural communications with deaf infants than with hearing infants. This could reflect an important adjustment by the hearing mothers with deaf infants, who may be better attuned at this age to the heightened visual needs of their deaf child. Many babies in this group had only recently been identified with a hearing loss, so their hearing mothers perhaps needed the intervening months to modify their own behaviors in subtle ways to meet the infant's perceptual needs more effectively.

Mothers' Tactile Behaviors. Additional differences were found in mothers' tactile behaviors.[2] As Table 4-5 illustrates, when infants were 6 months old, deaf mothers used more active/moving touches and touches of short duration compared to hearing mothers. Perhaps these behaviors are the early forms of the more formalized tapping behaviors employed by deaf mothers to obtain the attention of their toddlers.

In addition, the 6-month pattern of frequency of passive touch differed across the groups: Dd and Hh mothers increased this behavior from

Table 4-4. Maternal behaviors with infant
(1) At age 6 months: Exaggerated face, Visual-gestural, Talk/narrate, Vocal play,
(2) At age 9 months: Smile, Talk/narrate, Visual-gestural, Vocal play, Passive/observe,
Episodes 1 and 3, normal interaction (Mean frequency or duration)

Age 6 Months

Exaggerated Face[a*]		*Visual-Gestural*[a***]	
Dd	3.0	Dd	9.0
Hd	1.0	Hd	1.5
Dh	3.5	Dh	6.5
Hh	1.0	Hh	1.5
Talk/Narrate[b***]		*Vocal Play*[b***]	
Dd	6.0	Dd	6.0
Hd	35.0	Hd	45.0
Dh	20.5	Dh	18.5
Hh	49.5	Hh	63.0

Age 9 Months

Smile[a***]		*Talk/Narrate*[b***]	
Dd	5.0	Dd	6.5
Hd	7.0	Hd	42.5
Dh	4.5	Dh	9.5
Hh	8.5	Hh	42.0
Visual-Gestural[a*]		*Vocal Play*[b**]	
Dd	7.5	Dd	6.5
Hd	6.0	Hd	29.5
Dh	5.0	Dh	22.0
Hh	4.0	Hh	15.0

Passive/Observe[b**]	
Dd	26.5
Hd	47.5
Dh	22.0
Hh	38.0

[a]Frequency.

[b]Duration

*$p \le .05$.

**$p \le .01$.

***$p \le .001$.

See Table 4-2 for group definitions and Ns.

the first to the second interaction episode, whereas Hd mothers and Dh mothers (who had the lowest rate overall) decreased this behavior slightly from the first to the third episode.

At 9 months, Hd mothers were most likely to employ touch involving moving the infant's body or limbs with Dh mothers being next most

Table 4-5. Maternal tactile contact with infant
(1) At age 6 months: Active/moving, Short Duration, Passive,
(2) At age 9 months: Moving body/limbs, Touch to head/face,
Episodes 1 and 3, normal interaction (Mean frequency)

	Episode 1	*Episode 3*
Age 6 Months		
Active, Moving Touch^{G*}		
Dd	12.5	11.5
Hd	6.0	5.6
Dh	10.0	9.3
Hh	6.7	4.7
Short Duration Touch^{G*}		
Dd	6.3	5.2
Hd	5.0	1.6
Dh	5.2	3.3
Hh	1.8	1.8
Passive Touch$^{G\times E**}$		
Dd	5.8	7.5
Hd	8.8	7.2
Dh	3.2	2.7
Hh	3.5	10.7
Age 9 Months		
Moving Body/Limbs^{G**}		
Dd	3.3	5.5
Hd	10.8	11.4
Dh	8.5	6.5
Hh	4.0	6.2
Touch to Head/Face$^{G\times E*}$		
Dd	3.0	.8
Hd	2.2	2.4
Dh	1.0	2.0
Hh	.5	2.7

^{G}Group.

$^{G\times E}$Group-by-Episode.

$^{*}p \leq .05$.

$^{**}p \leq .01$.

N: Dd = 6; Hd = 5; Dh = 6; Hh = 6.

likely. Finally, patterns of frequency of touches to infants' head and face at the first and third episode differed at 9 months, with increases seen for Hd, Dh, and Hh mothers, but a decrease for Dd mothers. However, this behavior occurred rarely for every group.

Responses to Infants' Gaze Averts. Intriguing differences were also found at 9 months in mothers' reactions to their infants' averting gaze from them. Deaf mothers (Dd, Dh) were, of course, more likely than hearing mothers to respond to this behavior with a visual strategy, whereas hearing mothers (Hh, Hd) were more likely to react with a vocal behavior (see Table 4-6). (This was most frequent for Hh mothers, however.)

An analysis of the percentage of infant gaze averts to which mothers made an active bid to regain attention showed the mothers in unmatched hearing status groups (Hd, Dh) to be more likely to do this than mothers in the other two groups. As a corollary, this means that deaf mothers tended to wait patiently more often when their infants visually explored the surroundings.

Some of these maternal differences were related to mothers' hearing status and habitual communication mode. However, on other measures, the match or absence of match in mother and infant hearing status seemed to influence mothers' behaviors. In at least some situations (i.e., increased vocalization by Dh mothers; increased visual–gestural behaviors by Hd mothers), adaptive influences were evident. In other sit-

Table 4-6. Maternal behaviors during infant gaze aversions at age 9 months: Visual, Vocal, Bid for infant attention (Mean frequency or percent)

*Visual Response/Strategy**	
Dd	4.7
Hd	1.3
Dh	4.8
Hh	1.4
*Vocal Response/Strategy****	
Dd	.7
Hd	5.7
Dh	4.1
Hh	10.3
*Bid for Infant Attention**	
Dd	69%
Hd	93
Dh	86
Hh	76

*$p \leq .05$.

***$p \leq .001$.

N = 10 per group.

uations (i.e., tendency to actively attempt to redirect infants' attention), it is not clear whether these differences were adaptive or indicated mothers' exaggerated concern with maintaining contact with their infants.

Conclusion

It is evident that during face-to-face interaction deaf mothers incorporate more varied forms of stimulation and in different modalities than do hearing mothers, particularly when interacting with a 6-month-old infant. These activities include smiling, highly animated facial expressions, visual-gestural games and sign communication, and frequent, energetic tactile stimulation. However, this pattern changed somewhat at 9 months, at which point both groups of hearing mothers increased smiling and group differences in frequency of behaviors decreased.

Although the deaf mothers provided more frequent multimodal input (especially in the variety of their facial expressions and tactile communications), their infants engaged in more frequent repetitive physical activity such as kicking their legs, rhythmically extending and flexing their arms and hands. One interpretation of this finding is that the apparent similarity in mother and infant activity level, broadly defined, indicates an "attunement" similar to that described by Stern (1985). Although directionality cannot be assumed, it appears that deaf mothers and their infants share or match each other's level of physical engagement during these early face-to-face interactions. Because the deaf mothers are frequently signing to their infants, the infants may be responding to this communication in a "mirroring" fashion by frequently moving their hands and arms. If this infant movement is sensed and responded to by parents, such activity may become the precursor to sign communication regardless of an infant's hearing status; this is because hearing infants who are born into these deaf families are likely to grow up using sign language within the home even though they may also learn spoken language.

Our videotapes provide vivid examples to illustrate this point. In one case, a deaf mother responds to an infant who is waving his hands by signing to the baby, "Wow, you're signing so fast! You're learning to sign!" In another example, a deaf mother observes her infant, hand outstretched, opening and closing her fists repeatedly in a pattern quite similar to that of American Sign Language; the mother signs back "Milk? Do you want your milk? Are you trying to sign 'milk'?"

It is also interesting that infants with deaf mothers display the most repetitive physical activity during the Still Face episode, compared to their behavior during the interaction episodes. Possibly the highly active and animated interactive displays by the deaf mothers are more entertaining and engaging for infants; if so, then the Still Face episode in which the mother is no longer responding may represent a greater deviation from that which the infant has learned to expect, therefore eliciting a more vigorous response.

Contrary to expectation, results for infants rather than mothers show a greater number of correlations among individual behaviors from one age of observation to the next. The implication of this finding is that mothers of young infants are continually responding to the changing behavioral repertoire of the child: as the infant develops and the forms of certain behaviors evolve, parents adapt or refine their own interactive behaviors accordingly. The consistency seen in infant behaviors is most likely a reflection of temperament characteristics, which have been shown to be relatively stable over time. It is also of interest that the deaf babies with deaf mothers are the ones who exhibit the most stability in their behaviors. For this group, significant positive correlations are found for frequency of smiling and of looking at self; duration of looking at other and of repetitive physical activity both approach significance for this group when correlated from age 6 to 9 months. No other dyadic group had more than one significantly correlated behavior across the two observations.

Finally, it must be emphasized that although many differences existed among the four groups of mothers and infants, there were even more similarities in their behaviors. Evidence shows that hearing mothers with deaf infants are adapting to their infants' hearing loss, increasing their use of visual-gestural input from 6 to 9 months, while continuing to utilize the vocal signals that are habitual to them (but also supported by most early intervention specialists who recommend "speech plus sign" for deaf babies). Although the hearing status of infants and their mothers is an important behavioral influence, there are a myriad of other factors. Two of these, infant temperament and maternal interpretation of temperamental tendencies, are discussed in the following chapter.

Acknowledgments

Material in this chapter was extracted from the following sources:

Koester, L. S. (1994, July). The vocal environments of deaf and hearing infants and mothers. Poster presented at the International Society for the Study of Behavioural Development biennial meetings, Amsterdam, The Netherlands.

Koester, L. S. (1995). Characteristics of face-to-face interactions between hearing mothers and their deaf or hearing 9-month-olds. *Infant Behavior and Development, 18* (2), 145–153.

Koester, L. S., Brooks, L. R., & Karkowski, A. M. (1998). A comparison of the vocal patterns of deaf and hearing mother–infant dyads during face-to-face interactions. *Journal of Deaf Studies and Deaf Education, 3* (4), 290–301.

Koester, L. S., Brooks, L. R., & Traci, M. A. (2000). Tactile contact by deaf and hearing mothers during face-to-face interactions with their infants. *Journal of Deaf Studies and Deaf Education, 5* (2), 127–139.

Koester, L. S., Karkowski, A. M., & Traci, M. A. (1998). How do deaf and hearing mothers regain eye contact when their infants look away? *American Annals of the Deaf, 143* (1), 5–13.

Smith-Gray, S. K., & Koester, L. S. (1995). Defining and observing social signals in deaf and hearing infants. *American Annals of the Deaf, 140* (5), 422–427.

Notes

1. Raspberries are sounds made by blowing through pursed lips.
2. Tactile Contact Interrater Reliability. Six videotapes (26% of total sample) were randomly selected to be coded by each of two observers and compared for interrater reliability. Results indicated mean scores of 85% agreement for type of contact; 98% for location of contact; and 77% for intensity of contact.

5

Interactions of Hearing Mothers and 9-Month-Old Infants

Temperament and Infant Stress

Lynne Sanford Koester and Kathryn P. Meadow-Orlans

An infant's unique characteristics, such as irritability and adaptability, influence the interactive patterns of parent–infant dyads from birth onward. Often referred to as "temperament," this constellation of reactions to environmental cues has particular significance for a child with a disability (Chess & Thomas, 1996). "Temperament is a way of seeing the child as bringing unique social contributions to the world" (J. E. Bates, 1987, p. 1101). Temperament as a concept was effectively barred from scientific discourse for decades, when psychologists emphasized the role of the environment in human development. This prohibition was breached by "[t]he intellectual courage of Alexander Thomas and Stella Chess [1977], who introduced the idea of infant temperament in the late 1950s" (Kagan, 2001, p. 45). Prolonged debates about *Difficult* and *Easy* temperamental differences recur, and these often continue to be based on disagreements about the relative importance of "nature" and "nurture" (J. E. Bates, 1987, 1994; Belsky & Rovine, 1987; Goldsmith et al., 1987; Calkins & Fox, 1992). Some researchers have identified relationships between temperament and autonomic activity, noting the impact of an infant's self-regulatory abilities on processes such as selective attention and social interactions (Huffman et al., 1998).

Thomas and Chess (1977, Chess & Thomas, 1996) emphasize that temperamental characteristics are evident early; they consist of behavioral tendencies that are constitutionally derived and influence subsequent development because they shape early social relationships. By combining ratings of individual behaviors (e.g., distractibility, activity level, intensity of response, general mood, predictability), Thomas and Chess derived three general categories of temperament, which they refer to as "*Easy*," *Difficult*," and "*Slow-to-Warm-Up*." (In an effort to portray each style as having potentially positive qualities, the term "*Exuberant*" is sometimes being used now instead of the more negative term "*Difficult.*") Buss and Plomin (1984) took a more biological approach, emphasizing the child's general level of activity, energy, and tempo. They agreed, however, that these characteristics have significant consequences for the quality of early social interactions and are not immutable.

Differences in infant and maternal temperament are either explicit or implied in much of the research on mother–infant interactions. An important theme in recent developmental research is the degree to which parent and infant respond to *and* influence the other's behavior or contribute to dyadic interaction. This bi-directional influence has been documented in studies of normal (nondepressed) mothers and their infants (Brazelton, Koslowski, & Main, 1974; Tronick, Ricks, & Cohn, 1982) as well as in studies of infants and depressed mothers (Cohn, Matias, Campbell, & Hopkins, 1990).

Individual temperament patterns can have either a positive *or* a negative influence on a child's psychological development, regardless of a disability (Chess & Thomas, 1996). In the case of a *Difficult* or an *Easy* child the attitudes and responses of adults toward these temperamental expressions influence the direction and nature of that child's development. Furthermore, as with all children, a difficult child with a disability "is at greatest risk for evoking aversion in others. . . . New situations, people, and routines evoke withdrawal and protest [from the child], and adaptation takes a long time. . . . [W]hen stresses occur, stormy interactions are all too likely" (Chess & Thomas, 1996, p. 175).

Parental Responsiveness to Infant Signals

Some research suggests that disturbance in early nonverbal communication (such as difficult-to-read infant signals, or lack of responsiveness to caregivers' bids) may be important markers of interactional difficulties between parent and child, and they may presage future emotional problems (Mundy & Willoughby, 1996). Others (e.g., Papoušek, Papoušek, Suomi, & Rahn, 1991) have suggested that, alternately, a disturbance in the parent–child relationship may itself have a negative effect on early nonverbal communication. In either case, the situation may be exacerbated by a child's disabling condition.

Parents must perceive and interpret the infant's signals accurately if they are to respond appropriately. If the infant's cues are muted or ambiguous, communicative failures are more likely. That is, parents' responses are more likely to be based on inaccurate interpretations of the infant's signals:

> [M]isread signals may be particularly problematic for interactions with infants and children who have developmental delays, as the affective expressions of such children may be more difficult to discern. . . . Parents of children with developmental delays . . . have been shown to be more di-

rective in terms of the types of communications with their children as well as in the timing or contingency between child and parent behavior. (Walden & Knieps, 1996, p. 31)

Misread signals may also be more likely for mothers of deaf infants, and these miscues might contribute to the "directive" behaviors often attributed to these mothers (see Spencer & Gutfreund, 1990, for a review). Parental observations of their child's day-to-day behavior lead to a general perception of the child as *Easy* or *Difficult*. If the identification of an infant's hearing loss is particularly stressful, a *Difficult* child may make an already fragile relationship even more vulnerable.

Chapter 4 reviewed in detail the analyses of mother–infant patterns of face-to-face interactions at ages 6 and 9 months. Here, some of the 9-month interaction data are related to mothers' perceptions of their infants as generally of *Difficult* or *Easy* temperament. Because temperament data were not collected from the two groups of deaf mothers, this discussion includes only hearing mothes, groups Hd and Hh.

Methodology

Participants

Data were analyzed from thirty-eight hearing mothers and their 9-month-old infants, nineteen who are deaf (Hd) and nineteen who are hearing (Hh).

Procedures

Here, two measures of infant behavior are related to maternal judgments of child temperament. Thus, three variables are described: child repetitive activity, child gaze avert, and maternal response to a questionnaire assessing parenting stress.

Infant Behaviors During Face-to-Face Interaction. Data collection and coding procedures are described in Chapters 3 and 4. Infants' *Repetitive Activity* (e.g., cycling feet, kicking, waving arms, closing/opening fists, rocking) is utilized here to differentiate those with varying levels of activity during interactions with mothers. *Gaze Avert* (*Look Away* from mother) is the second infant behavior, indicating infant visual attention to the mother or to the environment in general. Because heightened or reduced infant *Repetitive Activity* and *Gaze Avert* could be expected to differentiate *Difficult* and *Easy* babies, these two behaviors were selected for this analysis.

Maternal Perceptions of Infants' Characteristic Behaviors. The *Parenting Stress Index* (PSI) (Abidin, 1986) was completed by hearing mothers only, after the 9-month laboratory visit. (The resources for translating the PSI into ASL on videotape were not available, and it was decided that deaf mothers' responses to a lengthy English-language questionnaire would produce data of questionable validity.) The Child Domain, used for this analysis, contains six subscales: Adaptability, Acceptability, Mood, Demandingness, Reinforces Parent, and Distractibility/Hyperactivity. Although this was not specifically designed as a measure of temperament, according to its author (Abidin, 1986) it is based on Thomas and Chess's (1977) earlier work. A Child Domain total score was created by summing the six subscale scores. Infants whose scores were above the median *for their group* (Hd or Hh) were defined as *Difficult*; those with scores below the group median were defined as *Easy*.

Results

Infant Behaviors by Hearing Status

Analysis of the mean durations of time spent in *Repetitive Activity* by infants in the two groups during each episode revealed that deaf infants with hearing mothers engaged in significantly longer durations of these activities when compared to hearing infants with hearing mothers [F (1,34) = 10.94; $p < .001$]. These rhythmic activities increased significantly for the deaf infants during the Still Face episode [t (38) = 2.37; $p < .05$].

The frequency of *Gaze Averts* by infants in each group was also compared during the three observation episodes. Results indicate that hearing infants looked away from their mothers significantly more often than did the deaf infants [F (1,34) = 7.76; $p < .01$].

Parenting Stress Index (Child Domain)

The only variable on which perceptions of mothers with deaf or hearing infants differed significantly on the PSI was the subscale "Distractibility/Hyperactivity." In this case, Hd infants were perceived as being more distractible or hyperactive than were their Hh counterparts [t (38) = 2.22; $p < .05$].

Infant Behaviors by PSI Scores: *Difficult* versus *Easy* Babies

Repetitive Activity was analyzed with the two groups of babies divided into those perceived as *Difficult* or *Easy* by their mothers. The Hd infants perceived as *Difficult* by their mothers engaged in significantly more *Repetitive Activity* during the first interaction episode compared to the three other subgroups: *Easy* deaf infants (Hd), *Easy* and *Difficult* hearing (Hh) infants [F (3,34) = 6.37; $p < .01$] (see Fig. 5-1).

During the Still Face episode however, *Repetitive Activity* of the *Easy* Hd babies increased to the level of the *Difficult* Hd infants, while all Hh

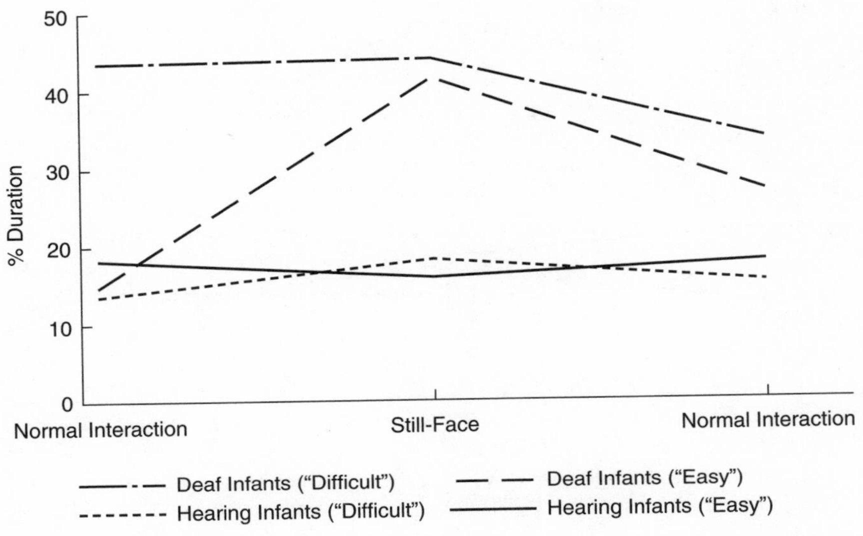

Figure 5-1. Repetitive physical activity by *Difficult* and *Easy* deaf and hearing infants.

babies exhibited significantly less repetitive activity than either Hd subgroup [F (3,34) = 4.08; $p < .01$]. This pattern was consistent through the final normal interaction period, although differences were not significant. Both Hd and Hh *Difficult* babies looked away from their mothers more frequently during episode 1, compared to the two groups of *Easy* babies [F (3,34) = 3.94; $p < .05$] (see Fig. 5-2).

The *Difficult* hearing infants continued this high level of gaze aversion during the Still Face episode [F (3,34) = 8.30, $p < .001$], but the *Difficult* Hd babies actually decreased their gaze aversions to the levels of the *Easy* babies during the episode of maternal nonresponsiveness (Still Face).

Discussion

Repetitive physical activity may be a response to interactive stress, particularly for infants who are deaf. If this interpretation is correct, it appears that the *Difficult* deaf infants may be experiencing some degree of stress during normal play interactions with their hearing mothers. By contrast, the *Easy* deaf babies, like both groups of hearing infants, exhibited relatively low levels of physical activity during the first episode of face-to-face interaction with their mothers. However, during the Still Face episode, the physical activity level of the *Easy* Hd babies rose sharply (compared to that of the *Difficult* Hd babies), whereas physical activity remained the same for both groups of hearing infants. Although physical behaviors declined somewhat when maternal interaction returned to

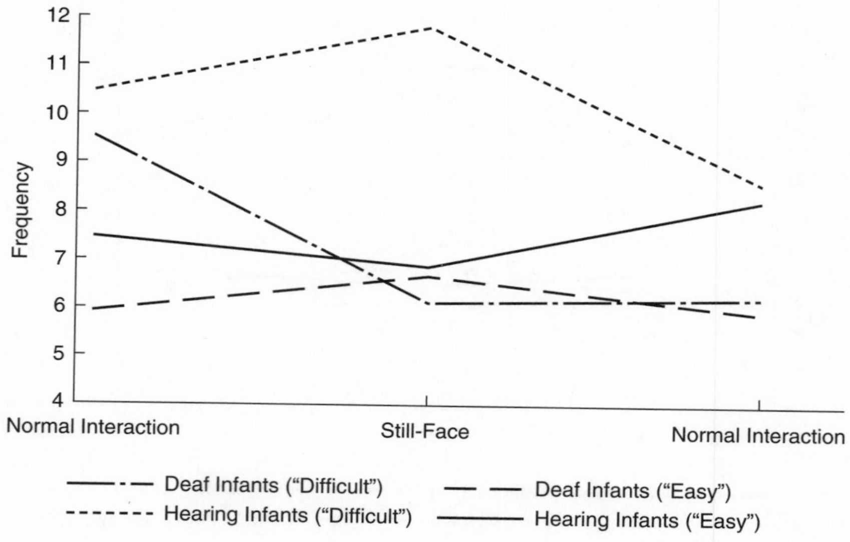

Figure 5-2. Frequency of gaze aversion by *Difficult* and *Easy* deaf and hearing infants.

normal in episode 3, this activity by deaf infants continued to be higher than that of the hearing babies. These findings suggest that even the temperamentally calm Hd infants may find it more difficult to recover from stress or harder to calm themselves after emotional upsets.

A number of researchers have reported a higher incidence of impulsive behaviors among older deaf children, compared to those with normal hearing (e.g., Altshuler et al., 1976; R. I. Harris, 1978; Meadow, 1984; Mitchell & Quittner, 1996). These results are usually explained as a response to the absence of elaborated communication between children who are deaf and their hearing parents. Such an interpretation is bolstered by several studies reporting that children who are deaf and have signing deaf parents do *not* exhibit the same behavioral problems commonly reported among children who are deaf and have hearing parents (Weisel, 1988; Calderon & Greenberg, 1993).

The results reported here, however, suggest that heightened physical excitation in response to stress can be observed in deaf children even before the age of language acquisition. It is of particular interest that this heightened activity is also associated with hearing mothers' perceptions of these infants as *Difficult*. Whether *Difficult* temperament reflects an innate biological tendency or is a response to environmental stimuli is a question that cannot be addressed with these data. Nevertheless, it is clear that an infant's predispositions play an important role in shaping caregiver responses and perceptions of a child's "soothability" and adaptability.

Calkins and Fox (1992) report a relationship between maternal assessment of hearing infants' activity level at 5 months and attachment classification at 14 months (insecure/avoidant infants were rated by mothers as being most active). However, no relationship was found between physiological measures (vagal tone and heart period) at 2 days, at 5 months, or at 14 months and attachment classification at 14 months (Calkins & Fox, 1992). Cohn, Campbell, and Ross (1992) propose that the face-to-face paradigm is analogous to the Strange Situation Procedure for the assessment of attachment in the sense that the Still Face episode corresponds to separation and the third interaction episode corresponds to the reunion. Following this logic, it would appear that the differential responses of the *Easy* and *Difficult* infants reported here may have important implications for later socioemotional outcomes for deaf infants with hearing mothers.

Braungart-Rieker, Garwood, Powers, and Notaro (1998) assert that while mothers often assist the infant in regulating arousal levels during normal interactions, when the mother is *not* responsive (as in the Still Face episode) the infant "may resort to more internally driven regulatory behaviors such as self-comforting and gaze averting" (p. 1428). Similarly, other researchers have examined infant responses to the maternal Still Face in terms of affective expressions, gaze behaviors, postural changes, and self-comforting strategies (Toda & Fogel, 1993). Their results lead to the conclusion that such behaviors are not only a reflection of the infant's own emotional responses to frustration, but also can serve as important signals to the caregiver about the infant's reactions and expectations.

Gaze behaviors have very different implications for children who are deaf compared to those who are hearing (see Chapter 11). Children with normal hearing can look away from their mothers and continue to be in communicative contact through audition, whereas those who are deaf are unable to attend to or easily perceive an oral communicative message while looking away (Wood, Wood, Griffiths, & Howarth, 1986). In either case, when deaf or hearing infants look away from their social partner, this behavior serves as an important social cue indicating either a change in focus of interest or a need to withdraw from an overload of stimulation. Results presented here show that both deaf and hearing *Difficult* infants look away from their mothers significantly more often during the first interaction than either group of *Easy* infants; these findings thus have more negative implications for the deaf than for the hearing infants (because of the deaf infants' increased dependence on vision for receptive communication). During the Still Face episode, the *Difficult* hearing babies continue their gaze aversion at the same level as in episode 1, but the *Difficult* deaf infants' gaze aversion levels drop to those of the *Easy* babies. This suggests that the earlier interaction may have been overstimulating or in some other way stressful and that with reduced maternal input the *Difficult* Hd babies might be better able to reengage with a social partner.

Conclusion

For these hearing mothers of deaf infants, infant behavioral characteristics such as repetitive motor activity and frequent looking away from the partner are related to mothers' perceptions of their infants as *Difficult.* Both of these behaviors can also be interpreted as indicators of the infant's response to mildly stressful interactions (for example, if the physical activity is diffuse, random, and disorganized, or if averting the gaze is a mechanism to avoid sensory overload). Alternatively, they may be nonverbal cues or signals to the caregiver, indicating a desire to control the level of stimulation and arousal during social interactions. Of particular interest here is that mothers' perceptions of their children's temperament are related to the two behaviors examined. That is, the deaf child who is physically active and who frequently averts his or her gaze is often perceived by hearing parents as being Distractible/Hyperactive (summarized here as *Difficult*).

Early intervention specialists may be able to use this information in two ways. First, they can encourage parents to perceive these behaviors as positive efforts of their infants to influence the environment and to communicate their feelings and wishes. Second, professionals can look carefully at the dynamics of dyadic interactions in an effort to determine whether changing maternal behaviors (such as reducing highly stimulating activities) results in modifications of the infant's "difficult" behavior patterns. Alternatively, early intervention specialists might help mothers to view active and distractible infants as "exuberant" and "curious" rather than *Difficult.* Caregivers need to recognize that individual infant differences in these behaviors are to be expected, and that although parents are not the *cause* of difficult behaviors, they may be able to influence them in a positive direction. That is, infants who are temperamentally *Difficult* may be harder to soothe and need calm and predictable environments as they learn to regulate their own physical and emotional responses to stimulation. For example, the Hd-*Difficult* infants in this study appeared to benefit from the reduced levels of maternal stimulation during the Still Face episode, reflected in the infants' heightened visual attention to the mother.

The definition of the infant as an active participant in social dialogue can contribute to increasingly positive dyadic interactions, and also a heightened recognition by parents that their infant's communicative efforts will occur in many different modalities during the early prelinguistic months. Most helpful to parent–infant interaction will be increased sensitivity by caregivers, an enhanced ability to "read" the infant's nonverbal cues, and to support the child's emerging self-regulatory capacities regardless of temperamental style.

Acknowledgments

Data presented in this chapter were published in:

Koester, L. S., & Meadow-Orlans, K. P. (1999). Responses to interactive stress: Infants who are deaf or hearing. *American Annals of the Deaf, 144,* 395–403.

6

Hearing Parents' Reactions to the Identification of Deafness and Cognitive or Motor Disabilities

Kathryn P. Meadow-Orlans, Birgit Dyssegaard, and Sybil Smith-Gray

Part I of this chapter deals with the responses of hearing parents to questionnaires about stress associated with hearing loss in a young infant and about sources of support that might alleviate the stress. Part II describes parents and their children who had cognitive or motor disabilities in addition to deafness. These families were excluded from other analyses reported in the book, but their experiences are valuable and rarely examined in detail, even though approximately one-third of all deaf and hard-of-hearing children have additional conditions that can influence their development (Wolff & Harkins, 1986; Schildroth & Hotto, 1993; Meadow-Orlans, Mertens, & Sass-Lehrer, 2003; Jones & Jones, 2003).

Regulations associated with Public Law 99-457, the Education of the Handicapped Act Amendments of 1986 (Gallagher, 1990; Black, 1991), mandate development of an Individual Family Service Plan (IFSP) to address the needs of an entire family (Dokecki & Heflinger, 1989). One effect has been a growing body of research on parental stress resulting from a child's risk or disability status (Abidin, 1986; Quittner, Glueckauf, & Jackson, 1990; Dyson, 1991; Quittner, 1991) and on support that can contribute to positive family coping (Beckman, Pokorni, Maza, & Balzer-Martin, 1986; Crnic, Greenberg, & Slough, 1986; Feiring, Fox, Jaskir, & Lewis, 1987; Beckman, 1991).

Research shows that parental stress may increase marital conflict (Bristol, Gallagher, & Schopler, 1988) and depression (Goldberg, Marcovitch, MacGregor, & Lojkasek, 1986; Beckman, 1991) for parents of children with disabilities. Stress is more severe among parents of children who have delayed rather than prompt diagnoses and unknown rather than specified etiologies (Goldberg et al., 1986), and it is more evident among parents of children with severe or profound conditions rather than those that are mild or moderate (Frey, Greenberg, & Fewell,

1989). Like mothers of nondisabled children, mothers of children with disabilities in father-absent homes experience more stress than do mothers whose partners are present (Beckman, 1983; Weinraub & Wolf, 1987; Salisbury, 1987), reflecting the increased importance of a supportive spouse for parents of children with special needs (Bristol et al., 1988; Gowen, Johnson-Martin, Goldman, & Appelbaum, 1989). Although researchers as well as practitioners often exclude fathers (Crowley, Keane, & Needham, 1982), some research has shown that mothers of children with disabilities report more depressive symptoms than do fathers (Goldberg et al., 1986; Prior, Glazner, Sanson, & Debelle, 1988; Beckman, 1991) and feel more overwhelmed by the additional demands of a child's disability (McLinden, 1990).

Some investigators question the importance placed on stress as a parental response to the identification of a child's disability, reporting that family stress and marital conflict are no more prevalent in families with special needs than in the general population (Freeman, Malkin, & Hastings, 1975; Henggeler, Watson, Whelan, & Malone, 1990). It has also been proposed that families may be strengthened and drawn together in the process of coping with childhood disability (Gallagher, Beckman, & Cross, 1983; Koester & Meadow-Orlans, 1990). The authors of recently published studies of families with deaf and hard of hearing children, who found no differences in the stress levels of these families and those of the general population, suggest that earlier identification of hearing loss and more effective intervention have helped to reduce parents' stress levels (Lederberg & Golbach, 2002; Pipp-Siegel, Sedey, & Yoshinaga-Itano, 2002).

Social support is recognized as a factor in reducing stress and improving well-being in families with special needs (Dunst & Trivette, 1986; Hauser-Cram, Warfield, Shonkoff, & Krauss, 2001), and most early intervention programs have this as a major goal (Krause & Jacobs, 1990). In one early intervention study, participating mothers gave heightened importance to emotional support from professionals and exhibited lower stress levels when they received that support, in contrast to fathers, who valued information more highly than support and were not greatly influenced by its availability (Upshur, 1991; Shonkoff, Hauser-Cram, Krauss, & Upshur, 1992). Other researchers, however, have found that social support reduced stress and depression for fathers as well as for mothers of children with disabilities (Vadasy et al., 1986; Beckman, 1991). Effective ways of managing stress are important concerns for parents of children with disabilities, and for the professionals who serve them.

Part I—Mothers' and Fathers' Stress and Support Levels

Participants and Procedures

Participants include the forty hearing-parent families who formed the core research group. All forty mothers (Hd and Hh) returned four questionnaires dealing with stress or support: two after the 9-month interview and two after the 15-month interview. Sixteen fathers of deaf children (Hd) and fifteen fathers of hearing children (Hh) completed the forms. Stress and support data were not collected from deaf parents for two reasons: *(1)* resources to translate and administer the questionnaires in American Sign Language (ASL) were not available, and *(2)* there is ample evidence that identification of hearing loss does not usually create stress for deaf parents (Meadow-Orlans, 2002; Meadow-Orlans, Mertens, & Sass-Lehrer, 2003). (The response of deaf parents to the identification of hearing in a newborn is less clear. This is a fertile area for future research [see Preston, 1994].)

The 9-month questionnaires were the *(1) Parenting Stress Index* (PSI; Abidin, 1986) and *(2) Stress of Life Events* (SLE), based on the Social Readjustment Rating Scale (Holmes & Rahe, 1967; Dohrenwend, 1973; Thoits, 1983). The PSI consists of 101 items divided between the Child Domain (Adaptability, Acceptability, Demanding, Mood, Distractibility/Hyperactivity, Reinforces Parent) and the Parent Domain (Depression, Attachment to Child, Restriction of Role, Competence, Social Isolation, Relations with Spouse, Health). Child Domain ratings are, therefore, indicative of the parents' evaluation of child characteristics and an indirect measure of the stress associated with parenting the child. The SLE consists of a list of twenty-eight events with potential for stress, covering *relationships, newborn care, health, finances, and work.* Stress levels are rated on a scale of 1 for "very little stress" to 5 for "a great deal of stress."

The 15-month questionnaires were the *(1) Family Support Scale* (FSS; Dunst, Jenkins, & Trivette, 1984), and *(2) Parenting Events Inventory* (PEI) adapted for younger children from *Parenting Daily Hassles* (Crnic & Greenberg, 1990). The FSS assesses eighteen sources of potential social support available to families of preschool children (family members, friends, work associates, and professionals). Respondents are asked to consider support received from the time the mother became pregnant with the target child on a scale of 1, "not at all helpful," to 5, "very very helpful." The PEI includes twenty statements for assessing the level of stress associated with the minor irritants of childrearing, on a scale of 1 (NOT difficult) to 5 (VERY difficult).

Interviews were conducted with mothers during the laboratory visit when infants were 9 months old, and again during a home visit when infants were 15 months old. Questions in the interview guide included some designed to elicit parents' responses to the identification of deafness, to subsequent events related to hearing loss, and to the presence or absence of intervention and support designed to ameliorate stress.

Results

Questionnaire Data

Parenting Stress Index (PSI). Overall scores on the PSI Child plus Parent Domains did not differ significantly for mothers versus fathers, or for

Hd versus Hh parents. Scores on the PSI for participants in this study are quite similar to those of Abidin's normative groups. However, there is greater variability in the scores of Hd parents compared to Hh parents. According to the guidelines established for the PSI (Abidin, 1986), scores above the 80th percentile are cause for concern about a parent's state of mind, and referral for counseling is recommended: 25% of Hd mothers and 24% of Hd fathers were "at risk" by this definition, compared to 5% of Hh mothers and none of the Hh fathers. Because mean scores were not significantly different, a larger proportion of Hd than Hh parents also had low scores, possibly indicating some "denial" of stress. That is, the range of scores was more extreme for group Hd than for group Hh.

Despite the lack of significant differences between groups in overall scores, subscale scores on the PSI Parent Domain show a number of significant differences between mothers and fathers (Fig. 6-1). Fathers of deaf infants reported marginally less "Attachment" compared to their wives. Mothers of deaf infants were marginally more "Depressed" than their husbands. Mothers of both deaf and hearing infants reported more stress related to "Restriction of Role" and to "Relations with Spouse" than did their husbands.

Subscale scores on the PSI Child Domain (Fig. 6-2) showed that fathers with deaf infants found them significantly less "Acceptable" and more "Demanding" than did fathers with hearing infants. Both mothers and fathers with deaf infants found them more "Distractible/Hyperactive" than did parents with hearing infants.

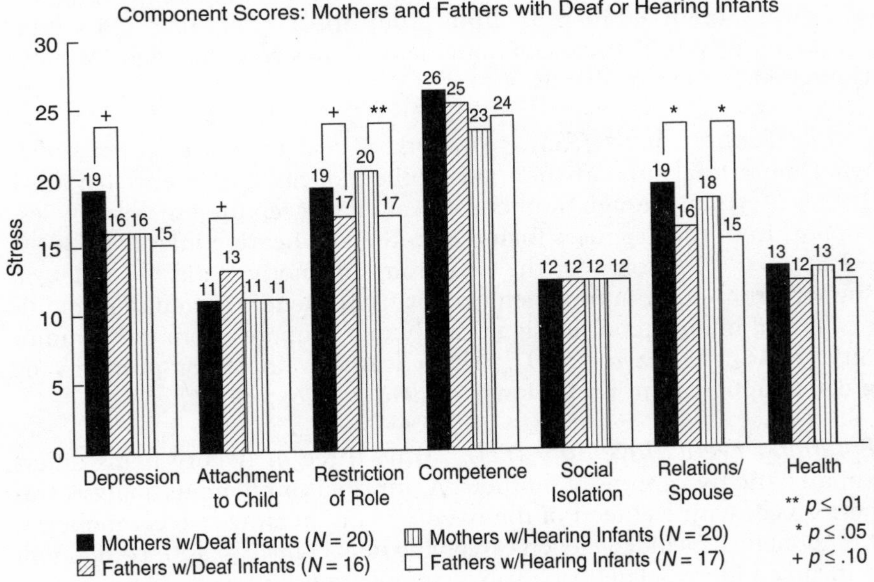

Figure 6-1. Parenting Stress Index: Parent Domain.

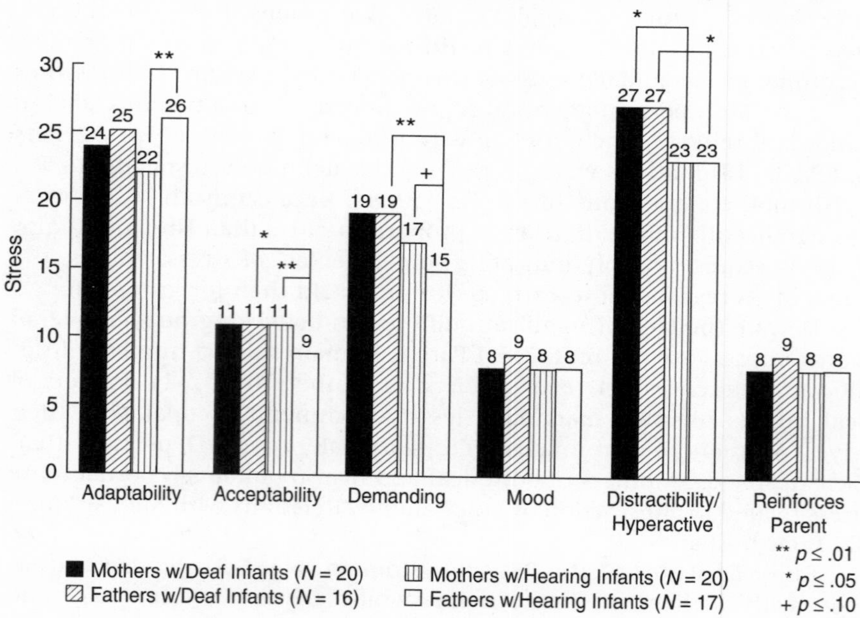

Figure 6-2. Parenting Stress Index: Child Domain.

Stress of Life Events (SLE). On this scale, mothers of deaf infants reported significantly more stress related to the "Care of Newborn" and marginally more stress about their own "Health" compared to mothers of hearing infants. (Fig. 6-3). Both groups of mothers reported significantly more "Work" stress and marginally more stress related to "Money" compared to their husbands.

Family Support Scale (FSS). Mothers of deaf infants reported somewhat more total support than did mothers of hearing infants [t (36) = 1.92; $p \leq .10$]. Although mothers of deaf infants reported marginally less support from their spouses than did mothers of hearing infants [t (36) = −1.88; $p \leq .10$], scores for the two groups of mothers did not differ on support from other family members or from friends. In addition, mothers of deaf infants reported significantly more support from the community [t (36) = 5.56; $p < .001$], which was accounted for primarily by greater support from professionals [t (21) = 1.96; $p \leq .10$].

Parenting Events Inventory (PEI). Only three of twenty items differentiated the two groups of mothers. A principal components analysis was performed, with eighteen of the twenty items creating two components. Component 1 included eleven caregiving items (*alpha* = .88); component 2 included items related to a baby's temperament (*alpha* = .78).

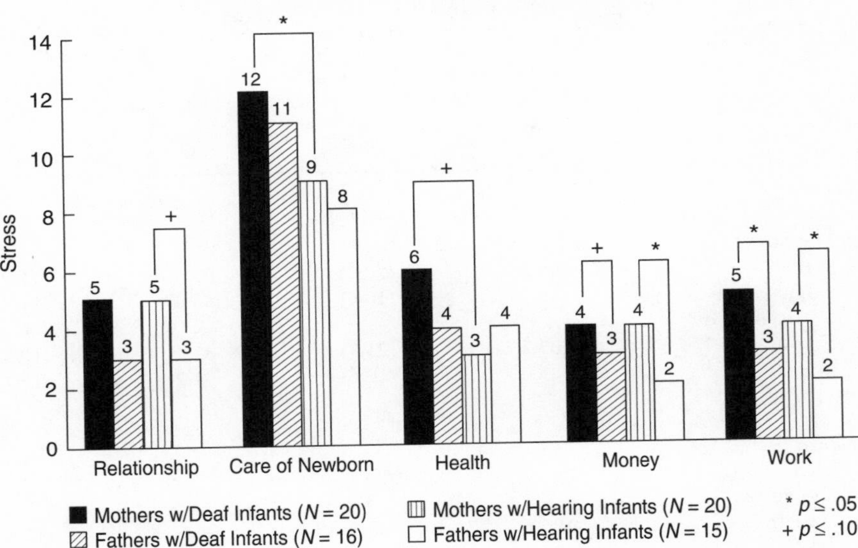

Figure 6-3. Stress of Life Events: Component Scores.

Composite Indices. To reduce the questionnaire data to manageable proportions, two composite indices were constructed. *The Life Stress Index* combined four scales or subscales with moderate correlations (mean Pearson $r = .29$): total scores from the Stress of Life Events Scale; Health subscale and Sense of Competence subscale from the Parent Domain of the Parenting Stress Index; and the Caregiving subscale (component 1) from the Parenting Events Inventory (PEI). The *Social Support Index* combined three scales (mean Pearson $r = .24$): Relationship with Spouse and Social Isolation subscales from the Parent Domain of the Parenting Stress Index and the mean total score from the Family Support Scale. Scores from each component of the two indices were divided into quintiles, and ordinal rankings for each participant were summed to yield index scores. No differences between the two groups of mothers or of fathers were found for either index score.

Relationship of PSI Child Domain Scores to Index Scores. Data in Table 6-1 show PSI Child Domain (PSI-CD) scores by levels (high or low) of the *Life Stress Index* and by levels (low or high) of the *Social Support Index,* first for mothers, then for fathers of infants who are deaf or hearing. Two-way ANOVAs were performed to test relationships of PSI-CD with *Life Stress* and *Social Support* levels.

Mothers' PSI-CD scores were significantly related to *Life Stress Index* level [F (1,36) = 18.05; $p < .001$], but not to infants' hearing status. Mothers' PSI-CD scores were significantly related to *Social Support Index*

Table 6-1. Parenting Stress Index (child domain) scores, by Life Stress level and Social Support level, for parents of infants who were deaf or hearing

	Infant hearing status			
	Deaf		*Hearing*	
	M	*(SD)*	*M*	*(SD)*
Mothers	*n* = 20		*n* = 20	
Life Stress				
High	109.2	(20.7)	97.6	(11.9)
Low	85.1	(10.6)	83.4	(11.3)
Social Support				
Low	103.5	(21.7)	87.1	(10.1)
High	85.4	(10.6)	91.2	(15.1)
Fathers	*n* = 16		*n* = 15	
Life Stress				
High	105.6	(20.4)	86.6	(11.4)
Low	91.1	(14.9)	91.8	(12.9)
Social Support				
Low	106.9	(19.1)	91.9	(10.6)
High	91.6	(17.0)	87.1	(13.9)

Note: Higher PSI scores = greater parenting stress.

level, with higher levels of support associated with lower stress, but only for mothers with deaf infants. [F (1,36) = 4.13; p = .05]. Thus, mothers' parenting stress scores reflecting evaluations of infant characteristics were highly related to levels of life stress, whether their infants were deaf or hearing, and levels of social support were related to mothers' PSI-CD scores only if their infants were deaf.

Fathers' PSI-CD scores were marginally related to *Life Stress Index* levels, only in interaction with infants' hearing status [F (1,28) = 3.13; $p <$ .10]. That is, high life stress levels were associated with child stress only for fathers with deaf infants. Likewise, there were only marginal main effects of infant hearing status [F (1,28) = 3.18; $p <$ .10] and *Social Support Index* level [F (1,28) = 3.35; $p <$ .10] on fathers' PSI-CD scores, and there were no interaction effects.

Interview Data

Although scores on stress measures were not significantly higher for the parents of deaf children compared to those of hearing children, many of their interviews reflected considerable personal and family stress. These personal accounts add to the understanding of the experience of deafness in hearing families. The initial identification of deafness in a young infant usually is an experience associated with considerable trauma, often experienced differently by a husband and wife, as described by these two mothers:

> While [my husband] wasn't as outwardly grievous, there was no question that he was miserable too. But I think he allowed me to be more expressive while he was more supportive.

> [The diagnosis] didn't really hit me until we got in the car. I felt like I didn't want to live. My husband was with me and he said something like, why was I so upset, I already have one deaf child. I don't really know how I worked out of it. . . . My husband has accepted it—he accepts a lot. So I think he just accepted it and decided we will deal with it. Oh, he was shocked, but he accepts easier than I do. . . . Actually, I don't think he really has any stress about anything.

One area of stress for the mothers of deaf infants was that of finances. A child's hearing loss can exacerbate these concerns. The following family had opted to use sign language with their deaf infant and her older deaf sister, complicating the mother's decision about working outside the home:

> Financially, we're struggling. It's really a strain. I can't decide if I should sacrifice the signing and go back to work or if I should continue to stay at home so they [her two children] can have the sign communication. . . . I can honestly admit that there's a strain on the marriage. My husband's working constantly, and I'm feeling guilty that I'm not working and helping him to support us.

Asked what areas of her life were causing stress for her, another mother replied:

> Finances and babysitting. Babysitting, it's finding people capable of caring for the kids. In terms of finances, there are always extra expenses connected to deafness. We put special lights in the house, that was a nice $400. The TTY [telecommunication device] cost $300. There are extra expenses like batteries for the hearing aids. . . . Lots of expenses for doctors.

A single working mother of a child deafened by meningitis also reported difficulties finding appropriate childcare. Asked how she felt about combining motherhood and a career, she responded:

> It's awful. I didn't think it was that terrible before his hearing loss, but you know, coordinating the home visit [with the teacher] is hard. I'd like to go to the parent–infant program half a day, but you can't get paid for all the time off you take, and then, he's had a lot of earaches, so there's been doctor's visits, and they seem to all come at one time. Or him being sick, or this or that.

This mother also described the professional advice and sources of support she had received:

> From the teachers and the family learning vacation. I think the advice has been [the most] support. Probably the best thing they keep saying is, "Remember you're a mother first, not a sign teacher, not a hearing impaired teacher." Because you kind of feel that way sometimes. The fact that you can change your decisions, nothing is concrete.

Holidays can be both a time of increased stress for families and one of celebration. For this mother, her child's hearing loss became the focus of holiday stress:

> Everything at the holidays came to a head. I was just burned out. Christmas does that to you anyway. Finally I just broke down. I just had had it. This wasn't the way it was supposed to be. I felt too much of the responsibility for his success, whether he was going to speak or not and do well in school was all in my lap. . . . We were just very sad that all this [the illness leading to hearing loss] had happened to him. I just was upset that he has to work all that much harder and it has changed his life tremendously. . . . You know, it was his first Christmas. It was supposed to be wonderful, and there I was feeling absolutely horrible. It's true, you have to go to the bottom to get your way back up again. Things got healthier for [both my husband and me] after that happened.

Discussion

Contrary to expectations and much of the research literature, mothers of infants who are deaf did not score significantly higher on measures of parenting stress (PSI and PEI) or of general life stress (SLE), compared to mothers of hearing infants. The general support levels of the two groups of mothers were similar, although mothers with deaf infants reported more support from professional sources, and their increased support was significantly related to less reported stress associated with their infant. Fathers with deaf infants did not differ significantly from their wives. As far as we know, no other studies of parenting stress have included data from fathers of children with hearing loss. However, these results are similar to those of a study of mothers and fathers whose children were developmentally delayed (Beckman, 1991).

Quittner's (1991) data showed Canadian mothers of children with a hearing loss ($n = 96$) to have significantly higher scores on the PSI than comparable mothers of hearing children ($n = 118$). However, the Canadian mothers and children differed in several important respects from those in this study, any one of which might contribute to the differing results: Canadian children were older (mean age = 4 years) and their hearing loss was diagnosed as late as age 3 years, whereas infants in this study had a hearing loss identified before 9 months of age. Canadian mothers, on average, had almost 3 years less education than the Gallaudet mothers, and they were more likely to be unmarried.

Two studies conducted recently include participants who are more comparable to the Gallaudet families (Lederberg & Golbach, 2002; Pipp-Siegel, Sedey, & Yoshinaga-Itano, 2002). Both used the PSI short form to assess maternal stress: Pipp-Siegel with 186 children (mean age 13.6 months), Lederberg with 23 children at age 3 and again at age 4. Stress among mothers with deaf and with hearing children in the Lederberg study did not differ, nor did stress levels increase from the time children were age 3 until they were age 4.

Pipp-Siegel and colleagues reported subscales for the PSI short form (Parental Distress, Parent–Child Dysfunctional Interaction, and Difficult Child), plus Parenting Daily Hassles (similar to the PEI scale), the Family Support Scale (FSS), and the Expressive Language Scale from the Minnesota Child Development Inventory. Mothers of children with and without hearing loss had similar scores on the three PSI subscales, but mothers with more intense daily hassles reported more stress. Other predictors of maternal stress were absence of social support and low income. Predictors of Dysfunctional Parent–Child Interaction were *(1)* disabilities in addition to hearing loss, *(2)* delayed language relative to age, and *(3)* less severe deafness.

Thus, mothers of children with hearing loss in all three recent studies (Gallaudet, Lederberg, and Pipp-Siegel) reported stress levels no higher than comparable mothers of children without hearing loss. Some circumstances were found to increase stress (financial problems, ambivalence about employment); others were found to alleviate stress (especially the support of professionals). Larger numbers and greater heterogeneity of participants enabled the Pipp-Siegel group to document the heightened stress contributed by conditions in addition to deafness, greater language delays, and less severe hearing losses. (This last feature seems counterintuitive, but results from another recent study suggest that stress in parents of children with mild and moderate hearing loss is often related to lengthy diagnostic delays [Meadow-Orlans, Mertens, & Sass-Lehrer, 2003].)

Part II—Stress and Support in Parents of Children with Additional Conditions

Approximately one-third of all children who are deaf or hard of hearing have additional physical, cognitive, or emotional conditions requiring special education services (Schildroth & Hotto, 1993; Meadow-Orlans, Mertens, & Sass-Lehrer, 2003). This figure has remained constant for many years, despite changes in the medical causes of deafness and treatment of illnesses and conditions producing hearing loss (Schein, 1996; Holden-Pitt & Diaz, 1998). However, only 20% of children with hearing impairments are diagnosed with additional disabling conditions during preschool years, reflecting the lower probability of identification of conditions such as "learning disability" or "emotional disturbance" at younger ages (Craig, 1992). Despite the high prevalence of multiple disabilities within this population, almost no research has been reported describing the behavioral or interactional consequences of additional disabling conditions, especially in very young children (Jones & Jones, 2003).

One purpose of this chapter is to provide detailed pre- and postnatal histories and observational descriptions of deaf or hard-of-hearing infants with additional conditions whose hearing loss was identified by the age of 9 months. Because of the small number of children, reported results are only suggestive and should not be generalized.

Participants and Procedures

The core group of twenty infants with hearing loss and hearing parents (Hd) was divided into those whose pre- or postnatal histories placed them at-risk (AR) for additional disabilities (Hd-AR, n = 10) and those who were not at risk (Hd-NR, n = 8). (Some data were missing for two Hd-NR infants who were therefore excluded from these analyses.) Five additional Hd infants recruited for the project were excluded from the general analyses reported in other chapters because of diagnosed motor or cognitive disabilities. These infants with additional conditions (Hd-AC) and their mothers are described in detail here. Table 6-2 shows selected characteristics of these three groups of infants and their parents plus the group of Hh infants.

Congenital cytomegalovirus (CMV) was confirmed for two of the Hd-AC infants (40%). Two of the Hd-AR infants were confirmed for CMV and a third had CMV as a suspected diagnosis. Significant group differences appeared in birth weights of the four groups of infants, with those of the multiply disabled and at-risk deaf infants significantly below the birth weights of the nonrisk deaf group and the hearing group. Mothers of Hd-AC babies were significantly younger than mothers of hearing infants, and mothers and fathers of multiply disabled infants had significantly fewer years of education compared to other groups.

Five of the ten at-risk deaf infants whose histories were most similar to those of the excluded (Hd-AC) infants were selected for observational description: two with confirmed CMV and three with very low birth weights (780, 1051, and 1108 grams [g]). For these five infants and for the infants with additional conditions, medical histories were extracted from interview transcripts. Descriptions of developmental levels and interactive behaviors were derived from watching the entire video record filmed during the laboratory visit when infants were 12 months old. These included presentation of four toys for mastery motivation, mother–infant free play, and the Ainsworth Strange Situation Procedure (not attempted for the two most delayed Hd-AC infants).

Table 6-2. Characteristics of subjects: Sex, hearing level, etiology, birth weight, parental age, and education

	Hd-AC (*n* = 5)	*Hd-AR* (*n* = 10)	*Hd-NR* (*n* = 8)	*Hh* (*n* = 20)
Sex				
Boys	3	6	4	12
Girls	2	4	4	8
Hearing Level				*NA*
Mild	—	1	—	
Moderate	—	—	2	
Moderate/Severe	2	2	—	
Severe	1	2	—	
Severe/Profound	1	3	5	
Profound	1	2	1	
Etiology of Hearing Loss				*NA*
Unknown	1	—	4	
Heredity	—	—	4	
Cytomegalovirus	2	3	—	
Rh incompatibility	—	1	—	
Prenatal prescribed drug	—	1	—	
Prematurity	—	2	—	
Birth trauma	2	—	—	
Meningitis	—	2	—	
Jaundice	—	1	—	
Birth Weight[a]				
Mean weight (grams)	2559	2587	3581	3482
(SD)	(820)	(1199)	(620)	(506)
Age (years)				
Mothers[b]	27.4	31.6	31.0	32.2
Fathers	30.6	34.4	32.6	33.8
Education (years)				
Mothers[c]	13.6	16.7	15.0	16.6
Fathers[d]	13.0	16.0	14.4	17.9

[a]Hd-AC and Hd-AR < Hd-NR and Hh groups, $F(3,39) = 4.80$; $p < .001$.

[b]F NS; Hd-AC < Hh: Duncan's post hoc range test, $p < .05$.

[c]$F(3,39) = 3.38$; $p \leq .05$; Hd-AC < Hd-AR and Hh groups.

[d]$F(3,39) = 8.12$; $p \leq .001$; Hd-AC < all others; Hd-AR and Hd-NR < Hh group.

Results

The Parenting Stress Index (PSI) scores were subjected to Kruskal-Wallis one-way Analysis of Variance tests. Table 6-3 shows no significant overall differences among the four groups of mothers for mean rank of PSI scores.

To the extent that infant potential for developmental difficulties influences mothers' stress, stress levels could be expected to increase with the risk or identification of additional disabilities for the infant. Thus, stress was expected to be greatest for Hd-AC mothers, somewhat less for group Hd-AR, followed by groups Hd-NR and Hh. Although differences in observed stress scores were small, it is notable that the trend for the mothers' scores for stress (from Parent Domain subscales) failed to support predictions: Hd-AC mothers show the least stress, followed by Hh mothers, Hd-AR mothers, and Hd-NR mothers. Closer examination of scores revealed these anomalous patterns to be a function of a bi-modal distribution of scores for this group of parents, with scores clustering either in the extremely high range ("recommend for clinical referral") or extremely low range ("suspect denial of stress"). Mothers of Hd-AC infants tended to have either very high or very low stress scores, reflecting either expressed or repressed stress that might place the family unit at risk for mental health problems. Because of this unusual distribution of scores, the group means masked the extremities of individual scores (suggesting the

Table 6-3. Parenting Stress Index (PSI) scores (child and parent domains) for mothers and fathers: Mean ranks of four groups: Deaf or hard-of-hearing with additional conditions (Hd-AC), at-risk (Hd-AR), or not at risk (Hd-NR) and hearing (Hh)

	Hd-AC (*n* = 5)[a]	*Hd-AR* (*n* = 10)	*Hd-NR* (*n* = 8)	*Hh* (*n* = 20)[b]	*K-W*[c]
Child Domain					
Mothers	21.4	23.1	24.9	19.4	1.39
Fathers	23.0	20.1	23.9	15.6	3.87
Parent Domain					
Mothers	17.7	23.3	27.3	19.2	3.20
Fathers	24.1	17.6	22.1	17.8	1.90

[a]Data missing for one mother.

[b]Data missing for three fathers.

[c]Kruskal-Wallis one-way ANOVA (corrected for ties).

need to attend closely to standard deviations in studies of atypical groups).

In addition, lower than expected stress scores for some mothers of Hd-AC infants (and some with Hd-AR babies) may reflect their relief that their infants survived traumatic births or postnatal illnesses. This colored their response to the child's physical and mental status. In comparison with death, disabilities seemed easier to bear. Finally, consistent with other reports (e.g., Pipp-Siegel, Sedey, & Yoshinaga-Itano, 2002; Meadow-Orlans, Mertens, & Sass-Lehrer, 2003), early diagnosis and intervention were helpful in relieving distress for mothers in this study.

Medical Case Histories and Behavioral Descriptions

Frequently, statistical summaries mask the individual nature of the experiences of infants and parents as they are combined for research reports. Tables 6-4 and 6-5 illustrate the diversity of pre- and postnatal experiences of deaf and hard-of-hearing infants.

Table 6-4 shows a wide range of pre- and postnatal difficulties for both groups of infants, with little overlap in particular conditions that were the probable cause of infants' hearing losses. Two Hd-AC babies (Cindy and Robby) and two Hd-AR babies (Kerry and Larry) had positive tests for CMV after birth, although only one of the four mothers was aware that she was infected with the virus during pregnancy. (One other Hd-AR infant was not tested for the virus, but mother gave CMV as a "possible" cause of deafness.) Mothers of the three other Hd-AC infants all reported multiple difficulties during their pregnancies, as did the mother of one Hd-AR infant (Sharon, Table 6-4). Two other Hd-AR infants were members of twin sets and had low birth weights (Julian, 1051 g, and Bruce, 780 g). The mother of one of these infants reported the cause of his deafness as a medication given during pregnancy. Because of the many difficulties experienced by the infants, all ten received early hearing tests, and no diagnosis was delayed. The medical and audiological histories of the babies in these two groups were not markedly different.

However, their observational summaries, shown in Table 6-5, reflect the significantly lower functioning of the five Hd-AC infants. They were described as developmentally delayed and disinterested in interaction (Robby, Johnny, Jimmy), possibly autistic (Johnny), with short attention spans (Cindy and Karen) and showing little or no attention to mother or to objects (Robby, Johnny, Jimmy). The five at-risk children, in contrast, were more often described as "normal," although Kerry had a high level of nonpurposive activity, and Larry's mother gave him little opportunity for self-initiated behavior because her attention shifted rapidly from one object to another.

Table 6-4. Medical and audiological histories

Name	*Prenatal history*	*Birth events*	*Birth weight*	*APGAR scores*	*Postnatal events*	*Audiological diagnosis*	*Hearing level*	*Intervention*
Part I: Deaf Infants with Additional Conditions (Hd-AC)								
Cindy #022	No significant difficulties: cold and bronchitis; probably symptoms of CMV.	Labor induced because of fetal weight loss.	1792 grams	9 and 10	Tests done to determine reason for low birth weight at full term: CMV positive.	Hearing loss detected at 6 days.	Severe to profound loss (left ear); moderate to severe loss (right ear).	Fitted with two hearing aids at 3 months; oral educational program.
Robby #031	Multiple difficulties: Mother at high risk for Down syndrome; placenta too large; fluid around infant's heart, abdomen, brain.	C-section at 32 weeks.	1580 grams	6 and 8	ICU; transfused; bilirubin 11; heart monitor; assisted breathing; CMV positive	Failed hearing screening at 3 days.	60 to 70 dB loss.	Two hearing aids by 9 months; oral educational program; no sign language.
Johnny #034	Maternal toxemia and high blood pressure.	Delivery by C-section; child "limp and blue"; ears malformed.	3136 grams	1 and 7	TORCH[a] tests negative.	Mother suspected hearing loss; tests at 2 months confirmed; paternal aunt profoundly deaf (measles at 3 months); mother attributes J's deafness to perinatal difficulties.	Severe to profound loss.	Hearing aids fitted at 3 months; auditory-verbal educational program (no sign or lipreading, only sound).

Jimmy #093	Bleeding during pregnancy.	Delivery by C-section (baby experienced distress after 5-hour labor); anoxic; "small mouth"; stiffness.	2940 grams	N/A	Seizure.	Hearing tested at 4 days because of anoxia. Loss confirmed at 6 weeks.	Profound (90 dB).	"Planning to get hearing aids." Enrolled in parent–infant program. Physical therapy.
Karen #101	Bleeding during pregnancy; fetus not attached to uterine wall.	Labor induced; congenital facial malformation ("face tag").	3360 grams	8 and 8	ICU for nasal and feeding difficulties.	Facial malformation prompted hearing test at 6 months.	Severe to profound loss.	Hearing aids at 7 months; oral educational program (sign language recommended, parents prefer to "try oral first").
Part II: Deaf Infants at Risk (Hd-AR)[b]								
Kerry #002	Mother tested positive for cytomegalovirus (CMV) infection early in pregnancy.	Infant delivered at 37 weeks gestation.	2528 grams	9 and 9	Low platelet count required a transfusion 24 hours after birth.	Hearing test at 3 months.	Severe.	Enrolled in total communication program.
Larry #009	No known risk factors.	Nothing significant.	2670 grams	N/A	Baby tested positive for CMV at about 6 months.	Hearing test after discovery of CMV.	Profound bilateral loss.	Hearing aids by 9 months; oral education program.

(*continued*)

Table 6-4. Medical and audiological histories (*Part II continued*)

Name	*Prenatal history*	*Birth events*	*Birth weight*	*APGAR scores*	*Postnatal events*	*Audiological diagnosis*	*Hearing level*	*Intervention*
Julian #028	Pregnancy complications include spotting, gestational diabetes, and loss of amniotic fluid. Mother placed on bedrest.	Twins (one with normal hearing) delivered by C-section at 28 weeks.	1051 grams	2 and 5	Jaundice, problems w/ breathing and swallowing; placed on IV feeding for 6 weeks, released from hospital at 9 weeks; received oxygen until 3½ months.	Tested at 2 months.	Bilateral loss, severe to profound.	Hearing aids by 9 months; oral education program.
Sharon #084	Mother diagnosed with an "incompetent cervix"; bedrest prescribed at 6 months. Hospitalized when contractions began 2–3 weeks later.	Attempts to postpone labor failed; infant delivered at 28 weeks gestation.	1108 grams	N/A	Jaundice; intestinal condition required surgery (20% chance of survival). Hospitalized for several months.	Tested at 2 months.	Severe to profound loss.	Hearing aids by 12 months; oral education program.
Bruce #087	At 24 weeks gestation mother received medication to delay labor.	Twins (one with normal hearing) delivered by C-section at 27 weeks.	780 grams	"low" and "almost normal"	Jaundice and breathing difficulties. Infant placed on respirator periodically until 6 weeks old.	Tested at 6 months because of malformation of left ear.	Moderate to severe loss (left ear); profound loss (right ear).	Hearing aids by 7 months; oral education program.

[a]TORCH, toxoplasmosis, other, rubella virus, cytomegalovirus, herpes simplex viruses. This group of agents can infect the fetus or newborn, causing a constellation of morbid effects that may or may not be symptomatic. Several of these infants were suspected of TORCH syndrome and were tested accordingly.

[b]Five of the ten at-risk infants are described: those with etiologies of low birth weight or cytomegalovirus selected as most comparable to the five multiply handicapped infants.

Table 6-5. Videotape observations at 12 months

	Cindy #022	*Robby #031*	*Johnny #034*	*Jimmy #093*	*Karen #101*
Part I Deaf Infants with Additional Conditions (Hd-AC)					
Motor development	Cindy cannot sit alone or crawl, but she moves quickly, effectively, and purposively by rolling. She can reach and grasp, but fine motor coordination is not well-controlled or effective. She can bring objects to her mouth.	Robby has little or no control over his gross motor movements, cannot roll over or sit alone, has no head control. He cannot grasp or hold toys, nor does he reach for them. He does bring his hands to his mouth and suck his thumb.	Johnny rolls over from stomach to back and reaches to the side but mostly lies flat on his back. He sits without help and with his legs wide apart. He does move his arms, but does not change position without help, cannot stand, crawl or turn over. His fine motor control and coordination are poor, although he reaches for and grasps objects that are close to him.	Jimmy's motor development is severely delayed. He lies flat on his back with very little movement of his legs and arms. He moves both arms/hands at the same time, seems unable to use one hand at a time. Neither reaches for nor grasps objects, nor does he hold them even when an object is placed in his hand. Lifted his head a little and held it up for a few seconds twice during the observation. He rolled to one side once.	Karen sits in exactly the same position (both legs stretched in front of her) throughout the play session. She appears delayed in gross motor development, muscle strength and tone (hypotonia) and she may have problems with head and neck control. She can reach for and pick up toys.
Play	She exhibits no real play with toys, only mouths them. However, she has the beginning of play interactions with mother, removing a blanket from her face and from a spoon, and she responds to tickling games.	He shows no interest in toys and does not look at them. He responds to body contact and enjoys Mom's tickling and cuddling.	There is almost no real play, only some shaking and mouthing. When lying down, he tried to bite or mouth a doll. Did not or could not bring objects to his mouth while sitting.	No play was observed	Functional play is at a low level with banging and shaking but no mouthing. There is some representational play: Karen copies mother's demonstration with brush and comb and tries to bring the spoon to her mouth.

(*continued*)

Table 6-5. Videotape observations at 12 months (*Part I Hd-AC continued*)

	Cindy #022	*Robby #031*	*Johnny #034*	*Jimmy #093*	*Karen #101*
Attention	Cindy's attention span is quite short. She becomes bored and tires easily. She pays attention to mother for a longer period when there is body contact.	In the tickling play, Robby laughs and appears to anticipate the tickling. No other apparent interest or attention.	There was no meaningful attention. He engaged in obsessive rocking, looking at lights, holding on to spoon and brush. Johnny was able to find the spoon and the brush in the toy basket after mother took them away from him.	Nothing appeared to engage his attention.	Attention span is quite short. In the free play situation, she was neither selective nor especially interested in any of the toys. In the mastery situation she seemed more focused on the task and appeared to understand it, but did not sustain interest long and pushed the toy away.
Activity level	Gross motor activity level is normal in quantity but at a low developmental level, although there are long intervals during which she lies on her back, biting or mouthing her shoes or toys.	Very passive, he has neither the ability nor motivation to be active. He sucks or mouths thumb or hands.	Activity level is very low apart from self-stimulating behaviors.	Jimmy moves very little and with no apparent intent.	Activity level is low. She has obvious gross motor problems, but she does not try to move and seems very low key with no sign of curiosity about toys in the free play situation. She waits for people and objects to come to her.

Interaction	She interacts quite well with mother for her developmental level: She rolls to mother when her name is called. However, there is little communication or interaction apart from physical contact.	There is little or no response to the environment, toys, or activities. His social interaction with mother is limited to response to her body contact.	There was almost no interaction with mother. The only instance occurred when mother blew at him and he mimicked her. Johnny looked to the research assistant but did not interact with her.	Mother attempted repeatedly to elicit a response from Jimmy who did not react to her efforts. No means of interaction has been established between Jimmy and his mother. Eye contact was observed briefly only once. Jimmy pushed away toys placed on his body and face, but it was not clear if these were voluntary movements.	Mother is very tense and intrusive. She does not capitalize on Karen's few efforts to initiate interaction or her small signs of interest. Mother's timing is much too fast and does not give Karen a chance to react or respond. Mother talks to Karen most of the time without checking to see if she understands. Very little eye contact. Karen checks with her mother and smiles at her a few times. Repeats "up, up" and "bye, bye."
Affective tone	Cindy seems quite content and somewhat placid. Her level of social involvement is good, she smiles at mother and research assistants, and she initiates contact with others.	No clear affect is shown, although he does cry when tired.	Very flat. There is no response to social contact from others and no effort to initiate affective contact.	Jimmy displays no affect towards his mother. He cried in his infant seat and was clearly uncomfortable. When lying on the floor, he showed no emotion.	Neutral to flat. Karen shows no excitement or enjoyment during the free play interaction. In the mastery situation, Karen smiled at mother and at the research assistant a few times, when she succeeded in solving her task.

(*continued*)

Table 6-5. Videotape observations at 12 months (*Part I Hd-AC continued*)

	Cindy #022	*Robby #031*	*Johnny #034*	*Jimmy #093*	*Karen #101*
Overall impressions	Cindy is clearly a child with developmental delays/mental retardation, perhaps with a syndrome. Her desire to become socially involved is appropriate for her developmental level; she initiates contact and responds to those around her. Mother has good contact with her and understands how to get her involved and how to support her. Development of more formal communication skills should be encouraged through use of all available modes.	Robby has severe delay/retardation in all areas of development. His passivity, lack of involvement or interest in the environment, including his mother, seem more serious threats to his functioning and future development than his hearing impairment.	Johnny's motor, social, emotional, and communicative development and functioning are all very low. The absence of social involvement or interest in the environment constitutes a risk to his overall development. He exhibits possible autistic traits.	Jimmy has multiple disabilities, with serious delays in all developmental areas.	Karen is delayed in gross motor development and functioning. Subdued activity and energy level, passivity, and limited interest are additional concerns.

	Kerry #002	*Larry #009*	*Julian #028*	*Sharon #084*	*Bruce #087*
Play	Representational: Bites on spoon and plate, sucks on doll's bottle, drinks from cup. Symbolic: feeds doll from bottle (copying mother), hugs doll.	Larry shows functional play in banging and shaking. Examples of representational play: comb and brush, doll's bottle.	Julian is at the functional play stage, bangs, shakes, and mouths toys.	Sharon at functional play level, mouths brush and phone, handles beads. No clear observation of representational play.	Functional play is at a high level. He puts blocks in shape box; also explores, bangs, and mouths. Representational: Drinks from doll's bottle (mother handed it to him, but did not demonstrate).
Attention	Kerry constantly returned to mirror and heat vent, but she was not attentive to mother or to the toys.	Larry does not have much opportunity to attend to his own activities, but he spends much time watching mother's activities. In mastery situation he quickly loses interest in tasks.	Julian has a fairly short attention span, does not show intentional play, and loses interest quickly.	Sharon stayed with same activity for fairly long periods (dancing, beads, brush). After mother put brush away, Sharon found it again and continued former activity.	Stays on task for a long time and returns to game and tasks; good level of interest and motivation.
Activity level	Kerry has a high motor activity level, is constantly on the move, crawling, circling around without specific aim or purpose.	Larry's activity level is normal but he is not left much room because of his mother's hyperactive behavior.	Normal activity level, much banging.	Normal activity level; Sharon moved around but sat on mother's lap for a long period.	Normal activity level, interested in toys and play, can explore and play on his own.

(*continued*)

Table 6-5. Videotape observations at 12 months (*Part II Hd-AC continued*)

	Kerry #002	*Larry #009*	*Julian #028*	*Sharon #084*	*Bruce #087*
Interaction	No real interaction, no intentional eye contact, no social initiative and very few responses to mother's few initiatives.	Mother shows no sensitivity to Larry's needs nor does she respond to his initiatives and signals. Larry's interaction seems to be appropriate given the circumstances: He is calm but overwhelmed. It is difficult to know if and how Larry communicates with mother: There is no indication in the video.	No real communication with mother, appears more interested in things than people.	Sharon does not often take the initiative, but she usually responds to mother and clearly enjoys the interaction, including physical contact with mother. Is less interested in play with toys.	Good interaction and basic communication with mother, also good social interaction with researchers. Enjoys play and successful achievements.
Affective tone	Quite flat affective tone, no smiling or protesting during free play. However, in the Strange Situation, she protested and cried bitterly.	It is difficult to judge the affective tone of this mother–child relationship.	Flat affective tone: He smiles at his own reflection in mirror and a few times at mother and researchers, but he protests and gets off mother's lap when she is hugging him, does not want "rough" play. In the Strange Situation, Julian appears quite sad.	Sharon's affective tone is neutral, rarely smiles. Not clear if smiles were for mother or for mirrored reflection of self. Mother is warm, hugs and kisses Sharon, but she is not able to communicate play ideas or involve Sharon with toys.	Animated affective tone. Bruce is responsive, alert, active, involved with environment, toys and people.

Overall impression	Increased motor activity, crawling, rocking behavior, limited interest in social interaction.	Mother's strange and hyperactive behavior and insensitive relationship to Larry places him at risk. There is a great need for support of this mother–child dyad, not only in terms of development of communication and language but also in social and emotional involvement from mother.	Julian's weak social involvement and interaction are reason for concern. There is little mutual communication between Julian and his mom, except for very basic physical contact and some facial expressions. Their lack of any communication mode or technique is likely to place his general development at risk.	Low level of interest in interaction and toys. Responds positively to mother's initiation of body contact but negatively to initiation of play with toys. Seems not to understand mother's intent for play.	Bruce seems to have developed very well and age appropriately. He needs to be exposed to consistent and more formal communication, which also should develop at a normal rate.

Discussion

Discussion of these analyses must be only suggestive because of the small numbers included in each group. However, because of the paucity of data on these important subgroups of children with hearing losses—that is, on those who are at risk for additional disabilities or who have additional disabilities identified during infancy—it seems important to report the information. It is striking that the (very small) group of mothers with multiply disabled infants in this study had fewer personal resources, as measured by their educational levels, compared to mothers in the other groups. This undoubtedly complicated parents' responses to their children's problems. The mothers of deaf infants with additional conditions had an average age of 27-plus years, so they certainly were not adolescents, nor were they poorly educated, with an average education of almost 2 years beyond high school. Nevertheless, they were about 4 years younger than mothers of other deaf infants, and 5 years younger than mothers with hearing infants. They had significantly less schooling than two of the other three groups of mothers.

Low socioeconomic status is associated with many medical and parenting difficulties, and the usual context for discussion of these problems is that of "poverty" (Halpern, 1993). However, the middle- or lower-middle class mothers of Hd-AC infants in this study were not at the poverty level. Nevertheless, the financial and emotional demands of their multiply-disabled infants placed them at substantial risk and in need of the emotional and material support that might be less available to mothers of sick or premature infants than to mothers of healthy full-term babies (Feiring, Fox, Jaskir, & Lewis, 1987). Another study found that mothers of children with additional conditions reported less rather than more support from professionals and family members (Meadow-Orlans, Mertens, & Sass-Lehrer, 2003).

Of the twenty-three deaf infants described in Part II of this chapter, fourteen (56%) had medical histories placing them at risk for a variety of disabilities. (One of the Hd-AC children, Julian, had disabilities with unknown etiology.) It is of considerable importance that ten of these fourteen at-risk infants (71%) displayed no apparent developmental anomalies by 12 months of age. Of the five infants whose hearing loss was related to congenital CMV (four confirmed, one suspected), three had escaped disabilities other than hearing loss. It has been known for many years that CMV causes deafness (and other disabilities), but the virus received serious attention beginning only in the 1980s (Fischler, 1985). In the 1991–92 Annual Survey of Hearing Impaired Children and Youth, conducted by Gallaudet University's Center for Assessment and Demographic Studies, hearing loss in 34% of children younger than age 6 was attributed to CMV. Fifty percent of CMV children were reported to have at least one additional condition (Schildroth, 1994).

Prematurity has been associated with retarded physical growth (Mohay, Hindmarsh, & Zhao, 1994), increased behavioral problems (Minde et al., 1989) and early delays (often reversed) in motor, cognitive, and language development (Greenberg & Crnic, 1988). Because deafness places children at risk for pervasive language delay, the relationship of prematurity or biological risk to language development is of particular concern for this population. One comparison of early- and later-identified deaf children with additional conditions showed that those identified, like these GIS (Gallaudet Infancy Study) children, by the age of 6 months, "had remarkable similarities in language quotients to [children identified later] with hearing loss only" at ages 31 to 36 months (Yoshinaga-Itano, 2003, p. 26). Thus, Universal Newborn Hearing Screening could be especially beneficial for that large group of deaf children with co-occurring conditions.

Conclusion

Much of the data from hearing mothers in this study reinforces findings reported by other researchers suggesting that early identification and intervention serve to reduce the stress related to hearing loss. Our reports from fathers of deaf infants suggest that they find hearing loss of their children less stressful than do their wives, but that they are, indeed, negatively affected. It is encouraging that support has a mediating influence on the stress of parents with deaf infants. This echoes results reported in a later chapter emphasizing the importance of support for families. The demands placed on parents whose children have physical or cognitive conditions in addition to hearing loss make support even more important for them, but too frequently such support if unavailable.

Acknowledgments

This chapter incorporates material from four sources:

Meadow-Orlans, K. P. (1991). Stress and support in families with deaf infants. In K. P. Meadow-Orlans, R. H. MacTurk, P. E. Spencer, & L. S. Koester, *Interaction and support: Mothers and deaf infants*. Final Report to Maternal and Child Health Research Program.

Meadow-Orlans, K. P. (1994). Stress, support, and deafness: Perceptions of infants' mothers and fathers. *Journal of Early Intervention, 18*, 91–102.

Meadow-Orlans, K. P. (1995). Sources of stress for mothers and fathers of deaf and hard of hearing infants. *American Annals of the Deaf, 140*, 352–357.

Meadow-Orlans, K. P, Smith-Gray, S., & Dyssegaard, B. (1995). Infants who are deaf or hard of hearing, with and without physical/cognitive disabilities. *American Annals of the Deaf, 140*, 279–286.

7

Mastery Motivation at 9 and 12 Months

Traditional and Nontraditional Approaches

Robert H. MacTurk, Jennifer L. Ludwig,
and Kathryn P. Meadow-Orlans

Mastery motivation, as exhibited in infants and young children, has been defined as "a psychological force that originates without the need for extrinsic reward and leads the . . . child to attempt to master tasks for the intrinsic feeling of efficacy rather than because of current reward" (Morgan, MacTurk, & Hrncir, 1995, p. 6). This chapter presents the results of two separate but related approaches to the examination of motivated behavior in deaf and hearing infants. For Part I, a traditional approach to the conceptualization of mastery motivation is employed. This approach views mastery motivation as an underlying construct that can be assessed by observation of discrete behaviors (McCall, 1995). Therefore, a coding system was utilized to identify and quantify mastery-related behaviors: exploration, persistence, successful achievement of a goal, and social orientation. The system was used to code mastery behaviors in groups Hd (deaf infants with hearing parents) and Hh (hearing infants with hearing parents) at ages 9 and 12 months.

In Part II, a different, nontraditional approach was used to assess mastery. This approach focuses on the *organization* of behaviors rather than the discrete behaviors themselves. For this analysis, a global coding scheme was used to identify mastery motivation oriented primarily toward either social or object-related aspects of the environment. Mastery motivation was assessed using this approach at age 12 months with all four groups of infants—deaf and hearing infants with deaf parents (Dd and Dh) and deaf and hearing infants with hearing parents (Hd and Hh).

Interest in mastery motivation was sparked by several influential papers by Robert White (e.g., 1959, 1963), in which he conceptualized the existence of an intrinsic drive to engage and control the environment, a motive that was not explained by traditional drive theories. Efforts to operationalize his concept of Effectance Motivation and to develop an appropriate methodology began in the early 1970s. These efforts with normally developing and developmentally delayed hearing infants resulted in an assessment methodology that showed moderate relationships to standardized measures of competence (Yarrow et al., 1983; Messer et al., 1986), and linked parental behaviors to infants' motivation to master the environment (Jennings et al., 1979; Yarrow et al., 1982, 1984; McCarthy & McQuiston, 1983).

Two aspects of these early investigations are relevant here. First, their primary focus was on infants' motivation to explore the inanimate environment, with relatively little attention paid to social motivation or socially mediated expressions of motivated behavior. Second, the validation studies employed samples of infants with known or suspected cognitive and/or physical impairments as well as infants without disabilities.

Although these early mastery assessments minimized interaction with testers and mothers, several researchers have since explored the social aspects of motivated behavior (MacTurk et al., 1985; Maslin & Morgan, 1985; Vondra & Jennings, 1990; Morgan, Maslin-Cole, Biringen, & Harmon, 1991). Wachs and Combs (1995) proposed that children have a primary orientation toward either the object or the social environment, and they can be reliably classified on the basis of that orientation, citing evidence that social and object mastery motivation styles are separate constructs associated with different developmental and environmental correlates. They defined social mastery motivation as an interest in interacting competently with other people, shown by persistent attempts to initiate social interactions and by attempts to maintain social interactions while displaying positive affect. These investigations established the importance of the social domain and prompted further interest in the integration of infants' socially oriented and object-related activities.

The rationale for previous investigations with atypical populations rested on the assumption that children with some disabilities demonstrate reduced motivation perhaps because they benefit less from their mastery efforts. Support for this assumption is found in reports on the motivational characteristics of infants with Down syndrome (MacTurk et al., 1985, 1987). Studies of premature infants (Harmon & Murrow, 1995) and physically handicapped children (Jennings et al., 1985; Jennings & MacTurk, 1995) can provide convergent evidence that infants and children with disabilities exhibit deficits in motivated behavior.

The relationship of maternal behavior to mastery and achievement motivation in typically developing infants has been documented in several studies (Harmon & Culp, 1981; Butterfield & Miller, 1984; Redding, Harmon, & Morgan, 1990). However, it is difficult to draw firm conclusions concerning the origins of the observed deficits in atypically developing children because of the interaction between their functional limitations and their parents' reactions to those limitations. Emphasis on a deficit model of development can lead one to disregard atypical children's strengths that ameliorate the effects of disabling conditions. This point was demonstrated vividly by Fraiberg (1977), who found that blind infants used their hands to communicate a wide range of affective emotions that are expressed on the face by sighted infants.

Deaf infants, like blind infants, may develop compensatory behaviors, obtaining the same information from two sensory channels (visual and tactile) that hearing infants obtain from three. However, the lack of audition may be especially problematic because an important precursor of intellectual competence (exploratory behavior) is a responsive environment, and deaf infants have less access to responsiveness expressed through the auditory channel. Most previous studies of the effects of responsiveness on hearing infants' mastery motivation employed measures based on auditory contact—for example, parental vocal responsiveness (McCarthy & McQuiston, 1983), or measures that confound physical responsiveness and vocal responsiveness (Bell & Ainsworth, 1972; Riksen-Walraven, 1978). Previous research has not addressed the possible effects of deafness in an effort to understand the range of adaptive skills that infants may develop. Vision is the most obvious channel for deaf infants' adaptations, and pilot studies for the research reported here indicated important differences between deaf and hearing infants in the use of visual cues. Normally developing deaf infants provide the opportunity to add to our understanding of motivated behavior and factors that may influence such development.

A recent study examined the relationship of language achievement and mastery motivation in 200 children with hearing loss, mean age 26 months (Pipp-Siegel, Sedey, VanLeeuwen & Yoshinaga-Itano, 2003). The hearing mothers completed a Minnesota Child Development Inventory, Expressive Language Scale (Ireton & Thwing, 1974) and Dimensions of Mastery Motivation Questionnaire (DMMQ; Morgan et al., 1992). When demographic variables, child's general competence and degree of hearing loss were controlled, expressive language was significantly predicted by social/symbolic persistence and marginally predicted by object-oriented persistence. Gross motor persistence and mastery pleasure did not predict expressive language.

Educators of deaf children have long been concerned about low academic achievement in this population (Moores, 2001; Marschark, Lang, & Albertini, 2002; Lang, 2003). Although many studies have been conducted of achievement motivation, few have included deaf children (Marschark, 1993b). However, Stinson (1974, 1978) reported that hearing mothers of young children with hearing loss were less likely to demand or expect achievement motivation than were hearing mothers of hearing children. Motivation in hearing children was found to be stable from middle childhood to late adolescence (Gottfried, Fleming, & Gottfried, 2001) and to be associated with academic achievement and interpersonal functioning in school-age children (Roesser & Eccles, 2000). Further investigation of mastery motivation in deaf children is, therefore, of practical as well as theoretical significance. The analyses summarized in this chapter are the first to be reported that are based on direct observation of behavior and include both deaf and hearing infants.

Data Collection. As described in Chapter 3, infants were videotaped from behind a one-way mirror in laboratory sessions as they were seated on their mothers' laps at a table facing a staff member/experimenter. When the infants were age 9 months and again at age 12 months, four age-appropriate toys were presented, one at a time, and demonstrated by the experimenter (Fig. 7-1). (These toys are described in Appendix 7-1). These videotapes were used to generate the data reported below in Parts I and II.

Part I—A Traditional Approach to Assessment of Mastery Motivation

Rationale for Traditional Measures of Mastery Motivation

Previous investigations of mastery motivation in hearing children (Jennings et al., 1979; Yarrow et al., 1983), identified four important indicators:

1. exploratory behavior (Explore);
2. persistence on task-related activities (Persist);

Figure 7-1. This is one of the 9-month mastery tasks, "Toy Behind a Barrier." The infant is seated on his mother's lap in front of a table. On the other side of the table, a staff member is holding a clear plastic board between the baby and an attractive toy. This baby was about to push the board aside and "succeed" in reaching the toy. (Illustration by Liz Conces Spencer)

3. task completion (Success);
4. social behaviors that co-occurred with positive affect (Social Smile).

Exploratory behaviors are common measures of infants' behaviors with objects and have often been employed as a measure of their interest in learning about characteristics of objects and the environment (McCall, Eichorn, & Hogarty, 1977; Ruff, 1986). Persistence in goal-directed behavior, that is, task persistence, has long been considered a primary indicator of motivation (e.g., Tolman, 1932; Atkinson, 1957; Weiner, Kun, & Benesh-Weiner, 1980). Persistence is defined as the duration or frequency of attempts to master a task. Success—that is, producing an effect or solving the problem presented by a toy—has been considered an index of the child's competence. In addition, several reports (MacTurk, et al., 1985, 1987) suggest that the ability to integrate socially oriented behaviors into the stream of object-related activities is an important dimension of motivation. These reports prompted a closer examination of the social component of motivated behavior. Affect was included in the social measure because facial expressions are considered a "window" to the emotional meaning of events to an infant.

Participants and Procedures. The focus of this first analysis was identification of infants' motivational behaviors during the data collection situation. The group comparisons presented in this section are based on data collected from nineteen deaf infants (Hd) and twenty hearing infants (Hh), all with hearing parents. The videotapes were coded using a remote-controlled Panasonic AG-6300 videocassette recorder connected to an IBM-compatible personal computer (PC) running a data acquisition and recording program. The onset of each behavior change was keyed into the PC keyboard while the time (in 1/30-second intervals) was obtained from the video time code. The resulting data set represented a time-based, sequential record of the infant's actions during the mastery motivation assessment session.

Coding Scheme. The coding scheme was designed to capture the full range of an infant's behaviors in the mastery motivation session: exploration, persistence, success, and social expression. There were three coding categories: *(1)* behaviors directed toward the objects; *(2)* behaviors directed toward the mother or experimenter; and *(3)* expressions of affect: crying/fussing, neutral, interest/excitement, and smiling/laughing.

The object-related behavior codes were derived in part from studies of exploratory behavior (Switzky, Haywood, & Isett, 1974; Belsky, Garduque, & Hrncir, 1984) and served as the basis for the first three levels of object-associated activities (Look, Explore, and Manipulate). The next two levels (Task- and Goal-directed) were derived from general theories of motivation (Piaget, 1952; Atkinson, 1957; Hunt, 1965) and from observations of infant behavior during the administration of standardized developmental assessments (Yarrow, Rubenstein, & Pedersen, 1975). The levels were conceived as a hierarchy, with the categories Look, Explore, Manipulate, Task-, and Goal-Directed ordered in relation to the degree of skill required of the infant. Success reflects infant competence in solving the problem presented by the object.

Behaviors directed toward the examiner and/or mother were considered to be a form of social referencing in which infants use adults' emotional responses as guides to continued interaction with the objects (Wenar, 1972; Feinman, 1982; Clyman, Emde, Kempe, & Harmon, 1986). The integration of social-directed and object-directed acts have been shown to constitute an important element of infants' persistent attempts to master the environment (MacTurk et al., 1985; Wachs, 1987).

The three categories of behavior in the coding scheme were mutually exclusive and exhaustive within a category but not between categories. Because the categories represent three relatively independent behavioral systems that could logically co-occur, the coding system was designed to record and tally the number of changes and durations of infants' socially oriented behaviors as they were actively engaged with the toy while simultaneously recording changes in facial expression (see Appendix 7-2 for the complete code). The actual coding was performed at the individual behavior level and combined during the initial data processing phase by adding the frequencies and durations to yield the primary measures of mastery motivation: Explore, Persist, Success, and Social Smile.

Reliability. Two trained observers independently coded 17% (n = 13) of the seventy-eight mastery assessment videotapes (thirty-nine at age 9 months plus thirty-nine at age 12 months). Interrater reliability estimates were computed on the frequencies of the individual measures. Pearson product-moment correlations ranged from .60 for Explore to .96 for Success, with a mean correlation of .82.

Analysis. The data were analyzed in several phases. The descriptive phase consisted of a 2 (group)-by-2 (age) repeated measures analysis of variance (RM-ANOVA) to test for the presence of significant group and age differences. In addition, correlations were computed to examine associations between the measures for each group at each age. The final analysis examined the predictive relations between measures for each group.

Results and Discussion

Group Differences. The RM-ANOVA revealed neither significant group differences nor a group-by-age interaction for any measure of task involvement or social behavior (Table 7-1). A main effect for age was de-

Table 7-1. Mastery motivation for deaf and hearing infants at 9 and 12 months: Means, Standard Deviations, and Repeated Measures ANOVA

	Deaf infants (n = 19)		*Hearing infants (n = 20)*		*ANOVA effects*		
	9 months	*12 months*	*9 months*	*12 months*	*Group*	*Age*	*Group × Age*
Explore	13.61 (3.57)	14.89 (4.42)	13.79 (2.71)	12.78 (4.02)	NS	NS	NS
Persist	14.20 (3.66)	17.55 (6.14)	13.99 (3.16)	15.90 (5.98)	NS	<.01[a]	NS
Success	3.00 (1.77)	4.08 (2.20)	3.50 (1.76)	4.65 (2.60)	NS	<.01[b]	NS
Social Smile	1.41 (1.52)	2.46 (1.94)	1.72 (1.52)	1.69 (1.96)	NS	NS	NS

[a] $F\ (1,37) = 7.81$ (combined means = 14.10–16.73).

[b] $F\ (1,37) = 8.00$ (combined means = 2.33–4.37).

tected for the frequencies of Persist and Success. Both groups of infants displayed a significant increase in these two measures from 9 to 12 months. These results supported the expectation that the hearing status of normally developing children with hearing mothers affects neither their motivation to explore objects nor their engagement with the social environment.

Nine-Month Intercorrelations. Despite group similarities for individual indicators of mastery motivation (Table 7-1), relationships between pairs of mastery-related behaviors were different for the deaf and hearing infants, as shown by the correlations in Table 7-2. Correlations among measures for the deaf infants revealed one significant relationship, Explore with Persist. Others were statistically independent, except for a moderate relationship between the frequency of Social Smile and Persist. This contrasted sharply with the pattern of relationships found for the hearing infants.

For hearing infants, the correspondence among behaviors reflecting different levels of task engagement was not as differentiated. All of the object engagement measures were highly intercorrelated and independent of Social Smile, suggesting that the hearing infants were more focused on the tasks than were their deaf peers. This speculation is supported by *(1)* the high correlations among the task-related measures of

Table 7-2. Intercorrelations for the 9-month measures of mastery motivation and social smile, deaf and hearing infants

	Explore	*Persist*	*Success*	*Smile*
Explore	—	**.72*****	**.60****	**−.08**
Persist	.81***	—	**.70*****	**−.31**
Success	.35	.22	—	**−.11**
Social Smile	.26	.40†	−.04	—

Correlations for the deaf infants (n = 19) are below the diagonal; correlations for the hearing infants (n = 20) are above the diagonal in boldface.

†$p < .10$.

**$p < .01$.

***$p < .001$.

Explore, Persist, and Success, and *(2)* the low correlation between social smiling and task engagement for the Hh group.

Although smiling and persistence were not related at the .05 level for either group, they were similar in magnitude for both groups but in opposite directions. The correlation was negative for the hearing infants, which suggests that social smiling is not associated with their involvement with the tasks, a finding consistent with earlier reports (Yarrow et al., 1983). Conversely, deaf infants displayed a positive relationship between their persistent, goal-directed activities and social smiling, suggesting a greater integration of the two domains. Infants in both groups also made similar efforts to master the environment, but the results suggest that the deaf infants display greater diversity in their explorations compared to the hearing infants. Thus, although the deaf infants appear to incorporate more "social" behaviors in their object-related activities, these social behaviors do not reduce their efforts to solve the toy problem (their persistence). This supports the idea that deaf infants' social behaviors are for the purpose of social referencing rather than bids for social interactions, and may reflect an adaptation to decreased auditory information from the environment.

Twelve-Month Intercorrelations. The primary differences between the groups at the 12-month mastery assessment are seen in the relationships between social smiling and task-related activities (see Table 7-3). The hearing infants displayed a pattern of significant positive correlations between social and object-related behaviors that was absent at 9 months, while maintaining the same level of task involvement found at the earlier age. In contrast, deaf infants displayed a reduced differentiation between their object-related activities, as evidenced by significant correlations between Explore/Persist and Persist/Success and by socially directed behaviors that are more independent of the task-related measures.

Results of the data obtained from the 12-month-old hearing infants imply that the relative importance of socially directed behaviors in the

Table 7-3. Intercorrelations for the 12-month measures of mastery motivation and social smile, deaf and hearing infants

	Explore	*Persist*	*Success*	*Smile*
Explore	—	**.90*****	**.78****	**.53***
Persist	.81***	—	**.88*****	**.44***
Success	.19	.62**	—	**.38**†
Social Smile	.29	.26	.26	—

Correlations for the deaf infants (n = 19) are below the diagonal; correlations for the hearing infants (n = 20) are above the diagonal in bold face.

†$p < .10$.

*$p < .05$.

**$p < .01$.

***$p < .001$.

context of attempts to master the environment undergoes a significant transformation during the interval from 9 to 12 months. This finding (that is, greater integration of social and mastery behaviors) is similar to that found in previous research with 6- and 12-month-old hearing infants (MacTurk et al., 1987). The original conclusion was that the 6-month-old infants were not as adept at integrating the social aspects of their behavioral repertoire into an ongoing stream of task-related activities. The current results offer support for the conclusion that the time frame for this important developmental transformation may be shorter than previously believed. This contrasted with the finding of a shift toward increased domain-specific independence for the deaf infants over the same time span. For deaf infants at 9 months, Social Smile accounted for 16% of the observed variance in the index of mastery motivation, whereas at 12 months, only 7% of the variance in mastery motivation was explained by Social Smile.

Cross-Age Correlations. An interesting pattern of group differences emerged in the predictions between the measures. For the hearing infants, all of the significant cross-age correlations were between measures of task involvement (see Table 7-4). Not only did Explore, Persist, and Success show a high degree of cross-age stability, but Persist at 9 months predicted Success at 12 months as earlier Success predicted later Persist. These results were similar to the 9-month intercorrelations for the hearing infants. Task engagement appeared to be relatively undifferentiated, both contemporaneously and predictively. The deaf infants, in comparison, had significant cross-age correlations that were restricted to the frequency of early social smiling and later exploration and persistence with a moderate level of stability for Social Smile (see Table 7-5). These differences did not affect overall distribution of mastery-related behaviors between the groups but did affect the relative importance of specific behaviors.

Table 7-4. Cross-age correlations for the hearing infants

	12 months			
9 months	*Explore*	*Persist*	*Success*	*Smile*
Explore	.60**	.33	.35	.18
Persist	.56**	.46*	.48*	.30
Success	.72***	.63**	.61**	.39†
Social Smile	.08	.06	−.02	−.06

†$p < .10$.

*$p < .05$.

**$p < .01$.

***$p < .001$.

Correlations for the hearing infants showed that they focused on interactions with the objects. Conversely, deaf infants displayed a more diffuse pattern, suggesting a greater commingling of their object-related and socially directed activities. For example, one deaf child frequently glanced at the experimenter and smiled while pushing hard at the plastic barrier that shielded the toy lion. This pattern of social-plus-exploratory mastery behaviors suggests that social smiling may serve a different psychological function for the deaf infants. Social smiling for the hearing infants may represent an invitation to the social partner to participate in their exploration of the object. In contrast, the deaf infants may be seeking visual feedback concerning their performance in an effort to reduce situational ambiguity, that is, the absence of adult participation. In this sense, the formal definition of social referencing may be a more appropriate explanation for the relationships between social and object behaviors. If social referencing does, indeed, represent an adaptive coping strategy, then the deaf infants who were able to integrate social/coping behaviors into their object-related activities at 9 months should have been able to devote more of their efforts to exploration and goal-directed activities at 12 months.

Table 7-5. Cross-age correlations for the deaf infants

	12 months			
9 months	*Explore*	*Persist*	*Success*	*Smile*
Explore	−.01	.18	.11	.00
Persist	.19	.22	−.03	.17
Success	.14	.19	.01	.09
Social Smile	.56**	.55**	.34	.44†

†$p < .10$.

**$p < .01$.

Part II—A Nontraditional Approach to Mastery Assessment

Rationale for an Organizational Construct Approach to Mastery Motivation

A focus on the frequency and duration of mastery motivation behaviors may mask important differences in how children approach and engage the environment (see also Barrett, MacTurk, & Morgan, 1995.) Messer (1995) affirmed that important differences in children's object mastery efforts may be qualitative rather than quantitative. It is proposed that children can be classified according to their general style of mastery motivation (social- versus object-oriented) just as they can be classified according to their style of attachment (secure versus insecure).

Ainsworth, Blehar, Waters, and Wall (1978) and Sroufe and Waters (1977) used an *organizational* construct approach to define the construct of attachment, as separate from other domains of functioning. The approach placed a greater focus on attachment styles or classifications with stability across time and situations, and it conceptualized attachment as a global internal characteristic of the child. The approach views domains of functioning as expressions of integrated behavior systems organized by an underlying strategy. By understanding the strategy, it should be easier to predict how behaviors will change in a different social or physical context (Seifer & Vaughn, 1995).

This organizational construct approach was utilized to develop a revised definition of mastery motivation:

> Mastery motivation is a behavioral system that promotes adaptability within changing environments. At the individual level, this is achieved by monitoring and appraising novel environmental events, with the set goal of achieving feelings of efficacy. Mastery motivation behaviors are used to achieve the set goal. These behaviors serve the function of initiating and maintaining interactions with and responding to the environment. Based on the organization of the relationships between these functional mastery motivation categories, infants can be classified in terms of certain consistent styles of mastery motivation (e.g., social- or object-oriented). (Ludwig, 1999, pp. 25–26)

Note that the emphasis here is on the *organization* of behavior in the service of the underlying motivational system. This approach contrasts with that taken in Part I. There, mastery motivation was conceptualized as representing a continuous measure with the implication that "more" mastery behavior was "better."

The major hypothesis of this second analysis is that deaf infants' adaptation to their limited access to auditory input results in their being more likely to "specialize" in social mastery behaviors. It was proposed that deaf infants' mastery motivation styles are organized in a manner similar to that of hearing infants, but they are more likely than hearing infants to develop a *social* mastery motivation style. However, another possibility must be considered: deaf infants' adaptation to and experience of the world may be so different from that of hearing infants that their organization of mastery behaviors is also radically different. Therefore, the possibility that the social mastery motivation construct may be very different for deaf and hearing infants must be considered; that is, similar mastery behaviors may have different meanings for deaf and hearing infants. If this is the case, different styles of mastery would be observed for the deaf and the hearing infants.

In this analysis, therefore, two different hypotheses are considered: *(1)* the organization of mastery behaviors is similar across groups of deaf and hearing children, but deaf children are more likely to show more socially related behaviors than hearing children; *(2)* deaf and hearing children show different organizations of their mastery motivation behavior, especially related to the meaning of social behaviors. These two hypotheses led to two different models of the organization of mastery motivation as reflected in the behaviors of deaf and hearing children. These models are illustrated in Figure 7-2. Additionally, Figure 7-2 represents a model for a general null hypothesis, which is that deaf and hearing infants show similar styles of social and object mastery motivation and are equally likely to show either style—that is, neither quantity nor quality of mastery motivation differs between deaf and hearing children.

Participants. All four groups of infants and mothers were included in this second analysis of the data for mastery motivation. The data from nineteen hearing infants of hearing parents (Hh), sixteen hearing infants of deaf parents (Dh), twenty-one deaf infants of deaf parents (Dd), and nineteen deaf infants of hearing parents (Hd) were analyzed.

Coding. Functional mastery motivation categories were created based on the organizational construct approach to mastery motivation. Rating scales were formed for each of the functional mastery motivation categories according to the degree of activity, promptness, strength, persistence, and/or consistency of the functional mastery behaviors. (A detailed description of the rating scales is reproduced in Appendix 7-3.)

Videotapes of the mastery motivation assessment session were coded using these rating scales. Each infant had four scores on each rating scale, one for each of the four toys. These four scores were averaged to obtain one score for each mastery variable. Five variables passed tests of interrater reliability and data screening. Therefore, the data for each infant consisted of averages of three object variables and two social variables:

1. Object Initiation: promptness, and activity level of toy interactions ($\kappa = .86$);
2. Object Engagement: sustained and varied goal-directed behavior with toy ($\kappa = .74$);

Null Hypothesis: Deaf and hearing infants show similar styles of mastery and are equally likely to show either style.

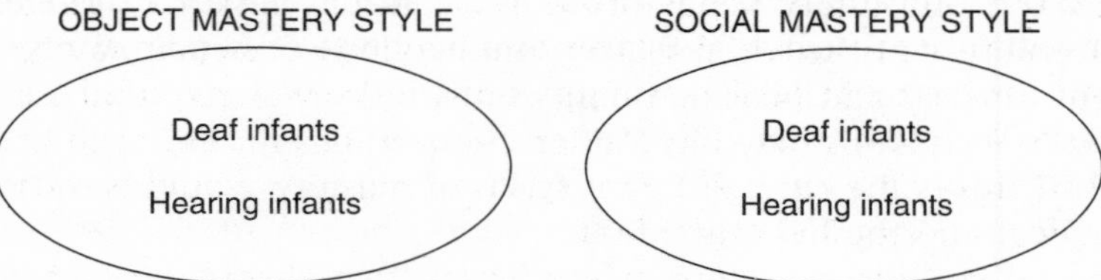

Model 1: Deaf and hearing infants show similar styles of mastery but deaf infants are over-represented in the social mastery category.

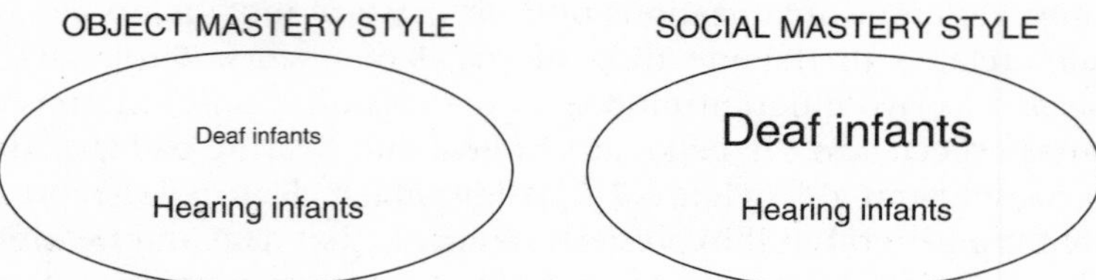

Model 2: Deaf and hearing infants show similar object mastery styles but non-overlapping styles of social mastery motivation.

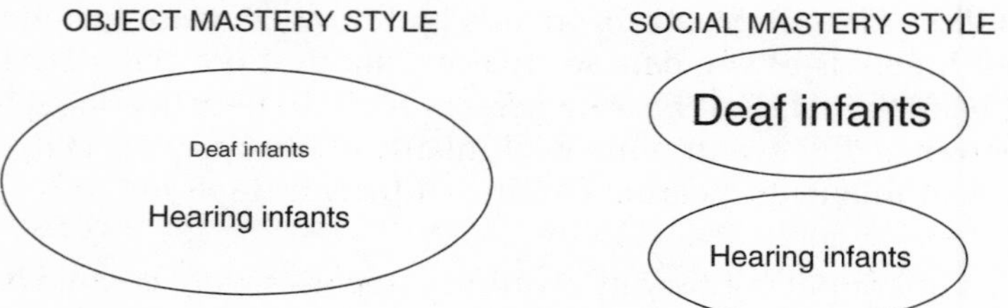

Figure 7-2. Two models of deaf infants' styles of social mastery motivation. *Note:* Differences in text size convey the relative difference between the numbers of deaf infants compared to hearing infants expected to be in each category. Print size does not convey information about the hearing infants' mastery motivation.

3. Object Engrossment: time, and enthusiasm with toy (κ = .78);
4. Social Signaling: instrumental/informational signaling to an adult (κ = .74);
5. Social Mutuality: attainment of joint activity with adult (κ = .71).

Reliability. Two graduate and one undergraduate research assistants were trained by the experimenter (Ludwig) to code the data. The mastery motivation behavioral system rating scales were used to code the videotapes with respect to the infant's behavior with the toys and with the two adults. Coders remained blind to the infant's hearing status, to the extent possible (some infants wore hearing aids).

Interrater reliability comparisons were made between the experimenter and three research assistants and between each pair of research assistants. Interrater reliability was assessed on the first seven infants and then every second to fourth infant, resulting in comparisons on 27% of the data (twenty infants). The five mastery motivation rating variables selected for analysis had mean Cohen's κ coefficient reliabilities greater than .70, with minimum and maximum coefficients that ranged from .62 to .93. This is comparable to reliability reported in another study using rating scale measures of mastery motivation (Maslin-Cole, Bretherton, & Morgan, 1993).

Analysis

The goal of the analysis was to determine whether the distribution of mastery styles across the hearing status groups most nearly reflected Model 1 (i.e., all groups showing similar mastery styles represented in an object vs. social orientation, but with more deaf than hearing children showing a social orientation), or Model 2 (i.e., more than one mastery style identified, with that of deaf and hearing children differing), or the null hypothesis (i.e., no significant differences in styles represented or distribution across those styles).

First, a cluster analysis was performed, incorporating the five social and object mastery scores from all infants. This analysis determined how many primary mastery style groupings existed, and it categorized each infant according to type of mastery orientation.[1] After infants were assigned to primary mastery style groups, logistic regression was used to determine whether hearing status related to the group to which an infant was assigned. This allowed determination of whether mastery style was best represented by Model 1, Model 2, or whether there was no significant hearing status/mastery style relation. Logistic regression was selected because sample size was relatively small and the variables were mutually exclusive categories (infant hearing status, style of mastery motivation) and because it does not require a normal distribution, equal variance, or a linear relationship between the predictors and the outcome variable (Tabachnick & Fidell, 1996). Logistic regression results are expressed in terms of odds ratios that indicate whether children from one hearing status group were more likely than expected by chance to be represented in one of the mastery style groups.

Additional analyses were conducted to determine whether variables other than infant hearing status explained significant variance in social mastery style. These other variables included *(1)* child sex because previous studies (e.g., Harter, 1975) found differences in social and object orientation for school-age girls and boys and *(2)* parent hearing status because differences in social interaction patterns had been previously reported for deaf children with deaf or hearing parents (Meadow, Greenberg, Erting, & Carmichael, 1981; Spencer & Gutfreund, 1990; Erting, Prezioso, & Hynes, 1994). It was predicted that deaf infants, girls, infants with deaf mothers, and deaf infants with deaf mothers would be more likely than comparison groups to develop a social mastery style. Odds ratios were calculated for these three additional analyses as well, with hearing mothers, girls, and hearing infants of hearing mothers arbitrarily chosen as the reference group, respectively, for each of the additional analyses.

Results and Discussion

Cluster analysis identified clear social and object mastery orientation clusters in which children from each of the four groups were represented. No different organization was found in mastery motivation between the groups. That is, orientations were represented by the same categories across groups. Because only one social mastery cluster was found, and deaf and hearing infants therefore did not show different social mastery styles, hypothesis 2 (represented in Model 2) was not considered further (Fig. 7-3 illustrates the two clusters graphically).

What remained to be tested was hypothesis 1 (represented in Model 1), which would be supported if it were found that deaf infants had a greater likelihood of exhibiting a social mastery style of motivation compared to hearing infants. To test this hypothesis, infant hearing status was used to predict the likelihood of an infant's having a social mastery style. Separate analyses used parent hearing status, infant sex, and the

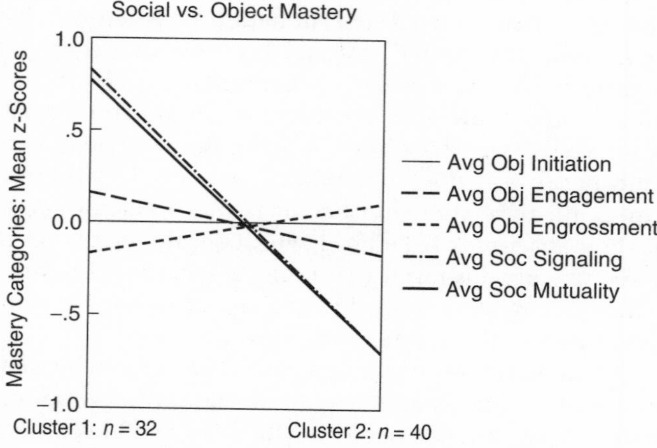

Figure 7-3. Graph of mean *z*-scores for infants in social versus object clusters.

interaction between parent and infant hearing status as predictors. These logistic regression results are shown in Table 7-6. The results are reported in the form of odds ratios.

As shown in Table 7-6, some relationships were found between tendency to show social orientation mastery style and infant hearing status, parent hearing status, and infant sex. For example, infants (whether deaf or hearing with deaf mothers), were three times as likely as those with hearing mothers to be identified as having this social orientation. However, the 95% confidence interval for all these odds ratios included the reference level of 1.00. Therefore, these relationships were nonsignificant. Neither infant hearing status, parent hearing status, nor infant sex, considered independently, increased the likelihood that an infant would demonstrate a social mastery style. In contrast, a significant interaction effect was found between infant hearing status and parent hearing status, but this interaction was significant only for Dd infants, for whom the 95% confidence interval around the odds ratio did not include the reference level of 1.00. The odds ratio for the deaf infants of deaf par-

Table 7-6. Relationship between social mastery style and hearing status and sex: Odds ratios

Social mastery's relations		*Lower 95%*	*Upper 95%*
With Infant Hearing Status	*Odds Ratio*	*Limit*	*Limit*
Deaf infant	1.46	.76	2.80
Hearing infant	1.00	1.00	1.00
With Parent Hearing Status	*Odds Ratio*	*Limit*	*Limit*
Deaf mother	3.18	.39	25.97
Hearing mother	1.00	1.00	1.00
With Infant Sex	*Odds Ratio*	*Limit*	*Limit*
Male	1.56	.56	4.37
Female	1.00	1.00	1.00
The "Interaction" Between Parent and Infant Hearing Status	*Odds Ratio*	*Limit*	*Limit*
Deaf mother/deaf infant	3.93	2.07	7.45*
Deaf mother/hearing infant	.45	.09	2.29
Hearing mother/deaf infant	1.05	.36	3.06
Hearing mother/hearing infant	1.00	1.00	1.00

*Significant result; 95% confidence interval does not contain the value 1.00.

ents (Dd) suggests that they were almost four times as likely to demonstrate a social mastery style of motivation when compared to the reference group, hearing infants of hearing parents (Hh). Deaf infants of hearing parents (Hd) and hearing infants of deaf parents (Dh) were not more likely to demonstrate a social mastery style than were those in the Hh reference group. Therefore, Model 1 was only partially supported. As the model predicted, deaf and hearing infants showed similar styles of mastery; however, Dd infants but not Hd infants were overrepresented in the social mastery category. Deafness predicted social orientation mastery style, but only when the deaf infant had deaf parents. (When variance due to sex was accounted for, this result remained statistically significant.)

The robustness of this significant finding was demonstrated through several unplanned analyses, which were conducted to determine whether the relationship between dyadic hearing status and social mastery was confounded by other factors. Even after the variance due to mother–father education and age, infant birth weight, birth order, and Alpern-Boll Physical/Self-Help scores were accounted for, the results remained the same. Therefore, it is likely that Dd infants' overrepresentation in the social mastery style group was attributable to the interaction between parent and infant hearing status, not to the potential effects of these other variables. Distributions of infants' object and social mastery style, by group, are shown in Table 7-7. This distribution illustrates the dramatic difference between the deaf infants with deaf parents (71% of whom demonstrated social mastery styles) and the three other groups of infants (no more than 40% of whom demonstrated a social mastery style). A striking example can be recounted from a videotape of one Dd infant: when he successfully mastered one task he applauded himself while smiling and gazing at the experimenter. Continuing to applaud, he twisted toward his mother and smiled broadly at her.

Table 7-7. Infants with social and object mastery styles, by group (percent, number, adjusted residual)

	Social mastery style			*Object mastery style*		
Group	%	*(n)*	*Adj. Res.*	%	*(n)*	*Adj. Res.*
Deaf infants, deaf mothers	71.4%	(15)	3.0	28.6%	(6)	−3.0
Deaf infants, hearing mothers	22.2	(4)	−2.2	77.8	(14)	2.2
Hearing infants, deaf mothers	40.0	(6)	−0.3	60.0	(9)	0.2
Hearing infants, hearing mothers	38.9	(7)	−0.5	61.1	(11)	0.5

Note: Pearson and likelihood-ratio chi-square analyses confirmed that an association existed between hearing status and mastery style of motivation, χ^2 (3) = 10.138, $p < .05$. Examination of adjusted residuals (Adj. Res.) showed that deaf infants of deaf mothers were more likely to demonstrate a social style of mastery (3.0, Adj. Res. > ± 2.0), and deaf infants of hearing parents were more likely to demonstrate an object style of mastery (2.2, Adj. Res. > ± 2).

Conclusion

In this chapter, two different measurement models were employed to describe mastery motivation. In the analysis reported in Part I, mastery motivation was conceptualized and measured using a traditional classical testing theory framework. The analysis presented in Part II addressed social mastery motivation directly by adopting a nontraditional organizational construct approach that parallels that used with a related construct, Attachment Theory. The first analysis (Part I) did not find significant differences between deaf and hearing infants with hearing parents on the quantity of behaviors indicating mastery motivation. This included indications of exploration, persistence, success, or social interest. However, the same analysis suggested that the deaf infants with hearing parents may *organize* their efforts to master the object environment differently from the hearing infants with hearing parents. Specifically, although socially oriented behaviors seemed to interfere with mastery success for the hearing infants, this was not the case for the deaf infants, who appeared to integrate the social and object-oriented modes of exploration. It was suggested that this integration of social and object mastery reflected an adaptation of the Dh infants to their reduced auditory contact with the environment. In support of this interpretation, it was also found that, although hearing infants' (Hh) *object* mastery behavior at 9 months predicted object mastery behavior at 12 months, deaf infants' (Hd) *social* mastery behavior at 9 months predicted object mastery behavior at 12 months.

The two additional groups of infants (Dd, Dh) were added to the analysis presented in Part II. Using a global rating scale to assess mastery behavior at 12 months, it was again found that both hearing and deaf infants were represented in the object and social style schemas. The mastery style of only one of the four groups differed significantly from those of the other three: the deaf infants with deaf parents. These Dd infants were significantly more likely to exhibit a social mastery style, whereas the infants in the three other groups were either just as likely to demonstrate an object mastery style, or more likely to demonstrate an object mastery style, rather than a social mastery style.

The analyses reported in Parts I and II both suggested that deaf infants incorporated "social referencing" or visual checking (accompanied by positive social affect), as a mechanism that is adaptive for hearing loss. It was suggested that Dd infants are especially likely to develop a social mastery style because they have been socialized to expect visual cues and responses from people by their deaf parents whose intuitive parenting draws upon their own adaptation to a sound-free (or reduced-sound) environment. (See Chapter 11 for additional evidence that Dd infants are more likely than Hd infants to integrate visual attention to *persons* with episodes of attention to *objects*.) It is possible that, as they accrue more visual communication experience and develop additional adaptive skills, deaf infants with hearing parents may move toward a social mastery style.

The analyses in this chapter provide important support for the notion that it is not hearing status alone but characteristics of deaf infants' interactive and communicative experiences that influence patterns of development. Thus, here as in other chapters in this book, differences were found that related to the combination of (thus the interaction between) infant and parent hearing status. This implies that characteristics of infants' interactive experiences, as well as their sensory processing abilities, are reflected in their adaptations to their social and object-related worlds.

Acknowledgments

The Introduction and Part I are adapted from:

MacTurk, R. H. (1991). Mastery motivation in deaf and hearing infants. In K. P. Meadow-Orlans, R. H. MacTurk, P. E. Spencer, & L. S. Koester, *Interaction and support: Mothers and deaf infants*. Final Report, Grant MCJ-110563. Washington, DC: Gallaudet University.

Part II is based on:

Ludwig, J. L. (1999). *An organizational construct approach to the study of mastery motivation in deaf and hearing infants*. Unpublished doctoral dissertation, Purdue University, West Lafayette, IN. Dr. Ludwig acknowledges the assistance of her dissertation committee: Gerald Gruen (chair), Judith Conger, Theodore Wachs, Karen Diamond, and Robert MacTurk. Coding assistance was provided by Carrie Watkins, Michele Banner, and Jiao Ziyi.

Note

1. Methods were chosen that did not produce overlapping clusters; therefore, no infant could be placed in more than one group. Both Ward's minimum variance method and the complete linkage method were used in order to confirm that the cluster pattern was stable across more then one type of analysis. These clusters or groups were the basis for determining style of mastery motivation. It was expected that clusters would form based on either a social or object mastery style (Model 1) or that more than one style of social or object mastery might be found (Model 2).

Appendix 7-1. Structured tasks used to assess mastery motivation

Nine-Month Toys

1. Toy behind barrier: An attractive lion squeeze-toy is placed behind a clear plastic rectangular screen (6" × 18") within reach of the child. The infant may obtain the toy by reaching around the barrier.
2. Busy poppin' pals: A yellow rectangular box with five pop-up doors can be opened by operating the push buttons, dials, or levers.
3. Peg board: This is a yellow plastic rectangular board with six holes on top with six yellow pegs, which fit into the holes. The toy is presented with the pegs in the holes and the infant is to remove the pegs.
4. Farm: This consists of a plastic barn with double doors on the front that are latched. A small plastic animal is hidden inside and can be obtained by unlocking the latch and opening the doors.

Twelve-Month Toys

1. Farm (same as 9-month)
2. Busy poppin' pals (same as 9-month)
3. Discovery cottage: This is a brightly colored house with a small front door and a hinged roof. Two dolls are hidden in slots located behind the door and under the roof, and they can be obtained by opening the door or raising the roof.
4. Shapes and slides: This brightly colored box has three holes on the top where dolls of different shapes are located. Levers are provided that, when pressed, release the doll down a slide.

Appendix 7-2. Traditional mastery code categories

Look	Only look at object
Explore/Manipulate	Only touch apparatus
	Only mouth apparatus
	Only passively hold apparatus
	Manipulate
	Examine
	Bang
	Shake
	Hit or bat
	Drop object
Persistence	
Task directed	Task-related activity
	Grasping or holding
	Reach for apparatus
Goal-directed	Goal-directed activity
	Resets/replaces toy
Success	Obtains toy
Social	Looks at experimenter
	Vocalizes to experimenter
	Looks at mirror
	Looks at mother
	Vocalizes to mother
	Leans back on mother
	Offers, gives object
	Rejects object
Off-task	Engages with nontask object
	Other

Facial Expressions

Negative (cry, fuss)
Obscured
Neutral
Interest/Excitement
Positive (smile, laugh)

Appendix 7-3. Nontraditional mastery rating scales

Social Signaling

Crying, active fussing, or attachment behaviors should not be scored.
4 Infant uses eye gaze accompanied by more active forms to attempt to initiate instrumental interactions with adults, such as offering toys, or initiating games. If attempts to initiate interactions with adults are unsuccessful, the infant shows persistence in trying to obtain an instrumental response from the adult by repeating the same request or changing the type of signal used.
OR
Infant uses eye gaze accompanied by more active forms, such as reaching for an adult, offering toys, or initiating games, to attempt to obtain instrumental responses from adults.
If attempts to initiate interactions with adults are unsuccessful, however, the infant does not persist in attempts to gain adult attention.
3 Infant repeatedly uses eye gaze accompanied by emotional expression (smiles, laughs, frowns) to initiate interactions. Does not use more active attempts to gain attention.
2 Infant repeatedly uses eye gaze to attempt to initiate interactions. May occasionally use emotional expression to initiate interactions.
1 Infant displays no or few attempts to get an adult's attention. May use eye gaze or other passive methods occasionally, but shows no consistent attempts.

Social Responsivity

Adult initiations consist of instrumental behaviors such as pointing, offers of objects, and demonstrating toys.
3 Infant is much more likely to comply than noncomply with adult requests.
2 Infant sometimes responds and sometimes does not respond to adult requests.
1 Infant is much more likely to noncomply than comply with adult requests.

Interactional Mutuality

4 Infant and adult engage in some sort of game that involves taking turns, such as handing objects back and forth or peek-a-boo. Infant must show positive expression and eye gaze toward the adult at least once to designate the activity a game. Each participant has at least two turns.
OR
Adult responds more than once to infant requests such as giving an object or reaching for an adult. Interactions do not involve turn-taking.
3 Adult responds once to infant verbal or nonverbal requests, such as giving an object or reaching for an adult. Interactions do not involve turn-taking.

2 Adult never responds to infant verbal or nonverbal request, such as giving an object or reaching for an adult.
1 Infant never makes an instrumental request of the adult.

Object Initiations

Scored during examiner initial presentation and demonstration of the object. Scoring begins when the examiner sets the object down on the table and ends 5 seconds after the examiner finishes demonstrating the toy.
4 Infant assertively reaches for the toy before or almost before the examiner begins demonstrating the object. The infant contacts the toy or shows an assertive attempt to obtain the toy if it is out of reach. Once the infant has the toy, the infant begins actively manipulating the toy.
3 Infant hesitates before assertively reaching for the toy, but does so before the demonstration is completed. The infant contacts the toy or shows an assertive attempt to obtain the toy if it is out of reach. Once the infant has the toy, the infant begins actively manipulating the toy.
2 Infant waits until after the examiner has completed the demonstration before contacting the toy. Infant then actively manipulates the toy.
1 Infant assertively attempts to contact the toy before or after the demonstration, but the infant only touches/holds the toy.
OR
Infant does not touch, hold, or manipulate the toy during or after the examiner demonstration.

Object Engagement

4 Infant shows instances of goal-directed behavior that are primarily demonstrated during lengthy bouts of goal-directed behavior. Infant also shows a great variety of types of goal-directed behaviors.
3 Infant exhibits instances of goal-directed behavior that are demonstrated during lengthy bouts of goal-directed behavior. Infant shows less variety in the types of goal-directed behaviors.
2 Infant reveals instances of goal-directed behavior that are demonstrated during short bouts of goal-directed behavior. Infant displays a great variety of types of goal-directed behaviors.
1 Infant exhibits instances of goal-directed behavior during short bouts of goal-directed behavior. Infant exhibits less variety in the types of goal-directed behaviors.
OR
Infant shows no instances of goal-directed directed behavior or a variety of goal-directed behavior that is of a repetitive nature.

Object Engrossment (Riksen-Walraven, Meij, van Roozendaal, & Koks, 1993)

4 Infant devotes much of the time to exploration. Throughout the session, the infant reveals consistent pleasure and excitement if effects are discovered. Infant displays little or no frustration and does not give up easily.
OR
Infant devotes much of the time to exploration. Infant occasionally shows pleasure and excitement if effects are discovered. Infant may or may not demonstrate some frustration or give up easily.
3 Infant spends relatively long periods of time in exploration. Infant may or may not show some moments of active interest—for instance, when repeating an effective

manipulation, but never shows enthusiasm or excitement. Infant may or may not demonstrate some frustration or give up easily.
2 Infant spends relatively little time on exploration, but shows moments of active engagement and enthusiasm during exploration. May or may not demonstrate some frustration or give up easily.
1 Infant spends relatively little time on exploration. Exploration is superficial, sometimes seemingly "mechanical." Infant may show some moments of active interest, but never displays enthusiasm or excitement. Infant may or may not demonstrate some frustration or give up easily.
OR
If the infant shows any exploration of the object, it is in a passive and listless manner. No evidence of pleasure or excitement. Sometimes the object seems to elicit negative emotions in the infant.

Active Object Inattention

Infant drops, throws, or pushes away toys. Instances where the infants let go of the object and it rolls or bounces onto the floor are not scored. Instances where the infant pushes the toy toward the adult as a request for help are not scored.
4 Infant displays repeated instances of dropping, throwing, or pushing away toys. Infant display some negative affect or frustration.
OR
Infant shows repeated instances of dropping, throwing, or pushing away toys. Infant displays neutral affect.
3 Infant displays a few instances of dropping, throwing, or pushing away toys. Infant displays some negative affect or frustration.
2 Infant shows few instances of dropping, throwing, or pushing away toys. Infant shows neutral affect.
1 Infant shows no instances of dropping, throwing, or pushing away toys.

8

Mother–Infant Interactions at 12 and 18 Months

Parenting Stress and Support

Kathryn P. Meadow-Orlans and Annie G. Steinberg

Most research investigating the impact of deafness on early mother–child interaction has compared hearing mothers and their deaf infants or toddlers (Hd) to hearing children and hearing mothers (Hh). Early studies found interactions of Hd dyads problematic compared to those of Hh dyads. Mothers' spoken language was found to be more antagonistic and included less praise (Goss, 1970), in a manner described as less flexible and approving, more didactic and intrusive (Schlesinger & Meadow, 1972). Later studies reported similar results (e.g., Brinich, 1980; Greenberg, 1980; Wedell-Monnig & Lumley, 1980; Nienhuys & Tikotin, 1983; Nienhuys, Horsborough, & Cross, 1985; Power, Wood, Wood, & MacDougall, 1990; Spencer & Gutfreund, 1990). All of these studies were conducted either with children older than 18 months or with fewer than six subjects.

One larger study of maternal conversational control included thirty-four hearing mothers with deaf children, first at ages 3 to 5 years, then at ages 5 to 7 years (Musselman & Churchill, 1992, 1993). Low levels of maternal control were associated with greater gains in expressive (but not receptive) language. Maternal control decreased over time, but reductions were not commensurate with the growth in children's language, nor did control decrease to the extent that has been reported for hearing mothers with hearing children. Another study (n = 24) found that maternal sensitivity, a subscale of a larger construct, "emotional availability," which describes emotional communication, at ages 21 to 33 months predicted expressive language in deaf and hard-of-hearing children at ages 33 to 41 months (Pressman, Pipp-Siegel, Yoshinaga-Itano, & Deas, 1999). Language differences were greater for children with a hearing loss (n = 21) than for their hearing peers (n = 21), suggesting that maternal emotional availability is more critical when the child has a hearing loss (Pressman et al., 2000).

Lederberg and Mobley's (1990) research included the largest number of deaf children younger than age 2 with hearing mothers (n = 41; median age = 22 months). They found no differences between groups of deaf and hearing children in quality of attachment but reported a significant difference in the quantity of communicative interactions experienced by deaf and hearing toddlers with hearing mothers. The deaf children spent less time interacting with their mothers and more time in solitary play with toys compared to their peers. Mothers of the children with hearing loss initiated more interactions with their children than did mothers of hearing children; Hd toddlers were more likely than Hh toddlers "to terminate an interaction because they did not see or hear the last communication by their mothers" (p. 1600). However, they found no differences in the kinds of maternal behaviors cited by other researchers, and they suggested that the communicative frustrations that lead to intrusive, apparently insensitive behaviors in the hearing mothers of deaf children emerge later, when language delays become more apparent and interfere more seriously with reciprocal communication and interaction.

Authors of the earlier studies often attributed the differences or difficulties of the hearing-mother-deaf-child dyads to stress produced by the diagnosis of deafness or to the effect of diminished parent–child communication resulting from the child's deafness. The actual or expected language delay in deaf children can contribute to maternal stress that has a negative impact on mothers' behaviors. Schlesinger (1985) proposed that failure to generate reciprocal communication elicits a sense of powerlessness in a hearing mother, leading to heightened efforts to control the deaf child and to the self-perpetuating cycle of reduced interactive language stimulation. The emotional impact of the identification of deafness on hearing parents may also contribute to ambivalence, grief, anger, guilt, or denial with negative effects on dyadic interactions (Moses, 1985; Mindel & Feldman, 1987; Harvey, 1989), although response to a family crisis can also elicit family cohesiveness (Koester & Meadow-Orlans, 1990). Authors of two recent studies report stress levels of mothers with hearing-impaired children to be no different from those of mothers whose children are hearing, suggesting that recent improvements in age at identification and support services may have had a positive impact (Lederberg & Golbach, 2002; Pipp-Siegel, Sedey, & Yoshinaga-Itano, 2002; see Chapter 6).

Other studies suggest factors that may ameliorate stress experienced by parents of young children who are at risk or whose disabilities have been identified. Boukydis, Lester, and Hoffman (1987) argued that social support promotes psychological adjustment in mothers of neonates, as well as positive mother–infant interactions and optimal infant development. Crockenberg (1987) and Weinraub and Wolf (1987) reported that the responsiveness of social networks can mediate potentially problematic parental interactions with infants of young or single mothers, who experience more stress with a child's disability than do mothers whose spouse is present (Beckman, 1983). Support may buffer the stress of a premature birth (Crnic et al., 1983), and professional support has special significance for high-risk premature infants (Crnic, Greenberg, & Slough, 1986). Feiring and colleagues (1987) found that high-risk mothers with adequate emotional and material support engaged in more episodes of appropriate face-to-face stimulation with their 3-month-old infants. Mothers of preschool deaf children who received counseling demonstrated increased praise, enjoyment, and communicative complexity, and decreased maternal directiveness in interactions with their children, compared to a control group of mothers with deaf children who received no counseling (Greenberg, 1983; Greenberg, Calderon, & Kusché, 1984).

Deaf Children, Deaf Mothers. Less research with deaf mothers and their deaf infants is available, compared to the number of studies cited above. In the 1970s, the first study of young deaf children with deaf parents was conducted by a group of psychiatrists at a strictly oral school for deaf children. Four children, ages 7 to 31 months, were observed. During their second year, the children exhibited severe separation anxiety and sleep disturbances, which the researchers concluded were the result of disturbed mother–infant relationships (Galenson, Miller, Kaplan, & Rothstein, 1979). A later study reported differing results, namely, that neither the attachment patterns (Meadow, Greenberg, & Erting, 1983) nor the social behaviors (Meadow, Greenberg, Erting, & Carmichael, 1981) of preschool children who were deaf and had deaf parents differed from those of the comparison group of hearing children with hearing parents. Authors of the second set of studies suggested that participating subjects were drawn from populations that differed from those in the other study in two important ways: *(1)* the second set was more highly educated, and *(2)* they participated in an environment where the educational use of sign language was both accepted and encouraged, unlike the situation in the other school.

More recently, our pilot studies of very early interaction (infants at ages 3 to 12 months) suggested that mothers who were deaf were highly responsive to the communication needs of their deaf infants, exhibited prolonged positive facial expressions, and often mimicked their infants' facial expressions (Meadow-Orlans et al., 1987b). They also were found to modify their signed communication to maximize infants' visual input (Erting, Prezioso, & Hynes, 1990, 1994; Spencer, Bodner-Johnson, & Gutfreund, 1992). Jamieson's intensive studies of small groups of dyads (Dh, Dd, Hh), including mothers with 4- to 5-year-old children, showed that deaf mothers were more likely than hearing mothers to adapt discourse strategies to their child's visual needs, to establish joint visual attention, and to use appropriate scaffolding behaviors that facilitate the child's independent exploration (Jamieson & Pedersen, 1993; Jamieson, 1994a, 1994b). Deaf mothers have also been observed to use more tactile contact with their infants compared to others (Maestas y Moores, 1980; Rea, Bonvillian, & Richards, 1988).

These studies report the positive impact of interactions for children who are deaf, despite the difficulties inherent in the communicative situation of those with diminished auditory access to the environment. Wood and his colleagues were the first to focus on and emphasize this element in the acquisition of communicative competence by deaf children: the importance of dividing visual attention between the person communicating and the object being discussed (Wood, 1982; Wood, Wood, Griffiths, & Howarth, 1986). The deaf child is usually unable to attend both to her conversational partner and to the object of the conversation simultaneously. She must divide her attention, addressing the person and the object consecutively. Before this "habit" is acquired and becomes automatic, shifting attention slows a conversational exchange. This is reflected in the reports from two studies showing that deaf infants with deaf parents were exposed to fewer and briefer maternal utterances than were hearing infants with hearing parents (Gregory & Barlow, 1989; Harris, Clibbens, Chasin, & Tibbitts, 1989; Harris, 1992).

Hearing Children, Deaf Mothers. Social-psychological research with hearing children and deaf parents is very sparse indeed. Most research with this group has focused on speech or language development, and some reports have not provided separate analyses for hearing and deaf children with deaf parents, especially if the research focus was sign language acquisition (Maestas y Moores, 1980; Woll & Kyle, 1989; Bonvillian, Orlansky, & Folven, 1994). Indeed, much attention has been given to the relative speed of acquisition of speech by hearing children and sign language by deaf children (Petitto, 1986; Bonvillian & Folven, 1993).

Hearing children with deaf parents have been found to code- or mode-switch appropriately from speech to sign, depending on the hearing status of their conversational partners, by the age of 19 months (Prinz & Prinz, 1979, 1981; Griffith, 1990). One interesting case of code/mode-switching is provided by a study of twins (one deaf, one hearing) with deaf parents. Between 16 and 24 months, the hearing twin received more total utterances and more vocal utterances from adults than did the deaf twin. Almost all the deaf twin's utterances were in sign only, whereas the hearing twin used no vocal utterances to her mother, a few to her father (who used voice plus sign to her), and most to the hearing researchers who used voice plus sign (Gaustad, 1988).

There is little research on the nature of discourse between deaf parents and their hearing or deaf children, but a recurring focus of study with hearing children of deaf parents is their acquisition of speech. A comprehensive literature review identified sixteen studies of this kind, conducted between 1971 and 1985 (Schiff-Myers, 1993). Only two of these were conducted with more than eight subjects; one found the receptive language abilities of hearing preschoolers (n = 56) with deaf parents to be equal to, and articulation to be better than, those measured in the general population (Brelje, 1971). The other study showed that twenty-three of forty children who could be tested appropriately had speech or language delays, but only eleven of these had problems that related only to their parents' deafness. The others had previously undetected hearing losses or were diagnosed with cognitive or emotional problems (Schiff & Ventry, 1976).

Studies that might illuminate family dynamics or interactions of deaf parents with hearing children are difficult to locate. Those available have been conducted with older children or collected retrospectively from adults. These suggest few serious problems with this population (Meadow-Orlans, 2002; see also Rienzi, 1990; Buchino, 1993; E. G. Jones, 1995). The personal accounts of children of deaf adults (CODAs) usually report positive family experiences; they did not as children, nor do they as adults, consider their parents "handicapped" (Hoffmeister, 1985). They may recount the burdens of interpreting for parents (Mallory, Schein, & Zingle, 1992), the need to protect parents from cruel strangers or insensitive family members (including hearing grandparents), but without exception they express strong affection and close emotional ties (Fant & Schuchman, 1974; Royster, 1981; Walker, 1986; Sidransky, 1990; Davis, 2000). Preston's study (1994), based on 150 interviews with hearing adults who have deaf parents, provides the most comprehensive picture of this family constellation. He cites both negative and positive accounts from informants, concluding that their views about childhood experiences range as broadly as those of any other group.

Clinicians who have worked with families comprised of deaf parents and hearing children (by definition, those who are experiencing relational or behavioral difficulties) suggest that their problems are frequently related to role reversals and power struggles, to parents' lack of self-confidence in their childrearing abilities, or to the negative influence of hearing grandparents (Robinson & Weathers, 1974; Rayson, 1987; Harvey, 1989; Hindley, 2000). Although inferences might be drawn from these retrospective studies, narrative accounts, and clinical descriptions of family dynamics, they neither address nor can they be compared directly to research that examines early parent–child communication and interactions.

Deafness and Interaction. In the aggregate, these studies of deaf/hearing, hearing/deaf, and deaf/deaf interaction reflect the remarkable complexity of linguistic, emotional, and communication modality issues that have an impact on parents and children when deafness is involved. Much remains to be learned about the positive strategies of early interaction and socialization that enable most deaf parents to rear, and most deaf children to become, healthy and contributing members of society.

Data on Mother–Child Interaction and Support

Methodology

Participants. Participants included the core groups of mothers and children: nineteen dyads with a deaf mother and hearing baby (Dh), twenty-one dyads with a hearing mother and baby (Hh), and twenty dyads from each of the groups with deaf mothers and deaf babies (Dd) and hearing mothers and deaf babies (Hd).

Procedures. Mother–child free play with toys was videotaped for 15 minutes at the 12-month data collection session and for 20 minutes at the 18-month session. Questionnaires were completed by hearing parents after the 9-month and 15-month interviews. (These data were not collected from deaf parents.)

Rating Scales. Rating scales for mother–infant interaction drew from protocols used previously with infants or toddlers (Crawley & Spiker, 1983; Greenberg & Crnic, 1988; Crnic & Greenberg, 1990) or specifically with mothers of infants with hearing loss (Schlesinger & Meadow, 1972; Lederberg & Mobley, 1990). The rating scales were designed to be completed by experienced, clinically trained observers after a global viewing of the entire sequence of interaction. A persuasive rationale for this approach was provided by Bakeman and Brown (1980):

> . . . [I]t may be more fruitful to think of characteristics of early interaction, like responsiveness, not as frequencies or sequences of particular acts but, rather as a disposition which permeates all of the mother's and/or all of the baby's interactive behavior. And in that case, global rating scales, and not sequential recording of minute particular behaviors followed by various microanalyses, might be the method of choice. (p. 445)

Primary scales used in these analyses were completed after viewing the entire sequence of interaction. These included six behavior ratings for mothers (use of touch, sensitivity, participation, flexibility, affect, consistency), four behavior ratings for infants (compliance, affect, participation, gentleness), and three behavior ratings for dyads (enjoyment, communicative understanding, reciprocal turntaking). The rating for mothers' "use of touch" was only marginally reliable and was excluded from the "summary rating" of mothers' behaviors. (The complete coding scheme is reproduced in the appendix to this chapter.)

Training of Raters and Rating Procedures. In addition to the chapter authors, three other professionals contributed to coding the 160 interaction sessions.[1] They were trained in the use of the scales by viewing and rating videotapes of four dyads excluded from the database. All had lengthy personal experience with young deaf children and were fluent in sign language; all except the first author were clinically trained. As nearly as possible, raters were blind to the hearing status of both mothers and children. Limitations were significant with the deaf mothers, all of whom used some sign language, but the hearing and deaf children were indistinguishable on videotape, with the exception of those children who wore visible hearing aids.

Two raters watched each tape together and completed evaluations independently on scales of 1 (negative) to 5 (positive). Scores were then compared, and any discrepancies greater than 1 scale point were discussed and agreement (within 1 point) was negotiated.

Reliability was calculated for each of the thirteen subscales, with scale scores within 1 scale point defined as "agreement." Cohen's kappa, a test of intercoder reliability, was calculated at .94 for 12-month tapes and .81 for 18-month tapes. (These values were computed from the initial scores entered by the two raters, not the final, negotiated scores.) Summary scores for mothers, infants, and dyads were created by summing relevant components from both raters and dividing to achieve a mean (range = 1 to 5). Cronbach's alpha was calculated for mothers' summary scores on five dimensions: .92 at 12 months; .94 at 18 months. Infants' summary scores on four dimensions were .89 at 12 months; .87 at 18 months. Dyads' summary scores on three dimensions were: .92 at 12 months; .93 at 18 months.

Index of Maternal Support. This Index was created by combining (hearing) mothers' responses to the Family Support Scale (FSS), completed when infants were 15 months old, and two subscales of the Parenting Stress Index (PSI), also completed when infants were 15 months old. Items on PSI subscales Relationship with Spouse and Social Isolation are relevant to social support from spouse and from friendship networks. The FSS contains items designed to tap family support (parents, spouse, in-laws, other relatives), friends' support (personal friends, co-workers, social groups), and community/professional support (church, physician, professional helpers, schools/day care centers, write-in "others"). Mothers were divided into those who fell above and below the median on the Maternal Support Index, defined as "high support" and "low support," respectively.

Analyses. For analyses of differences in mother–child interaction ratings for the four groups at ages 12 and 18 months, repeated-measures analyses of variance (ANOVAs) were performed on the *summary* ratings, with group as the between-subject factor and age as the within-subject repeated measure. These analyses were followed by one-way ANOVAs with Duncan's range tests to evaluate between-group differences and *t* tests to evaluate 12- to 18-month differences. One-way ANOVAs were performed on individual components of rating scales, also followed by Duncan's range tests. For analysis of the effect of social support on interaction ratings of hearing mothers and infants, a repeated measures MANOVA was performed, with hearing status (deaf vs. hearing) and support level (high vs. low) treated as between-group factors and behavior ratings treated as levels of the within-group factor.

Results

Interaction Ratings: Four Groups, Two Ages. For mothers' Summary ratings, significant group-by-age interaction effects were found [F (3,76) = 3.61; $p \leq .05$]. Main effects were significant for group [F (3,76) = 4.33; $p \leq .01$]. For infants' Summary ratings, no group-by-age interaction effects were found; only group effects were significant [F (3,76) = 3.09; $p \leq .05$]. For dyadic Summary ratings, interaction (group-by-age) effects and age effects were only marginally significant ($p \leq .10$), but main effects for group were significant [F (3,76) = 7.03; $p \leq .001$].

Mothers' Ratings. The Hd mothers' Summary ratings were significantly below those of Hh mothers' at both the 12-month and the 18-month assessments (see Table 8-1). No other significant Summary group differences emerged at 12 months. However, at 18 months Dh mothers were rated significantly below both Dd and Hh mothers. Ratings of Dd, Hd, and Hh mothers were somewhat (though not significantly) higher at 18 months than at 12 months, whereas ratings for Dh mothers were significantly lower at 18 months than at 12 months [t (18) = −2.27; p = .04]. Differences in mothers' Involvement in their children's play activities did not influence these ratings, either for the first (12-month) or the second (18-month) assessment. Likewise, differences in positive Affect had little or no influence on Summary scores. At 12 months, Hd and Dh mothers were rated significantly below Hh mothers for Flexibility and Hd mothers significantly below Hh mothers for Consistency. At 18 months, the magnitude of differences among mothers' ratings for Sensitivity, Flexibility, and Consistency increased: Hd mothers were rated significantly lower than Hh mothers for Sensitivity and Flexibility, but Dh mothers were rated significantly below both Hh and Dd mothers for Sensitivity and Flexibility, whereas Dh mothers were rated significantly below those in all three other groups on Consistency.

Infants' Ratings. Differences among groups of mothers increased from 12 to 18 months, but the opposite was true for infants. Summary ratings for infants at 12 months were significantly different [F (3,76) = 4.34; $p \leq .01$], with Hd infants rated less positively than infants in groups Dd, Dh, and Hh. At 18 months, no significant differences existed between any of the groups. At 12 months, Hd infants were marginally less Compliant and significantly less Involved than were Dd or Hh infants. They showed significantly less positive Affect than did infants in any other group, and

Table 8-1. Interaction ratings of mothers, infants, and dyads, by mother–infant hearing status, ages 12 and 18 months: Means (SD) one-way ANOVAs (*F*), *Duncan's multiple range test*

	Age 12 months					*Age 18 months*				
	Dd	*Hd*	*Dh*	*Hh*	*F (3,76)*	*Dd*	*Hd*	*Dh*	*Hh*	*F (3,76)*
Mothers										
Use of touch	3.3 (.9)	2.7 (1.1)	3.2 (1.1)	3.1 (1.1)	NS	3.4 (1.1)	2.8 (1.2)	2.6 (1.0)	3.7 (1.2)	3.70* *g*
Sensitivity	3.3 (1.2)	2.9 (1.3)	2.9 (1.1)	3.8 (1.1)	2.55† *g*	3.7 (.9)	3.4 (1.4)	2.7 (1.2)	4.2 (1.0)	6.58*** *a,j*
Involvement	4.3 (.9)	3.7 (1.0)	3.9 (.8)	4.0 (1.2)	NS	4.2 (.8)	3.8 (1.3)	3.3 (1.2)	4.0 (1.3)	NS
Flexibility	3.3 (1.3)	2.7 (1.2)	3.0 (1.0)	3.8 (1.2)	3.34* *g*	3.5 (1.1)	3.0 (1.4)	2.5 (1.0)	3.9 (1.1)	5.18** a,j
Affect	3.7 (.9)	3.2 (1.1)	3.6 (.9)	4.0 (1.1)	2.57† *a*	3.8 (1.0)	3.2 (1.4)	3.2 (.9)	4.0 (1.2)	2.34†
Consistency	3.7 (1.0)	2.8 (1.3)	3.2 (1.0)	3.8 (1.2)	3.77** *c*	3.9 (.8)	3.8 (1.0)	2.8 (1.1)	4.4 (1.0)	8.55*** *k*
Summary	3.7 (.9)	3.1 (1.0)	3.3 (.8)	3.9 (1.0)	2.83* *a*	3.8 (.8)	3.4 (1.2)	2.9 (.9)	4.1 (1.0)	5.30** *a,j*

(continued)

Table 8-1. Interaction ratings of mothers, infants, and dyads, by mother–infant hearing status, ages 12 and 18 months: Means (SD) one-way ANOVAs (*F*), *Duncan's multiple range test* (*continued*)

	Age 12 months					*Age 18 months*				
	Dd	*Hd*	*Dh*	*Hh*	*F (3,76)*	*Dd*	*Hd*	*Dh*	*Hh*	*F (3,76)*
Infants										
Compliance	3.3 (1.0)	2.6 (1.2)	3.3 (.9)	3.4 (1.0)	2.57† *c*	3.3 (1.0)	2.9 (1.1)	2.7 (.9)	3.5 (1.2)	2.64† *h*
Affect	3.4 (1.0)	2.5 (.9)	3.3 (.8)	3.4 (1.1)	3.76** *e*	3.4 (.8)	2.6 (1.1)	3.3 (.9)	3.1 (1.2)	NS
Involvement	3.9 (.9)	3.1 (1.1)	3.6 (.7)	3.9 (1.0)	3.07* *c*	3.8 (.7)	3.6 (1.0)	3.4 (1.1)	3.7 (1.3)	NS
Gentleness	3.5 (.8)	3.0 (1.0)	3.7 (.7)	3.8 (.8)	4.43** *l*	3.2 (1.0)	3.1 (.8)	3.0 (1.1)	3.6 (1.3)	NS
Summary	3.5 (.8)	2.8 (.9)	3.5 (.6)	3.6 (.8)	4.34** *e*	3.4 (.8)	3.1 (.9)	3.1 (.8)	3.5 (1.1)	NS
Dyads										
Enjoyment	3.3 (1.1)	2.3 (1.1)	3.4 (.9)	3.5 (1.1)	6.00*** *e*	3.6 (.9)	2.8 (1.3)	2.9 (1.1)	3.5 (1.3)	2.14†
Understanding	3.7 (1.1)	2.4 (1.0)	3.4 (1.0)	3.9 (.9)	8.33*** *e*	4.4 (.9)	2.6 (1.2)	3.5 (1.2)	3.8 (1.2)	8.56*** e,i
Turn-taking	3.2 (1.3)	2.2 (1.1)	2.9 (1.1)	3.5 (1.2)	4.58** *e*	3.9 (.8)	2.8 (1.2)	2.8 (1.3)	3.5 (1.3)	4.29** *f*
Summary	3.4 (1.1)	2.3 (1.0)	3.2 (.8)	3.6 (1.0)	7.20*** *e*	3.9 (.8)	2.7 (1.2)	3.1 (1.1)	3.6 (1.2)	4.86** *c,i*

[a]Hd < Hh. [e]Hd < Dd Dh Hh. [i]Dh < Dd. †$p \leq .10$.
[b]Hd < Dd. [f]Hd Dh < Dd. [j]Dh < Dd Hh. *$p \leq .05$.
[c]Hd < Dd Hh. [g]Hd Dh < Hh. [k]Dh < Hd Dd Hh. **$p \leq .01$.
[d]Hd < Dh Dd. [h]Dh < Hh. [l]Hd < Dh Hh. ***$p \leq .001$.

significantly less Gentleness than Dh or Hh infants. This absence of Gentleness was illustrated most clearly in one child who received low ratings at both 12 and 18 months. During the second play session, he repeatedly banged a doll's head on the floor. When the mother reprimanded him, the child bit the doll's head. A few minutes later he took several aggressive bites from a sponge that was part of the toy set.

Dyadic Ratings. Summary ratings at 12 months show Hd dyads significantly below each of the three other groups [F (3,76) = 7.19; $p \leq .001$]. At 18 months, these differences were somewhat less extreme [F (3,76) = 4.86; $p \leq .01$), and the pattern of group comparisons was somewhat different: Hd dyads continued to be rated below Dd and Hh, but Dh dyads ranked significantly below Dd dyads. Ratings improved significantly from 12 to 18 months for group Dd [t (19) = 2.20; p = .04] and to a substantial degree for group Hd [t (19) = 2.04; p = .055]. The Dh dyads had essentially the same ratings at 18 months as at 12 months; that is, their interactions had not improved, whereas those of Dd and Hd dyads improved considerably and Hh ratings did not change. At 12 months, ratings of Hd dyads for Enjoyment, Understanding, and Turn-taking were significantly below those of the three other groups. At 18 months, ratings for Enjoyment did not differ for any two groups. For Understanding, group Hd dyads continued to be rated significantly below the three other groups, and Dh dyads were rated below Dd mothers and infants. Both Hd and Dh dyads were rated below group Dd dyads for Turn-taking.

Relationship of Hearing Mothers' Interaction Ratings to Maternal Support

A 2 (Group) × 2 (Support) × 6 (Maternal Behaviors) repeated measures MANOVA was performed, with hearing status (deaf vs. hearing) and support level (high vs. low) treated as between-group factors and maternal behaviors treated as levels of the within-group factor. As expected, this analysis revealed a significant group-by-support interaction [$F(1,36)$ = 4.45; $p < .05$]. Additional MANOVAs for ratings of infants and dyads were not significant.

Mothers' Ratings. One-way ANOVAs for individual behavior ratings (see Table 8-2) showed that (hearing) mothers of deaf infants receiving low levels of support were rated significantly below other mothers on five of the six behavioral dimensions. Involvement was the single behavior that did not differentiate the low-support hearing mothers from others. Differences were significant for ratings of Use of Touch, Sensitivity, Flexibility, Affect, and Consistency.

Infants' Ratings. Mothers with low support levels had deaf infants who were significantly less compliant than were deaf or hearing infants whose

Table 8-2. Interaction ratings at 18 months for hearing mothers, infants, and dyads, by infant hearing status, by mothers' support level: Means, one-way ANOVAs (*F*)

	Deaf Infants		*Hearing Infants*		
Mothers' Support	*Low (N = 13)*	*High (N = 7)*	*Low (N = 7)*	*High (N = 13)*	*F (3,36)*
Mothers					
Use of touch	2.3	3.8	3.9	3.6	4.8**[a]
Sensitivity	2.7	4.4	4.2	4.2	6.0**[a]
Involvement	3.3	4.2	4.0	4.0	NS
Flexibility	2.4	3.9	4.0	3.8	4.5**[a]
Affect	2.7	4.0	4.1	4.0	3.1*[a]
Consistency	3.3	4.4	4.4	4.4	3.4*[a]
Summary	2.9	4.2	4.1	4.1	4.0**[a]
Infants					
Compliance	2.4	3.7	3.4	3.7	3.6*[b]
Affect	2.2	3.4	3.0	3.2	NS
Involvement	3.0	4.4	3.4	3.8	NS
Gentleness	2.7	3.4	3.5	3.8	NS
Summary	2.5	3.7	3.3	3.6	3.4*[b]
Dyads					
Enjoyment	2.2	3.7	3.4	3.5	3.1*[b]
Understanding	2.1	3.5	3.4	4.0	6.2**[a]
Turntaking	2.0	3.7	3.4	3.6	4.8**[a]
Summary	2.1	3.6	3.4	3.7	5.0**[a]

*$p \leq .05$.

**$p \leq .01$.

[a]Mothers or dyads w/ low support and deaf infants < all others.

[b]Deaf infants or dyads of low-support mothers < deaf or hearing infants of high-support mothers (Duncan's Multiple Range Test).

mothers had high support levels. Support did not differentiate infants for Affect, Involvement, or Gentleness. The cumulative effect of lower ratings on all four infant scales led to a significantly different infant Summary score, with low-support deaf infants rated below deaf and hearing infants of high-support mothers.

Dyadic Ratings. Dyads with deaf infants and low-support mothers were rated below dyads with deaf or hearing infants and high-support mothers for Enjoyment. These dyads were rated below the three other groups of dyads for Understanding and Turn-taking, and for the Summary rating.

Discussion

In almost every significant difference reported above, interactions of the members of matched hearing-status dyads were rated more positively than those for unmatched hearing-status dyads. That is, deaf infants and their deaf mothers (Dd) and hearing infants and their hearing mothers (Hh) engaged in more positive interactive behaviors, compared to dyads with unmatched hearing status: deaf infants and their hearing mothers (Hd) or hearing infants and their deaf mothers (Dh).

A good deal of relevant theory can be cited to help explain the importance of matched hearing status for deaf/hearing dyads. Erikson's (1959, 1963) epigenetic theory of life-cycle development emphasizes the importance of prior experiences of intimacy for successful parenting during midlife, and the urge for generativity that leads parents to hope for offspring like themselves. Parents often pattern their parenting styles on their own childhood experiences, labeled by one author as "the reproduction of mothering" (Chodorow, 1978). This repetition of one's own socialization experience is implied in the theory of "intuitive parenting" (Papoušek & Papoušek, 1987). This proposes that parents draw on intuitive or unconscious resources to monitor their infants' exposure to environmental stimuli, and that successful caregiving behaviors are then reinforced by infants' responses. In unmatched hearing-status dyads, parents have fewer intuitive experiences or techniques for fostering visual proficiency (Koester, 1992, 1994). The concept of "affective attunement" is also relevant here. This occurs between parent and child when the parent begins to expand his or her behavior from imitation to cross-modal matching, thus allowing for the recasting of an emotional experience in another form (Stern, 1985, 2002). This becomes more important when parent and child do not share the same sensory environment, and the most comfortable linguistic mode for the parent may not be the one most appropriate for the child.

Hearing Mothers, Deaf Infants. The ratings of hearing mothers and their deaf infants are consonant with the findings of most studies cited earlier in this chapter. It is noteworthy that the interactions of these deaf babies and hearing mothers improved during the period from 12 to 18 months (although the improvement was seen in expressive or emotional interactions rather than in the cognitive dimension defined as "mutual understanding"). This improvement in mother–child interaction may stem from three sources: the greater distance of mothers from the initial diagnosis of their infants' deafness, an improvement in the mothers' expressive communication skills, or the effects of an additional 6 months of social support.

An important finding that came from these data, in terms of potential application as well as the literature on mother–deaf-child interaction, is the significant positive effect of social support on behaviors of the hearing mothers with deaf children. Indeed, the differences between mothers with deaf and hearing children discussed in the preceding section resulted only from the ratings of mothers who reported low levels of social support. Ratings for hearing mothers of deaf children with high support levels were no different from those of mothers with hearing children. Except for Greenberg's (1983) experimental intervention study showing the positive effects of counseling on interactions of mothers and their deaf toddlers, we know of no other research with deaf children that has examined this relationship. However, evidence from research with other groups of high-risk dyads documents the positive effects of social support on mother–child interaction. Support for adolescent mothers, related to positive mother–infant interaction when stress levels were low, included caregiving help from husbands or boyfriends, role modeling by the infant's maternal grandmother, and parenting advice from professionals (Crockenberg, 1987). Stress was related to negative interactions with young children only for unmarried mothers; parenting support was marginally related to positive behaviors for both single and married mothers (Weinraub & Wolf, 1987). Mothers of children with mental retardation, physically handicapping conditions, and developmental delays were found to be more responsive during interactions with their children if they perceived their support systems to be adequate, compared to mothers who perceived those systems as inadequate (Dunst & Trivette, 1986).

A study of poor, inner-city, largely Hispanic mothers of sick and healthy, term and preterm infants showed the importance of both the type and source of support to proximal (near to child) and distal (farther from child) maternal behaviors (Feiring, Fox, Jaskir, & Lewis, 1987). For these mothers, support received closer to the identification of the child's deafness had a greater impact on behaviors at 18 months than support received later in the child's developmental trajectory, further evidence of the importance of early intervention with deaf children (Meadow-Orlans, 1987). Level of support rather than the number of separate support sources was more important, and the combination of support over time and across sources strengthened the relationship between support and maternal behavior.

Deaf Mothers, Hearing Babies. The comparatively poor performance of the Dh dyads might be seen as reinforcement for suggestions that a part of the explanation for the interactive difficulties of hearing mothers with deaf children was their emotional response to the diagnosis of deafness as difference, or their need to adjust to the notion of parenting a child unlike themselves in an important respect. Deaf mothers with hearing children, who do not face the communicative difficulties of Hd mothers because their children are quite capable of processing their signed communication, appear to demonstrate similar difficulties. The ratings of the Dh mothers are cause for some concern, especially as the interactions at 18 months were significantly less positive than interactions at 12 months, unlike those of mothers in other groups. One especially poignant and painful play session of a deaf mother and 18-month-old hearing child consisted almost entirely of the child talking into a toy telephone while the mother tried repeatedly to interest her in other activities. Eventually the mother sat back with a helpless demeanor, watching her child.

Conclusion

The wide variation within each of the four groups of dyads participating in this research project must be emphasized. Many deaf mothers with hearing children and hearing mothers with deaf children exhibited appropriate interactive behaviors and reinforced their child's positive responses. However, the striking group differences in mean scores between the matched hearing status dyads and those for the unmatched hearing status dyads raise a flag of concern. Hearing mothers with deaf infants routinely receive support services, mandated by federal law. This research suggests that deaf mothers with hearing infants could well benefit from similar services to help them deal with the practical and the emotional challenges of parenting a child whose communicative needs and abilities differ significantly from their own.

Acknowledgments

Some material in this chapter was adapted from the following sources:

Meadow-Orlans, K. P., & Steinberg, A. G. (1993). Effects of infant hearing loss and maternal support on mother–infant interactions at 18 months. *Journal of Applied Developmental Psychology, 14,* 407–426.

Meadow-Orlans, K. P. (1997). Effects of mother and infant hearing status on interactions at twelve and eighteen months. *Journal of Deaf Studies and Deaf Education, 2,* 26–36.

Note

1. Steinberg rated 69 dyads, Carol Erting 27, Sybil Smith-Gray 39, and Carren Stika 25. Meadow-Orlans rated all 160 videotapes.

Appendix 8–1. Mother–child Interaction Rating Scale: Definitions

Mothers

1. *Use of Touch*
   High rating: Touch is both frequent and positive. Includes body contact such as cuddling and sitting on Mom's lap.
   Low rating: Very little touching or any negative use of touch.
2. *Sensitive Versus Intrusive*
   High rating: Mother responds to child's interest and is willing to continue activity initiated by child. Gives child time to absorb one offered object/activity before beginning another. Provides appropriate structure and opportunity for child to pursue a variety of toys. Selects objects that stimulate child. Does not interrupt one child-initiated activity with another. Appears to play rather than teach. Pacing seems appropriate for child's age and situation.
   Low rating: Mother constantly intervenes or intrudes on child's attention or self-initiated exploration or activity. Doesn't wait for a lull to introduce a new object. Insensitive to child's interest; may appear anxious or frantic in introduction of new activity. Teaches or instructs rather than plays.
3. *Participatory and Involved Versus Passive and Disengaged*
   High rating: Mother expresses interest in play activities. Responds with pleasure to child's overtures or initiates playful activities of her own design.
   Low rating: Seems passive and lacking in interest. May appear to define situation as one in which the child plays and she watches without participating.
4. *Flexible and Creative Versus Rigid and Unimaginative*
   High rating: The flexible mother may set rules for safety and behavior but is willing to bend them at times. She is willing to accept a child's expression of disinterest in her proposed activity. She has imagination in getting child to follow the rules or in getting the child to perform a task. Creativity may also be evidenced in use of materials and play.
   Low rating: The rigid mother is unwilling to change a routine that has begun, is strict in the letter of the rule she has made, and does not cajole or try to redirect child's attention from a forbidden behavior. She may also lack imagination in use of materials, in capturing child's attention, or in finding interesting play.
5. *Overall Affective Tone*
   High rating: Facial, vocal, tactile, and body language for entire viewing time seems positive, warm, and pleasant.
   Low rating: Seems negative and lacking in warmth.
6. *Consistent Versus Inconsistent*
   High rating: Affect (positive or negative), flexibility/rigidity, and responsiveness/nonresponsiveness not subject to quick changes. Mother's behavior is consistent throughout the entire period of play.
   Low rating: Changes frequently/abruptly from positive to negative, permissive to strict, smiling to frowning. Neither behavior nor affect is predictable and/or "the words are right but the music is wrong."

Children

1. *Compliant Versus Resistant*
   High rating: Child is cooperative, acquiesces to mother's verbal or nonverbal requests/demands, and does not disobey or fail to respond to a request for participation in an activity. Compliance is cheerfully, happily given.
   Low rating: Child refuses to give in to mother's requests and may respond with defiance or ignore a request. If mother requests and child does not comply, rating

should be low whether or not observer believes that child understood. That is, compliance should be rated from the mother's perspective.

2. *Overall Affective Tone*
   High rating: Frequent smiling and laughter. Expressions of pleasure in activities. Communicates a sense of happiness.
   Low rating: Affect ranges from neutral to sad. Few expressions of pleasure. Absence of spontaneous joy.
3. *Participatory and Involved Versus Passive and Disengaged*
   High rating: Expresses interest in activities. Responds to mother's overtures and initiates activities reflecting the child's own interest and independence. Not bored.
   Low rating: Passive and lacking interest. Content to watch mother or to do nothing. Bored; perhaps tries to leave room. Dependent on mother for activities.
4. *Gentle Versus Aggressive*
   High rating: Child's manner is gentle, sweet, kind, and loving. (This may be expressed toward mother and/or toward toys.)
   Low rating: May be difficult to control, throws objects, or hits mother or doll. Angry, mean, or hostile quality to behavior.

Dyads

1. *Enjoyment Versus Nonenjoyment*
   High rating: Both mother and child enjoy the activities/interaction. Neither is bored; they take pleasure in each other's company and the activities each initiates.
   Low rating: Little or no pleasure/interest displayed by either member of the mother–child pair.
2. *Mutual Communicative Understanding Versus Little or No Understanding*
   High rating: Both mother and child understand the other's cognitive/linguistic meaning, as shown by behavioral, facial, or gestural/verbal response.
   Low rating: Neither mother nor child understands the other's cognitive/linguistic meaning. Absence of response.
3. *Reciprocity of Interaction Versus No Reciprocity*
   High rating: Dyad engages in turn-taking and shared initiations of new activities. May be seen in verbal communication or in behavioral or object turn-taking. Neither has a disproportionate share of initiation.
   Low rating: One or the other member of the pair does most of the initiating of conversation or activity, or there are monologues with no change of speaker/initiator.

9

Attachment Behaviors at 18 Months

Lynne Sanford Koester and Kathryn P. Meadow-Orlans[1]

For at least 30 years, infant–caregiver attachment has been a primary focus of developmental psychologists, and the Ainsworth Strange Situation Procedure (SSP) has been utilized in literally hundreds of research studies (Ainsworth, Blehar, Waters, & Wall, 1978; Solomon & George, 1999). The SSP involves a series of separations from and reunions with the mother, as well as episodes during which a stranger is also in the room with the infant. This procedure has enabled researchers to observe infants (typically 12- to 20-month-olds) in a standardized laboratory situation consisting of the following 3-minute episodes (Ainsworth & Wittig, 1969; Sroufe & Waters, 1977; Solomon & George, 1999):

1. mother and infant enter unfamiliar playroom, staff member explains procedure, then departs;
2. mother sits in chair and pretends to read a magazine while infant plays with toys;
3. stranger enters room, engages mother in conversation;
4. mother leaves infant with stranger;
5. mother returns, stranger exits;
6. mother leaves infant alone;
7. stranger returns, comforts infant if needed;
8. mother returns, stranger leaves.

In this chapter we describe the theoretical and methodological background for this assessment; the results from other studies linking attachment outcomes to earlier face-to-face interactions, play behaviors, and family stress; the relevance of attachment to the study of deaf children; and results from analyses of attachment data from this project.

Conceptual Background

Based on the theoretical work of British psychoanalyst John Bowlby (1958, 1969), attachment has been defined as an enduring affectional tie binding two people together, and it is characterized by maintenance of close physical contact and frequent communication. Behavioral indicators of attachment in the infant include efforts to seek and to maintain proximity such as approaching, following, and clinging, or to influence maternal responses by crying, smiling, or vocalizing (Bowlby, 1969; Ainsworth & Bell, 1970). Implications of this process extend beyond early socioemotional development. The infant who forms a healthy attachment to a caregiver can use this bond for further exploration and mastery of the environment, a quality that also serves well in later stages of development. Because moving further into the world includes risks, the secure infant may use the attachment figure for reassurance, returning to this "secure base" during times of distress or uncertainty. When reunited after a separation from the caregiver, the securely attached infant actively reestablishes proximity and comfort, and is then able to resume play and exploration with the knowledge that a trusted caregiver is available for protection when needed. The availability of a "safe harbor" may also promote affective competence that involves "being able to feel and process emotions for optimal functioning while maintaining the integrity of self and the safety-providing relationship (i.e., attachment)" (Fosha, 2000, p. 42). In some infants, reunion with the attachment figure does not effectively terminate the behaviors elicited by separation:

> . . . [T]he inability to find comfort in contact with an attachment figure is an important sign that the attachment behavioral system is not serving the integrative/adaptive function that it does for most infants. Insecurely or maladaptively attached infants may need contact even when environmental stress is minimal, may be unable to regain security or resume exploration upon reunion, or may actively avoid contact or interaction upon reunion. (Sroufe & Waters, 1977, p. 1186)

Most securely attached infants are able to play independently in an unfamiliar setting, but will eagerly seek contact after the attachment figure has been absent, and can then use her (or him) as a base from which to resume exploratory play. Insecurely or anxiously attached infants show quite different patterns both before and after reunion with the mother.

The standard SSP coding procedure classifies infant participants into three (or four) groups: Group A, "Avoidant" infants, separate readily and seek little contact throughout the procedure, show little distress, and appear somewhat indifferent to the changes taking place in each episode. These infants show little joy at the mother's return, sometimes not even acknowledging her, or overtly turn and move away from her especially after the second departure. The attachment system for these babies appears to elicit maladaptive behaviors, in that increased distress provokes increased distancing from the mother. "The insecure, avoidant child sacrifices his affective life in order to function. Throughout, . . . he exhibits neither distress at separation nor joy at reunion, as if he were indifferent to the caretaker's goings and comings" (Fosha, 2000, p. 43).

Group B, "Secure" babies, are prepared to explore the room and the toys when the mother is present, perhaps checking back with her occasionally. When the mother leaves the room, the child probably becomes overtly distressed, although willing to be comforted by the stranger. When the mother returns, the infant will seek contact with her and return to play with the toys after a short time (Weinfield, Sroufe, Egeland, & Carlson, 1999).

Group C babies are the "Insecure/Ambivalent" infants (also termed "Resistant"), whose exploration is minimal even when the mother is present. They are often uneasy with the stranger and may be upset even before the mother leaves. The most distinguishing characteristic of these infants is their inability to take comfort in the mother's return, or to settle down and resume play after the reunion. Even when the attachment figure is present, there is little evidence that she effectively provides a secure base for the child. (Most studies have investigated attachment in relation to the child's biological mother, although this does not mean that others, such as fathers, grandparents, adoptive parents, or siblings, are insignificant in the infant's socioemotional world.) The infant demonstrates ambivalence by a confusing mixture of both seeking and resisting contact. These infants typically continue to be distressed in their mother's presence, or express their ambivalence by angry outbursts of hitting, pushing, or kicking the mother or toys. These behaviors neither support a positive relationship with the attachment figure nor facilitate the infant's exploration of a new environment. Furthermore, the contradictory messages from the child are difficult for the caregiver to read and may thus exacerbate an already ineffectual dyadic communication pattern.

A category of "Disorganized/Disoriented" attachment (Group D) was added to the schema more recently in an effort to account for children who are not easily classified in one of the three original categories (Main & Solomon, 1986, 1990; Lyons-Ruth & Jacobvitz, 1999). Infants in this group "appear to have no coherent strategy for handling separations and reunions" (Colin, 1996, p. 47).

Whereas Group A babies appear to display predominantly defensive reactions, Group B (Secure) infants have coherent strategies that assist them in using the attachment figure as a secure base from which to venture forth again despite temporary separations. Conversely, Group C infants exhibit a more extreme form of dependence on the attachment figure, whereas Group D babies do not consistently employ any of these behavioral approaches—hence the appearance of being disorganized or disoriented (Colin, 1996).

Precursors to Attachment: Early Maternal Behaviors

Several studies have examined the relationship between the quality of attachment and the infant's earlier interactions with the attachment figure. It is assumed that sensitive, reciprocal, and contingent interactions with the caregiver during the first year enhance the probability of an infant's secure attachment at the end of that year. As Blehar, Lieberman, and Ainsworth (1977) reported, mothers of anxiously attached infants in their study "more frequently initiated face-to-face interaction with a silent, impassive face and more often failed to respond to their babies' attempts to initiate interaction than did mothers of infants who were later judged to be securely attached" (p. 190). In contrast, mothers of babies later classified as securely attached had been more contingent and facilitative of interaction in the previous observations. Similarly, Egeland and Farber (1984) found that securely attached infants had mothers who were sensitive to their infant's needs, and who encouraged reciprocity during earlier feeding and play situations.

Other researchers examining behaviors similar to those coded in our face-to-face interactions have found that mothers who were particularly skilled at modifying their behaviors according to the infant's visual attention were less likely to have avoidant babies at 12 months (Langhorst & Fogel, 1982). That is, sensitive caregivers decreased their activity when the infant looked away, and increased it when the infant looked back. This point has particular salience for interactions with a deaf infant, as will be discussed in a later chapter.

A number of other maternal behaviors in the first year have been linked to secure infant attachment: prompt responsiveness to distress; moderate, appropriate stimulation; interactional synchrony; warmth, involvement, and responsiveness (see Belsky, 1999, for an extensive review.) Nevertheless, a meta-analysis of sixty-six studies of parental behaviors and attachment found only a small effect size (DeWolff & van IJzendoorn, 1997).

Cross-Cultural Studies of Attachment. Ainsworth and her colleagues presented attachment theory as "biologically based and adaptive in the evolutionary sense," in which case the theory "should apply . . . in all cultures, races, and ethnic groups" (Colin, 1996, pp. 145–146). Most U.S. studies with the Strange Situation Procedure utilizing three classifications (that is, without the D/Disorganized) have reported about 65% of infants as B/Secure, with 20% A/Avoidant and 15% C/Ambivalent. This is the distribution of 106 infants reported by Ainsworth and her colleagues, and "is usually employed as the standard against which distributions obtained in other studies are compared" (Lamb, Thompson, Gardner, & Charnov, 1985, p. 182). Despite the early emphasis on attachment as a "universal" construct, there has been increasing interest in cross-cultural studies of attachment, and criticism of the emphasis on results from studies in the United States (Rothbaum et al., 2000).[2] Another observer suggests that "however reliable and theoretically rationalized, [the SSP] might still represent the moral judgments of a particular society at a particular moment in history rather than indicate normality and pathogenesis for all humans at all times" (LeVine, 1995, p. x).

Much of the questioning of the "universal" or "ethnocentric" nature of Ainsworth's attachment formulations emerged from reports of Israeli, Japanese, and German investigators. In the Israeli study, for the three-way attachment classification, infants living in a kibbutz were classified as 80% B/Secure, 0% A/Avoidant, and 20% C/Ambivalent if they slept at home and 48% B/Secure, 0% A/Avoidant, and 52% C/Ambivalent if they slept in a communal nursery (Sagi et al., 1994). A review of studies that focused on infants classified as C/Ambivalent concluded that "this pattern may result from relatively low or inconsistent maternal involvement . . . [leading] to increased attention to mother and decreased exploratory competence" (Cassidy & Berlin, 1994, p. 985).

A more recent Israeli study (n = 758), conducted with urban rather than kibbutz participants, reported 70% B/Secure, 2% A/Avoidant, 19% C/Ambivalent, 7% D/Disorganized and 2% CC (Can't Code). "[C]enter-care, in and of itself, adversely increased the likelihood of infants developing insecure attachment to their mothers . . ." (Sagi et al., 2002, p. 1166).

In Japan, the Sapporo study showed 72% of infants to be B/Secure, 0% A/Avoidant, and 28% C/Ambivalent (Miyake, Chen, & Campos, 1985). Researchers have interpreted this distribution in relation to observations that Japanese babies are rarely exposed to strangers or separated from their mothers during the first year, so that the Strange Situation may be unusually stressful for them (Fogel, 2001). Although Kagan and his colleagues have found that Asian infants are generally less active, less irritable, and more easily comforted in comparison to Caucasian babies (Kagan et al., 1994), this may assume prompt responding by the mother, which is not typically possible during the Strange Situation Procedure.

German infants in the Bielefeld study were classified as 33% B/Secure, 49% A/Avoidant, and 12% C/Ambivalent (Grossmann et al., 1985). (Presumably, 6% of these infants were "not classified.") The investigators note that German mothers are greatly concerned about independence training and begin such training earlier than do American mothers: all mothers in their sample were engaged in training their infants for independence by the age of 10 months. Though these infant behaviors are viewed, within the context of attachment theory, as negative indicators of insecure attachment, they might also be viewed as positive indicators of independence.

Another group of investigators utilized a very different approach to studying attachment in Anglo and Puerto Rican groups (Harwood, Miller, & Lucca Irizarry, 1995). They interviewed middle-class and working-class mothers "to examine indigenous perceptions of adult socialization goals, child behavior, and desirable and undesirable attachment behavior" (p. 39), concluding that culture was even more significant than social class in differentiating the views of mothers about the nature of desirable attachment behaviors, and that "we need culturally sensitive models" for conceptualizing attachment (p. 81).

Attachment Research with Deaf Children

Deaf Children, Deaf Mothers. Increasingly, the Deaf community is recognized as having a distinct culture or subculture, although there have been few efforts to identify childrearing practices or beliefs among deaf parents (Meadow-Orlans & Erting, 2000). However, "there may be cultural factors in the deaf community, relative to the hearing community, that shape maternal attitudes toward mother–child interactions. There is considerable evidence that mothers' conceptions of attachment depend on societal norms as well as the nature of their relationships with their own mothers . . ." (Marschark, 1993a, p. 14). The one published study of attachment in deaf children with deaf mothers reported proportions of secure attachment like those reported for hearing children (Meadow, Greenberg, & Erting, 1983). However, participants in that study were preschoolers rather than infants, and the coding scheme utilized was based on the presence of a "goal-directed partnership" (Marvin, 1977; Marvin & Britner, 1999), rather than on the traditional Ainsworth classification. In that system, an important component was the presence of "preseparation planning" during which the mother urges the child to give her "permission" to leave the room.

Deaf Children, Hearing Mothers. Two published studies have utilized the SSP with deaf children and their hearing mothers. In both, participants were preschoolers. One study utilized the "goal-directed" coding approach, and reported that deaf preschoolers with poor communication skills were often insecurely attached, but those with good communication skills developed secure attachments (Greenberg & Marvin, 1979). The other study (Lederberg & Mobley, 1990) recruited eighty-two participants, evenly divided between Hd and Hh dyads. Using traditional SSP coding and classifications, the investigators reported 56% of Hd children and 61% of Hh children as B/Secure, 22% Hd and 32% Hh as A/Avoidant, and 22% Hd and 7% Hh as C/Ambivalent. When this study was combined with others as part of a meta-analysis of attachment in "children with problems," the standardized residuals indicated that "Deaf children show an overrepresentation of C classifications" (van IJzendoorn, Goldberg, Kroonenberg, & Frenkel, 1992, p. 851).

Mavrolas (1990), for her unpublished dissertation, studied forty mother–infant dyads, evenly divided between Hd and Hh toddlers, with groups matched for sex, race, and SES (socioeconomic status) when children were 24 to 36 months old. The Hd toddlers were reported as 40% B/Secure, 20% A/Avoidant, and 40% C/ Ambivalent; Hh toddlers were reported as 80% B/Secure, 10% A/Avoidant, and 10% C/Ambivalent ($p < .05$). Thus, attachment data for deaf toddlers with deaf parents or hearing parents are not clear-cut and no data have yet been reported for deaf infants.

The idea that hearing mothers may play a more active and directive role in orchestrating the behaviors of a deaf child is discussed elsewhere (Chapters 4 and 8), and seems to be consistent with findings regarding parents of children with a variety of developmental and physical disabilities. Hauser-Cram, Warfield, Shonkoff, and Krauss (2001) attribute this to parental beliefs that these children need more intense stimulation in order to elicit a response, and to the fact that the child's own signals may be more difficult for parents to read. Marschark (1993a, 1997) suggests that when a hearing mother's attention to her infant is disrupted or withheld (as in both the Strange Situation and the Still Face Procedures), a deaf child might perceive this as a greater departure from normal than would a hearing child.

Although previous studies have failed to demonstrate strong effects of childhood deafness on attachment ratings, there is sufficient evidence to assume that a history of asynchronous or poorly coordinated interactions could have a negative effect on this process. As Marschark (1993a) pointed out, little progress has been made to date to advance our understanding of the dynamics of the attachment process for parents and their deaf infant.

Methodology

Participants

When infants were 18 months old, seventy-five mother–infant dyads participated in the Strange Situation Procedure (SSP), producing videotapes that were complete and could be reliably coded: deaf infants with deaf mothers (Dd, n = 19); deaf infants with hearing mothers (Hd, n = 20); hearing infants with deaf mothers (Dh, n = 16); hearing infants with hearing mothers (Hh, n = 20).

Procedures. When mother and her 18-month-old child arrived at the project office, they were immediately ushered into the playroom/laboratory and the SSP was explained to the mother while the child was placed on the floor to play with toys. Hearing research assistants or project investigators managed the SSP and served as "strangers" for the hearing mothers and their infants. Deaf research assistants, proficient in sign language, managed the procedures and served as "strangers" for the deaf mothers and their infants. The stranger made an effort to turn the deaf infants toward the door in preparation for the first reunion, so they would see their mothers reentering the room, but of course this was not possible when infants were alone during the second separation. For a variety of reasons, the SSP was placed at the end of procedures, after Mastery and Free Play, for the 12-month-old infants. It was later decided to exclude the 12-month SSP data.

Coding. Scoring of the Strange Situation Procedure is highly standardized and is based primarily on the degree to which the infant seeks and maintains proximity to the mother after her two absences. The two reunions (episodes 5 and 8) are crucial in determining infants' responses to these brief separations, and their use of the mother as a base for further exploration and play. Attachment classifications (A/Avoidant, B/Secure, C/Ambivalent, D/Disorganized) are based primarily on infants' behaviors during the two reunions. The reunions and the overall SSP are utilized to code infants' interactive behaviors: Proximity-Seeking, Contact-Maintenance, Resistance, and Avoidance (see Ainsworth et al., 1978, for detailed descriptions of coding procedures for these interactive behaviors). Also coded are finer gradations of the A/B/C classifications: there are two gradations of A/Avoidant babies, four of B/Secure, and two of C/Ambivalent/Resistant. Of the four "Secure" distinctions, B3 is considered the "most Secure."

Coding of Infants with Hearing Mothers. Videotapes of infants with hearing mothers were coded by developmental psychologists on the Gallaudet research team (Drs. Lynne Sanford Koester and Robert H. MacTurk—both hearing) who were trained in SSP scoring procedures by Dr. Alan Sroufe at the University of Minnesota. They coded thirty-nine videotapes: twenty deaf infants with hearing mothers (Hd) and nineteen hearing infants with hearing mothers (Hh). Interrater reliability was established by first coding six videotapes separately, then meeting to discuss each code category and overall classification. (This coding was completed before the D/Disorganized classification was formalized.) Disagreements were resolved by discussion. Thereafter, each coder was randomly assigned half the tapes from each of the two groups. Tapes judged to be difficult to classify were reviewed by both coders, and any uncertainties were resolved by consensus.

Coding of Infants with Deaf Mothers. Subsequent coding of the hearing and deaf children with deaf mothers was done by Dr. Brian Vaughn, then at Auburn University, under a contractual arrangement. Dr. Vaughn, an experienced and certified coder of the Strange Situation, has been involved with attachment research for many years, although never with deaf participants. That is, he has completed the highest level of training in this coding system, but has little or no experience with deafness and its cultural and communicative implications. One can therefore assume that the coding of deaf mothers and their infants in this study was done accurately according to procedures standardized with hearing dyads. Dr. Vaughn provided thirty-five SSP classification codes (Dd = 19; Dh = 16), and interactive codes for twenty-one infants with deaf mothers (Dd = 12; Dh = 9). (He also coded twenty 12-month-old infants with deaf mothers, but noted infant fatigue and some procedural problems in the videotapes, contributing to the decision to exclude those data from analysis.)

Results

Attachment Classifications

Distribution of infants in Secure/Insecure categories was not significantly different when the four groups were compared (see Table 9-1, Part A). Because the D category was not utilized for infants with hearing parents, the statistical test was based on two groups only: Secure (B) versus Insecure (A + C + D). The chi-square (χ^2) computation showed that differences are not significant. However, the difference in proportions of Insecure Dd infants (43%) compared to that of Hh infants (11%) is striking. The B3 code is for the "most Secure" infants. Proportions of infants in the four groups receiving this code are: Dd 5%, Hd 25%, Dh 13%, Hh 45%. (When Hh and Dd infants are compared, with Hd and Dh infants excluded, $\chi^2 = 5.27$; $df = 1$; $p = .025$.)

Utilizing a more differentiated coding that incorporates two levels of Avoidant (A) infants, four levels of Secure (B) infants, and two levels of Ambivalent (C) infants, a numerical code of 1 (least secure) to 5 (most secure) can be recorded (Maslin-Cole & Spieker, 1990). When this more differentiated coding procedure is followed, (see Part B, Table 9-1), means for the four groups of infants differ significantly, with Dd and Dh infants being coded as less secure than Hd and Hh infants.

Table 9-1. Strange situation classifications, by mother–infant hearing status (Part A, number and percent; Part B, mean and SD)[a]

*Part A**

Group	*A (Avoidant)*	*B (Secure)*	*C (Ambivalent)*	*D (Disorganized)*	*Total*
Dd	16% (3)	58% (11)	11% (2)	16% (3)	101% (19)
Hd	20 (4)	75 (15)	5 (1)	NA	100 (20)
Dh	19 (3)	69 (11)	6 (1)	6 (1)	100 (16)
Hh	— (0)	89 (17)	11 (2)	NA	100 (19)

*Part B***

Group	*Mean*	*(SD)*	*(n)*
Dd	3.26	(1.19)	(19)
Hd	3.75	(1.12)	(20)
Dh	3.50	(1.15)	(16)
Hh	4.32	(.82)	(19)

[a]Score 5 = most secure or B3; score 4 = B1, B2, B4; score 3 = A2, C1; score 2 = A1, C2; and score 1 = least secure or D, A/C mix (Maslin-Cole & Spieker, 1990).

*Secure vs. Insecure $\chi^2 = 5.00$; $df = 3$; NS.

**$F(3,70) = 3.29$; $p = .026$; Duncan's post hoc: Dd, Dh < Hd, Hh.

Interactive Codes. Additional details of behavioral differences among infants in the four groups are provided by analyses of the interactive codes, as reported in the section on "Coding." (Comparison of infants with deaf mothers for whom interactive codes were and were not available shows similar distributions for Secure/Insecure classifications [χ^2 = <1.0; *df* = 1; *p* = 1.0]).

Hearing infants with hearing mothers (Hh) are significantly more likely to Seek Proximity after the second reunion (episode 8), compared to deaf infants with deaf mothers (Dd) [F (3) = 5.05; $p < .01$]. Infants in the Hh dyads were also more likely to engage in Contact Maintenance after the two reunions, compared to both groups of infants with deaf mothers (Dd and Dh) (F [3] = 3.92; $p < .01$; and F [3] = 5.13; $p < .01$ for reunions in episodes 5 and 8, respectively) (see Fig. 9-1). Group differences for Resistance were not significant, either for the first or second reunions, but deaf infants with hearing mothers (Hd) were significantly more likely to be Avoidant after the first reunion, compared to the three other groups of infants (Dd, Dh, Hh) [F (3) = 5.47; $p < .01$]. (Fig. 9-2).

Discussion

As noted earlier, the usual distribution of North American infants classified by the Strange Situation Procedure is approximately 65% Secure

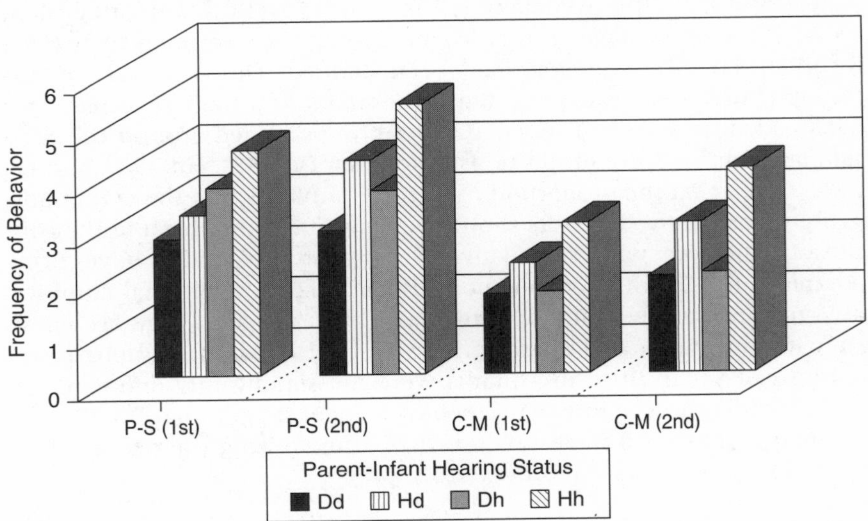

Proximity-seeking (P-S) – First reunion – *F* NS
Proximity-seeking (P-S) – Second reunion – F [3, 70] $p \leq .01$ Dd < Hh**
Contact-maintenance (C-M) – First reunion – F [3, 70] $p \leq .01$ Dd < Hh,** Dh < Hh*

Figure 9-1. Proximity-seeking and contact-maintenance during reunions: 18 months.

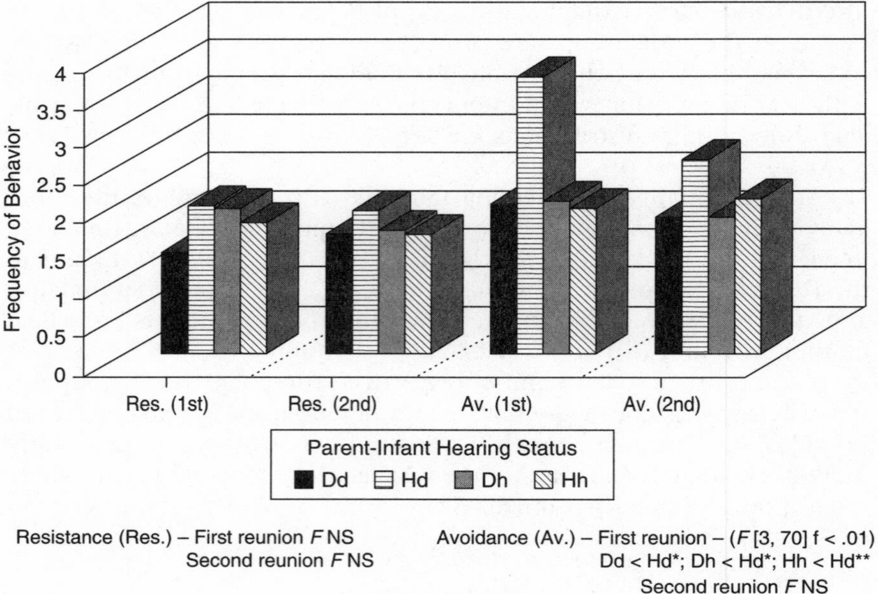

Figure 9-2. Resistance and avoidance during reunions: 18 months.

(category "B"), 20% Avoidant ("A"), and 15% Resistant/Ambivalent ("C"); these percentages are based on averages determined before the Disorganized ("D") category had been defined. Our "control" infants (group Hh) were considerably above the standard usually reported, with 89% coded as Secure. The three other groups circled around the 65% standard, with Secure proportions as follows: Dd 58%, Hd 75%, and Dh 69%. Given that the proportion of secure Hh infants was above that normally reported, these results should be viewed as tentative and the conclusions still somewhat speculative. Because so few studies have incorporated the SSP with a population of deaf infants, additional empirical investigations are warranted, particularly by researchers who are familiar with the needs and characteristics of deaf children. Although proportions of Secure/Insecure infants were not significantly different, significant differences in interactive behavior codes suggest that Dd, Dh, and Hd infants may each have unique ways of organizing their secure-base relationships with their mothers.

Infants with Deaf Mothers: Deaf Culture and Independence

Our data suggest that both hearing and deaf infants with deaf mothers had somewhat different reactions to the Strange Situation Procedure than did infants with hearing mothers: Dd infants were found to be significantly less likely than Hh infants to be Proximity Seeking. Both groups of infants with deaf mothers (Dd and Dh) were less likely than Hh infants to promote Contact Maintenance. Perhaps these results reflect the efforts of deaf mothers to promote independence in their young children, somewhat like the German mothers in Grossmann and colleagues' (1985) Bielefeld study described above. In an early study (Meadow, 1967), deaf mothers reported earlier completion of bowel training by their children, and hearing mothers of deaf children reported later completion, compared to a large childrearing study conducted with hearing mothers of hearing children (p. 280). These deaf mothers "followed a deliberate policy of fostering early independence" (p. 288).

Although studies of deafness are not always considered under the rubric of cross-cultural research, it is generally accepted that there is a Deaf culture existing alongside or within the dominant or host hearing culture. Little or no research has been reported on parenting beliefs and practices in the Deaf community, but it is possible that differences in childrearing patterns might influence the behaviors of children with deaf mothers in the Strange Situation. Anecdotal evidence leads to the proposal that independence is a major value, and is viewed as a quality essential to socialization, especially for a child who is deaf. One deaf mother participating in this study articulated this perspective in relation to her infant, who was then 9 months old, indicating that it was her conscious practice to promote independence even before her child could walk.

Erting (1994) discusses the experience of deaf people within a framework of ethnicity, proposing that although "deaf people experience the world and structure their lives differently from those who are not deaf" (p. 4), they must adapt to a world designed for hearing people. This means that the "dependency constraint" is a constant in their lives; they are forced to rely on hearing interpreters in many situations, to ask friends to make telephone calls, to depend on hearing relatives for many day-to-day chores. This enforced dependence "create(s) a dynamic tension that underlies and shapes the daily lives of deaf people" (Erting, 1994, p. 5), and may lead to determined efforts toward self-reliance and independence wherever possible both for themselves and their children.

Deaf Infants, Hearing Mothers, and Avoidance

The Hd infants showed significantly more avoidance of their mothers compared to the three other groups during the first reunion, and 20% of Hd infants were classified as A/Avoidant compared to 0% of Hh infants. Nevertheless, the proportion of Secure Hd infants (75%) is not significantly below that of the Hh infants (89%). Both of these proportions are elevated compared to those of three other studies of deaf children with hearing mothers reviewed above (Greenberg & Marvin, 1979; Lederberg & Mobley, 1990; Mavrolas, 1990).

The higher rates of avoidance coded as one of the interactive *behaviors* (not the A/Avoidant *classification*) by infants in the Hd pairs in our study might suggest an increased risk of disturbed relationships. Colin (1996) states that it is appropriate to enquire (albeit cautiously) whether overstimulation leads to avoidance. Another source for this reaction, especially for a deaf infant, might be the difficulty in establishing an effective, accessible, and contingent system of communication with a primary caregiver who is hearing. However, the mediating effect of other forms of contingent responsiveness can temper a child's anger (illustrated, for example, by resistant behavior during the Strange Situation Procedure), and lead to a positive relationship, as suggested by the deaf infants' generally secure overall attachment ratings.

An elaborate meta-analysis of attachment compared twenty-one studies where mothers had problems (e.g., mental illness, drug abuse) to thirty-four studies where children had problems (e.g., prematurity, physical or sensory disability), finding that children whose mothers had problems were "highly divergent" from the A/B/C distributions, whereas in studies with "problem children" distributions were similar to those expected in nonproblematic populations. Investigators concluded that "the mother plays a more important role than the child in shaping the quality of relationships. Logically, the mother's more mature capacities allow her to be guided by infant needs, while the infants are not capable of comparable adaptation" (van IJzendoorn, Goldberg, Kroonenberg, & Frenkel, 1992, p. 855).

Several researchers have concluded that, for children at developmental risk, "constraints on behavioral and relationship patterns implicit in the traditional categories of attachment may not operate" (Vondra & Barnett, 1999, p. v). This is a suggestion that must be considered in relation to deaf children with hearing parents.

Conclusion

A number of theoretical and methodological issues arise in the use and interpretation of the Strange Situation Procedure (SSP) when one or both members of a mother–infant dyad are deaf. One procedural question that must be raised when deaf infants participate in the SSP is whether they are actually aware of the mother's leave-taking and return, as most will not hear the door open and close and some will be unable to understand a mother's reassurance that she will "return soon." These behavioral differences related to hearing loss may have adverse effects on behavioral coding if the child does not react to the mother upon her return (thus appearing to avoid her), when in fact the deaf baby may simply not have noticed her presence.

When a child makes no response to the mother's departure or is more oriented toward the toys or the stranger, he or she may be coded as indifferent. A delayed reaction during these 3-minute episodes can influence the ratings of attachment behaviors and raise a question regarding the validity of the SSP coding for this population. As Marschark (1993a) notes, the deaf child's seeming indifference to a mother's leave-taking or distress at her subsequent return may be due to factors different from those observed in hearing dyads. Perhaps deaf children are left alone less often than hearing children of the same age, or perhaps a deaf child is more likely to be unaware that the mother has left the room and is therefore more distressed when her absence is then realized. A deaf infant may not have yet learned to scan the environment periodically for valuable visual clues.

Waxman, Spencer, and Poisson (1996) cautioned that coding systems developed for hearing dyads may be insensitive and problematic when applied to infants or parents who are deaf. In that study, mother–child interactions initially deemed to be noncontingent were found, upon further analysis, to be actually adaptive for deaf babies. As other researchers have noted, because research with children who have disabilities is often based on small, nonrandom, perhaps nonrepresentative samples, "individual studies therefore can yield quite diverging attachment classification distributions, even if they belong to the same [population]" (van IJzendoorn, Goldberg, Kroonenberg, & Frenkel, 1992, p. 854).

It would be worthwhile to investigate attachment with this population using a Q-set (Vaughn & Waters, 1990) or parent interviews regarding the child's typical responses to separations and reunions in more naturalistic situations (Harwood, Miller, & Lucca Irizarry, 1995; Hauser-Cram, Warfield, Shonkoff, & Krauss, 2001). These types of studies, emphasizing childrearing practices and beliefs in the Deaf community, are especially important for interpreting attachment behaviors in children of deaf parents. Such data could also provide important insights for early interventionists in their efforts to support optimal parenting and healthy social-emotional development in young deaf children.

Acknowledgments

Some data in this chapter were previously reported elsewhere:

Koester, L. S., & MacTurk, R. H. (1991, July). Predictors of attachment relationships in deaf and hearing infants. Paper presented at the XIth Biennial Meetings of the International Society for the Study of Behavioural Development, Minneapolis, MI.

Koester, L. S., & MacTurk, R. H. (1991). Attachment behaviors in deaf and hearing infants. In K. P. Meadow-Orlans, R. H. McTurk, L. S. Koester, & P. E. Spencer, *Interaction and support: Mothers and deaf infants* (Chapter 7). Final Report to Maternal and Child Health Research Program.

Notes

1. Robert H. MacTurk helped to supervise the data collection and coding for the Strange Situation Procedure.

2. This paper elicited spirited comments in defense of attachment as a universal construct (Chao, 2001; Gjerde, 2001; Kondo-Ikemura, 2001; Posada & Jacobs, 2001; van IJzendoorn & Sagi, 2001), with a reply by Rothbaum et al. (2001).

10

Language at 12 and 18 Months

Characteristics and Accessibility of Linguistic Models

Patricia E. Spencer

Traditionally, language development has been a great concern for those working with deaf and hard of hearing children. Even youngsters with a relatively mild hearing loss are at risk for difficulties in language development (Davis, Elfenbein, Schum, & Bentler, 1986; Bess, Dodd-Murphy, & Parker, 1998; Meadow-Orlans, Mertens, & Sass-Lehrer, 2003). Delays have been noted in the acquisition of vocabulary (see Lederberg & Spencer, 2001, for a review), syntax (Lederberg, 2003; Schick, 2003), and some aspects of pragmatics (the expression of communicative intentions) (Day [Spencer], 1986; Nicholas, Geers, & Kozak, 1994; Lederberg & Everhart, 2000).

Studies showing language delays for deaf children have focused on those with hearing parents. No such delays have been reported for deaf children with deaf parents. In general, those children are exposed to sign language from birth and have been reported to acquire sign language at the same age or even somewhat earlier than the age at which hearing children typically acquire spoken language (Meier & Newport, 1990; Volterra & Iverson, 1995; Spencer & Lederberg, 1997; Morford & Mayberry, 2000; Anderson & Reilly, 2002; Schick, 2003). These reports indicate that there is nothing inherent in hearing loss that constrains language development; rather, the delays and differences that are typical for deaf children with hearing parents reflect their delayed exposure to a language model that they can process effectively.

Identification of hearing loss for deaf children with hearing parents has, in fact, traditionally occurred after the age at which hearing children acquire language (Moores, 2001; Meadow-Orlans, Mertens, & Sass-Lehrer, 2003). Thus, before the early twenty-first century, deaf or hard-of hearing children with hearing parents often already had significant language delays before intervention was initiated. There are indications that identification and intervention during the first year of life leads to earlier language acquisition for Hd children. For example, Yoshinaga-Itano and her colleagues in Colorado reported that language skills, as measured by the Minnesota Child Development Inventory (a parent report instrument), developed more rapidly when identification of hearing loss occurred before rather than after 6 months of age (Yoshinaga-Itano, Sedey, Coulter, & Mehl, 1998; Snyder & Yoshinaga-Itano, 1999; Yoshinaga-Itano, 2003). Results from the Colorado studies have shown the mean language functioning of deaf children with hearing parents to be in the "low average" range expected for hearing children of the same age.

Moeller (2000) used existing data from administrations of a standardized receptive vocabulary test, the Peabody Picture Vocabulary Test, to evaluate language skills of Hd children. She found that age at of intervention was significantly associated with the vocabulary measure at 5 years. In Moeller's study, the "early" intervention group included children who entered a program by 11 months of age. Their mean vocabulary scores "approximated those of their hearing peers" (Moeller, 2000, p. e43); the scores of children who were identified later did not. Neither the Moeller nor the Yoshinaga-Itano studies, both of which focused on deaf children with hearing parents, showed any association between quality of language outcomes and the language modality used by the family or intervention program.

Moeller (2000) found that a measure of family involvement with the child and the child's program was associated with 5-year vocabulary levels even more strongly than age of intervention. Other more specific parenting behaviors have also been reported to be associated with the language outcomes of children who are deaf or hard of hearing. Spencer (1998), for example, found that a measure of maternal responsiveness was significantly associated with deaf children's language skills at 18 months. Pipp-Siegel, Sedey, and Yoshinaga-Itano (2002) found that a measure of maternal emotional availability was also associated with later language functioning.

A number of studies have found Hd mothers to be less responsive and more directive during interactions with their children than is typical for Hh mothers (Cross, Johnson-Morris, & Nienhuys, 1980; Spencer & Gutfreund, 1990). Early interactions between deaf children and hearing mothers have been characterized as having a lower frequency of maternal communication (Lederberg, Binz, McIntyre, & McNorton, 1989) or, alternatively, such high rates of maternal communication that there is little chance for the child to take communicative turns (Wedell-Monnig & Lumley, 1980; Kenworthy, 1986). These types of maternal interactive style can limit opportunities for children's early acquisition of language skills (Tomasello, 1988). However, in an excellent review of wide-ranging sources, Gallaway and Woll (1994) argue that many of these studies "present what we now know to be an oversimplified picture" and that "the essential question of what may or may not be facilitative in this atypical context of childhood deafness has barely been considered" (pp. 217–218).

Not all researchers have reported negative interactive patterns for Hd mothers. Lederberg and Everhart (2000) found no differences in responsiveness between Hd and Hh mothers in their study of mother–child dyads at about 2 and 3 years. In addition, Pipp-Siegel and colleagues (2002) did not find emotional availability ratings of Hd mothers with early identified deaf children to be lower than in the normative population. It is possible that identification of hearing loss within the first year of life leads to more positive language-learning environments for deaf infants and young children because it increases parents' knowledge about hearing loss and their feelings of competence to support their deaf child's development.

Such feelings of parenting competence, as well as a more positive view of deafness are common among deaf parents of deaf children (see Chapters 8 and 9). Perhaps due in part to these attitudes and expectations, deaf mothers have been reported to participate in highly responsive interactions with their deaf infants and young children (Erting, 1994; Meadow-Orlans & Erting, 2000; Harris, 2001). They have also been observed to modify their communication behaviors and sign language in ways appropriate for enhancing deaf infants' attention to and learning of sign language (Maestas y Moores, 1980; Kantor, 1982; Harris, Clibbens, Chasin, & Tibbits, 1989; Erting, Prezioso, & Hynes, 1990/1994; Masataka, 2000). For example, the sign language deaf parents address to infants tends to be produced in a slow, highly rhythmic manner, and the signs tend to be made larger than is usual (Erting et al., 1994). Especially with the youngest infants, deaf mothers often sign directly on the infant's body or even move a compliant infant's hands in the action representing a sign (Maestas y Moores, 1980; Mohay, 2000). Just like the high-pitched rhythmic spoken language hearing parents address to infants, these "motherese" modifications in sign serve to direct and to hold infants' attention (Masataka, 1992). Deaf mothers also tend to produce fewer signed utterances in a given time frame compared to hearing mothers' usual rate of production of spoken utterances. This may reflect patterns of visual turn-taking specific to conversing in a visual instead of an auditory language (Spencer, 2003).

The language environment and developmental progress of hearing children of deaf parents has been documented less extensively than that of Hd and Dd children. Most reports indicate no delay in language for Dh children. This has been shown for small numbers of Dh children's acquisition of sign language (see Bonvillian, Orlansky, & Folven, 1994) and generally for their development of spoken language, which may initially be somewhat delayed but later is equal to that of Hh children (Meadow-Orlans, 2002). Bornstein and colleagues (1999) found, in fact, that deaf mothers reported higher language levels for hearing children than for deaf children at two years of age. (These data came from written questionnaires completed by deaf mothers reporting both signed and spoken language for their hearing children.) Rea, Bonvillian, and Richards (1988) and Koester (see Chapter 4) reported more vocal communications from Dh than from Dd mothers during interactions with their infants and toddlers. Other interactive differences have not been reported except for a decreased level of general responsiveness or sensitivity noted by Meadow-Orlans for Dh mothers (see Chapter 8).

This chapter focuses on children's language acquisition in relation to the language models provided by their mothers. Like those studied by Moeller (2000), all of the deaf children considered in this chapter had their hearing loss diagnosed and intervention services started before 1 year of age. In fact, all of the deaf children included here were diagnosed with a hearing loss by 6 months of age, making them similar to the population of early diagnosed children on which Yoshinaga-Itano and her colleagues have focused (Yoshinaga-Itano, 2003). Unlike the Yoshinaga-Itano and Moeller reports, the present study provides information about language functioning from direct observations of deaf children with deaf parents (Dd) and hearing children with deaf parents (Dh) as well as a comparison group of hearing children with hearing parents (Hh).

Methods

Characteristics of Participating Dyads

From the perspective of language development, it is especially important to reiterate that mothers in all groups were unusually well-educated and that children had no conditions other than deafness that might interfere with language acquisition. Almost all children were first- or second-born, and families were financially comfortable, suggesting that most mothers had both time and resources to devote to supporting their children's development (see Chapter 3 for details).

Deaf and Hearing Children, Hearing Mothers. Eighteen Hd dyads and eighteenth Hh dyads were included in the language analyses. Hearing loss in Hd children ranged from moderate to profound. Two Hd children with a mild hearing loss were excluded from language analyses, and one Hd child could not be included because of a flawed videotape. One Hh child was excluded because her mother signed fluently to her during the interaction session. Another Hh child was excluded because he was later found to have significant delays in receptive and expressive language and thus to demonstrate atypical development for a hearing child (Paul, 1996; Weismer & Evans, 2002). As stated above, all Hd children were identified with a hearing loss by age 6 months, and all were enrolled in intervention programs by age 9 months.

Deaf and Hearing Children, Deaf Mothers. Data were obtained from the sixteen Dd dyads and fifteen Dh dyads for whom tapes were available at both 12 and 18 months. All of the children had audiological testing. Hearing loss in the Dd group ranged from mild to profound, with most of the children functioning at severe-profound or profound levels. No Dh child gave evidence of a hearing loss.

Deaf mothers reported that American Sign Language (ASL) was their preferred language, but they used forms of contact ASL–English signing when interacting with hearing people. Although most of the Dd mothers did not use voice while signing with their children, there were exceptions. This was most obvious in a dyad in which both mother and child had hearing levels in the severe range. This mother frequently accompanied her signs with spoken words. Her child was doing the same by 18 months, although visual communication predominated. Mothers in the Dh group were somewhat more likely to accompany their signs with vocalizations, but there was great variability in both frequency and intelligibility of their vocal productions.

Procedures

Data Collection. Data were collected during 15 minutes of mother–child free play at the 12-month visit and 20 minutes of free play at the 18-month visit. Toys provided at each visit were appropriate for both manipulative and symbolic (pretend) play. Information about mother–child communicative and language behaviors was taken primarily from the first 10 minutes after mothers joined the children in play. (An initial 5-minute segment of child-alone play, which allowed children to become familiar with the toys, was not included in the analyses.) Additional information for some analyses was drawn from interviews conducted with mothers when infants were 9, 12, 15, and 18 months old. Hearing families were re-contacted when children were 2 and 3 years old, and those who could still be located completed the English language version of the MacArthur Communicative Development Inventory, Toddler Edition (CDI) (Fenson et al., 1993) to provide assessments of their children's vocabulary development.

Coding of Data. Although the collection of data for these analyses was relatively simple, consisting primarily of videotaping unstructured dyadic play, data coding required lengthy and intensive effort. For *mothers*, communication acts were identified in the stream of ongoing behaviors, and descriptive codes were then applied to vocal and/or signed language and to other communications that were not expressed formally. These codes provided information about the modality, complexity, and frequency of communication produced by mothers during the interaction.

Gestural–tactile communication behaviors were categorized according to their form, including: *signed expressions, gestures without objects* (conventional gestures, points, pre- or nonconventional gestures), *gestures with objects* (showing, demonstrating, moving objects to get attention), *visual or physical attention-directing signals* (waving or tapping on the infant), or *physical manipulation of the infant.*

Signed and vocal language productions were categorized as *nongrammatical* (nonsense vocalizations, exclamations [e.g., "ooh!"] and imitations of animal and vehicle sounds), *single-element* (single-sign or single-word), or *multielement* (grammatical) *expressions.*

Identification and coding of *infants'* communications proceeded in a similar manner, although identifying intentionally communicative behaviors from their ongoing stream of behaviors was conceptually more complex. Gestural behaviors that were coded included:

- *Preconventional gestures* (such as reaching). These behaviors were coded if they were *(1)* accompanied by eye gaze to mother, *(2)* produced after mother's attention was obtained or accompanied by effort to obtain her attention, *(3)* followed by the infant's waiting for a response from mother, *(4)* repeated if she made no response, or *(5)* followed by some kind of consummatory behavior after a response.
- *Conventional gestures* (such as pointing and "so tall").
- *Signs* or recognizable attempts to produce signs.

Infant vocal behaviors that were coded included the following:

- *Preconventional vocalizations.* These were considered to be intentional communication efforts and were coded if they were accompanied [within 2 seconds] by eye gaze to the mother or by an intentionally communicative gestural behavior. Preconventional vocalizations were also categorized according to their metaphonological characteristics as follows:
    - *Canonical syllables* consisted of consonant-vowel combinations (such as "bah-bah" or "da-da-da") in which the timing and "sound envelope" closely approximated possible English syllable structure. (This form of babbling is considered to be an important precursor of spoken language in hearing children [Oller, 1980; Oller & Eilers, 1988].)
    - *Precanonical vocalizations* lacked such an organized structure and could not have functioned as syllables in spoken English.
- *Conventional vocalizations* (such as imitations of vehicle sounds).
- *Spoken words* or recognizable approximations.

Because infants' vocal and manual productions both reflected age-related articulatory constraints, the determination of operational definitions for "word" and "sign" was critical for this study. It was decided to follow the definition of a "word" provided by Huttenlocher and her colleagues (Huttenlocher et al., 1991), who defined a "word" as a vocal production that occurred in a nonimitative communicative context, made sense in that context, and contained at least two of the phonemes in the presumed target word. A parallel operational definition was developed to aid in the identification of signs produced by the children in the current study. To be considered a "sign," a manual gesture had to be produced in a nonimitative situation occurring in a communicative context. In addition, the supposed sign had to "make sense" in context, and at least two of the three primary parameters of the sign (location of production, handshape, or direction/type of movement used) had to match those expected in the presumed sign's canonical or adult form. This definition was more specific and perhaps more restrictive than that used by a number of other researchers, but it allowed direct comparison of deaf and hearing infants.

Because the coding was technically arduous, separate teams focused on visual–tactile and vocal behaviors. Approximately 10% of the time on tape that was used for analysis was coded independently by two trained individuals to check reliability (or agreement). For hearing mothers, this included a total of 1214 maternal vocal behaviors and 601 maternal gestural–tactile communication acts; 373 vocal and 253 gestural acts were coded for the infants. Agreement on categories of communicative acts ranged from adequate to high, that is, from 73% agreement on production of nongrammatical utterances to 97% for production of conventional gestures. Agreement on infant communications ranged from 75% for preconventional gestures to 100% for conventional gestures. Cohen's kappa for categorization of infant vocalizations was .88.

For Dh and Dd dyads, transcription and coding of the play sessions proceeded as with that for the dyads in which mothers were hearing. However, staff members fluent in ASL were responsible for the coding. Children's signs were reviewed by a specialist in child language who was experienced with the modifications in form common in the "baby talk" of young signers.[1] Tapes were also reviewed by a hearing researcher accustomed to spoken language of young deaf children to assure that vocalizations and spoken words produced by the children were identified. Levels of intercoder agreement exceeded 80% on all measures, and Cohen's kappa was .65 or greater.

Analysis. Differences for related sets of dependent variables across groups were analyzed by first calculating multivariate analysis of variance (MANOVA) and following up significant results with univariate analysis of variance (ANOVA) to locate the source of differences.

Results and Discussion

Deaf and Hearing Children with Hearing Mothers

Mothers' Communications. An initial MANOVA indicated group differences within the set of gestural–tactile behaviors coded, and follow-up tests identified several differences between Hh and Hd mothers' use of these communicative acts. Compared with mothers of hearing infants, mothers of deaf infants (Hd) produced more gestures with objects [F (1,34) = 17.5; $p < .001$], were more likely to tap on their infants' bodies to obtain their attention [F (1,34) = 5.7; $p < .05$], and more likely to physically manipulate their infants [F (1,34) = 11.1; $p < .01$]. These differences suggest that hearing mothers understood the need to obtain their deaf infants' visual attention before communicating with them. The mothers used many visual object-related behaviors and tactile behaviors in attempting to accomplish this. (See Chapter 11 for more about hearing and deaf mothers' use of these and related strategies.)

Some important aspects of mothers' communication did *not* differ significantly between the two groups. For example, no group difference was found in the frequency of mothers' language directed to the children. In addition, the proportion of mothers' utterances falling in the nongrammatical, single-element, or multielement categories were similar, and nongrammatical utterances decreased for both groups of mothers from the 12- to 18-month sessions [F (1,33) = 7.8; $p < .01$]. Both groups of mothers produced fewer linguistic utterances at 18 months compared to 12 months (Hd 12-month mean = 153.6; 18-month mean = 141.7; Hh 12-month mean = 158.6, 18-month mean = 141.9). These reductions reflect mothers' recognition of the children's increasing ability to contribute to and take turns in communicative interactions. No difference was found in topic responsiveness, or degree to which the content (or topic) of the language of these two groups of mothers matched (or followed) their children's already-established focus of attention.

In sum, communication and language behaviors of the Hd and Hh mothers differed in the degree to which they relied on gestural and/or tactile communications, but they did not differ on frequency or responsiveness of linguistic productions. However, because signing was relatively infrequent, and not all of mothers' language was actually accessible to their infants, the language-learning environment of the Hd and Hh infants differed overall. Hd infants' access to their mothers' language was more limited.

Infants' Communications. Despite similarities in mothers' communications, the deaf and hearing infants differed significantly on several important measures that reflected the Hd infants' reduced auditory access. There was a group difference in the production of vocalizations (F [2,33] = 6.9; $p < .01$); follow-up analysis showed that hearing infants significantly exceeded deaf infants in production of babbled syllables with canonical metaphonological structure [F (1,34) = 12.4; $p = .001$], in which clear consonant and vowel sounds are sequentially combined. However, despite the overall difference between deaf and hearing infants in production of this relatively mature form of babbling, both groups' production of canonical syllables increased from 12 to 18 months [F (1,34) = 16.7; $p < .001$] (see Table 10-1).

Table 10-1. Mean frequency of gesture and vocal production of hearing and deaf infants with hearing mothers during 10 minutes of interaction

	12 months		*18 months*	
Communication behavior	*Hd*	*Hh*	*Hd*	*Hh*
Preconventional gesture	8.8	6.0	9.6	7.5
Conventional gesture/sign	2.3	3.0	2.7	3.1
Precanonical babbled vocalization	37.1	38.1	33.6	24.0
Canonical babbled vocalization[a]	1.6	8.6	10.7	33.4
Conventional vocalization/word[b]	.3	6.7	2.9	24.9

[a]18 months > 12 months, F (1,34) = 16.7; p = .001; Hh > Hd, F (1,34) = 12.4; p = .001.

[b]Hh > Hd, F (1,34) = 6.7; p = .01; 18 months > 12 months, F (1,34) = 13.9, p < 001; Age-by-Hearing Status Group interaction, F (1,34) 4.15; p = .05.

Not surprisingly, group patterns for the mean frequency of production of conventional-level vocalizations (e.g., animal and motor sounds, exclamations such as "uh-oh!") mirrored the patterns for babbling. Few conventional vocalizations were produced by either group at 12 months. Although production increased for both groups by 18 months, the increase was more rapid for hearing infants than for deaf infants (age-by-hearing status group interaction [$F(1,34) = 4.15$; $p = .05$]).

The groups also differed in linguistic-level productions at 12 months: half of the Hh children produced one or more spoken words during the interaction period, but none of the Hd children produced any signs or spoken words. At 18 months, hearing infants were, on average, distinctly advantaged compared to their deaf peers, with Hh children producing a mean of 21.9 linguistic utterances during the 10 minutes of interaction, while Hd children produced a mean of 4.5 words or signs [$F(1,34) = 5.6$; $p < .05$]. Despite this statistical difference, considerable within-group variability existed. Some hearing children produced many spoken multiword utterances during the 10 minutes of coded interaction, but others produced none. Although no Hd infant matched the language levels of the more linguistically advanced hearing children, a number of Hd infants produced enough language to match the *average* hearing children. Table 10-2 (section A) shows the distribution of Hh and Hd children at 18 months across three language groups based on naturally occurring breaks in the frequency and symbolic level of their communications during the coded interaction: children in the "low" or Level 1 group produced primarily prelinguistic communications; children in the "middle" or Level 2 group produced primarily single spoken words and/or signs; children in the "high" or Level 3 group produced at least two multisign or multiword combinations and ten or more linguistic-level utterances.

The distribution of the two groups of 18-month-old children across the three language levels is similar to that reported by Lederberg and Everhart (2000) for children at about 22 months of age. The majority of

Table 10-2. Frequency and percentage of children performing at each language level during interactions at 18 months

Group	*Level 1*	*Level 2*	*Level 3*	*Total*
A. (Children with Hearing Mothers)				
Deaf children/Hearing mothers	12 (66.7%)	6 (33.3%)	—	18
Hearing children/Hearing mothers	6 (33.3%)	8 (44.4%)	4 (22.2%)	18
B. (Children with Deaf Mothers)				
Deaf children/Deaf mothers	4 (25%)	6 (37.5%)	6 (37.5%)	16
Hearing children/Deaf mothers	3 (20%)	9 (60%)	3 (20%)	15

Kruskal-Wallis test comparing all four groups, chi-square = 10.212; $p = .017$; follow-up Mann-Whitney U tests between pairs, Dd, Hh, Dh > Hd.

Level 1 = prelinguistic; Level 2 = single word or sign; Level 3 = multiword or sign utterances.

Hd children are in the "low" or beginning category, fewer are in the "middle" category, and none reach the "high" levels shown by almost one-quarter of the hearing children. Language modality used in the Hd children's intervention programs was not systematically associated with the language levels attained at this age. Furthermore, language levels of the Hd children were unrelated to the degree of their hearing loss: two infants in the middle group had a profound hearing loss, one had a severe-profound loss, two had a severe loss, and one had a moderately severe loss. Hearing level of Hd children was, however, associated with the production of canonical syllables at 12 months and with *oral* language production at 18 months.

Despite the different distributions of language levels attained by the Hh and Hd infants, there were some important measures on which no significant differences were found. For example, frequency of gestural communication was the same in both groups. This probably reflects the extent to which gesture forms a basis for children's language development regardless of hearing status or the modality of their formal expressive language (Singleton, Goldin-Meadow, & McNeill, 1995). In addition, when symbolic levels and modalities were combined, the two groups of infants did not differ significantly in total quantity of communicative acts. Thus, there was no evidence of decreased effort to communicate on the part of infants with hearing loss.

The data available from the infants' communication behaviors during the interaction session are in some ways consistent with the reports by Moeller (2000) and the Yoshinaga-Itano research team (e.g., Mayne, Yoshinaga, & Sedey, 1999; Yoshinaga-Itano, 2003). Among the group of early identified Hd children described in this chapter, a significant number fell within the low-average or even the average range of expressive language functioning observed for hearing peers. However, quite significant delays remained for a large portion of the Hd group, leading to significant differences in mean scores between this group and the Hh children. The current observation-based data show higher linguistic functioning for the Hd children, on average, than was expected in the past when identification occurred later. However, by no means were all of their language acquisition and development problems resolved.

Association between Mother and Infant Language. An association was expected between the frequency of maternal linguistic utterances at 12 months and that of the infants at 18 months. This association was found only for the subgroup of Hd dyads participating in intervention programs using signed language, or total communication, at both 12 and 18 months. Because the total number of signed utterances from these mothers was significantly lower than that of other groups (see below), it is possible that effects of frequency of language input are critical only when the rate of input is quite low.

Learning to Sign from the Models Presented by Hearing Mothers: A Closer Look at a Special Subgroup. Seven of the infants included in group Hd (five girls and two boys, all with severe or profound hearing loss) had participated with their families in intervention programs using some form of total communication (signs produced more or less simultaneously with spoken language) from at least 9 through 18 months of age. This subgroup provided an opportunity to assess the effects of extended sign-based intervention on mothers' production of signed language and to identify associations between mothers' signing and their children's language development. For these analyses, in addition to the 10-minute communication samples discussed above, the entire data-collection session at each age (generally lasting between 1 and 2 hours) was reviewed to assure that patterns observed in the free play session were representative of communication over a longer period of time and in varied contexts. Mothers also reported on their own skills and those of their children during interviews.

Families of the seven children considered here received between 3 and 5 hours of direct intervention services each week. Professionals in the intervention programs were not deaf, but sign language instruction was included in the services offered in addition to information about deafness and language development.

Despite similar times of participation in intervention programs emphasizing signed communication (sign accompanying speech), there was great variability in the frequency of signed utterances produced by the mothers during the free play sessions. For the purpose of this analysis, utterances were counted as "signed" if at least one content word (adjective, adverb, noun, verb) was signed. During the interaction at 12 months, two of the mothers produced no signed utterances and two additional mothers produced only five to eight signed utterances; however, three mothers produced between twenty-five and fifty-one signed utterances. At 18 months, one of the initially nonsigning mothers still produced no signed utterances. The other six mothers increased their sign production at the 18-month sessions, producing between nine and fifty-seven signed utterances. The range in the frequency of signed utterances indicates that the intervention programs were relatively ineffective in promoting use of signed language for at least two of the families. In addition, a strong correlation between mothers' frequency of signed productions at the two infant ages ($r_s = .88$; $p < .05$) suggests that the mothers' tendencies to incorporate signs into their communications could be observed fairly soon after intervention had begun. It was also noted that mothers' reports in interviews about the proportion of spoken utterances that they accompanied with signs failed to match their actual performance. This was most clearly the case for the mothers who signed little if at all during the play session.

As is typical of new signers, the mothers tended to make mistakes in their sign production. In addition, although the mothers were receiving training in sign systems that used invented signs to represent (English) grammatical morphemes for verb tense, noun plurals, articles, and prepositions, they almost always omitted these special markers. The signed language model demonstrated by these mothers did not, therefore, provide a particularly consistent or complete picture of English. Neither did it provide a model of American Sign Language (ASL), which represents these grammatical meanings in different ways.

Regardless, some of the children used these incomplete and inconsistent language models as a bridge to production of their first expressive signs. Three Hd children (those whose mothers signed with at least 40% of their spoken utterances at 12 months and 70% at 18 months) produced their first signs by 13 months of age. These three children produced between five and thirteen signed utterances during 10 minutes of coded interaction from the 18-month play session. All of the children were reported by their mothers to be producing at least one sign by 18 months. However, three children were not observed to sign during the entire recorded session at that age. Communicative attempts of the child whose mother was not observed to sign during the play sessions at either age actually decreased between 12 and 18 months.

For this subgroup of the Hd children, language production at 18 months was strongly related to mothers' frequency of sign production at both 12 ($r_s = .87$, $p < .05$) and 18 months ($r_s = .93$; $p < .01$). Mothers' use of signs, in turn, appeared to be influenced by having other adults with whom to sign. The three mothers who signed most frequently reported having relatives, spouses, and friends who were also learning and using signed language.

Expressive Vocabulary at 2 and 3 Years. Parents of eleven of the Hd children and eleven of the Hh children reported their children's vocabulary (by completing the Toddler version of the Communicative Development Inventory, developed for children learning spoken English) when the children were 24 and 30 months old. According to these reports of expressive vocabulary (considering signs as well as spoken words), the Hd children were progressing but continued to trail their hearing peers significantly. Vocabulary size of Hd children in oral programming ranged between 16 and 328 words at 30 months of age. The range reported for Hd children in total communication (sign plus speech) programs at that age was 97 to 232 signs or spoken words. In contrast, the 30-month vocabularies of Hh children ranged from 465 to 661 words. Most of the hearing children had larger expressive vocabularies at 24 months than the most linguistically advanced deaf children at 30 months.

Summary: Hd Children. In general, it appears that early identification and intervention for the Hd children participating in this study resulted in more positive prelinguistic communication than has been reported in many previous studies. This reflects in part the more positive characteristics observed in their mothers' communications. That is, these Hd mothers were sensitive to their children's focus of attention, increased their use of object-related gestures and tactile behaviors, and produced communications and spoken language with their deaf children at a rate similar to that of the Hh mothers. However, the modifications adopted by the Hd mothers often did not include significant production of visually salient language. Participation in an intervention program promoting use of signs to accompany speech did not consistently result in frequent signing by the mothers. This is unfortunate, because the children responded positively when even minimally salient models of language were provided. This finding illustrates the importance of focusing intervention efforts on increasing Hd parents' use of signs or other visual language systems when auditory information cannot be received and processed by the child.

Despite the progress shown by many of the Hd children, a sizable subgroup continued to show language development that was significantly delayed compared to their Hh peers. Early identification and intervention, therefore, did not assure age-appropriate language development. It is important for future researchers to focus on characteristics of intervention programs that effectively support hearing parents' provision of fluent language models to their infants after early identification of hearing loss.

Deaf and Hearing Children with Deaf Mothers

Mothers' Communication. The most striking aspect of the communication of the deaf mothers observed in this study was the relatively small number of linguistic messages they produced compared to that of the hearing mothers (of either deaf or hearing infants). The hearing mothers produced, on average, over 150 spoken utterances (with or without signs) during the 10-minute coded observation period at 12 months, but the deaf mothers produced an average of only 50. Unlike the hearing mothers (whose utterance frequency tended to decrease from 12 to 18 months), the deaf mothers increased the frequency of their signed utterances from 12 to 18 months. However, the utterance frequency of deaf mothers remained significantly below that of both groups of hearing mothers.

Other differences were evident in the patterns of communication behavior of deaf and hearing mothers. Signed productions of the deaf mothers tended to be shorter than the oral language production of hearing mothers, and usually consisted of one or two formal signs combined with points or other signals to direct the infants' attention to the referenced object or activity. Signs were often repeated many times, a communicative strategy that has been reported by other researchers (e.g., Harris, Clibbens, Chasin, Tibbits, 1989; Swisher, 2000). This strategy seems to give deaf infants or toddlers increased opportunities to see a communication even if they are not visually focused on their mother for an extended period. Processes of simplification and establishing a clear reference for language were characteristic of hearing mothers (both Hh and Hd). However, these processes were even more striking in deaf mothers' language.

Deaf Infants with Deaf Mothers. The Dd mothers were especially inclined to tap on their infants' arms, shoulders, or legs to signal infants to look up to see communication (Waxman & Spencer, 1997) (see Figs. 10-1 and 10-2). The Dd mothers produced such behaviors significantly more often than did hearing mothers of deaf children at all ages and, at 12 months, more often than Dh mothers. Also, Dd mothers were highly consistent in providing linguistic information when children responded to an attention signal by looking at mother. The language produced by the Dd mothers was also highly responsive to their children's visual attention focus (or the focus just before they looked up at mother) and "followed" that focus more than 80% of the time (Wilson & Spencer, 1997). Thus, although the Dd mothers did not typically sign about something *while* their children looked at it, they consistently signed about it immediately *after* the child looked at it and then looked up to receive a message.

The picture of communication presented by Dd mothers was often one of watchful waiting and responding to their children's interests when presented with an opportunity to communicate. The Dd mothers' communications were almost always visual and tactile, with little vocal language used. The Dd children themselves rarely vocalized, with the exception of one child who had significant aided hearing and whose mother spoke while signing. (This was the only Dd child who produced canon-

Figure 10-1. During the free play situation, this deaf mother tapped her 9-month-old child's shoulder. Failing to get a response, she moved a doll past the child's face and held it next to her own face. The child's gaze followed the moving toy. (Illustration by Liz Conces Spencer)

ical babbling or spoken words.) The relative absence of vocalizations compared to Hd children probably reflects the fact that most of the Dd children did not use amplification consistently and that their mothers rarely used spoken language.

Despite their lack of spoken language, the Dd children's signed language was developing at a rate parallel to that of Hh children's learning of spoken language. The Dd children produced frequent prelinguistic gestural communications at 12 months, and about half of the children produced at least one sign during the 12-month interaction. Based on mothers' reports during interviews at 15 months and the children's language performance during the interactions at both 12 and 18 months, the Dd children showed no delay in onset of expressive sign language. However, in contrast to some earlier reports (e.g., Bonvillian, Orlansky, Novack, & Folven, 1983; Meier & Newport, 1990), there also was no evidence of precocity (see also, Volterra & Iverson, 1995). The proportion of Dd children who produced formal signs at 12 months was the same as Hh children who produced formal spoken words. In addition, the two groups did not differ significantly on the proportions of their linguistic productions that were single-element (one word or sign) or multielement ut-

Figure 10-2. After having obtained her infant's visual attention, the mother signs "baby" to label the toy she holds. (Illustration by Liz Conces Spencer)

terances at 18 months (see Table 10-2, Section B). However, in addition to modality, the Dd children's language differed from that of the Hh children in another way: their average number of utterances was significantly lower than that of the Hh children (Hh median = 12, range 0–134; Dd median = 9, range 0–39). That is, although the level of complexity of language produced by Dd and Hh children did not differ, the frequency of production did. This difference mirrored the difference in the frequency of production of hearing and deaf mothers.

Clearly the pace of linguistic turn-taking in the first year of life is slower for dyads in which child and mother are deaf than for dyads in which both are hearing. This difference in pace is to be expected because deaf persons must divide their visual attention between exploring objects in the environment and receiving communications. This effect is not obvious in adult signed conversations, but is a pervasive characteristic of signed conversations with infants and toddlers who have not yet developed the ability to make smooth changes in focus of visual attention (Bakeman & Adamson, 1984; see Chapter 11 this volume). A conversation that depends on visual attention is likely to proceed at a slower pace with a deaf child if the adult partner is sensitive to that child's need for dual use of vision. Dd children's rate of expressive communication may also be reduced because of their reluctance to interrupt manual exploration or object play to use their hands to communicate—and possibly also because of temporal matching of the slow turn-taking pace set by the mother.

Association between Mother and Child Language. Despite the relatively low rate of maternal signing in the Dd group, within-group analysis showed that frequency of mothers' signed utterances correlated significantly with child language level as measured by the number of different signs used and the complexity of signed utterance structure. Although all deaf mothers signed less often than hearing mothers spoke, Dd children whose mothers signed the most were the most linguistically proficient (Wilson & Spencer, 1997).

How were such relatively low rates of maternal language able to support typical rates of language acquisition by deaf children? The deaf mothers' language topics tended to be highly responsive to their children's interest, and mothers were generally careful to ensure that children could actually see language addressed to them. Thus, each message addressed to deaf children by their deaf mothers was highly supportive of language development. It is tempting to conclude that the rate of production by these deaf mothers is actually a "good enough" rate to support language development of all children, and that much of the spoken language addressed to hearing children by their more verbose mothers is simply ignored and developmentally irrelevant. This could explain the importance to language development of maternal language that is contingent upon or responsive to an interest already expressed by the child (e.g., Tomasello & Farrar, 1986). Such "interest matching," or responsive language, may be preferentially attended to by a hearing child—and therefore be especially beneficial input. However, it is also conceivable that there is a modality effect, with less input being necessary for visual than for auditory language development. The visual signals of a signed message, especially in the slowed and exaggerated form often produced when addressing infants, may be "in the child's attention" longer and be more readily processed than the same message produced in the rapidly changing and fading signals of auditory language.

Hearing Children with Deaf Mothers. Dh children have language-learning environments that differ in some important ways from those of the other three groups. Unlike Hh and many Hd children, Dh children are provided with sign language input in their daily interactions with parents. Unlike Hd children, hearing children with deaf parents have full, unrestricted access to their parents' primary language modality and can be presented with a complete language model. Therefore, for most Dh children, sign is their first language. Unlike Dd children, however, Dh children also have access to spoken language directed to them or occurring around them. For example, although Dh mothers' vocal language is often less intelligible than that of hearing mothers, it was reported in Chapter 4 that deaf mothers often vocalize to hearing infants. Also, Dh children usually have hearing children and adults in their extended family or community with whom they participate in vocally based interactions.

In some ways, therefore, Dh children's language development can be expected to mirror that of other hearing children in bilingual environments. Most available studies indicate that Dh children become fluent in both the sign language their parents use and the spoken language of the larger society (Meadow-Orlans, 2002). In fact, deaf mothers have reported that their hearing children have vocabularies at age 2 years that are larger than those of either Dd children or Hd children (Bornstein et al., 1999). It is possible that this finding reflects difficulties in comparing signing and speaking children because the first words learned are not necessarily identical in the two language modes. Also, it is possible that deaf parents (who lack full access to their hearing children's spoken productions) simply expect more differentiated vocabulary from them than from deaf children, and their responses to a vocabulary checklist reflect their expectations. However, it is also possible that Dh children have slightly accelerated vocabulary growth compared to their Dd peers because of their early access to two language systems.

At 12 months, ten of the fifteen Dh children produced at least one formal sign or intelligible spoken word during the 10 minutes of coded interaction. This is a somewhat higher percentage of children than in groups Dd or Hh but is not significantly different. It is, however, significantly higher than group Hd.

At 18 months, Dh children's language levels again failed to differ significantly from those of groups Dd and Hh, and all three groups tended to perform at higher language levels than group Hd (Kruskal-Wallis chi-square = 10.21; $p = .017$). When frequency of utterances was compared, however, group Dh (like Dd) produced significantly *fewer* linguistic utterances than did group Hh. The performance of group Dh, therefore, is consistent with a conclusion that use of sign as a primary language modality results in slower turn-taking and fewer linguistic turns than is typical for dyads in which auditory language is used.

However, Dh children may have been producing more language than these analyses reflect. By 18 months, most of the Dh children produced "babbled" sequences and vocalizations, only some of which were deemed to be intelligible and were thus counted as linguistic utterances. The impression gained from observation of the videotaped interaction was that these children, who were already capable of interacting with their deaf mothers using sign language, were now focusing on acquisition of oral language (see Chapter 8, p. 129, for an example of a Dh child who spent much of the interaction time "talking" on a toy telephone). A closer look at Dh children's transition from prelinguistic to mostly signed language to oral language with or without accompanying signs could provide information about competition or mutual support across different language modalities. This information might be especially useful to professionals considering issues related to language modalities for children who are hard-of-hearing or who are using cochlear implants and thus have some access to both auditory and visual language.

Conclusion

All four groups of mothers showed strong tendencies to modify the communication and language they directed toward their infants so that its form and syntactic structure differed from that used to communicate with other adults. A number of similarities were observed in the two groups of hearing mothers. Both those with hearing infants and those with deaf infants produced many vocal utterances. That is, talk was frequent. In addition, the hearing mothers' spoken utterances tended to be short, but lengthened as their children grew older and were apparently assumed to understand more complex structures. The frequency of hearing mothers' utterances decreased from 12 to 18 months, probably because their infants (hearing or deaf) were more likely to be taking communicative turns, even if still using primarily prelinguistic communications. Finally, both groups of hearing mothers used gestures and objects in their communications with their infants, and most of their utterances were responsive to their infants' apparent interest or activity.

Deaf mothers also tended to be highly responsive, producing signed utterances that were relevant to their children's interests. However, deaf mothers' language differed in some ways from that of both groups of hearing mothers, and these differences appeared to match the specific needs of an infant who relies primarily on vision for receptive communication. First, the deaf mothers did not produce as many utterances as did hearing mothers. This may initially seem to be detrimental to the language development of the infants of deaf mothers. However, a closer look suggests that it is necessary and appropriate with an infant or toddler who must use vision for receptive communication as well as general exploration of the surrounding environment. Therefore, the apparent reason for the relatively low frequency of utterances from the deaf mothers is that they did not "waste" them by signing when their infants could not see the signs. Second, deaf mothers did not always wait for spontaneous looks from their infants but skillfully employed a variety of communicative strategies for obtaining their infants' visual attention (see Chapter 11 for more details). Some but not all of these strategies were also used by hearing mothers of deaf infants. Third, the signed utterances of deaf mothers were shorter than the spoken utterances of hearing mothers, especially at 12 months when infant visual attention to mothers tended to be fleeting. In contrast to the hearing mothers, the deaf mothers *increased* the number of utterances between 12 and 18 months, apparently in response to their infants' increased visual attention to language.

This study replicates, with a larger number of subjects, earlier reports that deaf and hearing infants of deaf mothers produce expressive language at similar ages and with similar complexity to that of hearing infants with hearing mothers. However, the frequency of linguistic productions differed, with both Dd and Dh infants producing fewer utterances than Hh infants. The children's rates of production of linguistic communications, therefore, reflected those of their mothers. There may be several reasons for this, not the least of which could be that engaging manually with toys, and having to switch visual attention back and forth between mother and toy, simply made it physically more complicated for Dd and Dh children to produce signed utterances.

Although Dd, Dh, and Hh infants showed generally similar patterns of language development, this was not the case for the deaf infants with hearing mothers. Although Hd children's prelinguistic abilities to use gesture and vocalization to express interests and needs matched those of the other children, many of them experienced significant delays in development of formal language. Early identification as deaf or hard-of-hearing and subsequent early intervention and use of hearing amplification, therefore, did not fully prevent the delays traditionally experienced by this group of children. Two factors predicted language development in the Hd group: *(1)* production of canonical babbling at 12 months was associated with production of spoken words at 18 months; *(2)* frequency of mothers' signing was associated with production of signed language by 18 months. Thus, the most advantaged Hd infants either had sufficient hearing, when amplified, to provide a basis for spoken language development or they had access to a visual language model that, even if not fluent, was sufficient to provide a basis for the beginnings of signed language development. The increasing gap between Hd and Hh children in vocabulary by 3 years of age, however, indicates that access to less than a complete, fluent language model can have a cumulative effect of slowing important aspects of language development.

Findings from this study do not appear, overall, to be as positive about the language development of early identified Hd children as those reported by Moeller (2000) and Yoshinaga-Itano (Mayne, Yoshinaga-Itano, & Sedey, 1999; Mayne, Yoshinaga-Itano, Sedey, & Carey, 1999; Yoshinaga-Itano 2003) and her colleagues. This study differs from the others in that the focus was primarily on observed communication behaviors, with no direct testing and with parents' reports used only for assessment of 24- and 30-month vocabulary. Differences in methods may be reflected in the results. However, findings from the current study are consistent with the earlier reports in that a significant *proportion* of the Hd group was found to function within the range expected for hearing peers—at least up to the age of 18 months. The scores of a relatively large proportion of participants, those experiencing significant language delays despite early identification and intervention, created differences in the mean scores between Hd children and those in the other groups. Clearly, a continuing need exists for concern about and support for language development in deaf children with hearing parents. Continued efforts are needed in assisting hearing parents' acquisition and use of sign-language skills as well as ongoing efforts to develop technologies to enhance the infants' access to auditory language models.

Acknowledgments

Some of these findings have been reported previously:

Spencer, P. (1993a). Communication behaviors of infants with hearing loss and their hearing mothers. *Journal of Speech and Hearing Research, 36,* 311–321.

Spencer, P. (1993b). The expressive communication of hearing mothers and deaf infants. *American Annals of the Deaf, 138*(3), 275–283.

Spencer, P., & Lederberg, A. (1997). Different modes, different models: Communication and language of young deaf children and their mothers. In L. Adamson & M. Romski (Eds.), *Communication and language acquisition: Discoveries from atypical development* (pp. 203–230). Baltimore: Brookes.

Note

1. Sincere thanks to Karen Saulnier, who spent many hours reviewing and coding these tapes. Her expertise was invaluable. We also want to thank Natalie Grindstaff, Linda Stamper, Arlene Kelly, and Barbara Gleicher for assisting in transcriptions of the tapes of deaf mothers.

11

Visual Attention

Maturation and Specialization

Patricia E. Spencer, M. Virginia Swisher, and Robyn P. Waxman

Throughout infancy, "eye contact," or gaze between infant and caregiver, plays a meaningful role in interactions and, therefore, in social and emotional development. Vision and visual attention also play a critical role in cognitive and linguistic development by giving infants a way to learn about persons, objects, and events. This chapter begins with a brief summary of existing information about the development of visual attention by hearing children with hearing parents, on whom most studies have focused. That will be followed by a summary of available information about the development of visual attention by deaf children. There is relatively little existing information about these children, and much of that has focused only on deaf children with hearing parents. Analyses will then be presented of results from the longitudinal observational study of visual attention of infants in the four groups addressed in this book—and the maternal behaviors that appear to support development of visual behaviors by infants who are deaf or have deaf mothers. Because of the differing hearing status in dyads, the results suggest the degree to which interactive experiences, in addition to infant hearing status, influence attention development.

Development of Attention by Hearing Infants

From the earliest weeks of life, there appears to be some form of automatic or involuntary coordination between hearing a sound and looking toward it (Clifton, 1992; Ruff & Rothbart, 1996). Infants have also been found to visually track moving objects more readily and to focus on them longer when the presence of the object is accompanied by sound (Lawson & Ruff, 1984). This is the case even when the sound does not emanate from the same location as the visual display. Ruff and Rothbart suggested that these effects of sound on infants' visual attention may simply reflect heightened general arousal due to the stimulation of more than one sense. However, even if initially involuntary, associations between visual attention and environmental sounds provide opportunities for developing voluntary, active coordination of looking with listening.

Studies of development of visual attention, not surprisingly, show a general progression from simpler to more complex patterns. For example, during the early months, infants and their parents frequently engage in extended periods of face-to-face mutual gaze that do not require rapid shifts or redirection of gaze (Tronick, Als, & Brazelton, 1980). Although objects may be involved to some degree in these early face-to-face episodes, they are not usually the focus.

By 5 or 6 months of age, most infants show increasing interest in looking at objects (Trevarthen, 1979; Adamson & Chance, 1988), and the duration of direct gazes at caregivers decreases. Even in experimental face-to-face situations without toys, infants' attention to their mothers' faces drops dramatically between 6 and 26 weeks of age (Kaye & Fogel, 1980). According to Schaffer (1989), gazes at objects during this developmental stage, like the earlier extended face-to-face episodes, tend to have a single focus. That is, during episodes of attending to an object, the child does not shift gaze toward the communication partner. Schaffer attributes the "either/or" nature of hearing infants' visual attention at this age to limitations of general attentional capacity: the child can attend to "an object *or* a person but not to both" (p. 197).

Early in the second year of life, most hearing children show an important advance in their attention skills by switching (or coordinating) attention between an object or event and a communication partner within a single episode. This new development, sometimes referred to as "triadic" or "coordinated joint" attention (Bakeman & Adamson, 1984), presages the onset of expressive language (Carpenter, Nagell, & Tomasello, 1998). Coordinated joint attention is evident when children systematically look back and forth between a person and an object during a single communication or play episode. It is also evident when they modify their actions with objects in response to the spoken suggestions of a communication partner, thus actively coordinating visual attention with attention to vocal communications.

The Impact of Hearing Loss on Visual Attention

Coordinated Joint Attention episodes provide significant opportunities for learning when adults use these opportunities to suggest expanded activities or to describe and label salient characteristics of the objects or events involved. However, if a child cannot hear this linguistic input and fails to look up to see it when it is offered in visual form, the potential for learning diminishes accordingly. Therefore, learning to shift visual attention between objects and communication partners is especially important for deaf children, who must use vision for receptive communication while also using vision to explore the environment.

Because of the apparent close coordination between sound and vision in hearing infants and young children, questions have been raised about whether the lack of auditory reception will delay, or at least complicate, the development of visual attention by deaf children. Wood and his colleagues (Wood, Wood, Griffiths, & Howarth, 1986; Wood, 1989), in fact, reported that this ability was significantly delayed in a small group of orally-trained deaf children between 3 and 5 years of age, but, as with hearing children, it emerged just before expressive language. The children did not display temporal coordination of looking toward teachers who were speaking to them until immediately before they began to demonstrate expressive language skills. These deaf children showed a pattern, therefore, of delayed development of both visual attention and language.

Considering a different level of visual attention skill, Quittner and her colleagues (1994) reported an apparent deficit in *selective* attention to visual stimuli by deaf children compared with hearing children between 6 and 13 years of age. In addition, because a group of the oldest deaf children showed an acceleration in selective attention after receiving cochlear implants, these researchers proposed that audition plays an important role in its development.

Other investigators have indicated that deaf children's reliance on vision to monitor the environment for safety as well as communication will inevitably result in differences in development compared to hearing children. For example, Smith, Quittner, Osberger, and Miyamoto (1998) reinterpreted the Quittner et al. (1994) data by suggesting that deaf children's visual attention skills are selectively shaped by their need to monitor their environment visually, a requirement that can decrease the emphasis on selective attention to the discrete stimuli used in their investigation. Similarly, Swisher (1993) reported that deaf children ages 8 through 18 are able to identify signs that are presented well out in their peripheral visual fields. Swisher (1992) also found that some deaf children under the age of 3 years spontaneously responded to or shadowed signs seen in the near periphery in a natural communication situation. These observations suggest increased attention to signals in the peripheral visual field and illustrate a behavioral analog to reports by Neville and Lawson (1987) of electrophysiological evidence of increased attention to stimuli in the peripheral visual field by deaf compared to hearing adults.

An additional functional difference in patterns of visual attention for deaf and hearing conversational dyads is that in signed conversations, unlike spoken ones, visual attention to the person communicating is obligatory (Baker, 1977). Thus, a pattern of sustained visual attention to a signer is typical for older deaf children and adults. A pattern of such extended gaze during conversation would seem to run counter to the trend observed for hearing children, for whom the length of visual fixations decreases from infancy to the toddler years (Colombo, Mitchell, Coldren, & Freeseman, 1991).

Observations of small numbers of deaf children who have signing deaf parents, however, have failed to provide evidence of any delay or difference in visual attention development during the first few years of life. Observations of small numbers of these children have indicated that, by the age of 18 to 20 months, they make spontaneous shifts in visual attention to gaze at their mothers even while engaged in other activities (Woll & Kyle, 1989; Harris, 1992, 2001). These observations suggest that the deaf children's development of attention may progress at a rate similar to that of hearing children. If this is so, it indicates that Coordinated Joint Attention may be supported by a specific set of nonauditory attention-getting and directing strategies that deaf mothers are reported to use. These strategies include such behaviors as extended waiting for children's visual attention before communicating with them, moving the location in which signing occurs to accommodate the preexisting visual focus of the children, and tapping on children's bodies to direct their attention away from an object and back toward the mother (Maestas y Moores, 1980; Kantor, 1982; Harris et al., 1989; Spencer, Bodner-Johnson, & Gutfreund, 1992; Erting, Prezioso, & Hynes, 1990/1994; Mohay, 2000). These observations suggest that, when mothers use adaptive tactile and visual attention-related signals, deaf children's early development of visual attention proceeds as for hearing children.

Questions remain, therefore, about the early course of development of visual attention by deaf children and the degree to which it matches or diverges from that of hearing children. Because of the association between auditory and visual attention for hearing children, and because of deaf children's increased need to use vision for communication and for monitoring the environment, it might be expected that the two groups would show some differences in visual attention development. Conversely, given the importance of coordinated visual attention for language development (especially the pattern of switching gaze between object and person), it is reasonable to expect that this ability would be a priority for early development regardless of available communicative modalities.

Issues related to similarities or differences in development of visual attention in deaf and hearing infants and toddlers are addressed in this chapter. First, patterns of visual attention are compared at 9, 12, and 18 months of age in order to identify any differences in development that can be attributed to hearing status. Second, mothers' attention-related strategies are compared across groups, and associations between mothers' behaviors and children's development of visual attention are explored. Both of these analyses are of special importance because they include larger groups of children than previous studies, and because they include the four groups of mother–infant hearing-status dyads. Finally, we provide a closer look at the variability of attention strategies among deaf mothers with deaf children, and we discuss implications of those variations for children's visual attention and communication.

Analysis I. Visual Attention Development: Effects of Child and Mother Hearing Status

The purpose of the first analysis was to look for evidence of specialization and, alternatively, of common maturational effects on infant visual attention patterns related to hearing status and communication experiences. This analysis included all four of the groups participating in the longitudinal study.[1] Data were available for a total of seventy-seven dyads: nineteen deaf infants with deaf mothers (Dd), eighteen deaf infants with hearing mothers (Hd), nineteen hearing infants with deaf mothers (Dh), and twenty-one hearing infants with hearing mothers (Hh). (This included all dyads for whom data were available through the 18-month session at the time coding was performed.) Ten minutes of the free play sessions at 9, 12, and 18 months were coded for visual attention, based on a coding system that was developed initially for hearing infants by Bakeman and Adamson (1984) and pilot-tested for use with deaf infants by Spencer and Kelly (1993).[2]

Coding. Bakeman and Adamson (1984) conceived of attention as a series of states with a significant duration rather than as fleeting events. Accordingly, although each second of time received an attention-state code, a change in attention state was coded only when a new state endured for at least 3 seconds and was considered to be "established." The six attention states identified by Bakeman and Adamson are defined below. These states make up a mutually exclusive and exhaustive coding system that generally reflects a developmental progression. This is most evident in the two most complex states, namely *supported* and *coordinated joint attention*. The former is common at about 12 months of age, with the latter becoming increasingly evident after about 15 months of age. Categories of attention that were coded include:

- *Unengaged* (no clear attention focus).
- *Onlooking*. The infant watches mother's actions but does not actively engage with her.
- *Persons*. Infant and mother are actively engaged with each other, but no object is involved.
- *Object*. The infant is engaged with and attending to an object only.
- *Supported Joint*. Infant and mother are engaged with and focused on the same object, but the infant does not demonstrate any active attention to mother or her communications. (This state was originally called "passive joint" but was reconceptualized as "supported joint" by Prezbindowski, Adamson, and Lederberg, 1998.)

- *Coordinated Joint*. The infant and mother are actively engaged with each other as well as with an object. The infant shows interest in mother and her activities by switching visual attention between object and mother at least twice during the episode, by participating in an organized period of turn-taking with mother in actions or communications related to the object, or by actively responding (communicatively, or by modifying behaviors related to an object) to at least two communications from mother during the episode.

Second-by-second agreement on coding was calculated for thirty-seven of the play sessions (approximately 15% of the time on tape). Simple percentage of agreement between codes assigned by two coders ranged from 76% to 100% (mean = 88%). Cohen's kappa for agreement on individual tapes ranged from .61 to 1.00 (mean .80).[3]

Predictions. If infant hearing status has a unique effect on the development of visual attention, the two groups with deaf infants (Hd, Dd) should have similar amounts of time in the six attention states over time, and their pattern should differ from that of the groups with hearing infants (Hh, Dh). In contrast, to the extent that modality of communication experiences influences development of visual attention patterns, similarities should be found for groups based upon mothers' habitual communication system, with children of mothers who sign frequently (Dd, Dh) differing from those whose mothers tend to rely on vocal communication (Hh, Hd). Finally, to the extent that development of visual attention during infancy is primarily a maturational process, with biologically regulated "unfolding" of a developmental progression, the groups of children should not differ.

Analysis. Differences in time in the various states of attention were investigated using MANOVA for repeated measures, with time in the various attention states as dependent variables, dyadic hearing status as a between-subject variable, and age as a repeated within-subject variable. Univariate ANOVA and Duncan's post hoc multiple comparison tests were used to identify sources of significant MANOVA effects. Trend analysis was performed to describe changes in time in each attention state across the three ages.

Results. The MANOVA indicated differences in time spent in the attention states across groups [$F(9,219) = 3.214$; $p = .001$] and across ages [$F(2,72) = 44.281$; $p < .0001$]. There was no significant group by age interaction. These results indicate that, although the means for absolute times differ across groups for several of the attention states, the general trend, or developmental trajectory, is similar across groups. (This can be seen in Fig. 11-1.)

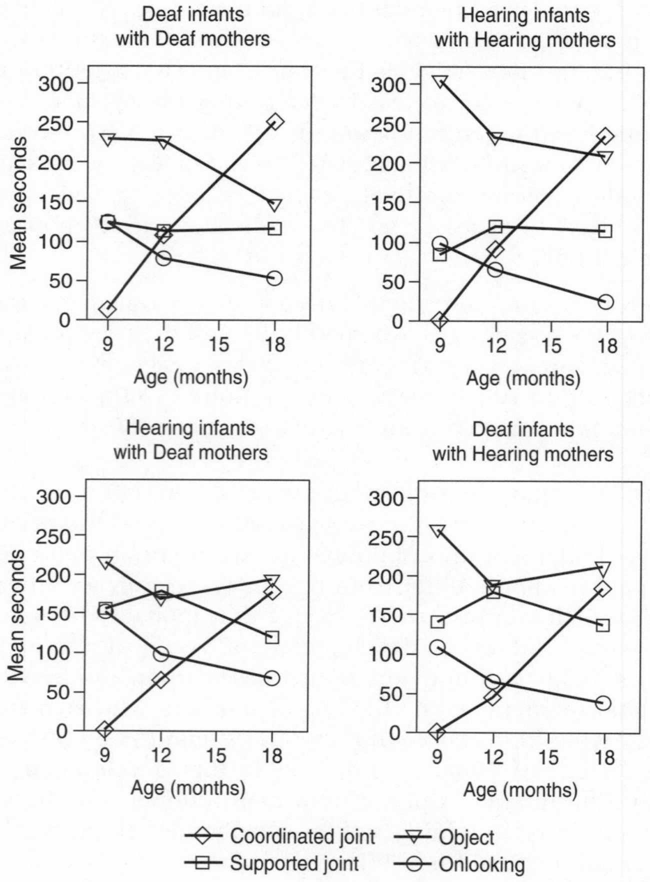

Figure 11-1. Group patterns of development of four states of visual attention at 9, 12, and 18 months.

The states of Unengaged and Persons attention were omitted from the figures and from follow-up analyses because of large within-group differences for the former state and a very small amount of time coded for the latter state. Overall, time in Onlooking decreased over time. This was also true for time attending solely to Objects, although the trend was less evident in the two groups in which infant and mother hearing status differed (Hd, Dh) than for the two in which infant and mother had the same hearing status (Hh, Dd). Time in Supported Joint Attention showed a quadratic trend, with time generally increasing from 9 to 12 months and then tending to decrease at 18 months. However, this trend was more evident in the groups with unmatched infant–mother hearing status. In contrast, all four groups showed a strong linear increase in time in Coordinated Joint Attention across the three ages.

Despite the similarities in trends over time, the groups differed significantly in mean time in three states: Onlooking (with both groups of children with deaf mothers [Dd and Dh] spending longer times than Hh children, and Dh children Onlooking longer than Hd children); Object Attend (with Hh children attending to objects for longer times than either group of children with deaf mothers); Coordinated Joint Attention (with Dd children having more time in this state than Hd or Dh children). One implication of these results is that factors in addition to infant hearing status were operating. Regardless of infant hearing status, those whose mothers often used sign language (and therefore provided frequent visual communications) looked at them for longer periods than did infants whose mothers were hearing and were less likely to present communications visually. Infants who were hearing and whose mothers' communications were usually oral (group Hh) were more likely than any of the other infants to maintain a focus on objects. These patterns for Onlooking and Object Attend states seem to be adaptive and responsive to the communicative conditions the infants typically experience. They also provide early evidence for some of the group differences in patterns of visual attention that have been reported for older deaf children, with children exposed primarily to visual communication (Dd and Dh) spending more time watching their mothers even at this early age.

The pattern of results for the Coordinated Joint Attention state was also complex. None of the other groups differed significantly from the hearing infants with hearing parents, who had the second highest mean time in this state. However, the deaf children with deaf mothers (who had the highest mean time in Coordinated Joint Attention at every age) differed significantly from children in the two groups in which infant and mother hearing status differed (Hd and Dh). A further analysis found the *frequency* of episodes of Coordinated Joint Attention to be similar across the four groups (ranging from 5.4 to 6.4 episodes in 10 minutes), but the mean *duration* of episodes was longer for the two groups with matched infant–mother hearing status (Hh = 48 seconds; Dd = 41 seconds) than the groups in which mother and infant hearing status was different (Hd = 34 seconds; Dh = 30 seconds). Thus, there were some indications of differences developing between the two groups of deaf children, Dd and Hd, and also between the two groups with signing mothers (Dd and Dh).

In an attempt to explain these complex differences among the groups of children, additional analyses focused in more detail on the communicative behaviors of the mothers in the four groups, especially their use of specific strategies for establishing shared visual attention. In addition to considering how differences in mothers' behaviors might relate to the differences in Coordinated Joint Attention between the two groups of deaf children (Dd, Hd), mothers' behaviors could also shed light on the unexpected finding that the hearing children whose mothers were deaf (Dh) also showed less time in Coordinated Joint Attention than the Dd children.

Analysis II. Mothers' Support for Joint Attention with Deaf and Hearing Infants

Various researchers have noted that deaf mothers use special communicative strategies to accommodate young deaf children's needs for visual attention to communication as well as exploration of objects and the environment. For example, deaf mothers have been reported to make frequent contact with their infants by signing on their bodies and by tapping or rubbing gently on the infants' arms, legs, or torsos to attract their attention (Maestas y Moores, 1980). In addition, deaf mothers have been reported to use especially strong and positive facial expressions (Meadow-Orlans et al., 1987b; Reilly & Bellugi, 1996), a characteristic that has been suggested to reinforce infants' gaze to mothers.

Special modifications have also been noted in the signed language produced by deaf mothers interacting with their young children. Signs are often produced with a slowed and highly rhythmic movement, and signs are often repeated a number of times. Relatively few signed utterances are produced compared to the number of spoken utterances expected from hearing mothers in the same length of time (Launer, 1982; Harris, Clibbens, Chasin, & Tibbits, 1989; Masataka, 1992; Erting, Prezioso, & Hynes, 1990/1994; Spencer & Lederberg, 1997). In addition, several researchers (Harris et al., 1989; Swisher, 1992; Prendergast & McCollum, 1996) reported that deaf mothers frequently move their hands and bodies to sign directly in children's line of sight or in their peripheral visual field in order to avoid the need to redirect their children's visual attention.

Koester (1992) provided a potential explanation for these modifications by comparing them to the intuitive modifications evident in the "motherese" (talk directed toward infants) of hearing mothers (Papoušek & Papoušek, 1987; see also Chapters 1 and 4, this volume). Because intuitive behaviors such as these are sensitive to differences in infants' reactions to them, they can be expected to change as infants mature and their responses reflect emerging abilities. However, it is possible that mothers' attention-related communicative strategies are also influenced by their own communicative experiences and not solely by responses produced by their infants. To the extent that this is the case, the choice and timing of a strategy would probably appear to be more appropriate and responsive when mother and child hearing status was the same.

Given the low incidence of deaf children with deaf parents, the observations of mothers' communicative modifications summarized above have been based on small numbers of dyads. Information about variations based on the combination of mother and infant hearing status, developmentally related changes in the modifications employed, or within-group variations in mothers' attention-related behaviors was not available before the analyses reported here were completed.

Participants. Use of the strategies discussed above by the four groups of mothers was investigated. Groups were compared on the frequency of production of each strategy during a play interaction and on changes over time in frequency of use of the strategies. These analyses were based on the same videotaped free play sessions as in the visual attention analysis presented above. Again, all dyads who had completed the entire series of visits by the time analyses began were included in these analyses. This resulted in complete data for nineteen Dd, nineteen Hd, eighteen Dh, and twenty-one Hh dyads at 9, 12, and 18 months.

Coding. Using information available from studies summarized above, plus information from preliminary viewing of the tapes, the following maternal behaviors were coded for each dyad:

- production of signs or gestures in the normal adult signing space;
- production of signs or gestures showing modification in location (on infant's body or in preexisting line of vision) to accommodate infant's attention;
- production of specific visual or tactile signals apparently designed to redirect infants' visual attention, including:
  —presentation of object (moving, shaking, manipulating object to direct attention to it);
  —tapping on or pointing to object;
  —tapping on infant's body to direct attention to mother;
  —waving hand in infant's line of vision; and
  —tapping on the floor.

Combinations of the above codes were made to provide additional measures of *(1)* the frequency of time segments containing signing or gesturing without overt attention accommodation or redirection and *(2)* the frequency of time segments in which an attention redirection signal occurred but was not followed by signing or gesturing. All coding was based on 15-second time samples. That is, the presence or absence of each strategy was noted for each 15-second segment across the 10 minutes of interaction that was coded. Behaviors were coded only once during a time segment, regardless of their frequency of occurrence within the time segment.

Approximately 20% of the tapes were coded independently by two coders. Simple percent of agreement was above 90% for all codes. Cohen's kappas ranged from .82 to .96. Intercoder reliability was, therefore, quite high.

Results. As expected, initial analyses showed that the frequency of signing and gesturing differed across the four groups of mothers [$F(3,73) = 71.60$; $p < .001$]. (This analysis included both signs produced in adult form and those modified to occur where infants were already looking.) Mothers in the groups with at least one deaf member (Dd, Dh, Hd) produced signs or gestures in more time segments at each age than did the hearing mothers of hearing infants. Furthermore, sign/gesture production was greater for the two groups in which mothers were deaf (Dd, Dh) than in the group in which mothers were hearing and infants deaf (Hd) (see Table 11-1).

An additional effect for the frequency of signs or gestures was found for infant age [$F(2,72) = 19.67$; $p < .001$], but this was complicated by a significant group-by-age interaction [$F(6,146) = 2.89$; $p = .01$]. There was a trend across the three groups with a deaf member (Dd, Dh, Hd) for more frequent signing or gesturing as the child's age increased. This was not the case for the Hh group, however, as the initially low frequency of maternal gesturing increased slightly at 12 months but then decreased again by 18 months.

Modification in location or production of signs or gestures to match the infants' line of gaze was compared only across the three groups with a deaf member because of the low rate of gesture production in the Hh group. Because mothers in the Hd group produced significantly fewer total signs and gestures than did the deaf mothers (Dd, Dh), the groups were compared using proportions (segments with a modified location sign or gesture/total segments with signs or gestures). No between-group differences were found based on the proportion of gestures/signs that were produced in locations modified to accommodate infants' attention focus. That is, hearing mothers of deaf infants, when they produced a sign or gesture, were as likely to modify its location as were deaf mothers. Furthermore, all three groups of mothers were found to decrease the proportion of signs and gestures with modified location as the children matured and presumably became better able to switch visual attention between objects and mothers' communications [$F(2,44) = 14.60$; $p <$

Table 11-1. Maternal signs and/or conventional gestures for hearing-status groups at three ages (means and SD)

	Frequency of 15-second time segments containing signs/gestures		
Group	*9 Months*	*12 Months*	*18 Months*
Deaf mothers/deaf infants (n = 19)	20.5 (8.0)	27.0 (6.7)	29.4 (4.6)
Hearing mothers/deaf infants (n = 19)	8.6 (7.8)	9.5 (7.8)	12.4 (10.5)
Deaf mothers/hearing infants (n = 18)	15.6 (7.2)	21.6 (9.0)	24.1 (8.4)
Hearing mothers/hearing infants (n = 21)	1.5 (2.5)	2.9 (3.7)	2.1 (3.3)

Frequencies are number of time segments containing one or more signs or gestures from total of forty time segments.

.001]. This result is consistent with a report from Harris (2001) that neither deaf nor hearing mothers of 18-month-old deaf children tended to displace their signs, preferring instead to sign in the usual space. The MANOVA with the five types of attention redirecting signals as dependent variables, hearing status group as the between-subject variable, and infant age as a within-subject (repeated measure) variable indicated a significant interaction among group, type of attention-redirecting signal, and infant age. Follow-up ANOVA identified the source of the interaction in the frequency with which mothers tapped directly on their children's limbs or bodies to redirect their attention [$F(6,146) = 2.56$; $p = .02$]. At both 9 and 12 months, group Dd had the highest mean frequency of maternal tapping for attention, followed by mothers in group Dh. However, at 18 months, the two groups with deaf mothers were approximately equal in the mean frequency of their tapping signals. The two groups of hearing mothers, even the group with deaf infants, produced significantly fewer of these signals than did the deaf mothers at all three sessions (see Table 11-2).

The maternal attention-redirecting strategy of moving objects to obtain or direct attention occurred frequently in all four groups, but mothers in the two groups with unmatched mother–infant hearing status (Hd, Dh) used the strategy more often than those with matched hearing status [$F(3,73) = 3.27$; $p = .03$]. However, the same trend for significant decreases in this behavior between 9 and 12 and between 12 and 18 months was found across groups [$F(2,72) = 12.01$; $p < .001$].

The strategy of pointing to or tapping directly on objects to redirect attention differed by infant age [$F(2,72) = 5.21$; $p < .01$], with significant increases occurring between 9 and 12 months ($t = -3.07$; $p < .01$). Differences were not significant, however, among the groups.

The strategy of tapping on the floor to redirect attention occurred very rarely during these play sessions. Waving in the infant's visual field occurred somewhat more often, and the two signals were combined for analysis. In fact, the maternal behaviors coded in this combined category consisted almost entirely of waves. The groups differed in the frequency of production of these signals, with Dd mothers most likely to produce them, followed by Dh mothers. In addition, production increased with child age [$F(2,72) = 3.81$; $p = .03$], especially between the 12- and 18-month sessions ($t = 2.57$; $p = .01$). Hearing mothers of deaf children rarely produced these signals, and the majority of them never used the signals.

Again looking at only the three groups with a deaf member (Dd, Dh, Hd), the frequency with which mothers produced one of the redirecting signals but failed to follow up with a gesture or signed language was compared. Significant effects were found for both group [$F(2,53) = 21.46$; $p < .001$] and age [$F(2,52) = 34.09$; $p < .001$]. Although the incidence of this pattern decreased with age for all groups of mothers, Hd mothers were the most likely to signal for attention but then fail to follow up

Table 11-2. Maternal attention-redirecting strategies for hearing status groups at three ages (means and SD)

	Deaf mothers/deaf infants (n = 19)			*Hearing mothers/deaf infants (n = 19)*			*Deaf mothers/hearing infants (n = 18)*			*Hearing mothers/hearing infants (n = 12)*		
Strategy	*9 Months*	*12 Months*	*18 Months*	*9 Months*	*12 Months*	*18 Months*	*9 Months*	*12 Months*	*18 Months*	*9 Months*	*12 Months*	*18 Months*
Present	25.5	23.6	20.7	30.8	23.8	24.6	27.0	26.1	22.2	21.4	21.8	19.1
object	(6.8)	(7.6)	(6.6)	(7.5)	(10.1)	(8.0)	(6.1)	(8.0)	(8.1)	(7.1)	(7.2)	(7.7)
Tap	2.4	5.8	5.7	2.4	3.8	1.9	4.3	4.0	4.7	2.1	3.8	3.7
object	(2.5)	(4.0)	(5.0)	(3.1)	(3.7)	(1.7)	(3.3)	(3.0)	(3.1)	(2.3)	(4.7)	(3.9)
Tap child	8.4	10.7	8.7	1.2	1.6	1.1	4.2	4.8	7.0	0.4	0.3	0.0
	(6.1)	(5.8)	(5.5)	(1.8)	(3.3)	(1.6)	(4.0)	(5.1)	(6.5)	(0.9)	(0.7)	(0.0)
Wave/tap	1.9	1.9	3.4	0.5	0.3	0.4	0.3	1.2	2.1	0.0	0.0	0.1
floor	(3.1)	(2.4)	(3.7)	(1.4)	(0.7)	(1.0)	(0.6)	(1.8)	(2.1)	(0.0)	(0.0)	(0.5)

Frequencies are number of time segments containing each strategy from total of forty segments.

with visual communication. Failure to follow attention signals with communication was next most frequent for mothers in group Dh but happened quite rarely in group Dd, especially at the 18-month session.

Finally, no significant difference was seen among the three groups in the proportion of signed/gestured communications that was produced without either an accommodation (such as moving to sign in the line of sight) or a preceding signal (like tapping on the child). However, the incidence of such "spontaneous" visual communications increased with infant age [$F(2,46) = 11.40$; $p < .01$], especially between 12 and 18 months ($t = 2.89$; $p > .01$). This change probably reflects mothers' reactions to the children's increasing ability to coordinate visual attention between objects and the communication partner. Such shifts of gaze from object to mother would result in more natural communicative turn-taking, making it less necessary for mothers to employ a strategy to establish joint attention before communicating. Again, by 18 months, the children may have become more alert to communication occurring in their peripheral vision, allowing mothers to sign without the need to overtly redirect attention.

This analysis of mothers' strategy use leads to several conclusions. There is evidence that differences in mothers' habitual communication experiences and their primary language modality affect their modifications in attention-related accommodations and redirections. For example, both groups of deaf mothers were more likely to use visual and tactile attention-directing signals than were hearing mothers.

However, mothers' hearing status did not completely dictate their use of such signals. For example, deaf mothers with hearing infants (Dh) were less likely to use these signals than were Dd mothers, especially before their children reached 12 months of age. This may have been due to deaf mothers feeling confused about how to interact with a hearing child who, although expected to learn sign language, is also expected to learn oral language. In addition, being hearing, these children may have presented somewhat different interactive behaviors than deaf children, because the hearing children would be responsive to sounds occurring in the environment. The Dh mothers' initial uncertainty seems to have resolved, however, by the 18-month sessions, when many of the Dh children were producing expressive signs. At this point, the Dh mothers may have felt more comfortable using their own habitual communication system, in part because the children's communication behaviors were now providing a better match with their own.

Hearing mothers with deaf children (Hd) faced a situation in which their habitual communication behaviors were a less-than-perfect match for their children's needs. The mothers were not oblivious to their children's needs for visual input and, indeed, they attempted to accommodate those needs in several ways. First, they used objects frequently in efforts to establish joint or shared attention. Second, when they gestured or signed, they were as likely as deaf mothers to accommodate immature attention patterns by moving into the child's existing focus. However, the Hd mothers did not spontaneously make complete adjustments or accommodations to their child's hearing loss. This is reflected, for example, in their relative lack of meaningful follow-up to signals for redirecting attention. It is also seen in their lack of use of the tapping signal that is so prevalent in deaf mothers' communication. Finally, even when they were learning signed language, Hd mothers produced signs less frequently than did deaf mothers, undoubtedly because of limited fluency.

Mothers' Attention-Related Communications and Children's Development of Visual Attention

If the attention-related strategies employed most frequently by deaf mothers represent intuitive adaptations to interacting with an infant who depends on visual communication, then it could be expected that those strategies would effectively promote or scaffold deaf infants' visual attention. Thus, more mature infant visual attention patterns would be expected in deaf children whose mothers make frequent use of visual communications (signs or gestures) and visual–tactile (waving/tapping on child) signals for obtaining and redirecting attention.

Quantitative analyses including the two groups with deaf infants (Dd, Hd) in fact showed that infant time in Coordinated Joint Attention at 18 months was significantly related to mothers' use of the visual-tactile signals ($r = .54$; $p < .01$) and to the frequency of mothers' gestures/signs ($r = .45$; $p < .01$). At 12 months, associations between Coordinated Joint Attention and these maternal communicative behaviors were also positive and statistically significant. In addition, mothers' use of visual–tactile signals to redirect infant attention at 9 months correlated positively, although nonsignificantly, with the children's time in Coordinated Joint Attention at 18 months. Therefore, substantial associations were found between mothers' attention-related communications and their children's visual attention behaviors. However, these associations (even when statistically significant) showed the mothers' communicative strategies to account for less than 25% of the variance in child attention. Large proportions of the variance in child Coordinated Joint Attention remain unexplained. Other factors must be involved.

Analysis III. The Role of Maternal Sensitivity

Mothers' sensitivity, or general responsiveness, to their infants has been shown to support development in a variety of areas (e.g., Slade, 1987b; Dunham & Dunham, 1992; Baumwell, Tamis-LeMonda, & Bornstein, 1997; Smith, Adamson, & Bakeman, 1998; and see Chapter 12, this volume). Because of the relatively small proportion of variance in infant attention accounted for by mothers' attention-related strategies, associations between ratings of maternal sensitivity and infants' time in the most advanced visual attention state (Coordinated Joint Attention) were explored. This component of mothers' communicative behaviors could provide additional explanation of effects of infants' communicative experiences on their visual attention development.

Participants and Procedures. Data for these analyses were available for eighty dyads across the four hearing status groups: twenty Dd, twenty Dh, nineteen Hd, twenty-one Hh. Ratings of maternal sensitivity were composite scores based on five dimensions of the rating scale described in Chapter 8: *(1)* sensitivity, *(2)* involvement, *(3)* flexibility, *(4)* positive affect, and *(5)* consistency. Each dimension was rated using a Likert-type scale with a range of 1 (most negative) to 5 (most positive). Cohen's kappa computations assessing intercoder reliability were .94 for the 12-month tapes and .81 for the 18-month tapes (see Chapter 8 for a detailed description of coding procedures).

Results. Significant group differences existed in the composite scores for the mothers [$F(3,76) = 3.61$; $p < .05$]. At infant age 12 months, Hh mothers' mean sensitivity rating was significantly higher than that for Hd mothers. At 18 months, Hh mothers' ratings were again significantly higher than those for Hd mothers. In addition, both Hh and Dd groups were rated significantly higher than were Dh mothers, who had the lowest average rating.

Infant time in Coordinated Joint Attention was calculated as explained earlier in this chapter. Because additional dyads were included in Analysis III, group mean times in Coordinated Joint Attention (hereafter CJA) differed slightly. However, Dd infants still had the highest mean time in CJA, significantly longer than that for either Hd or Dh infants [$F(3,73) = 3.35$; $p = .02$].

Correlations between time in CJA and ratings for maternal sensitivity were significant for two of the groups: Dh and Hd. At 18 months, maternal sensitivity predicted 36% of the variance in time in this attention state for group Hd ($r = .62$; $p < .01$) and 31% of the variance for group Hd ($r = .56$; $p < .01$). In contrast, the correlations for the other two groups, although positive, were not statistically significant, predicting approximately 10% of the variance for group Hh ($r = .31$) and 12% of the variance for group Dd ($r = .34$). Maternal sensitivity was, therefore, more closely related to infant visual attention in the two groups in which mother and child hearing status differed.

It will be recalled that mothers' use of visual–tactile attention-redirecting signals was significantly associated with 18-month time in CJA for both groups with deaf children (Dd, Hd). This association remained significant even when maternal sensitivity ratings were statistically controlled ($r = .44$; $p = .02$). A parallel analysis, measuring the relation between maternal sensitivity and CJA when mothers' frequency of redirecting signals was statistically controlled, also resulted in a significant, positive correlation ($r = .39$; $p = .02$).Therefore, mothers' use of specific attention-directed strategies and mothers' general interactive sensitivity contributed independently to deaf infants' time in CJA.

Analysis IV. Individual Differences in Deaf Mothers' Use of Attention-Getting Signals

As we have seen, infants' time in CJA was related to several factors, including the match (or absence of match) between mother and child hearing status. For deaf children, CJA related to the frequency with which mothers used tactile and visual signals to redirect visual attention as well as the degree to which mothers showed sensitivity to the infants' interests and activities.

These associations, based on group averages, indicate central tendencies within the groups. However, it is also the case that there was considerable within-group variability in infants' time in the various attention states and in mothers' production of attention-related strategies. Relying on comparison of group means could obscure important within-group variation. Furthermore, within-group variability could be a natural outcome of mothers' sensitivity to their infants' unique characteristics.

The purpose of a final analysis was to identify and describe in more detail some of the within-group variability. This analysis focused on the group of deaf mothers with deaf children because of their children having the largest mean time in CJA and their heavy reliance on vision for receptive communication. Results of the analysis provide a picture of the range of behaviors used by deaf mothers with deaf children as they fostered communicative turn-taking and shifts in visual attention.

Participants and Procedures. Nine Dd dyads were selected in which infants' time in CJA was above the median. By definition, all these infants showed optimal development of visual attention, and by implication it was assumed that their mothers would be skilled in strategies for fostering this ability. If the patterns of maternal attention-directing strategies were similar among these mothers, it would indicate that frequent use of these strategies could be recommended for other mothers of deaf infants. The analysis centered on mothers' use of the signal of tapping on the child to redirect attention because this signal occurred so frequently for this group, and because it was associated with time in CJA.

Coding. As in other analyses reported in this chapter, data were drawn from the recordings of mother–child play with toys at 9, 12, and 18 months. For comparability with other analyses, 10 minutes of interaction were coded for mothers' use of redirecting signals to gain the children's visual attention. In contrast with Analysis II, where a time-sampling approach was used, every instance of the redirecting strategy was counted. A coded "event " was a tap or multiple taps bounded by a pause. Though long series of taps sometimes occurred, the most common pattern of signaling was a two-beat tap. In each case, one event was coded.

In addition, 15 minutes of each dyad's play interaction were coded to determine the percent of time that each infant responded to attention-getting signals and to provide qualitative descriptions of the dyadic interaction. Infants' responses were coded as:

- child responds after redirecting signal (meaning the child oriented visually to either the mother's face or signing hand, or to an object she was holding);
- no response;
- other.

For three of the taped segments (one each of the 9-, 12-, and 18-month sessions), intrarater reliability for coding of mothers' signals and infants' responses was calculated and found to be 90%, 100%, and 89%.

Results. Even though these dyads were selected from only one group, and the infants were among those showing the highest amounts of CJA, much variability still existed among the mothers in use of the attention-directing tapping signal. The mean frequency of instances of attention getting was approximately fifteen in the 9-month session, seventeen in the 12-month session, and twenty in the 18-month session, but standard deviations approached the mean in the first and last sessions.

What the means obscure is that when the infants were 9 months old, some of the deaf mothers were doing very little tapping (from three to nine taps in 10 minutes by five of the mothers), whereas others were tapping very frequently (twenty and twenty-four taps by two mothers, thirty and thirty-five by two others). In the 18-month session, the number of taps ranged from eight to forty-four, and the two mothers who were tapping the most (thirty-nine and forty-four taps in 10 minutes) had been among those who tapped the least frequently at 9 months (when they tapped their children three and five times, respectively).

It is important to note that children need to learn that a tap is a signal for attention. This insight is neither intuitively obvious nor inborn. For example, if someone taps on the arm of a young infant, the infant often will not respond—or may even look at the place tapped instead of toward the person's face. In other words, making the connection that a tap means "Look up at me" or "Look at what I'm about to show you" is a cognitive achievement. It is not surprising, therefore, that infants often did not respond to taps in the 9-month session: the mean response rate was 23%, with a response rate ranging from 0% to 43%. Furthermore, when the 9-month-old infants looked at their mothers' faces, their glances tended to be fleeting, leaving mothers little time to make a signed comment. However, as the infants matured, responses were more common, with mean response rates of 50% at 12 months and 78% at 18 months.

These differences, as well as differences in the quality of the tapping seen across the sessions, suggest that tapping may have different functions at different points in development. Thus, at one extreme, a tap can be an attempt to get the attention of an infant who has not yet learned to coordinate looking at a person and an object in the same episode and, therefore, has not yet learned the patterns of conversational turn-taking required for visual language. At the other extreme, after the child has learned the role of tapping signals and has learned to alternate attention during a conversation, tapping becomes a conventionalized signal that is part of a well-established communicative routine. Technically it may not even be necessary for getting the infant's attention at this point, because the infant may have learned to recognize the typical rhythm of conversational turn-taking and may be alert to an array of signals, such as the mother leaning forward, raising her hands into the signing space, or beginning to sign. In fact, in the 18-month sessions, the tapping of those mothers who used it frequently is rapid and light, and turn-taking proceeded so quickly that it was difficult to determine a single cue to which the infant was responding.

What explains the variability within this group in the mothers' use of signals? One possibility might be the readiness with which individual infants responded to the signals, thereby shaping the mothers' behavior. However, it was notable that the variability among infants' response rates was much less than their mothers' production rates. In addition, the ratios of the standard deviations to the means for responses dropped steadily over time; that is, performances were becoming more similar over time. Therefore, it is not probable that differences in infant response rates influenced mothers' rate of signaling. Another possible influence on mothers' signaling rate is infant temperament or relative interest in objects and interaction. Maternal sensitivity to such factors could influence both the rate and the insistence with which the tapping signal is used. Yet another possible influence could be a mother's notion of appropriate behavior, and her beliefs about how she can best engage her infant and promote attention and communication. To date, no published study has addressed these possibilities.

Conclusion

These four analyses allow several conclusions about the development of visual attention during infancy. First, the similar trajectories of development of attention states by all four groups of infants indicate significant maturational effects beyond effects of communication experience and hearing status. Second, audition does not seem to play an obligatory role in acquisition of increasingly complex states of visual attention nor in the time engaged in Coordinated Joint Attention (CJA) during the infant–toddler period). This conclusion can be drawn from the fact that the deaf infants with deaf mothers (Dd) consistently had the highest average time in this state at each age, significantly more than Hd children. In addition, the fact that an infant was hearing did not assure high levels of time in CJA, as Dh infants ranked third or fourth among the groups on this measure at each age.

General effects of interactive experience were seen in the pattern of greater time in Onlooking for both groups of children whose mothers used visual language (Dd, Dh), and the greater time in Object Attend by Hh, who had less need to watch their mothers to obtain communicative information. Two other environmental factors were found to relate to the development of CJA. One of these factors was generalized maternal sensitivity or responsiveness to the infant during interaction, although this factor was significant only for children whose hearing status differed from that of their mothers. This may reflect the fact that sensitivity, as represented by a measure of quality of interaction, appeared to be lower in those two groups (Dh, Hd). Perhaps there is a threshold effect, and only significant deviations from typical sensitivity (as shown in the two groups in which mother and child hearing status were matched) have obvious effects on the child's visual attention.

The second factor that related to the infants' development and display of CJA was that of mothers' use of visual or tactile signals (waving in the child's visual field; tapping on the child) to redirect attention to the mother. The general lack of use of these signals by Hd mothers was associated with less time in CJA. It is also possible that the Dh mothers' relatively infrequent use of this signal at 9 and 12 months contributed to their infants' lesser time in CJA. Use of such signals, plus provision of a rich visual language environment, may be a necessary alternative to auditory signals for redirecting attention when an infant is learning a visual rather than an auditory language.

The qualitative analysis of interactive behaviors of Dd mothers suggested, however, that early high rates of use of these visual–tactile signals is not necessarily required for rapid development of this complex attention state when other aspects of the mothers' interactive behaviors are sensitive to the infants' reactions as well as to general demands of a visual language. The delays or disruptions in attention development that have been reported in earlier studies of somewhat older deaf children (e.g., Wood, 1989; Quittner et al., 1994) seem to be avoidable. However, appropriate rates of development may require exposure to a visually rich language model as well as experience in early interactions with persons sensitive to the demands of visual communication.

Acknowledgments

Data summarized in this chapter have been previously described in the following reports:

Meadow-Orlans, K., & Spencer, P. (1996). Maternal sensitivity and the visual attentiveness of children who are deaf. *Early Development and Parenting, 5,* 213–223.

Spencer, P. (2000). Looking without listening: Is audition a prerequisite for normal development of visual attention during infancy? *Journal of Deaf Studies and Deaf Education, 5*(4), 291–302.

Swisher, M. V. (2000). Learning to converse: How deaf mothers support the development of attention and conversational skills in their young deaf children. In, P. E. Spencer, C. J. Erting, & M. Marschark (Eds.), *The deaf child in the family and at school: Essays in honor of Kathryn P. Meadow-Orlans* (pp. 21–39). Mahwah, NJ: Erlbaum.

Waxman, R. P., & Spencer, P. E. (1997). What mothers do to support infant visual attention: Sensitivities to age and hearing status. *Journal of Deaf Studies and Deaf Education, 2,* 104–114.

Notes

1. Because the analyses reported in this chapter were performed at different times during the longitudinal study, slightly different numbers of participants are reported across the analyses discussed.

2. We greatly appreciate the assistance of Lauren Adamson, Georgia State University, in evaluating the appropriateness of the Bakeman and Adamson (1984) coding system for use with deaf infants and for training members of the Gallaudet research staff to use the system.

3. Many thanks to Devin Smith and Martha Bowles for their dedicated and very competent work coding infants' attention state.

12

The Development of Play

Effects of Hearing Status, Language, and Maternal Responsiveness

Patricia E. Spencer and Kathryn P. Meadow-Orlans

Children explore, investigate, manipulate, and play with objects from the earliest weeks and months of life. Numerous researchers have systematically observed the play behaviors of hearing infants and toddlers in order to understand and document developmental processes. Because it implies the absence of any externally supplied "agenda" and allows a child to follow his or her interests, play provides an especially powerful context for developing and practicing cognitive abilities (Piaget, 1952, 1962; Chance, 1979). In addition, because regularities have been identified in hearing children's play development over the first years of life, play behaviors also provide a "window" into cognitive development and skills of individuals or groups of children (Rubin, Fein, & Vandenburg, 1983; McCune, DiPane, Fireoved, & Fleck, 1994; Spencer & Hafer, 1998), thus providing a means for developmental assessment.

During the first 3 years of life, children's play typically advances from simple sensorimotor manipulation of objects, to the use of realistic objects in pretense or representational play, to incorporation in play of highly symbolic activities such as preplanning and intentional substitution of one object for another (Piaget, 1952; McCall, 1974; Lowe, 1975; Fenson & Ramsay, 1980; Belsky & Most, 1981; McCune-Nicolich, 1981; McCune, 1995). For typical hearing children, these advances are associated with advances in another symbolic ability—language. For example, the expression of single words emerges around 13 months of age, about the time that simple representational play with realistic objects is observed. The expression of word combinations in simple proto-sentences co-occurs with production of sequenced play later in the second year of life (Bates et al., 1980; McCune-Nicolich, 1981; Kelly & Dale, 1989; Ogura, 1991; Mayer & Musatti, 1992; McCune, 1995).

However, the relation between language and play skills does not always conform to this pattern, and more complex associations have been suggested. For example, some researchers have found that the play of year-old hearing children is related more strongly to their receptive language skills than to their expressive skills (Shore, O'Connell, & Bates, 1984; Vibbert & Bornstein, 1989). Additionally, Tamis-LeMonda and Bornstein (1994) found early play was related to the range of semantic cases (cognitive relations) children expressed linguistically, but not to the length, and therefore the syntactic complexity, of their utterances.

The picture is even more complicated when factors other than language are considered. A relatively large body of research indicates that the social history and experiences of hearing infants and young children are associated with or predict play behaviors. For example, Slade (1987a, 1987b) found that both the quality of mother–child attachment and the quality of mothers' contributions during play were related to the child's level of play. Others have reported that children's play was enhanced when a mother or other caregiver expanded on a child's play initiations (Vygotsky, 1978; O'Connell & Bretherton, 1984) or became otherwise engaged in the play (Slade, 1987a). Fiese (1990) commented that a mother's "willingness to allow the toddler self-direction within a context of turntaking and reciprocity" (p. 1654) was associated with higher levels of play. In contrast, Fiese noted that intrusive, nonresponsive behaviors from mothers actually lowered the level of play. Therefore, the play behaviors shown by a child at a specific point in time are influenced by the immediate social context as well as by more pervasive factors such as the child's history of interactive experiences and, perhaps, the child's language skills.

Compared to hearing children, deaf children often experience less satisfying social interactions, and dyads of deaf children and hearing mothers are frequently reported to demonstrate lower levels of maternal responsiveness or sensitivity (see Chapter 8). These children also typically show significant delays in language development (Chapter 10). Deaf children, regardless of parents' hearing status, rely more heavily on visual communication than is typical for hearing children. Given all these differences, it might be expected that deaf children's play will also differ from that of hearing children. Research about the play of deaf children younger than 3 years is rare, however, so characteristics of their play are yet to be described in detail. Such information would be useful for professionals and parents of deaf children, who are often encouraged to use play as a context for intervention activities (e.g., Hafer & Topolosky, 1995; Spencer & Hafer, 1998). Information about the development of play by deaf children can also illuminate the effects of sensory, linguistic, and interactive factors on the play of all children (including those who are hearing) during the early years.

Play of Deaf Toddlers and Young Children

Most published studies of deaf children's play have included participants who were at least 3 years old. In most cases, these children were reported to experience significant delays in language development and to have hearing parents, although some researchers have failed to provide such information. Many investigators have reported that the deaf children in their samples showed delays in cognitive aspects of their play (e.g., Singer & Lenahan, 1976; Darbyshire, 1977; Vygotsky, 1978; Gatty, 1990). That is, the children produced fewer object substitutions and less "make-believe" play than is typical for hearing children of the same age. Others have reported delays in social aspects of play, with deaf children tending to engage in more solitary play than is typical for hearing children of the same age (Higginbotham & Baker, 1981; Mann, 1985). Some researchers specifically addressed the relation between play and language skills of preschool-age deaf subjects, and they concluded that children with the most delayed language produced less imaginary, substitutional, sequenced, or preplanned play than did those with relatively advanced language skills (Vygotsky, 1978; Casby & McCormack, 1985; Schirmer, 1989; Selmi & Rueda, 1998; Brown, Prescott, Rickards, & Patterson, 1997). Because the nonverbal cognitive development of most deaf children proceeds at a rate similar to that of typical hearing children, these results suggest that language skills are closely tied to some aspects of play during the preschool years.

Gregory and Mogford (1983) reported on the play of a small group of younger deaf children who were observed at home at ages 15, 18, 24, and 30 months. All of the children were reported to have delays in language development. Gregory and Mogford found that these children were much like hearing peers in production of simple representational play using realistic toy objects—for example, pretending to eat using a toy spoon. However, the deaf toddlers were less likely than their hearing peers to engage in truly imaginary play with objects, to give evidence of planning play behaviors before they were produced, or to coordinate multiple objects in a play episode. These researchers concluded that even in children as young as 2 years, language skills play an important role by allowing children to benefit from verbal suggestions and prompts from their mothers during play; children with delayed language development are less likely than those with more advanced language to benefit from these kinds of maternal communications. In addition, Gregory and Mogford suggested that language skills support children's ability to plan sequences of play behaviors and that lack of language skills interferes with such planning.

Similar results were reported by Brown, Rickards, and Bortoli (2001), who compared the play of a group of ten deaf children with that of ten hearing children. The deaf children were in oral programming, had hearing parents, and had significantly delayed language. With data averaged over observations at 28, 29, and 30 months of age, the deaf children's play was delayed compared to that of the hearing children across a number of measures. In addition, the level of pretend-play demonstrated by the deaf children was significantly related to their expressive vocabulary, again suggesting a link between play and language skills. Yoshinaga-Itano and her colleagues (Snyder & Yoshinaga-Itano, 1998; Yoshinaga-Itano, Snyder, & Day, 1998) also reported a significant association between language skills and play behaviors of a large group of deaf children between the ages of 8 and 36 months.

In contrast with findings of most researchers, Bornstein and his colleagues (1999), found no significant difference in the amount of pretend-play or the highest level of play demonstrated by 2-year-old deaf children (with hearing or deaf parents) and hearing children with hearing parents.[1] However, as Brown, Rickards, and Bortoli (2001) noted, this lack of observed difference could reflect ceiling effects, because Bornstein and colleagues (1999) did not consider more symbolically advanced aspects of play (such as planning, substitutions, and ordered sequences) separately from play at the simple representational level. But, in agreement with many other studies, Bornstein's research team found that pretend-play was associated with language skills for the group of deaf children with hearing parents.

In a study that served as a pilot for the one reported here, Spencer and her colleagues also analyzed aspects of the play of 2-year-old deaf and hearing children (Spencer, Deyo, & Grindstaff, 1990, 1991; Spencer & Deyo, 1993; Spencer, 1996).[2] This study included ten children, ages 24 to 28 months, in each of three groups: deaf children with hearing parents (Hd), deaf children with deaf parents (Dd), and hearing children with hearing parents (Hh). The children were videotaped during 30 minutes of play with their mothers, using a standard set of toys. In addition to analysis of amount and level of pretend play, children's expressive language and aspects of mothers' interactive behaviors were assessed and compared across groups. Based on a coding system developed by McCune-Nicolich (1983),[3] a distinction was made between pretend-play at the simple representational level and that at more complex levels. The complex, or symbolic, level included (verbal or nonverbal) preplanned play, object substitutions, and canonical sequences (sequences of thematically related play behaviors that were produced in realistic or logical order).

Only one significant difference was found when the various play measures were compared across hearing status groups: the total duration, but not the frequency, of pretend play (with time in simple representational play and more complex symbolic play combined) was longer for the group of deaf children with deaf parents than for the other two groups. This difference may have reflected the generally slower turn-taking communication style in the dyads of deaf mothers and children, as the children divided their attention sequentially between objects and communications during a play episode (see Chapter 11). This is similar to Gregory and Mogford's (1983) suggestion that deaf children's developmental patterns might be influenced in subtle ways by their greater dependence on visual information compared to hearing children.

However, more differences were evident when play performance was analyzed across groups defined by language levels instead of hearing status, with hearing status disregarded. Language level was significantly associated with performance on the more complex symbolic play measures. Children with the highest-level expressive language (expressive lexicons of 200 or more words or signs and frequent production of multiword or sign utterances) produced a greater frequency of symbolic, or abstract, play (primarily play that showed preplanning) than did children in the other two language groups. Both the highest language group and the middle language group (with lexicons of fifty or more words or signs and occasional multiword or sign utterances) surpassed the lowest language group on frequency and duration of canonically sequenced play. (The order in which component actions are produced is critical in canonical sequences, and that order must represent a logical or "real life" progression.) These language–play relations could be identified, in part, because language levels of participants in this study were not uniformly associated with their hearing status. That is, although the highest language group was comprised of children from groups Hh and Dd only, approximately half of the Hd children in this study performed in the middle language group, along with children from both of the other groups. Only about half of the Hd children in this study demonstrated significant language delays at the assessed ages.

Another measure obtained across groups in this study was the frequency of play behaviors that were prompted or initiated by the mothers. No differences were found across hearing status or language groups on this measure. However, in a less formal qualitative analysis, Spencer and Deyo (1993) noted that the children of mothers who were fully engaged in and enjoyed dyadic play showed higher play levels. Based on these and other findings, a longitudinal study was planned to investigate more formally the potential effects of differences in the quality of mothers' interactive behaviors during play with their deaf children. The new play study was designed to assess associations between language skills and symbolic play behaviors as well as differences related to hearing status and language modality. It would focus on younger children, covering the important period during which both simple representational and higher-level symbolic play are expected to emerge.

Play, Hearing Status, Language, and Maternal Responsiveness

The Gallaudet Infancy Study (GIS) provided an opportunity for longitudinal investigation of the development of play, and factors associated with its development, in deaf infants and young toddlers.[4] This study began with infants at 9 months of age, before representational and symbolic play typically develop. Therefore, patterns of development of these more advanced play abilities could be observed as they emerged from a base of presymbolic level play. Because language abilities also often emerge during this age range, early relations between the two skills could be observed. Because children were observed in dyadic play with their mothers, mothers' contributions to play at different stages could also be also investigated.

Based upon previous research, we hypothesized that *(1)* deaf and hearing children's play at 9 and 12 months would be similar, but differences would be found in at least a subset of the deaf children by 18 months of age, when language becomes a more important component of the interactive context; *(2)* the level of play at 18 months would be strongly associated with toddlers' use of expressive language (regardless of modality), with higher language levels associating with higher play levels regardless of child hearing status; and *(3)* maternal interaction characteristics, especially those characterized as "sensitive" or "responsive," would be associated with children's play levels regardless of child hearing status.

Participants

Three groups of dyads were included in the play analyses: Dd, Hh, Hd.[5] Although the population of deaf children with deaf parents is much smaller than that of the other two groups, it was planned to include equal numbers of dyads in each group. When data collection began, there were only fifteen dyads available from group Dd, so fifteen dyads were selected randomly from the twenty or twenty-one available in each of the other two groups. Subsequently, two of the Dd dyads missed appointments and were deleted from the analyses, leaving thirteen dyads in that group for whom complete data were available. There were seven girls and eight boys in both Hh and Hd groups; group Dd included seven girls and six boys. These dyads' scores on the Alpern-Boll Physical and Self-Help scales (Alpern, Boll, & Shearer, 1980), their mothers' education levels, and their families' ethnic backgrounds were consistent with those of the larger groups participating in the study (see Chapter 3).

Families in group Dd reported that they used American Sign Language (ASL) at home. In group Hd, nine families were in early intervention programs using "simultaneous" or "total" communication (speech plus signs) and six were in programs using oral language only. Spoken English was the home language for all families in which parents were hearing.

Procedures

Longitudinal play data were obtained from the videotaped free play situation that is described in Chapter 3. A standard set of toys, selected to allow prerepresentational as well as representational–symbolic play, was provided for mother and child (see Table 12-1). The play sessions lasted 15 minutes at 9 and 12 months and 20 minutes at 18 months. Ten minutes from each session were analyzed for child play and language at each age. Ratings of maternal interaction characteristics, based on the entire time in the play sessions, were available for 12 and 18 months.

Coding Play Behaviors. The coding system for children's play behaviors was modified from those developed by McCune-Nicolich (1983), Belsky and Most (1981), and Fenson and Ramsay (1980). The resulting exhaustive and mutually exclusive coding system was detailed, and included prerepresentational, representational, and symbolic play levels. Care was taken to assure that all play levels could be identified without depending upon child language. The coding system included:

- No play
- Manipulation of single objects
  —Mouthing
  —Simple manipulation/examining
  —Differentiated manipulation/exploration
  —Complex manipulation—actions appropriate for specific object; part–whole relations
- Relational play with two or more objects
  —Simple, nonfunctional relational
  —Functional-relational based on visual or physical characteristics of objects
  —Complex-relational/construction (e.g., building, making designs)
- Representational play showing knowledge of object/identity or function
  —Inaccurate representations (object is apparently mistaken for another)
  —Emerging self-oriented representation (enactive naming, recognitory gestures or somewhat inaccurately produced actions typically performed in real life by child)

Table 12-1. Toys provided for play sessions

Shape and stir pot with lid	Tongue depressor
Blocks with wagon	Seashell
Toolbox with tools	Comb and brush
Tea set: *2 saucers, 2 cups, teapot, 3 bowls, 2 spoons, drinking glass*	Hand mirror
Baby doll with blanket	Sunglasses
Baby bottles for doll	Sponge
Telephone	3-wheeled car with bear
Adult male and female dolls	Pop beads
	Cloth monkey
	Book (at 18 months only)

—Emerging decentered representation (brief or inaccurately performed actions directed toward other person or doll and/or typically performed by other person, not by child)
—Established self-oriented representation (actions as in emerging self-oriented category but produced accurately and with clear evidence of pretend)
—Established decentered representation (actions as in emerging decentered category but produced accurately and with clear evidence of pretend)

- Sequenced representational play (combinations or sequences of thematically related representational actions)
—Same action repeated in different locations
—Same action repeated with different participants
—Different self-oriented actions
—Different decentered actions
—Book-handling actions (18 months only)
- Symbolic play (with evidence of mental transformations or symbolic activity)
—Ordered self-oriented sequences (canonical sequences)
—Ordered decentered sequences (canonical sequences)
—Nonverbally planned actions
—Verbally announced planned actions
—Nonverbally announced object substitutions
—Verbally announced object substitutions
—Attributional play (attributing feelings, agency to inanimate object or assigning "role" to self or other).

Both frequency and duration of play acts were recorded. Each second of time was given a code. Manipulative play was coded if it lasted for 2 seconds or longer. Relational play episodes were considered to continue through interruptions as long as 5 seconds if during the interruption the infant was attending to a communication from mother or manipulating an object to ready it for continued play. Following Slade (1987a, 1987b), representational play was coded as beginning at the time the child picked up an object if play began within 5 seconds. Once it began, representational play was coded until the child clearly redirected attention to another activity or stopped representational play for 10 seconds. Coding of symbolic play began when the child first gave clear indication of a canonically ordered, planned, or substitution episode. That is, the time coded for symbolic play included the "planning" as well as the object manipulation time.

Intercoder agreement on the set of codes across the tapes for eighteen dyads ranged from 75% to 86% (mean = 84%) for frequency of play behaviors across the various categories. Cohen's kappa for duration of play behaviors ranged from .64 to .95 (mean = .82). Additional intercoder agreement computations were performed for the categories of sequenced representational play (kappa = .86) and symbolic (preplanned/substitutional) play (kappa = .93) because separate analyses were planned for these categories.

Categorizing Children's Expressive Language Productions. No child was observed to produce expressive language (signed or spoken) during the play sessions at 9 months. All language (signed or spoken) produced by the children at 12- and at 18-month sessions was transcribed, with information recorded about frequency, length (number of signs or words), and utterance content. Language level at 12 months was characterized as either prelinguistic (no formal language expressed) or emerging-lexicon (one or more single word/sign utterances expressed). There was a group difference in language levels at 12 months (chi-square = 10.57, $df = 2$; $p < .01$), with 60% (nine) of the Hh children and 54% (seven) of the Dd children but only 6% (one) of the Hd children demonstrating an emerging lexicon. At 18 months, three language levels were identified: emerging lexicon; frequent single-words or signs; emerging syntax. A group difference was again found [$F(2,40) = 3.86$; $p = .02$; Dd, Hh > Hd] (see Table 12-2).

Rating Maternal Responsiveness. The Interaction Rating Scale developed by Meadow-Orlans and Steinberg (Meadow-Orlans & Steinberg, 1993; see Chapter 8) was used to rate maternal sensitivity during the play sessions at 12 and 18 months. A principal components analysis of the five aspects of maternal behavior rated on this scale (Sensitivity, Flexibility, Consistency, Overall Affect, and Involvement) showed that 78% of the variance in total score was contributed by three of the subscale ratings: *(1)* sensitivity (willingness to respond to the child's interests, willing to continue an activity initiated by the child), *(2)* flexibility (willingness to bend rules at times and to accept child's expression of disinterest in mother's proposed activity), and *(3)* consistency (affect, flexibility/rigidity, responsiveness/nonresponsiveness not subject to quick changes).

Table 12-2. Mean ratings of language performance levels at 18 months

Group	*Language level**
Hearing child/hearing mother (Hh) (n = 15)	2.1
Deaf child/deaf mother (Dd) (n = 13)	2.2
Deaf child/hearing mother (Hd) (n = 15)	1.5

*$F(2,40) = 3.86$; $p = .03$; Dd, Hh > Hd.

Ratings: 1 = emerging lexicon; 2 = established single word/sign productions; 3 = emerging syntax.

Together, these three subscales can be thought of as representing maternal "responsiveness." Group differences in composite responsiveness scores were found at 12 months [$F(2,40) = 7.31$; $p = .01$; Hh > Hd] and at 18 months [$F(2,40) = 3.69$; $p = .03$; Hh > Hd] (see Table 12-3).

Results

Results are presented in three sections. First, the sequence of development is addressed by reference to the number of children in the three groups who demonstrated each of the play levels at each age. Second, group comparisons are made on frequency and duration of play at various levels at the three ages. Finally, regression analyses are reported in order to provide information about the power of child language and maternal responsiveness to explain or predict individual children's time in higher levels of play.

Children Showing Each Level of Play at 9, 12, and 18 Months

For analysis purposes, subcategories of play were combined to represent the major categories or levels demonstrated. Thus, analyses focus on the categories of manipulation, relational, and representational/symbolic play. Table 12-4 shows the number of children in each group at each of the three ages who exhibited each of the major levels of play, with subcategories of the symbolic level further differentiated. As Table 12-4 indicates, a number of commonalities existed in the play produced by children in each group. For example, presymbolic play (manipulation, relational) had emerged and was displayed by most of the children at 9 months. Furthermore, presymbolic play was observed at all three ages. It did not disappear. Only a few children engaged in simple representational play at 9 months, but the majority of children in each group produced play at this level at 12 and at 18 months. Sequenced representational play emerged later, being noted first at the 12-month sessions but not becoming common until 18 months. With one exception, children did not engage in symbolic-level play until 18 months. Based on the data

Table 12-3. Mean ratings of maternal responsiveness at 12 and 18 months

Group	*12 Months***	*18 Months**
Hearing infant/hearing mother (Hh)	4.1	4.3
Deaf infant/deaf mother (Dd)	3.6	3.9
Deaf infant/hearing mother (Hd)	2.7	3.3

**$F(2,40) = 7.31$; $p = .01$; Hh > Hd.

*$F(2,40) = 3.69$; $p = .03$; Hh > Hd.

Ratings from 1 to 5, with 5 the most responsive.

Table 12-4. Number of children in each hearing status group at each age demonstrating each level of play

	Hearing child/ Hearing mother (n = 15) Age (months)			*Deaf child/ Deaf mother (n = 13) Age (months)*			*Deaf child/ Hearing mother (n = 15) Age (months)*		
Play levels	*9*	*12*	*18*	*9*	*12*	*18*	*9*	*12*	*18*
Presymbolic									
Manipulation	15	15	15	13	13	13	15	15	15
Relational	14	15	13	11	13	12	12	12	14
Representational									
Simple representation	4	15	15	5	11	13	5	8	14
Sequenced representation	0	9	14	0	5	13	0	3	12
Symbolic									
Canonical Sequence	0	1	8	0	0	3	0	0	6
Preplanned	0	0	13	0	0	13	0	0	6
Substitution	0	0	4	0	0	4	0	0	3
Attribution	0	0	5	0	0	2	0	0	0

reported in Table 12-4, the *order* of emergence of the major levels of play was similar across the three groups; thus, the general developmental trajectory was similar regardless of hearing status.

Table 12-4 suggests, however, that group differences existed in the age at which play levels emerged. For example, more Hh than Dd or Hd children demonstrated simple and sequenced representational play at 12 months. At the 18-month session, all of the children in groups Hh and Dd demonstrated some form of symbolic-level play, most typically by giving evidence of preplanning. However, less than half of the children in group Hd showed any symbolic-level play even at 18 months. This pattern suggests an initial advantage for the hearing children, a somewhat later acceleration for Dd children so that they perform on a par with Hh children at 18 months, with a continuing delay for the Hd children.

Frequency and Duration of Each Level of Play

Comparison of mean frequency and duration of each level of play provides more specific information about the play categories. Analysis of variance (ANOVA) showed significant effects for age and group, as well as a significant age-by-group interaction, on the distribution of time in the three major levels of play—manipulative, relational, representational/symbolic (see Table 12-5). Follow-up analyses indicated no group differences in time in manipulative or relational play, and the groups showed similar changes with age on these measures: mean time in manipulative play decreased across the three groups as age increased; time in relational play showed a curvilinear pattern, increasing from 9 to 12 months and then decreasing at 18 months. The significant interaction effect reflected different degrees of acceleration in the amount of representational/symbolic-level play across groups at the three ages: at 12 months, the average time that Hh children engaged in this level of play was significantly greater than for Dd or Hd groups. However, at 18 months, Dd and Hh children's mean time in representational/symbolic play was virtually the same, whereas time in this level of play was somewhat (but not significantly) lower for Hd children. Analyses of representational/symbolic play duration thus confirm the group differences suggested above.

Additional analyses indicated a significant difference between the three hearing-status groups at 18 months when time in symbolic-level play (with lower-level representational play excluded) was considered. When only this most advanced level of play was compared, Hd children's time was significantly below that of the other two groups. These results are also consistent with the pattern shown in Table 12-4 and are further evidence of a delay in a substantial number of the Hd children.

Explaining Individual Differences in Play at 12 and 18 Months

Because of these group differences, hierarchical multiple regressions were calculated to identify which variables (child hearing status, child language level, maternal responsiveness, dyadic hearing status) best accounted for the variance in children's time in the highest levels of play. At 12 months, child hearing status predicted a significant 28% of the variance in representational play. After hearing status was controlled, no other variable contributed significantly to the equation (see Table 12-6).

The result was different at 18 months, when the three variables were employed as predictors of time in preplanned symbolic play. (Preplanned play was chosen as the outcome variable because most of time in play observed at the symbolic level fell in this category.) At this level, child hearing status was not a significant predictor. After hearing status was controlled, child language level was a marginally significant predictor. Even after these two variables were controlled, however, maternal responsiveness contributed significantly to the prediction of time in preplanned play. Finally, a dummy variable representing the combination of mother and child hearing status (Dd, Hh, or Hd) was entered in the equation to see whether it would predict additional portions of the vari-

Table 12-5. Mean (SD) number of seconds in major categories of play by three groups during 10 minutes

	Hearing child/ Hearing mother (n = 15)			*Deaf child/ Deaf mother (n = 13)*			*Deaf child/ Hearing mother (n = 15)*			*Univariate effects*		
Play category[a]	*9 Months*	*12 Months*	*18 Months*	*9 Months*	*12 Months*	*18 Months*	*9 Months*	*12 Months*	*18 Months*	*Group*	*Age*	*Group-X-Age*
Manipulation	302.5 (79.0)	225.9 (107.0)	183.7 (86.7)	251.5 (115.0)	212.1 (113.5)	134.6 (59.4)	310.8 (117.4)	187.2 (82.8)	196.9 (68.9)	NS	<.001	NS
Relational	22.4 (15.3)	114.4 (89.6)	78.9 (72.1)	16.2 (19.2)	134.4 (93.1)	61.6 (78.4)	26.0 (38.4)	101.8 (118.1)	93.3 (87.4)	NS	<.001	NS
Representational/ Symbolic[b]	0.5 (1.1)	78.4 (70.5)	254.7 (79.5)	1.2 (3.0)	25.8 (32.5)	253.9 (99.9)	.7 (1.6)	13.3 (17.7)	193.9 (79.5)	<.01	<.001	<.05

[a]MANOVA: group, $F(2,40) = 4.76$, $p = .01$; age, $F(2,80) = 42.39$, $p < .001$; group-x-age, $F(4,80) = 2.91$, $p = .03$.

[b]12 months, Hh>Dd, Hd.

Table 12-6. Predicting (accounting for) variance in children's time at higher play levels: Predictor variables entered hierarchically in order listed

	Criterion variables			
	12 Months—Total representational play[a]		*18 Months Symbolic play*[b]	
Predictor variables	*Beta*	*t*	*Beta*	*t*
Hearing status (child)	.41	2.97*	.04	.28
Language level (child)	.19	1.36	.28	1.92†
Responsiveness (mother)	.14	.96	.38	2.58*

[a]Multiple $R = .58$, $R^2 = .34$, $F = 7.07$; $p < .001$.

[b]Multiple $R = .57$, $R^2 = .32$, $F = 6.24$; $p < .01$.

†$p = .06$. *$p \leq .01$.

ance. However, after the other variables were controlled, dyadic hearing status did not contribute significantly to the prediction of child time in advanced levels of play. In sum, the variables that were considered accounted for 34% of the variance (or individual difference) in representational play at 12 months and 32% of the variance in preplanned symbolic play at 18 months.

Discussion

A major goal of analyses of child play was to document stages in play shown by two groups of deaf children (Dd and Hd) and a group of hearing children (Hh) across the ages when play typically progresses from presymbolic to symbolic levels. Effects and interrelations of child and dyadic hearing status, child language production, and maternal responsiveness were investigated.

The children in all three groups were found to progress through similar steps in the acquisition and demonstration of representational and symbolic play, thus indicating the robustness of the developmental course of this ability. However, the age at appearance and the time spent in production of higher levels of play were associated with and apparently influenced by the other factors investigated. An effect of child hearing status was found at 12 months for the production of representational play, with hearing children more likely than either group of deaf children to play at this level. Neither child language level nor maternal responsiveness was significantly related to representational play at this age after child hearing status was controlled. At 18 months, however, neither child hearing status nor dyadic hearing status was associated with the production of simple representational-level play. Differences were found across the groups, but only at the higher, symbolic level: both Dd and Hh children exceeded Hd children in production of play at this level. This pattern suggests two conclusions: *(1)* The initial lag in representational play found for the Dd children represents an alternative, adaptive developmental path, because there was no delay at 18 months; *(2)* the initial lag in representational play found for Hd children, and the relative lack of symbolic play by that group at 18 months, presages continuing delays for that group.

To understand and explain these conclusions, it is important to remember that dyadic hearing status is, in fact, a "proxy" variable. It "stands in" for a number of processes that occur differently in the three groups of dyads. In this investigation, two of those processes were investigated and provide a more in-depth understanding of the differences observed. The first of those processes is the children's language production. As has been suggested elsewhere (Spencer, 1996), language skills may enable or at least facilitate symbolic levels of play that involve retrieval of remembered events or active mental planning of events. Indeed, expressive language was more strongly associated with symbolic play (occurring at 18 months) than with simple or even sequenced representational play (at either 12 or 18 months) that can be prompted by realistic objects that are present. (Of course, it is possible that this earlier level of representational play may have been associated more strongly with a measure of receptive language than with the expressive measure used here.)

Although results from this study agree with those of most previous studies in identifying a language–play association, that association was not as robust as the association between play and the other process measure—ratings of maternal responsiveness. This measure has been shown to associate both with language and with play, and it is generally reported that children whose mothers are more responsive advance more quickly in both areas. Findings from the current study indicate that this characteristic of maternal behavior is as important for understanding the development of deaf children as for hearing children. Therefore, despite the differences in the apparent rate of development of play skills, the underlying processes involved appear to operate similarly regardless of child hearing status—or of dyadic hearing status.

The characteristic of maternal responsiveness, which is defined here as a composite measure of maternal sensitivity to the children's interactive behaviors, may also relate to the apparent importance of child hearing status for play at 12 months. As was discussed in Chapter 11, infants of that age (whether deaf or hearing) are just beginning to be able to switch visual attention between an object they are exploring and a communication partner. Probably in reaction to this, deaf mothers have been observed (see Chapter 10) to produce relatively few communications in play-based interactions with deaf infants at that age. Mothers who are more aware of and sensitive to their deaf children's visual attention needs may be less likely (verbally or nonverbally) to prompt and guide play than are hearing mothers with hearing children who can assume that their children hear their communications while looking away. Given this difference, it is probable that the play of Hh children at this age more closely represented their "supported" play level than did the play of Dd children. In addition, the apparent focus of the deaf mothers on their deaf children's visual attention needs at 12 months appears to have adequately supported the children's development of higher-level play, as is shown in their similarity to Hh children at 18 months.

The continued delay of Hd children at 18 months probably reflects a number of factors. Although their hearing mothers tend to communicate frequently with them using vocal language, those communications are often not accessible to the children. In addition, the ratings showed that mothers in this group tended to be less responsive to their children and, not surprisingly, the children's language levels also lagged behind those of the children in other groups. However, it should be noted that not all of the children in group Hd showed this pattern. Some showed language production equal to that expected for age. In addition, some of the mothers were highly responsive. In these dyads, the children's play was more advanced. That is, the play of this group co-varied as in the other groups with maternal responsiveness and language.

Acknowledgments

Data reported in this chapter were previously published in:

Spencer, P. E., & Meadow-Orlans, K. P. (1996). Play, language, and maternal responsiveness: A longitudinal study of deaf and hearing infants. *Child Development, 67,* 3176–3191.

Notes

1. The study conducted by Bornstein et al. (1999) also included a group of hearing children with deaf mothers. Because the current chapter does not include analysis of this group, the findings of Bornstein and colleagues about this group are not included in the review.

2. David Deyo and Natalie Grindstaff were equal partners in this original research. They actively recruited subjects, collected data, coded data, and interpreted results. We greatly appreciate their help and the opportunity to work with them.

3. We are grateful to Lorraine McCune for visiting our research center and discussing the implications of hearing loss on early play, for training several researchers in the use of her coding system, and for allowing use of her coding scheme for the analyses reported in this chapter.

4. Coding of play and the analyses reported in this chapter were funded by a separate U.S. Office of Education grant, No. H023A10005, to Patricia Spencer, Kathryn Meadow-Orlans, and Donald Moores. Play coding was performed by Peishi Wang, Martha Bowles, Lynne Erting, and Erez Miller. We gratefully acknowledge their important contributions to this study.

5. The study of play reported here was developed to address a primary question about the effect of infant hearing loss on development of play. Hearing children with hearing parents were considered to be the appropriate and sufficient comparison group for addressing this question; therefore, analyses did not include the group of hearing children with deaf parents.

13

Relationships Across Developmental Domains and Over Time

Patricia E. Spencer, Kathryn P. Meadow-Orlans, Lynne Sanford Koester, and Jennifer L. Ludwig

Previous chapters focused on infant and mother interactive behaviors related to various developmental domains, including affect, cognition, socialization, and language. In most chapters, the focus was on a single domain, and analyses centered on differences between and among groups as defined by the combination of mother and infant hearing status. Group differences were commonly found. At 9 months, differences were seen across hearing status groups in affect, eye gaze, and communicative behaviors in the face-to-face situation. Differences were also found at 12 and 18 months, when data were gathered in a variety of other situations. At those two ages, groups with matched hearing status (Dd and Hh) exhibited more positive social interactions and more time in the most advanced attention state (Coordinated Joint) compared to groups with unmatched hearing status (Dh and Hd).

Other group differences were found in infants' visual attention behaviors, with infants with deaf mothers being more likely than those with hearing mothers to keep their gaze on their mothers and thus maintain access to mothers' signed communication. Play behaviors (analyzed for three groups only) were more advanced for the matched hearing status groups (Dd, Hh) than for the deaf children with hearing mothers (Hd). The pattern for language skills was a bit different, with only the deaf infants with hearing mothers (Hd) lagging behind the other three groups. Assessment of mastery motivation showed that deaf infants with deaf mothers (Dd) were most likely to have a social mastery style. Finally, the four groups differed on attachment behaviors, with children of deaf mothers more likely to be classified as "insecure" using the coding guidelines developed for a hearing North American population.

Although some variation existed, a common theme across domains was differences between the matched (Hh, Dd) and unmatched (Hd, Dh) hearing status groups. When such differences were found, however, the separation among the groups was not absolute: although strong and significant differences were seen when group averages were considered, some dyads in the unmatched groups performed like those in the matched groups, and vice versa. Although dyadic hearing status clearly influences infant development, the impact occurs through expression of behaviors and attitudes, some of which can be modified or adapted.

This chapter extends the analyses presented previously. First, intercorrelations among variables are investigated across behavioral and developmental domains at 18 months for all four groups. Second, two groups are created—one including all dyads with a deaf child and another including all dyads with a hearing child. Predictions of 12- and 18-month measures are then considered for all of the deaf children and, separately, for all of the hearing children. The focus of this set of analyses will be on the predictive power of specific observable mother and child behaviors, many of which are amenable to intervention, instead of the pre-existing, immutable characteristic of matched or unmatched hearing status. Mothers' hearing status (and, therefore, dyadic hearing status differences) will, however, be considered as a final potential predictor in most analyses. When mothers' hearing status fails to add significantly to a prediction after other variables are included, it can be assumed that dyadic hearing status differences reported in earlier chapters are effects of the behaviorally oriented variables considered here. In contrast, when mothers' hearing status adds to a prediction after other variables have been included, it will be evident that the set of behaviorally oriented variables employed fails to adequately represent some important aspects of differences in mother and child hearing status.

Relationships Across Domains at 18 Months

Five important outcome measures were available for all of the groups at 18 months: *(1)* child's expressive language levels; *(2)* child's time in Coordinated Joint Attention (CJA); *(3)* quality of child's interaction behaviors (obtained from the qualitative rating scale described in Chapter 8); *(4)* child's attachment classification (using the Maslin scoring system explained in Chapter 9); and *(5)* mother's general responsiveness (from the summary interaction rating that was drawn from the general "sensitivity" measure described in Chapter 12). Thus, children's linguistic, cognitive (attention), and social-affective (interaction, attachment) domains are represented, plus the important measure of maternal responsiveness.

Figure 13-1A–D shows the relationships identified among these five 18-month measures for the four groups of dyads.[1] All four groups show a pattern of significant association among a central "core" set of variables that includes the social measures of child interaction quality and maternal responsiveness, and the cognitive measure of attention. In addition, language is associated with attention for three of the groups (Hh,

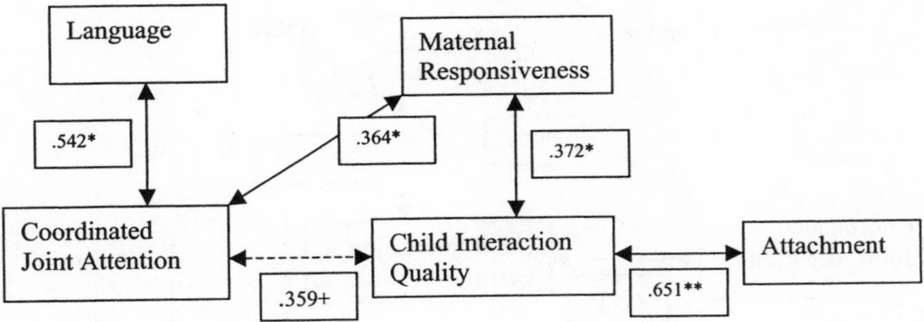

Figure 13-1A. Intercorrelations at 18 months for dyads of deaf infants and deaf mothers. **Pearson r, $p \leq .01$ (continuous lines) *Pearson r, $p \leq .05$ (continuous lines) +Pearson r, $p \leq .12$ and Spearman $rs \leq .10$ (dotted lines). Significance levels differ for values of r because of differences in the number of subjects available across bivariate analyses.

Dd, Dh), with that relationship being similar in strength across groups. The relatively strong attention–language relationship for the two groups with deaf mothers highlights the importance of visual attention behaviors for children learning sign as their first language when those children are provided a rich visual language model. Indirect effects on language from maternal responsiveness and child interaction quality are also suggested. For both groups with hearing mothers (Hh, Hd) there was a more direct relationship between maternal responsiveness and child language. For group Hd, this suggests that aspects of mothers' communicative behavior in addition to the use of visually salient communication are especially important for children who face challenges in acquiring language.

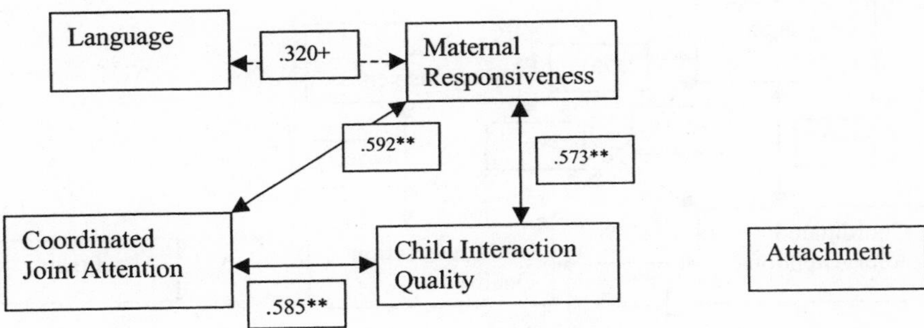

Figure 13-1B. Intercorrelations at 18 months for dyads of deaf infants and hearing mothers. **Pearson r, $p \leq .01$ (continuous lines) *Pearson r, $p \leq .05$ (continuous lines) +Pearson r, $p \leq .12$ and Spearman $rs \leq .10$ (dotted lines). Significance levels differ for values of r because of differences in the number of subjects available across bivariate analyses.

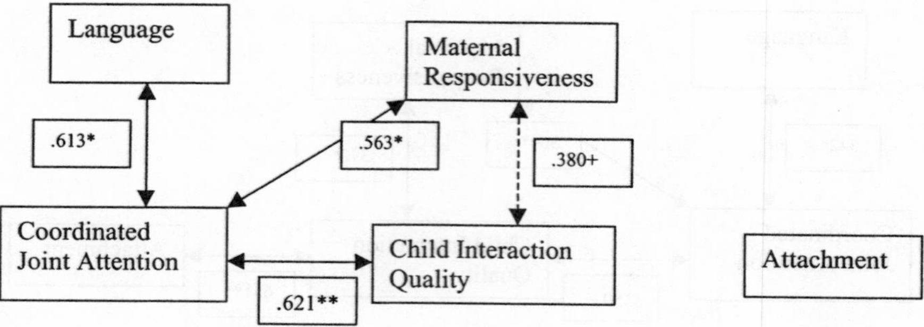

Figure 13-1C. Intercorrelations at 18 months for dyads of hearing infants and deaf mothers. **Pearson r, $p \leq .01$ (continuous lines) *Pearson r, $p \leq .05$ (continuous lines) +Pearson r, $p \leq .12$ and Spearman $rs \leq .10$ (dotted lines). Significance levels differ for values of r because of differences in the number of subjects available across bivariate analyses.

Two relationships were unique to a single group. Only group Hh showed a significant relationship between the social measure (child quality of interaction) and language, whereas attachment was associated with the social measure for group Dd only. Attachment was *not* significantly related to any other variable for any group. For the other three groups, it appears that the development of secure attachment proceeds independently of the variables that were available for analysis. The strong relationship between attachment and child interactive behavior in the Dd group is worthy of further investigation; however, even for this group, attachment did not relate directly to the maternal responsiveness measure or to language.

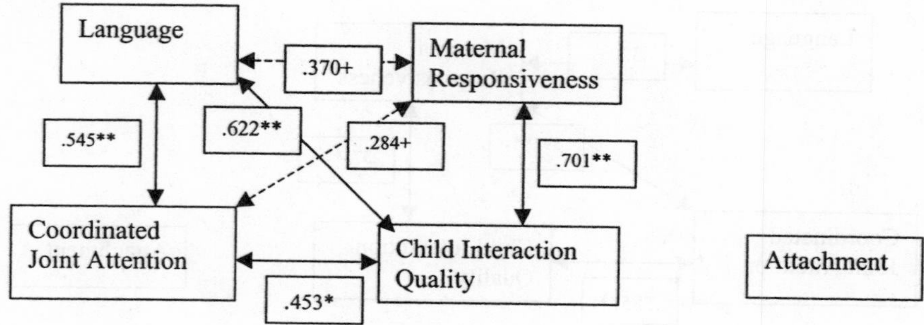

Figure 13-1D. Intercorrelations at 18 months for dyads of hearing infants and hearing mothers. **Pearson r, $p \leq .01$ (continuous lines) *Pearson r, $p \leq .05$ (continuous lines) +Pearson r, $p \leq .12$ and Spearman $rs \leq .10$ (dotted lines). Significance levels differ for values of r because of differences in the number of subjects available across bivariate analyses.

Finally, it is interesting that, with the exception of attachment, the picture of across-domain correlations is more complete for group Hh than for the other groups. Most developmental theory is based on this group, and the relationships observed here replicate those from previous reports. However, differences between the pattern of correlations for this group and that for the other three groups suggest that the developmental model derived from hearing child/hearing mother dyads may not be totally applicable for dyads in which one or both members are deaf.

Development Over Time: Longitudinal Analyses Across Domains

The analyses reported above showed both similarities and differences across groups in the web of intercorrelations among measures of child and mother functioning at 18 months. This section of the chapter will focus on measures obtained at 9 and 12 months, in an effort to understand to what degree they predict two of the important 18-month outcome variables: language and social interaction behaviors. Both of these outcome variables have been noted in our analyses and those of other researchers as being of particular importance for deaf children. In addition, they were not consistently related across the four groups in the analyses reported above; therefore, they may represent effects of somewhat different sets of predictor variables.

The analyses proceeded in two major steps. First, associations between 12 and 18 months were explored for each outcome measure. Then associations were examined between 9-month measures and those 12-month measures that had been found to relate to the 18-month outcome variables. The analyses presented and discussed below are based on correlation and regression procedures conducted separately for deaf children (with groups Dd and Hd combined) and hearing children (with groups Hh and Dh combined).[2] Dyadic hearing status is considered in the final regression analyses.

Before other analyses were conducted, a series of simple regressions were computed to determine whether background variables were related to the 18-month outcome measures. The background variables that were considered included infant sex and birth weight, mothers' years of education, mode of communication in an early intervention program, child's hearing level, and family socioeconomic status (SES). None of these variables were found to relate significantly to either 18-month language or social behaviors.

Prediction of Children's 18-Month Language Levels

Simple correlations were computed for deaf and for hearing groups between the 18-month language measure and 12-month measures of child functioning (mastery motivation style, social interaction rating, time in CJA) and maternal functioning (responsiveness, production of signs/gestures).

Deaf Children. As Table 13-1 illustrates, each one of these 12-month variables was significantly related to deaf children's language at 18 months. A social mastery style, more positive social interaction characteristics, and greater time in Coordinated Joint Attention (CJA)—as well as more frequent signing or gesturing by mothers and more maternal responsiveness—was associated with higher language levels for deaf children. A regression equation showed that the combination of 12-month variables provided a significant prediction of later language for this group [$F(5,19) = 4.223$; $p = .009$], and together the variables predicted 53% of the variance in the 18-month measure. The only unique predictor (that is, the only variable that contributed significantly to the variance in deaf children's language at 18 months after the variance contributed by all the other variables was taken into account) was mothers' production of signs/gestures at 12 months. As a final step, mothers' hearing status was added to the equation, but it failed to make a significant contribution.

Hearing Children. As shown in Table 13-1, neither mastery motivation style nor mothers' sign/gesture production related to hearing children's 18-month language. However, both child social ratings and attention were related to the language measure, and maternal responsiveness showed a marginally significant relationship.

A regression analysis was conducted using the three 12-month variables that related to the hearing children's language development: social interaction ratings, time in CJA, and maternal responsiveness. These three measures predicted approximately 41% of the variance in hearing children's 18-month language [$F(3,26) = 5.945$; $p = .003$]. Both the so-

Table 13-1. Associations between 18-month language and selected 12-month measures

12-Month measures	*Deaf children*	*Hearing children*
Mastery motivation[a]	.476**	.093
Social interaction behavior	.419**	.518***
Attention	.605***	.297*
Maternal responsiveness	.335*	.199†
Mother sign/gesture	.600***	.093

[a]For mastery motivation, R from simple regression; Pearson r, one-tailed, is reported for other variables

†$p \leq .15$.

*$p \leq .05$.

**$p \leq .01$.

***$p \leq .001$.

cial ratings and attention were unique contributors to the prediction. Mothers' hearing status did not add significantly to the prediction.

Predicting Child Social Behaviors (Quality of Interaction)

Simple correlations were computed separately for deaf and hearing children on 18-month child interaction ratings and the 12-month variables discussed above (see Table 13-2).

Deaf Children. As Table 13-2 shows, both the children's 12-month social interaction ratings and mothers' production of signs/gestures were related significantly to the 18-month social measure for deaf children. In addition, a marginally significant correlation was found between maternal responsiveness and the social measure. A regression analysis showed that the three 12-month measures predicted about 21% of the variance in the 18-month social measure [$F(3,35) = 3.108$; $p = .039$]. Mothers' production of signs and/or gestures was a uniquely significant contributor, adding to the prediction of variance even after other variables had been considered. After these measures had been considered, mothers' hearing status did not add significantly to the prediction of social interaction ratings.

Hearing Children. For hearing children, the 12-month ratings of social interaction, attention, and maternal responsiveness were correlated with the 18-month measure of social interaction. A regression equation showed that these three variables in concert predicted about 49% of the variance in the 18-month social measure [$F(3,32) = 9.647$; $p < .001$]. Both the 12-month social and attention measures were uniquely significant contributors. Mothers' hearing status did not increase the prediction significantly.

Table 13-2. Associations between 18-month social interactive behavior and selected 12-month measures

12-Month measures	*Deaf children*	*Hearing children*
Mastery motivation[a]	.014	.101
Social interaction behavior	.295*	.589***
Attention	.117	.367**
Maternal responsiveness	.165†	.510***
Mother sign/Gesture	.436**	−.045

[a]For mastery motivation, R from simple regression; Pearson r, one-tailed, is reported for other variables.

†$p \leq .15$.

*$p \leq .05$.

**$p \leq .01$.

***$p \leq .001$.

Summary: Predictions Based on Measures at 12 Months

Combinations of the three child and two maternal variables predicted 53% and 41% of the variance in language outcomes for deaf and hearing children, respectively. The 12-month measures of social interaction, visual attention, and maternal responsiveness were associated with the language outcomes for both groups. This finding reflects an underlying similarity in developmental processes regardless of child hearing status. For deaf children, two additional 12-month measures were associated with 18-month language: social mastery style (representing frequent gaze to the communication partner) and mothers' production of signs and/or gestures (representing provision of visually salient communication). After all these variables were considered, mothers' hearing status (and, therefore, matched or unmatched dyadic status) did not add to the prediction of language outcomes for either deaf or hearing children. Thus, the process-oriented measures used as predictors account fairly well for the differences in early language development that have been attributed to dyadic hearing status.

Combinations of the same 12-month variables predicted 21% and 49% of the variance in 18-month social interaction of deaf and hearing children, respectively. The same three variables (social interaction, attention, and maternal responsiveness) that were so important in language predictions for both groups are also predictors of hearing children's 18-month social behaviors. The variance accounted for in deaf children's social behavior is noticeably lower than that for hearing children, however, and the set of predictors was somewhat different, with attention not being a significant predictor but mothers' sign/gesture production implicated. This latter relation shows that provision of an accessible language model is important for deaf children's social interaction in general and not just for their language development. This is another indication of the importance of visual communication models for that group.

In general, 18-month language and social behaviors of deaf and hearing children can be predicted moderately well by observations at 12 months. The earlier ratings of child social behavior, mothers' responsiveness, and behaviors related to visual attention and/or provision of a visual communication model are particularly important indicators of later child language and social functioning. Early observations of these behaviors may, then, be especially useful in the identification of dyads that need intensified or modified intervention efforts.

Predictions of 12-Month Measures from Observations at 9 Months

There were many measures available from the microanalytic observations of face-to-face interaction when infants were 9 months old.[3] All measures used here were taken from the first episode in the face-to-face interaction, before stress had been introduced for the infant. The number of measures to be used in this longitudinal analysis were reduced by theoretical considerations, with care being taken to identify expected relationships over time. Bi-variate correlations were computed, relating the 9-month measures to the developmentally important 12-month measures of child social interaction, child visual attention, mothers' responsiveness, and mothers' production of visual communication. As a result of these exploratory investigations, a smaller set of 9-month variables was identified that showed potentially important relationships with the 12-month variables: *child activity level* (duration of infants' rhythmic limb and body movements), *child facial affect* (frequency of infant smiles), *mothers' facial affect* (frequency of mothers' exaggerated facial expressions), and *mothers' vocal communication* (vocal games plus vocal narration/talk).[4] The significant 9- to 12-month correlations are shown in Table 13-3. Regression analyses were conducted to follow up the initial correlations, primarily to determine whether mothers' hearing status (i.e., dyadic status) added significantly to predictions. (For the variable of 12-month maternal responsiveness, two additional variables were included—a mea-

Table 13-3. Associations between 9-month and 12-month measures for dyads with deaf and hearing infants

12-Month measure	*Correlation*	*9-Month measures*
A. Deaf Infants		
Mastery classification[a]		(None related)
Mother sign/gesture[a]	← (−.380*) ———	Mother vocal communication
Child attention	← (−.657**) ———	Mother vocal communication
Child social interaction[a]	← (−.309*) ———	Child activity
Mother responsiveness	← (.306*) ———	Mother's facial affect
"	← (−.276†) ———	Infant's activity
"	← (.346*) ———	Mother's support
"	← (−.282*) ———	Mother's stress
B. Hearing Infants		
Mastery classification		(None related)
Mother sign/gesture[a]	← (−.243†) ———	Mother vocal communication
Child attention		(None related)
Child social interaction		(None related)
Mother responsiveness	← (.243†) ———	Infant's facial affect
"	← (−.232†) ———	Infant's activity
"	← (.501**) ———	Mother's support

[a]Mother's hearing status added significantly to prediction of 12-month variable.

†p = .06–.10.

*p = .05.

**p = .01.

sure of mothers' perceptions of their level of support and a measure of their reported stress. These measures were obtained at 15 and 9 months, respectively.)

None of the 9-month variables were associated with mastery motivation style for either deaf or hearing children, although deaf children were more likely to have a social mastery style if their mothers were deaf. Mothers' frequency of vocal communications at 9 months was inversely related with their frequency of sign/gesture production at 12 months, regardless of child hearing status. That is, mothers tended to "specialize" in either vocal or visual communication, and that tendency was relatively stable over time. This specialization related to maternal hearing status, with deaf mothers producing much more visual communication than hearing mothers. Mothers' preferred communication modality related to child visual attention at 12 months, with children exposed to visual communication spending more time in the CJA state.

Deaf children's 9-month activity levels were related inversely with their 12-month social interaction ratings. It is possible that high levels of activity on the part of a deaf child may be an observable symptom of interactive difficulties that will continue to be manifested later in development. In contrast with results of analyses comparing 12- and 18-month behaviors, mothers' hearing status also contributed significantly to prediction of 12-month social ratings. This indicates the presence of early variables or predictors that were not included in the current analysis.

Hearing children's 12-month attention and social interaction ratings were not associated with any of the 9-month measures. Variations in the 9-month behaviors included in this analysis may not, therefore, be so critical for development when there is no particular communicative challenge for the dyad to overcome and infants have full access to their mothers' communications.

Maternal Responsiveness

Initial correlation analyses found that infant activity level and affect were associated with the maternal responsiveness measure. For example, child activity level at 9 months was negatively associated with 12-month maternal responsiveness for both groups. In addition, in dyads with deaf infants, mothers who displayed positive affect also tended to be responsive. Child affect was associated with maternal responsiveness for the group with hearing infants. In addition, the measures of stress and of support at approximately 12 months related significantly with the 12-month responsiveness of mothers of deaf children. Only the support measure, however, associated significantly with responsiveness of mothers of hearing children.

Regression analyses indicated that, for mothers of deaf children, a combination of infant activity level, mothers' facial expressions, mothers' reports of levels of support, and their degree of stress predicted about 30% of the variance in the 12-month responsiveness measure [$F(4,28) = 2.893$; $p = .04$]. Much shared variance existed among these variables, and none proved a uniquely significant predictor of responsiveness. Interestingly, at 18 months the stress measure did not relate to responsiveness of the mothers of deaf children. Therefore, time after diagnosis and concomitant provision of intervention support seems to overcome any importance of early expressions of stress—and, with time, support becomes a more important factor relating to maternal responsiveness.

The stress measure, in fact, failed to relate to responsiveness of mothers of hearing children even at 12 months. Infant activity level, infants' facial affect, and support reported by mothers accounted for about 35% of responsiveness in this group. Support was a uniquely significant contributor to the prediction. Mothers' hearing status did not add significantly to the prediction.

Summary: 9 to 12 Months

In sum, 9-month measures of child activity level and mothers' vocal communications were inversely related to several 12-month measures for deaf children. Child activity, mothers' support and stress, and mothers' facial affect were related to later maternal responsiveness. Predictions for responsiveness of mothers of hearing children were similarly related to child activity. For this group, children's smiling (expression of affect) was positively related to mothers' responsiveness, and the measure of maternal stress failed to correlate significantly with responsiveness.

Mothers' hearing status was directly related to several of the 12-month measures, including production of signs and gestures and, for dyads with deaf children, child social mastery style and social interaction ratings. This suggests that behaviors in addition to those included in these analyses should be investigated in order to further explain and predict dyadic functioning at 12 months.

Conclusion

None of the 9-month measures correlated significantly with the 18-month outcome measures; therefore, no direct relations were identified between the variables at those two ages. However, it was possible to identify across-age correlations in a stepwise manner. Links were shown between 9- and 12-month behaviors and between 12- and 18-month measures. An example of these linking correlations is given in Figure 13-2, which shows the series of interage associations related to 18-month language skills of deaf children. As the diagram shows, mothers' hearing status (that is, matched or unmatched mother–infant hearing status) related directly to some of the 12-month measures, but there was no evi-

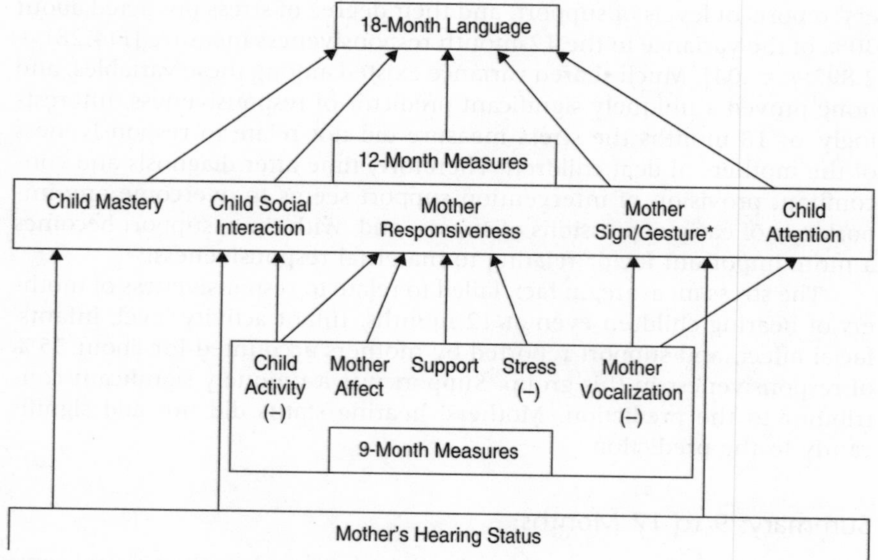

Figure 13-2. Predictors of deaf children's language development.

dence of direct influence of dyadic hearing status on the 18-month measures. The entire set of mother and child 12-month measures contributed to prediction of deaf children's language. Of these measures, a core set, including child social interaction ratings, child attention, and maternal responsiveness, was related to deaf and hearing children's language and to hearing children's social outcomes. Social interactions of deaf children at 18 months were also related to mothers' production of signs and gestures. Measures related to visual communication, mothers' visual expression of affect, and children's social mastery style (which includes frequent visual attention to persons) were of special importance for the development of the deaf children.

In general, it appears that mothers' communication modalities and dyadic expression of affect in early interactions indicate the degree to which those interactions support infants' development. By the time infants are 12 months old, observations of infant social and cognitive behaviors, as well as mothers' communication behaviors, provide significant information for predictions of developmental levels at 18 months. Such predictions can help parents and intervention professionals make decisions about modification of services provided to families.

Notes

1. The figures indicate Pearson *r* coefficients between variables. This statistic was used after initial analyses showed no nonlinear relationships between the various pairs of variables. However, given that two measures may be considered

to be ordinal in nature (attachment, language), Spearman rank correlations were also calculated. Results were similar for both strength of correlation and significance levels for parametric and nonparametric correlations, although in several cases, the Spearman r_s indicated significance at $p = .10$ when Pearson r significance was slightly higher. (Because mastery motivation is represented by a 2-level nominal code, correlations and significance levels reported for this variable are derived from simple regression calculations with mastery motivation as a dummy-coded independent or predictor variable.) Owing to the small number of subjects in some analyses, and the effect of n on significance levels of correlations, marginal significance above .05 and no greater than .15 is indicated as well as traditional significance levels for this first set of analyses. All significance levels are one-tailed, because it was possible to predict the direction of expected relationships. Log transformation was required for one measure, Coordinated Joint Attention, at 12 months, to normalize distribution. All reported calculations for this variable thoughout the chapter are based on the log-transformed measure.

2. Prior to conducting regression analyses, variables were again checked to assure that bivariate relationships were linear and that there were no extreme outliers. Collinearity tolerances were also assessed for variables in each equation, and problematic variables were deleted from analyses.

3. Distribution characteristics and bivariate linearity were also examined for all 9-month variables. The measure of mothers' exaggerated facial expressions required a square-root transformation to approach normality. All calculations involving that measure are, therefore, based on the transformed measure. Both frequency and duration measures were available for most of the 9-month variables. A choice was made between those two forms of the variable based on initial exploration of distributions and correlations between the two forms and the outcome variable being addressed.

4. Vocal games and vocal narration were strongly associated with each other and showed a similar pattern of associations with 12-month measures. A composite measure called "vocal communication" was therefore created by computing the mean of z-scores (standardized scores) calculated for these two measures. Measures of child vocal production and of mothers' visual–gestural production at 9 months did not relate significantly to later measures. A measure of duration of child gaze to mother during 9-month free play was associated with social mastery classifications at 12 months, but measures of child gaze during the face-to-face interaction failed to associate significantly with the 12-month variables on which analyses are focused.

14

Implications for Intervention with Infants and Families

Kathryn P. Meadow-Orlans, Patricia E. Spencer, Lynne Sanford Koester, and Annie G. Steinberg

The twenty-first century brought a new millennium and a new world for deaf infants. Both the timing and the nature of intervention in childhood deafness changed dramatically in the previous two decades, with a heightened awareness of the value of services for children with disabilities from birth onwards, rather than services previously mandated from age 3. Child development became an established subspecialty of pediatrics and psychology, consonant with increased recognition of the need for early identification and close monitoring of developmental delay. Although debates about specific communication choices in childhood deafness continue, there is general recognition that the primary goal is the development of a shared language between parent and child. Many parents today, like the parents in this study population, are offered some choice of communication mode, broadening the range of possibilities and areas in which parents can feel they have some influence and control over their children's lives.

One important change was triggered by Universal Newborn Hearing Screening (UNHS), a movement to identify hearing loss in any affected infant by the age of 6 months. Legislation to implement this mandate is already in place in many states (Hayes, 1999; Joint Committee on Infant Hearing, 2000). All infants participating in our study were identified with hearing loss by the age of 6 months, which made them unique for deaf infants with hearing parents at that time. (When these data were collected, the average age of identification was between 15 and 16 months [Mace, Wallace, Whan, & Stelmachowicz, 1991].) In 1999, one estimate of the average age at identification was 14 months (American Academy of Pediatrics, 1999). Another reliable source estimated average age at 12 to 25 months (American Speech-Language-Hearing Association, 2003). Many more infants now have a hearing loss identified earlier than was the case a decade ago, making the infant participants in our study closer to today's norm.

Much has been made of the advantages of early identification and intervention, especially for the acquisition of language. However, the language performance of our cohort of early identified deaf children with hearing parents leads us to a more cautious prognosis. Although some were at the level of hearing children, many exhibited serious language lags at age 18 months, continuing through age 3 for the smaller group followed until that time. This means that interventions to promote language development—delivered by knowledgeable professionals with the goal of enhancing both positive parent–child interactions and visual attention—remain a high priority.

Advances in technology led to the increasing utilization of cochlear implants, another important development for deaf children (Spencer, 2002; Spencer & Marschark, 2003). Some authorities predict (and some members of the Deaf community fear) that implants will eradicate profound deafness. However, uneven and unpredictable outcomes from use of implants make this seem unlikely, at least for the near future. Intervention to promote the visual attention and language of deaf children will continue to be beneficial and even necessary for large numbers of children.

In the following pages, we summarize the findings of the research reported in preceding chapters and suggest the implications of these results for parents and educators. We should reiterate that the infant and parent participants in this project were privileged in many ways. Except for the small subset of infants with multiple conditions reported separately in Chapter 6, no infants had known conditions other than hearing loss that might affect their development. Because one-third of all children with hearing loss have some additional condition (Schildroth & Hotto, 1993), this is an important exception to the general application of our results. The parents were highly educated, with English or ASL as their native language. Most lived in urban centers where excellent services were available. Almost all families were intact, with relatively secure economic positions. Parents were committed to providing the best possible care for their children. In short, these children could be expected to be "at the top of their class." With these caveats and exclusions, what recommendations can be inferred and proposed from the information provided by this intensive longitudinal study?

Accent Mothers' Innate Parenting Capabilities

Four groups of mother–infant dyads were recruited and observed in the course of the Gallaudet Infancy Study. One of these, hearing children and hearing mothers (Hh), was the control or comparison group. The dyads consisting of deaf children and deaf mothers (Dd) were considered to be least at risk of the three other groups because their "matched hearing status" was expected to produce a sense of parenting competence in mothers because they were equipped to communicate with their children. The dyads consisting of hearing children and deaf parents (Dh) are those for whom the least developmental research exists. There is ample evidence that most of these Children of Deaf Adults (CODAs) function as productive adults. Their early development has been the focus of little research, but it is possible that unmatched hearing status might lead to early parenting insecurity with a negative effect on dyadic interaction. The fourth group of dyads, comprised of deaf children with hearing parents (Hd), is the most problematic, the group at greatest potential risk, and the one for which intervention is most important.

We conclude, from several of the domains and analyses presented, that mothers in all four groups utilized "intuitive parenting" skills to the benefit of their infants, and that in many ways the infants were developing optimal social, cognitive, and linguistic skills. This is the case especially in the important area of *attachment* (Chapter 9). Attachment has become one of the most important indicators and predictors of current and future development. Infants who are securely attached to a caregiver whom they use as a base are more likely to venture into the world and to develop positive social skills and better psychological adjustment than infants who are insecure, although this relationship has been questioned and is certainly not immutable (Thompson, 1999). Our data showing no differences in security of attachment between deaf and hearing infants with hearing mothers is a heartening sign, and suggests that intuitive parenting among mothers of the at-risk infants has been a positive force, and/or that intervention services have been effective. (Differences in attachment classifications of infants with deaf and with hearing mothers may be related to Deaf cultural values and will be discussed below.) Differences in *mastery motivation* also were minimal, and were related to positive monitoring of the social environment by deaf infants, rather than to differences in the motivation to succeed in an object-related task.

Observations of maternal behaviors, especially during the early months when Hd mothers did not yet have much specific orientation to deafness, provide additional evidence of the power of intuitive parenting to provide "good enough" maternal support to promote positive development. When their deaf infants were only 6 months old, these hearing mothers were already providing some stimulation and communication via multiple modalities, even though none of the mothers had begun using sign language. When their babies were 9 months old, the hearing mothers had increased these combinations of vocal, visual, tactile and kinesthetic behaviors, thus enhancing the likelihood of mutually satisfying and reciprocal early interactions. We cannot say if this change was the result of exposure to intervention, to increasing comfort with their infant, or to increasing experience with the visual needs of their baby—but it clearly was a positive change.

For intervention professionals, our results support the importance of instilling confidence in hearing mothers, empowering them to know that they do indeed have the capability to provide the love, nurturance, security, and skills their deaf infant needs. Hearing parents turn to professionals for help in dealing with their feelings surrounding identification of a hearing loss as well as concrete but often confusing information about technology, communication choices, and interaction.

Deaf Children "Can Do Anything Except Hear"

King Jordan, the first deaf president of Gallaudet University, made this statement a favorite motto in the Deaf community (Christiansen & Barnartt, 1995). It is relevant here because it is important for hearing parents to know that their deaf infants have the potential to develop normally and to lead full, happy, productive lives. It is assumed that every effort is made by professionals to encourage parents to provide their deaf children with appropriate technology to maximize any residual hearing. Beyond this, they must demonstrate the infant's and toddler's capacity to use vision as a substitute for or supplement to audition to understand communicative signals through gestures, lip movements, or formal signs.

The importance of visual attention has been emphasized in several chapters of this book. A deaf child's ability to maintain protracted attention and shift attention between objects and people is highly related to positive language development and to positive social interaction skills. The Dd infants, exposed early to parents' attention-promoting communication devices, were more likely to exhibit social mastery styles at 12 months, suggesting that they had already incorporated social referencing into their repertoires. These infants were also more likely than any others to exhibit Coordinated Joint Attention (CJA), also highly related to mothers' production of signs and gestures, suggesting a reason for the Dd babies' emphasis on social mastery attention patterns.

Communicating to hearing parents that deaf babies have many normal abilities and are able to compensate for lack of sound is critical. Deaf infants have the same range of temperament styles as do other infants. First-time parents, especially, may wrongly believe that an infant's heightened activity or wakefulness is due to hearing loss. Hearing parents may also feel "rejected" by an infant who is "difficult" or often looks away from the parent. The greater need for some infants—deaf or hearing—to have a calm, soothing sensory environment can be expected; adjusting to an infant's individual temperament and rhythm is a normal part of parenting. Conversely, some children are more "spirited" and exuberant than others; regardless of their hearing status they respond better to vigorous stimulation by an animated, expressive partner. Finding the optimal match between an infant's interactive style and that of the parents can be challenging for any family, and one that can be facilitated by the sensitive guidance of early intervention specialists.

There is much encouraging information in our data, useful to parents and professionals: hearing mothers can and do modify their usual interactive styles to match the needs of their deaf infants; the infants can and do develop visual attention skills that help to compensate for their hearing loss. However, this good news is only part of the story.

Helping Parents Improve Their Interaction Skills

Although hearing parents have many of the intuitive skills that will promote their deaf infant's development, these can be complemented by behavioral modifications that may not occur to them, as lifelong members of a hearing-speaking culture. These complementary skills must often be proposed and demonstrated by intervention professionals.

Sensitivity to the developmental needs of a child requires careful attention to the signals provided by the infant. In some cases, infant signals are not easily perceived or interpreted by caregivers, and parents may need help through videotaped feedback of interactions or the example of experienced deaf mothers. Helping parents to see the many ways in which babies communicate nonvocally can provide important support for caregivers' efforts to accommodate to a deaf child's needs and signals. For example, repetitive physical activity observed in some 9-month-old babies suggested that they were temperamentally more active and might need a calmer, more soothing environment. These babies were more likely to have mothers judged to be less sensitive or responsive to their needs when they were 12 months old and to be less socially responsive themselves. Again, early intervention efforts with hearing parents can provide effective feedback to enhance parents' individual styles of interacting with their infant. This detailed level of analysis, therefore, supported other analyses reported in Chapter 4 that suggest a complex interaction between characteristics of mother and infant in the development and support of mature visual attention and social interaction.

Another finding that can provide helpful feedback to hearing mothers is the degree to which deaf mothers used animated, exaggerated facial expressions in their face-to-face interactions with their 9-month-old infants. Mothers' positive facial affect during interactions with their 9-month-old infants was related to their being judged "responsive" when infants were 12 months old. Thus, use of exaggerated and positive facial expression with a very young deaf child may demonstrate a mother's tendency to modify social/communicative behaviors to accommodate a child for whom visual information is critical. Observations of such accommodations may also provide an early measure of the degree of maternal involvement in interactions with the child.

One of the most powerful predictors of positive outcomes for deaf infants was the responsiveness of their mothers. For 18-month-old deaf infants with hearing mothers, maternal responsiveness was related to the infants' development of attention and social skills as well as to their language skills. Responsiveness and sensitivity are somewhat elusive qualities. Important is a mother's ability to respond to her child's interests, to be flexible and gear her pace to her child's preferred activity level. A mother who is comfortable and confident in her parenting role is most able to respond to her child in a sensitive way.

The strong relationship of positive maternal behaviors and social support among mothers participating in this study demonstrates that the emphasis on support in early intervention programs for infants with hearing loss is appropriate and can be effective. The data also show that support from a variety of sources leads to more positive mother–child interaction. Spouse, extended family, and friends continue to be the most important sources of support, suggesting that early intervention professionals should make a special effort to involve parents' social networks in the delivery of services to mothers and their deaf infants.

Our data show that husbands, compared to wives, generally do not feel (at least demonstrate or admit) the same level of stress related to the identification of an infant's hearing loss. Nevertheless, they also benefit from professional support, and their wives certainly benefit from their husband's support.

While several studies point to the significant benefits that accrue in areas such as language development when a child's hearing loss is identified in the first 6 months and the child receives early services, little is known about how parents can best be supported during these early months (Calderon & Naidu, 2000; Moeller, 2000). Only recently have studies on intervention services and the resulting reduction in family stress focused on families whose children were identified in the first 6 months of life. Beyond diagnostic evaluations and audiological interventions, these are the months critical to the formation of a healthy relationship with the primary caregivers.

Even in this privileged group of GIS mothers, support made a significant difference in a mother's ability to respond in a sensitive way to her deaf infant. Reported levels of stress played a relatively insignificant role in this respect. However, it can be assumed that for less privileged mothers, more severe socioeconomic stressors would signal an even greater need for intervention from the time of identification. One study of an indigent community demonstrated the importance of support not only in early intervention, but also in the screening and identification of infants with hearing loss (Connelly & Schneider, 2000).

It may be overly simplistic to propose that generalized "support" will promote parents' sensitive responsiveness to their infants (Sameroff & Fiese, 1990). There is a danger that an emphasis on the importance of stimulation and visual attention can result in increased maternal anxiety as they struggle to "do the right thing." This is the demon, the "rock and the hard place," the Scylla and Charybdis of early intervention practitioners. It is also common for professionals to emphasize that parents should "use every opportunity to provide linguistic input" to a deaf child. However, responsive deaf mothers with deaf infants used relatively few signed utterances in their early interactions with their babies. They were likely to wait until the infant was looking at them and could process a communicative act. Again, prescriptions and suggestions offered to hearing mothers should depend on their individual needs and abilities. For example, some hearing parents may be quite open to looking to deaf parents as models for interaction and attention-getting strategies, whereas others may not be ready soon after diagnosis of a child's hearing loss. The sensitive professional is more likely to provide appropriate guidance if he or she has observational experience with successful parent/infant interactions.

Choice of Communication Mode

The communication mode that is to be used with a deaf child remains a thorny issue for professionals and the hearing parents they serve. Incorporation of formal systems of visual communication into a hearing family requires an enormous commitment, regardless of their use of American Sign Language, an English-based sign system, or Cued Speech. The decision will continue to be (and should be) based on the preference of the individual family, and the extent of a child's residual hearing will influence a family's choice. This research focused on total language, that is, both spoken and signed, in evaluating linguistic progress. Families who focus primarily on developing speech should be informed about the collateral importance of visual attention for their child. Our research suggests that a strict adherence to an auditory–verbal regimen that decreases visual input, although it may be successful with a limited number of children or as an approach to speech therapy, is likely to delay the general language and social development of children with a hearing loss, especially those whose loss is severe or profound.

For deaf children in this study, the mother's use of signs and gestures when the child was 12 months old was strongly related to the child's language progress, social interaction ratings, and visual attention patterns at 18 months. In contrast, mothers' frequency of vocal communications with children at 9 months was inversely related to children's attention to communication at 12 months. Mothers' preferred language modality was consistent over time—for example, those who produced frequent vocal communication at 9 months tended to continue frequent vocal communication at 12 and 18 months, producing few signs and gestures.

Intervention and Assessment

The authors of a recent review of current approaches to early intervention note that an accepted principle is that intervention must be "assessment-based" (Sass-Lehrer & Bodner-Johnson, 2003). Results of this study have implications for assessment (often based on observations of play at these ages) and intervention efforts with deaf infants and toddlers. Data from these deaf children, whose interactive and language experiences differed in systematic ways from those typical for hearing children, can contribute to our understanding of factors influencing play in all children. Professionals who use dyadic play situations for assessing children's development levels must be sensitive to the interactive effects of child and mother behaviors; such an assessment represents a measure of the dyad's functioning, not just that of the child. Analyses in the current study showed a generally predictable developmental sequence for deaf children; however, the play of deaf children at 12 months, especially those with deaf mothers, was not associated significantly with their play levels at 18 months. That is, 12-month play observations did not predict 18-month functioning for these children, even when the mothers were highly sensitive to infants' need for a somewhat slowed pattern of turn taking in order to accommodate immature visual attention skills. In fact, this sensitivity might have led the mothers to interrupt less often and to make fewer suggestions during play sessions with their deaf children before patterns of CJA were established.

Intervention with Deaf Parents and Their Children

The tasks of an intervention specialist working with deaf infants and their deaf parents are quite different from those of working with hearing families. Unlike hearing parents, some deaf parents may welcome the diagnosis of deafness (Orlansky & Heward, 1981; Meadow-Orlans, Mertens, & Sass-Lehrer, 2003). They expect to be able to communicate freely with deaf children and to be competent in meeting their developmental needs. As suggested earlier, deaf children with deaf parents (Dd) were considered to be least at risk for developmental delays or difficulties compared with both Hd and Dh groups. For the most part, this prediction was supported by the data. In most analyses, Dd children were at, or close to, levels of performance of the Hh children (with somewhat higher levels of attention skills). One unexpected exception was the differences in behaviors seen during the Strange Situation Procedure (SSP), assessing the nature of the child's attachment to mother. In the SSP, Dd children were seen to be more "Resistant" than other children when they were reunited with mothers after a separation. It was suggested that deaf mothers might emphasize independence earlier than most hearing American mothers, especially in their deaf children, and that the usual classifications utilized for attachment might not be suitable, because Deaf culture may promote somewhat different childrearing values. This is a hypothesis that needs testing with research, but professionals might be alerted to the possibility of earlier independence training in deaf families.

Early intervention programs serving families with children up to age 3 play an important role in providing family support as well as assessment, programming, and follow-up for deaf infants and toddlers whose parents are hearing. These services form an important part of the social support that contribute to the interactive success of dyads in the Hd group. In contrast with the Hd group, hearing children and their deaf parents are not typically considered to be at risk and are not usually eligible for early intervention or special educational services available to deaf children with either deaf or hearing parents. (Exceptions are programs such as Head Start and the more recent *Early* Head Start, both of which provide services for families in which either a child or parent has a "handicapping" condition.) Like dyads with matched hearing status, Dh mothers and children have access to a shared communication-modality—vision. That is, they have the physical capacity to communicate as well as the Hh or Dd dyads. However, interactive difficulties appeared to emerge for many Dh dyads by 18 months, as communication and interpersonal interaction became more complex and as the children increased their use of vocal communications not accessible by their mothers. It appeared, therefore, that some of the Dh dyads were at risk for interactive difficulties, particularly, in the second year of life. This leads us to believe that deaf mothers with hearing babies can benefit from increased support services addressing parenting tasks and communication that may differ from their preferred and habitual communication modality.

Children with Additional Conditions

For the five infants with multiple disabilities, deafness was sometimes a secondary rather than a primary concern. The four with motor or psychomotor involvements were already receiving physical therapy in addition to special help related to hearing loss. When several different kinds of experts are utilized for intervention with a young child, other problems may emerge. One is related to communication between sets of professionals as well as between each professional and family members. If prescriptions for parental input conflict or if overwhelming demands are placed on parents, priorities must be set. Family members and professionals need to agree on the relative importance of various interventions for different ages and stages. A "case manager" becomes more important for these families.

One research group studied the impact of parent group attendance on families with infants and young children with severe cognitive and motor disabilities (Krauss, Upshur, Shonkoff, & Hauser-Cram, 1993). Researchers found that many parents gained positive benefits from increased peer support and reduced feelings of isolation, but problems were also noted. These included parents who felt they were pressured to discuss their feelings before they were prepared to do so, and some who felt out of place in a group because their child's difficulties either were more severe or were different from those of other group members. Parent groups were not rated as highly as home visits, child groups, and parent–child group activities (Upshur, 1991).

A holistic approach to the development of an Individual Family Service Plan, mandated by Public Law 99-457, is imperative for these children. It is important to learn more about the very early experiences of deaf infants with additional disabilities, and to engage specialists from various disciplines in efforts to develop an optimal intervention plan.

Conclusion

One important lesson to be learned from the infants participating in this study is the diversity of their experiences in the first weeks and months of life. They were born into relatively privileged environments: middle class, college-educated, two-parent families. They have the advantages of caring, nurturing parents, early diagnosis and prompt intervention, all of which combine to predict positive developmental outcomes despite the risk factors associated with their early histories. Nevertheless, their medical biographies, particular temperaments, and motor capabilities require individually designed programs for remediating existing difficulties and preventing future complications. All of this reinforces the mandate of Public Law 99-457, which requires an Individual Family Service Plan for young children with disabilities. Those with multiple disabilities require parents and caregivers to give special attention to their individual needs for human interaction, communication, stimulation, and nurturance.

Finally, investigations that focus on children whose experiences differ from those typical for hearing children can lend clarity to descriptions of associations between experiences and developing abilities. In this study, differences among the groups in sensory experiences, characteristics of maternal interactive behaviors, and rate of language development illuminated the interrelationships among those variables. The resulting picture supports the inclusion of multiple factors in these investigations. Simple bi-variate associations between one or more factors can be misleading.

Although technology exists for prompt detection of congenital deafness, many infants with a significant hearing loss continue to slip through the broad cracks in medical service delivery systems and remain undiagnosed during the important early months (even years) of their lives. This study and others conducted with children who experience different kinds of developmental risks demonstrate that maternal support benefits the parent–child relationship, freeing mothers to be more responsive to their child's interactive needs. However, the factors considered in this study explained only about 30% to 40% of the variance in children's performance. Additional longitudinal investigations of the impact of multiple factors are needed to explain this complex developmental process further. The goal is "to understand the processes that lead to [positive] outcomes, not just to generate indexes about them, so that problematic and compromised developmental outcomes can be prevented and remediated" (Tronick, 1989, p. 112). The world of deaf infants and toddlers is more positive today than in the past, partly because of research results incorporated into intervention programs for increasingly younger children. That world can and should be enhanced through an environment as positive as that of hearing peers. We hope this book helps to bring children closer to the goal through the efforts of parents and professionals, and that future research will broaden the world of deaf infants even further.

References

Abidin, R. R. (1986). *Parenting Stress Index—Manual (PSI)*. Charlottesville, VA: Pediatric Psychology Press.

Adamson, L. B., & Bakeman, R. (1991). The development of shared attention during infancy. *Annals of Child Development 8*, 1–41.

Adamson, L. B., & Chance, S. E. (1998). Coordinating attention to people, objects, and language. In A. M. Wetherby, S. F. Warren, & J. Reichle (Eds.), *Transitions in prelinguistic communication* (pp. 15–37). Baltimore: Brookes.

Ainsworth, M. D. S., & Bell, S. M. (1970). Attachment, exploration and separation: Illustrated by the behavior of one-year-olds in a strange situation. *Child Development, 41*, 49–67.

Ainsworth, M. D. S., Bell, S. M., & Stayton, D. (1974). Infant–mother attachment and social development: "Socialization" as a product of reciprocal responsiveness to signals. In M. P. M. Richards (Ed.), *The integration of the child into a social world* (pp. 99–135). London: Cambridge University Press.

Ainsworth, M. D. S., Blehar, M. C., Waters, E., & Wall, S. (1978). *Patterns of attachment: A psychological study of the strange situation.* Hillsdale, NJ: Erlbaum.

Ainsworth, M. D. S., & Wittig, B. A. (1969). Attachment and exploratory behavior of 1-year-olds in a strange situation. In B. M. Foss (Ed.), *Determinants of infant behavior,* (Vol. 4, pp. 129–173). London: Metheum.

Alpern, G. D., Boll, T. J., & Shearer, M. S. (rev., 1980). *Manual, Developmental profile* II. Aspen, CO: Psychological Development Publications.

Als, H. (1982). The unfolding of behavioral organization in the face of a biological violation. In E. Z. Tronick (Ed.), *Social interchange in infancy* (pp. 125–160). Baltimore: University Park Press.

Als, H., Tronick, E. Z., & Brazelton, T. B. (1980). Stages of early behavioral organization: The study of a sighted infant and a blind infant in interaction with their mothers. In T. M. Field, S. Goldberg, D. Stern, & A. M. Sostek (Eds.), *High-risk infants and children* (pp. 181–204). New York: Academic Press.

Altshuler, K. Z., Deming, W. E., Vollenweider, J., Rainer, J. D., & Tendler, R. (1976). Impulsivity and profound early deafness. A cross cultural inquiry. *American Annals of the Deaf, 121*, 331–345.

American Academy of Pediatrics (1999). Newborn and infant hearing loss: Detection and intervention. *Pediatrics, 103*(2), 527–530. *http://www.aap.org/policy/re9846.html* (available 1/13/03).

American Speech-Language-Hearing Association (2003). Newborns and infants. *http://www.asha.org/hearing/testing/index.cfm#newborn* (available 1/14/03).

American Psychological Association (1982). *Ethical principles in the conduct of research with human participants.* Washington, DC: Author.

American Psychological Association (1992). *Ethical principles of psychologists and code of conduct. http://apa.org/ethics.*

Anderson, D., & Reilly, J. (2002). The MacArthur Communicative Development Inventory: Normative data for American Sign Language. *Journal of Deaf Studies and Deaf Education, 7*(2), 83–106.

Atkinson, J. W. (1957). Motivational determinants of risk-taking behavior. *Psychological Review, 64,* 359–372.

Atkinson, L., Chisholm, V. C., Scott, B., Goldberg, S., Vaughn, B. E., Blackwell, J. Dickens, S., & Tam, F. (1999). Maternal sensitivity, child functional level, and attachment in Down syndrome. In J. I. Vondra & D. Barnett (Eds.), *Atypical attachment in infancy and early childhood among children at developmental risk* (pp. 45–66). *Monographs of the Society for Research in Child Development, 64* (3, Serial No. 258).

Bakeman, R., & Adamson, L. (1984). Coordinating attention to people and objects in mother–infant and peer–infant interaction. *Child Development, 55,* 1278–1289.

Bakeman, R., & Brown, J. V. (1980). Early interaction: Consequences for social and mental development at three years. *Child Development, 51,* 437–447.

Baker, C. (1977). Regulators and turn-taking in American Sign Language discourse. In L. Friedman (Ed.), *On the other hand: New perspectives on American Sign Language.* (pp. 215–241). New York: Academic Press.

Barrett, K. C., MacTurk, R. H., & Morgan, G. A. (1995). Concluding comments on mastery motivation: Origins, conceptualizations, and applications. In R. H. MacTurk & G. A. Morgan (Eds.), *Mastery motivation: Origins, conceptualizations, and applications* (pp. 339–359). Norwood, NJ: Ablex.

Bates, E. (1979). Pragmatics and sociolinguistics in child language. In D. Morehead & A. Morehead (Eds.), *Normal and deficient child language.* Baltimore: University Park Press.

Bates, E., Bretherton, I., Snyder, L., Shore, R., & Volterra, V. (1980). Gestural and vocal symbols at 13 months. *Merrill-Palmer Quarterly, 26,* 407–423.

Bates, J. E. (1987). Temperament in infancy. In J. D. Osofsky (Ed.), *Handbook of infant development* (2nd ed., pp. 1101–1149). New York: Wiley.

Bates, J. E. (1994). Parents as scientific observers of their children's development. In S. L. Friedman & H. C. Haywood (Eds.), *Developmental follow-up: Concepts, domains, and methods* (pp. 197–216). New York: Academic Press.

Baumwell, L., Tamis-LeMonda, C., & Bornstein, M. (1997). Maternal verbal sensitivity and child language comprehension. *Infant Behavior and Development, 20,* 247–258.

Beckman, P. J. (1983). Influence of selected child characteristics on stress in families of handicapped infants. *American Journal of Mental Deficiency, 88,* 150–156.

Beckman, P. J. (1991). Comparison of mothers' and fathers' perceptions of the effect of young children with and without disabilities. *American Journal of Mental Retardation, 95,* 585–595.

Beckman, P. J., Pokorni, J. L., Maza, E. A., & Balzer-Martin, L. (1986). A longitudinal study of stress and support in families of preterm and full-term infants. *Journal of the Division of Early Childhood, 11,* 2–9.

Bell, S., & Ainsworth, M. (1972). Infant crying and maternal responsiveness. *Child Development, 43,* 1171–1190.

Belsky, J. (1999). Interactional and contextual determinants of attachment security. In J. Cassidy & P. R. Shaver (Eds.), *Handbook of attachment: Theory, research, and clinical applications* (pp. 249–264). New York: Guilford.

Belsky, J., Garduque, L., & Hrncir, E. (1984). Assessing performance, competence, and executive capacity in infant play: Relations to home environment and security of attachment. *Developmental Psychology, 20,* 406–417.

Belsky, J., & Most, R. (1981). From exploration to play: A cross-sectional study of infant free play behavior. *Developmental Psychology, 17*(5), 630–639.

Belsky, J., & Rovine, M. (1987). Temperament and attachment security in the strange situation: An empirical rapprochement. *Child Development, 58,* 787–795.

Belsky, J., Taylor, D.G., & Rovine, M. (1984a). The Pennsylvania Infant and Family Development Project, II: The development of reciprocal interaction in the mother–infant dyad. *Child Development, 55,* 706–717.

Belsky, J., Taylor, D. G., & Rovine, M. (1984b). The Pennsylvania/Infant and Family Project, III: The origins of individual differences in infant–mother attachment. *Child Development, 55,* 718–728.

Blehar, M.C., Lieberman, A.F., & Ainsworth, M.D.S. (1977). Early face-to-face interaction and its relation to later infant–mother attachment. *Child Development, 48,* 182–194.

Bess, F. H. (1985). The minimally hearing-impaired child. *Ear and Hearing, 6*(1), 43–47.

Bess, F., Dodd-Murphy, J., & Parker, R. (1998). Children with minimal sensorineural hearing loss: Prevalence, educational performance, and functional status. *Ear and Hearing, 19*(5), 339–354.

Black, M. M. (1991). Early intervention services for infants and toddlers: A focus on families. *Journal of Clinical Child Psychology, 20,* 51–57.

Bonvillian, J. D., & Folven, R. J. (1993). Sign language acquisition: Developmental aspects. In M. Marschark & M. D. Clark (Eds.), *Psychological perspectives on deafness* (pp. 229–265). Hillsdale, NJ: Erlbaum.

Bonvillian, J., Orlansky, M., & Folven, R. (1994). Early sign language acquisition: Implications for theories of language acquisition. In V. Volterra & C. Erting (Eds.), *From gesture to language in hearing and deaf children* (pp. 219–232). Washington DC: Gallaudet University Press.

Bonvillian, J., Orlansky, M., Novack, L., & Folven, R. (1983). Early sign language acquisition and cognitive development. In D. Rogers & J. Sloboda (Eds.), *The acquisition of symbolic skills* (pp. 207–214). New York: Plenum.

Bornstein, M. H., Selmi, A. M., Haynes, O. M., Painter, K. M., & Marx, E. S. (1999). Representational abilities and the hearing status of child/mother dyads. *Child Development, 70,* 833–852.

Boukydis, C. F. Z., Lester, B. M., & Hoffman, J. (1987). Parenting and social support networks in families of term and preterm infants. In C. F. Z. Boukydis (Ed.), *Research on support for parents and infants in the postnatal period* (pp. 61–83). Norwood, NJ: Ablex.

Bowlby, J. (1958). The nature of the child's tie to his mother. *International Journal of Psychoanalysis, 39,* 350–373.

Bowlby, J. (1969). *Attachment and loss: Vol. I. Attachment.* New York: Basic Books.

Brasel, K. E., & Quigley, S. P. (1977). Influence of certain language and communication environments in early childhood on the development of language in deaf individuals. *Journal of Speech and Hearing Research, 20,* 81–94.

Braungart-Rieker, J., Garwood, M. M., Powers, B. P., & Notaro, P. C. (1998). Infant affect and affect regulation during the still-face paradigm with mothers and fathers: The role of infant characteristics and parental sensitivity. *Developmental Psychology, 34* (6), 1428–1437.

Brazelton, T. B. (1982). Joint regulation of neonate–parent behavior. In E. Z. Tronick (Ed.), *Social interchange in infancy: Affect, cognition, and communication* (pp. 7–22). Baltimore: University Park Press.

Brazelton, T. B., & Cramer, B. G. (1990). *The earliest relationship. Parents, infants, and the drama of early attachment.* Reading, MA: Addison-Wesley.

Brazelton, T. B., & Greenspan, S. I. (2000). *The irreducible needs of children. What every child must have to grow, learn, and flourish.* Cambridge, MA: Perseus Publishing.

Brazelton, T. B., Koslowski, B., & Main, M. (1974). The origins of reciprocity: The early mother–infant interaction. In M. Lewis & L. Rosenblum (Eds.), *The effect of the infant on its caregiver* (pp. 49–77). New York: Wiley.

Brelje, H. W. (1971). *A study of the relationship between articulation and vocabulary of hearing impaired parents and their normally hearing children.* Doctoral dissertation, University of Portland, Oregon.

Brinich, P. M. (1980). Childhood deafness and maternal control. *Journal of Communication Disorders, 13,* 75–81.

Bristol, M. M., Gallagher, J. J., & Schopler, E. (1988). Mothers and fathers of young developmentally disabled and nondisabled boys: Adaptation and spousal support. *Developmental Psychology, 24,* 441–451.

Brown, P. M., Prescott, S., Rickards, F., & Paterson, M. (1997). Communicating about pretend play: A comparison of the utterances of four-year-old normally hearing and hearing-impaired children in an integrated kindergarten. *The Volta Review, 99*(1), 5–17.

Brown, P. M., Rickards, F., & Bortoli, A. (2001). Structures underpinning pretend play and word production in young hearing children and children with hearing loss. *Journal of Deaf Studies and Deaf Education, 6*(1), 15–31.

Buchino, M. A. (1993). Hearing children of deaf parents: Perspectives on the parent–child relationship. *American Annals of the Deaf, 138,* 40–45.

Busch-Rossnagel, N. A., Knauf-Jensen, D. E., & DesRosiers, F. S. (1995). Mothers and others: The role of the socializing environment in the development of mastery motivation. In R. H. MacTurk & G. A. Morgan (Eds.), *Mastery motivation: Origins, conceptualizations, and applications* (pp. 117–145). Norwood, NJ: Ablex.

Buss, D. M., & Plomin, R. (1984). *Temperament: Early developing personality traits.* Hillsdale, NJ: Erlbaum.

Butterfield, P. M., & Miller, L. (1984). Read your baby: A follow-up intervention program for parents with NICU infants. *Infant Mental Health Journal, 5,* 107–116.

Calderon, R., & Greenberg, M. T. (1993). Considerations in the adaptation of families with school-aged deaf children. In M. Marschark & M. D. Clark (Eds.), *Psychological perspectives on deafness* (pp. 27–47). Mahwah, NJ: Erlbaum.

Calderon, R., & Greenberg, M. T. (2000). Challenges to parents and professionals in promoting socioemotional development in deaf children. In P. E. Spencer, C. J. Erting, & M. Marschark (Eds.), *The deaf child in the family and at school: Essays in honor of Kathryn P. Meadow-Orlans* (pp. 167–189). Mahwah, NJ: Erlbaum.

Calderon, R., & Greenberg, M. T. (2003). Social and emotional development of deaf children. In M. Marschark & P. Spencer (Eds.), *Oxford handbook of deaf studies, language, and education* (pp. 177–189). New York: Oxford University Press.

Calderon, R., & Naidu, S. (2000). Further support for the benefits of early identification and intervention for children with hearing loss [Monograph]. *Volta Review, 100*(5), 53–84.

Calkins, S. D., & Fox, N. A. (1992). The relations among infant temperament, security of attachment, and behavioral inhibition at twenty-four months. *Child Development, 63,* 1456–1472.

Carpenter, M., Nagell, K., & Tomasello, M. (1998). Social cognition, joint attention, and communicative competence from 9 to 15 months of age. *Monographs of the Society for Research in Child Development, 63* (Serial No. 255).

Carter, A. S., Mayes, L. C., & Pajer, K. A. (1990). The role of dyadic affect in play and infant sex in predicting infant response to the still-face situation. *Child Development, 61,* 764–773.

Casby, M., & McCormack, S. (1985). Symbolic play and early communication development of hearing-impaired children. *Journal of Communication Disorders, 18,* 67–78.

Cassidy, J. (1999). The nature of the child's ties. In J. Cassidy & P. R. Shaver (Eds.), *Handbook of attachment: Theory, research, and clinical applications* (pp. 3–20). New York: Guilford.

Cassidy, J., & Berlin, L. J. (1994). The Insecure/Ambivalent pattern of attachment: Theory and research. *Child Development, 65,* 971–991.

Chance, P. (1979). *Learning through play*. New York: Gardner.

Chao, R. (2001). Integrating culture and attachment. *American Psychologist, 56,* 822–823.

Chess, S., & Thomas, A. (1996). *Temperament: Theory and practice*. Philadelphia: Brunner/Mazel.

Chodorow, N. (1978). *The reproduction of mothering: Psychoanalysis and the sociology of gender*. Berkeley: University of California Press.

Christiansen, J. B., & Barnartt, S. N. (1995). *Deaf president now! The 1988 revolution at Gallaudet University*. Washington, DC: Gallaudet University Press.

Cicchetti, D., & Sroufe, L. A. (1976). The relationship between affective and cognitive development in Down's syndrome infants. *Child Development, 47,* 920–929.

Cleary, P. J. (1980). A checklist for life event research. *Journal of Psychosomatic Research, 24,* 199–207.

Clifton, R. (1992). The development of spatial hearing in human infants. In L. Werner & E. Rubel (Eds.), *Developmental psychoacoustics* (pp. 135–157). Washington, DC: American Psychological Association.

Clyman, R. B., Emde, R. N., Kempe, J. E., & Harmon, R. J. (1986). Social referencing and social looking among twelve-month-old infants. In T. B. Brazelton & M. W. Yogman (Eds.), *Affective development in infancy* (pp. 75–94). Norwood, NJ: Ablex.

Coates, D. L., Vietze, P. M., & Gray D. B. (1985). Methodological issues in studying children of disabled parents. In S. K. Thurman (Ed.), *Children of handicapped parents: Research and clinical perspectives* (pp. 155–180). Orlando, FL: Academic Press.

Cohn, J. F., Campbell, S. B., & Ross, S. (1992). Infant response in the still-face paradigm at 6 months predicts avoidant and secure attachment at 12 months. *Development and Psychopathology, 3,* 367–376.

Cohn, J. F., Matias, R., Campbell, S. B., & Hopkins, J. (1990). Face-to-face interactions of post-partum depressed mother–infant pairs at 2 months. *Developmental Psychology, 26,* 15–23.

Cohn, J. F., & Tronick, E. Z. (1982). Communicative rules and the sequential structure of infant behavior during normal and depressed interaction. In E. Z. Tronick (Ed.), *Social interchange in infancy* (pp. 59–78). Baltimore: University Park Press.

Colin, V. L. (1996). *Human attachment.* New York: McGraw-Hill.

Colombo, J., Mitchell, D. W., Coldren, J. T., & Freeseman, L. J. (1991). Individual differences in infant visual attention: Are short lookers faster processors or feature processors? *Child Development, 62,* 1247–1257.

Connelly, P. E., & Schneider, N. G. (2000, October). *Societal and cultural impact on effectiveness of newborn hearing screening in an urban teaching hospital.* Paper presented at the International Conference on Newborn Hearing Screening, Milan, Italy.

Craig, H. B. (1992). Parent–infant education in schools for deaf children before and after PL 99–457. *American Annals of the Deaf, 137*(2), 69–78.

Crandell, L. E., Fitzgerald, H. E., & Whipple, E. E. (1997). Dyadic synchrony in parent–child interactions: A link with maternal representations of attachment relationships. *Infant Mental Health Journal, 18*(3), 247–264.

Crawley, S. B., & Spiker, D. (1983). Mother–child interactions involving two-year-olds with Down syndrome: A look at individual differences. *Child Development, 54,* 1312–1323.

Crinic, K. A., & Greenberg, M. T. (1985, April). *Parenting daily hassles: Relationships among minor stresses, family functioning and child development.* Paper presented at the Biennial Meeting of the Society for Research in Child Development, Toronto, Ontario.

Crnic, K. A, & Greenberg, M. T. (1990). Minor parenting stresses with young children. *Child Development, 61,* 1628–1637.

Crnic, K. A., Greenberg, M. T., Ragozin, A. S., Robinson, N. M., & Basham, R. (1983). Effects of stress and social support on mothers and premature and full-term infants. *Child Development, 54,* 209–217.

Crnic, K. A., Greenberg, M. T., & Slough, N. M. (1986). Early stress and social support influences on mothers' and high-risk infants' functioning in late infancy. *Infant Mental Health Journal, 7,* 19–33.

Crockenberg, S. (1987). Support for adolescent mothers during the postnatal period: Theory and research. In C. F. Z. Boukydis (Ed.), *Research on support for parents and infants in the postnatal period* (pp. 3–24). Norwood, NJ: Ablex.

Cross, T., Johnson-Morris, J., & Nienhuys, T. (1980). Linguistic feedback and maternal speech: Comparisons of mothers addressing hearing and hearing impaired children. *First Language, 1,* 163–189.

Crowley, M., Keane, K., & Needham, C. (1982). Fathers: The forgotten parents. *American Annals of the Deaf, 127,* 38–40.

Cruttenden, A. (1994). Phonetic and prosodic aspects of baby talk. In C. Gallaway & B. J. Richards (Eds.), *Input and interaction in language acquisition* (pp. 135–152). New York: Cambridge University Press.

Darbyshire, J. (1977). Play patterns in young children with impaired hearing. *The Volta Review, 79,* 19–26.

Davis, J., Elfenbein, J., Schum, R., & Bentler, R. (1986). Effects of mild and moderate hearing impairment on language, education, and psychosocial behavior of children. *Journal of Speech and Hearing Disorders, 51,* 53–62.

Davis, L. J. (2000). *My sense of silence: Memoirs of a childhood with deafness*. Urbana: University of Illinois Press.

Day (Spencer), P. (1986). Deaf children's expression of communicative intentions. *Journal of Communication Disorders, 19,* 367–385.

D'Entremont, B., & Muir, D. (1997). Five-month-olds' attention and affective responses to still-faced emotional expressions. *Infant Behavior and Development, 20,* 563–568.

Department of Health and Human Services (1991). *Protection of Human Subjects*. Title 45, Code of Federal Regulations, Part 46. Rev. June 18, 1991. Washington, DC: U.S. Government Printing Office.

de Villiers, J., Bibeau, L., Helliwell, K., & Clare, A. (1989, April). *Speech and gestural communication between oral deaf children and oral deaf mothers.* Paper presented at the biennial meetings of the Society for Research in Child Development, Kansas City, MO.

DeWolff, M., & van IJzendoorn, M. (1997). Sensitivity and attachment: A meta-analysis on parental antecedents of infant attachment. *Child Development, 68,* 571–591.

Dohrenwend, B. S. (1973). Life events as stressors: A methodological inquiry. *Journal of Health and Social Behavior, 14,* 167–175.

Dohrenwend, B. S., Krasnoff, L., Askenasy, A. R., & Dohrenwend, B. P. (1978). Exemplification of a method for scaling life events: The PERI life events scale. *Journal of Health and Social Behavior, 19,* 205–229.

Dokecki, P. R., & Heflinger, C. A. (1989). Strengthening families of young children with handicapping conditions: Mapping backward from the "street level." In J. J. Gallagher, P. L. Trohanis, & R. M. Clifford (Eds.), *Policy implementation and PL 99–457* (pp. 59–84), Baltimore: Brookes.

Dore, J. (1974). A pragmatic description of early language development. *Journal of Psycholinguistic Research, 3,* 343–350.

Dunham, P., & Dunham, F. (1992). Lexical development during middle infancy: A mutually driven infant–caregiver process. *Developmental Psychology, 28,* 414–420.

Dunst, C. J., Jenkins, V., & Trivette, C. M. (1984). The Family Support Scale: Reliability and validity. *Journal of Individual, Family, and Community Wellness, 1,* 45–52.

Dunst, C. J., & Trivette, C. M. (1986). Looking beyond the parent–child dyad for the determinants of maternal styles of interaction. *Infant Mental Health Journal, 7,* 69–80.

Dyson, L. L. (1991). Families of young children with handicaps: Parental stress and family functioning. *American Journal of Mental Retardation, 95,* 623–629.

Egeland, B., & Farber, B. (1984). Infant–mother attachment: Factors related to its development and changes over time. *Child Development, 55,* 753–771.

Ellsworth, C. P., Muir, D. W., & Hains, S. (1993). Social competence and person–object differentiation: An analysis of the still-face effect. *Developmental Psychology, 29,* 63–73.

Elssmann, S. F., Matkin, N. D., & Sabo, M. P. (1987). Early identification of congenital sensorineural hearing impairment. *The Hearing Journal, 9,* 13–17.

Erikson, E. H. (1959). *Identity and the life cycle*. New York: International Universities Press.

Erikson, E. H. (1963). *Childhood and society*. New York: Norton.

Erting, C. J. (1994). *Deafness, communication, and social identity: Ethnography in a preschool for deaf children*. Burtonsville, MD: Linstok.

Erting, C. J., Johnson, R. C., Smith, D. L., & Snider, B. D. (Eds.). (1994). *The Deaf way. Perspectives from the international conference on Deaf culture*. Washington, DC: Gallaudet University Press.

Erting, C. J., Prezioso, C., & Hynes, M. O. (1990). The interactional context of deaf mother–infant communication. In V. Volterra & C. J. Erting (Eds.), *From gesture to language in deaf and hearing children* (pp. 97–106). Berlin: Springer-Verlag. (Reprinted Washington, DC: Gallaudet University Press, 1994.)

Erting, C. J., Thumann-Prezioso, C., & Benedict, B. S. (2000). Bilingualism in a deaf family: Fingerspelling in early childhood. In P. E. Spencer, C. J. Erting, & M. Marschark (Eds.), *The deaf child in the family and at school. Essays in honor of Kathryn P. Meadow-Orlans* (pp. 41–54). Mahwah, NJ: Erlbaum

Fant, L. J., Jr., & Schuchman, J. S. (1974). Experiences of two hearing children of deaf parents. In P. J. Fine (Ed.), *Deafness in infancy and early childhood* (pp. 225–229). New York: Medcom.

Feinman, S. (1982). Social referencing in infancy. *Merrill-Palmer Quarterly, 28,* 445–470.

Feiring, C., Fox, N., Jaskir, J., & Lewis, M. (1987). The relation between social support, infant risk status and mother–infant interaction. *Developmental Psychology, 23,* 400–405.

Fenson, L., Dale, P., Reznick, J., Thal, D., Bates, E., Hartung, J., Pethick, S., & Reilly, J. (1993). *The MacArthur Communicative Development Inventories: User's guide and technical manual.* San Diego, CA: Singular.

Fenson, L., & Ramsay, D. (1980). Decentration and integration of the child's play in the second year. *Child Development, 51,* 171–178.

Fernald, A. (1989). Intonation and communicative intent in mothers' speech to infants: Is the melody the message? *Child Development, 60,* 1497–1510.

Fewell, R. R. (1983). Working with sensorily impaired children. In S. G. Garwood (Ed.), *Educating young handicapped children, A developmental approach,* (2nd ed., pp. 235–280). Rockville, MD: Aspen.

Field, T. M. (1978). The three R's of infant–adult interaction: Rhythms, repertoires, and responsivity. *Journal of Pediatric Psychology, 3,* 131–136.

Field, T. M. (1980). Interactions of preterm and term infants with their lower- and middle-class teenage and adult mothers. In T. M. Field, S. Goldberg, D. Stern, & A. M. Sostek (Eds.), *High-risk infants and children* (pp. 113–132). New York: Academic Press.

Fiese, B. (1990). Playful relationships: A contextual analysis of mother–toddler interaction and symbolic play. *Child Development, 61,* 1648–1656.

Fischler, R. (1985). The pediatrician's role in early identification. In E. Cherow (Ed.), *Hearing-impaired children and youth with developmental disabilities* (pp. 101–121). Washington, DC: Gallaudet University Press.

Fogel, A. (1977). Temporal organization in mother–infant face to face interaction. In H. R. Schaffer (Ed.), *Studies in mother–infant interaction* (pp. 119–151). London: Academic Press.

Fogel, A. (2001). *Infancy: Infant, family, and society.* Belmont, CA: Wadsworth/Thomson Learning.

Fosha, D. (2000). *The transforming power of affect: A model for accelerated change*. New York: Basic Books.

Foster, S. (1993/1994). Outsider in the deaf world: Reflections of an ethnographic researcher. *Journal of the Deafness and Rehabilitation Association,* 27, 1–10.

Fraiberg, S. H. (1977). *Insights from the blind.* New York: Basic Books.

Freeman, R. D., Malkin, S. F., & Hastings, J. O. (1975). Psychosocial problems of deaf children and their families: A comparative study. *American Annals of the Deaf, 120,* 391–405.

Frey, K. S., Greenberg, M. T., & Fewell, R. R. (1989). Stress and coping among parents of handicapped children: A multidimensional approach. *American Journal of Mental Retardation, 94,* 240–249.

Galenson, E., Miller, R., Kaplan, E., & Rothstein, A. (1979). Assessment of development in the deaf child. *Journal of the American Academy of Child Psychiatry, 18,* 128–142.

Gallagher, J. J. (1990). The family as a focus for intervention. In S. J. Meisels & J. P. Shonkoff (Eds.), *Handbook of early childhood intervention* (pp. 540–559). Cambridge: Cambridge University Press.

Gallagher, J. J., Beckman, P., & Cross, A. H. (1983). Families of handicapped children: Sources of stress and its amelioration. *Exceptional Children, 50,* 10–19.

Gallaway, C., & Woll, B. (1994). Interaction and childhood deafness. In C. Gallaway & B. J. Richards (Eds.), *Input and interaction in language acquisition* (pp. 197–218). New York: Cambridge University Press.

Gatty, J. (1990). *The effects of deafness on play in four-year-old boys.* Unpublished doctoral dissertation, University of Massachusetts, Amherst.

Gaustad, M. G. (1988). Development of vocal and signed communication in deaf and hearing twins of deaf parents. In M. Strong (Ed.), *Language learning and deafness* (pp. 220–260). Cambridge: Cambridge University Press.

Gjerde, P. F. (2001). Attachment, culture, and *amae. American Psychologist, 56,* 826–827.

Goldberg, S., Marcovitch, S., MacGregor, D., & Lojkasek, M. (1986). Family responses to developmentally delayed preschoolers: Etiology and the father's role. *American Journal of Mental Deficiency, 90,* 610–617.

Goldsmith, H. H., Buss, A. H., Plomin, R., Rothbart, M. K., Thomas, A., Chess, S., Hinde, R. A., & McCall, R. B. (1987). Roundtable: What is temperament? Four approaches. *Child Development, 58,* 505–529.

Goss, R. N. (1970). Language used by mothers of deaf children and mothers of hearing children. *American Annals of the Deaf, 115,* 93–96.

Gottfried, A. E., Fleming, J. S., & Gottfried, A. W. (2001). Continuity of academic intrinsic motivation from childhood through late adolescence: A longitudinal study. *Journal of Educational Psychology, 93,* 3–13.

Gowen, J. W., Johnson-Martin, N., Goldman, B. D., & Appelbaum, M. (1989). Feelings of depression and parenting competence of mothers of handicapped and nonhandicapped infants: A longitudinal study. *American Journal of Mental Retardation, 94,* 259–271.

Greenberg, M. T. (1980). Social interaction between deaf preschoolers and their mothers: The effects of communication method and communicative competence. *Developmental Psychology, 16,* 465–474.

Greenberg, M. T. (1983). Family stress and child competence: The effects of early intervention for families with deaf infants. *American Annals of the Deaf, 128,* 407–417.

Greenberg, M., Calderon, R., & Kusché, C. (1984). Early intervention using simultaneous communication with deaf infants: The effect on communication development. *Child Development, 55,* 607–616.

Greenberg, M. T., & Crnic, K.A. (1988). Longitudinal predictors of developmental status and social interaction in premature and full-term infants at age two. *Child Development, 59,* 554–570.

Greenberg, M. T., & Marvin, R. S. (1979). Attachment patterns in profoundly deaf school children. *Merrill-Palmer Quarterly, 25,* 265–279.

Greenspan, S. I. (with Benderly, B. L.) (1997). *The growth of the mind and the endangered origins of intelligence.* Reading, MA: Perseus Books.

Gregory, S., & Barlow, S. (1989). Interactions between deaf babies and their deaf and hearing mothers. In B. Woll (Ed.), *Language development and sign language* (pp. 23–35). Monograph No.1, International Sign Linguistics Association. Bristol, UK: Centre for Deaf Studies, University of Bristol.

Gregory, S., & Mogford, K. (1983). The development of symbolic play in young deaf children. In D. Rodgers & J. Sloboda (Eds.), *The acquisition of symbolic skills* (pp. 221–231). New York: Plenum.

Griffith, P. L. (1990). Emergence of mode-finding and mode-switching in a hearing child of deaf parents. In V. Volterra & C. Erting (Eds.), *From gesture to language in hearing and deaf children* (pp. 233–246). Berlin: Springer-Verlag.

Grossmann, K., Grossmann, K. E., Spangler, G., Suess, G., & Unzner, L. (1985). Maternal sensitivity and newborns' orientation responses as related to quality of attachment in northern Germany. In I. Bretherton & E. Waters (Eds.), *Growing points of attachment theory and research.* (pp. 233–256). *Monographs of the Society for Research in Child Development, 50* (Serial No. 209, Nos. 1–2).

Gusella, J.L., Muir, D., & Tronick, E.Z. (1988). The effect of manipulating maternal behavior during an interaction on three- and six-month-old's affect and attention. *Child Development, 59,* 1111–1124.

Haekel, M. (1985). *Greeting behavior in 3-month-old infants' mother–infant interaction.* Poster presented at the Eighth Biennial Meeting of the International Society for the Study of Behavioral Development, Tours, France. (Abstracted in *Cahiers de Psychologie Cognitive, 5,* 275–276.)

Hafer, J., & Topolosky, A. (1995, June). *Facilitating language through play.* Paper presented at the Conference of American Instructors of the Deaf. Minneapolis, MN.

Halpern, R. (1993). *Poverty and infant development.* In C.H. Zeanah, Jr. (Ed.), *Handbook of infant mental health* (pp. 73–86). New York: Guilford.

Harmon, R. J., & Culp, A. M. (1981). The effects of premature birth on family functioning and infant development. In I. Berlin (Ed.), *Children and our future* (pp. 1–9). Albuquerque: University of New Mexico Press.

Harmon, R. J., & Murrow, N. S. (1995). The effects of prematurity and other perinatal factors on infants' mastery motivation. In R. H. MacTurk & G. A. Morgan (Eds.), *Mastery motivation: Origins, conceptualizations, and applications* (pp. 237–256). Norwood, NJ: Ablex.

Harris, M. (1992). *Language experience and early language development: From input to uptake.* Hillsdale, NJ: Erlbaum.

Harris, M. (2001). It's all a matter of timing: Sign visibility and sign reference in deaf and hearing mothers of 18–month-old children. *Journal of Deaf Studies and Deaf Education, 6,* 177–185.

Harris, M., Clibbens, J., Chasin, J., & Tibbitts, R. (1989). The social context of early sign language development. *First Language, 9,* 81–97.

Harris, M., & Mohay, H. (1997). Learning to look in the right place: A comparison of attentional behavior in deaf children with deaf and hearing mothers. *Journal of Deaf Studies and Deaf Education, 2,* 96–102.

Harris, R.I. (1978). The relation of impulse control to parent hearing status, manual communication, and academic achievement in deaf children. *American Annals of the Deaf, 123,* 52–67.

Harter, S. (1975). Developmental differences in the manifestation of mastery motivation on problem-solving tasks. *Child Development, 46,* 370–378.

Harvey, M. A. (1989). *Psychotherapy with deaf and hard-of-hearing persons. A systemic model.* Hillsdale, NJ: Erlbaum.

Harwood, R. L., Miller, J. G., & Lucca Irizarry, N. (1995). *Culture and attachment: Perceptions of the child in context.* New York: Guilford.

Hauser-Cram, P., Warfield, M. E., Shonkoff, J. P., & Krauss, M. W. (2001). Children with disabilities: A longitudinal study of child development and parent well-being. *Monographs of the Society for Research in Child Development, 66* (3, Serial No. 266).

Hayes, D. (1999). State programs for universal newborn hearing screening. *Pediatric Clinics of North America, 46*(1), 89–94.

Henggeler, S. W., Watson, S. M., Whelan, J. P., & Malone, C. M. (1990). The adaptation of hearing parents of hearing-impaired youths. *American Annals of the Deaf, 135,* 211–216.

Higginbotham, D., & Baker, B. (1981). Social participation and cognitive play differences in hearing impaired and normally hearing preschoolers. *The Volta Review, 83,* 135–149.

Hindley, P. (2000). Child and adolescent psychiatry. In P. Hindley & N. Kitson (Eds.), *Mental health and deafness* (pp. 42–74). London: Whurr.

Hoffmeister, R. J. (1985). Families with deaf parents: A functional perspective. In S. K. Thurman (Ed.), *Children of handicapped parents, research and clinical perspectives* (pp. 111–130). Orlando, FL: Academic Press.

Holden-Pitt, L., & Diaz, J. A. (1998). Thirty years of the Annual Survey of Deaf and Hard-of-Hearing Children and Youth: A glance over the decades. *American Annals of the Deaf, 142,* 72–76.

Holmes, T. H., & Rahe, R. H. (1967). The social readjustment rating scale. *Journal of Psychosomatic Research, 11,* 213–218.

Huffman, L. C., Bryan, Y. E., del Carmen, R., Pedersen, F. A., Doussard-Roosevelt, J. A., & Porges, S. W. (1998). Infant temperament and cardiac vagal tone: Assessments at twelve weeks of age. *Child Development, 69* (3), 624–635.

Hunt, J, M. (1965). Intrinsic motivation and its role in psychological development. In D. Levine (Ed.), *Nebraska symposium on motivation: Vol. 13. Current theory and research in motivation* (pp. 189–282). Lincoln: University of Nebraska Press.

Hupp, S. C. (1995). The impact of mental retardation on motivated behavior. In R. H. MacTurk & G. A. Morgan (Eds.), *Mastery motivation: Origins, conceptualizations, and applications* (pp. 221–236). Norwood, NJ: Ablex.

Huttenlocher, J., Haight, W., Bryk, A., Seltzer, M., & Lyons, T. (1991). Early vocabulary growth: Relation to input and gender. *Developmental Psychology, 27,* 236–248.

Ireton, H., & Thwing, E. (1974). *The Minnesota Child Development Inventory.* Minneapolis: University of Minnesota.

Isabella, R. A., & Belsky, J. (1991). Interactional synchrony and the origins of mother–infant attachment: A replication study. *Child Development, 62,* 373–384.

Isabella, R. A., Belsky, J., & von Eye, A. (1989). The origins of infant–mother attachment: An examination of interactional synchrony during the infant's first year. *Developmental Psychology, 25,* 12–21.

Jamieson, J. R. (1994a). Teaching as transaction: Vygotskian perspectives on deafness and mother–child interaction. *Exceptional Children, 60,* 434–449.

Jamieson, J. R. (1994b). Instructional discourse strategies: Differences between hearing and deaf mothers of deaf children. *First Language, 14,* 153–171.

Jamieson, J. R., & Pedersen, E. O. (1993). Deafness and mother–child interaction: Scaffolded instruction and the learning of problem-solving skills. *Early Development and Parenting, 2,* 229–242.

Jennings, K. D., Connors, R. E., Stegman, C. E., Sankaranarayan, P., & Mendelsohn, S. (1985). Mastery motivation in young preschoolers: Effect of a physical handicap and implications for educational programming. *Journal of the Division for Early Childhood, 9,* 162–169.

Jennings, K. D., Harmon, R. J., Morgan, G. A., Gaiter, J. L., & Yarrow, L. J. (1979). Exploratory play as an index of mastery motivation: Relationships to persistence, cognitive functioning, and environmental measures. *Developmental Psychology, 15,* 386–394.

Jennings, K. D., & MacTurk, R. H. (1995). The motivational characteristics of infants and children with physical and sensory impairments. In R. H. MacTurk & G. A. Morgan (Eds.), *Mastery motivation: Origins, conceptualizations, and applications* (pp. 201–219). Norwood, NJ: Ablex.

Joint Committee on Infant Hearing (2000). Year 2000 position statement: Principles and guidelines for early hearing detection. *Pediatrics 106*(4), 798–800.

Jones, E. G. (1995). Deaf and hearing parents' perceptions of family functioning. *Nursing Research, 44,* 102–105.

Jones. O. H. M. (1980). Prelinguistic communication skills in Downs syndrome and normal infants. In T. M. Field, S. Goldberg, D. Stern, & A. M. Sostek (Eds.), *High-risk infants and children* (pp. 205–226). New York: Academic Press.

Jones, T. W., & Jones, J. K. (2003). Challenges in educating young deaf children with multiple disabilities. In B. Bodner-Johnson & M. Sass-Lehrer (Eds.), *Early education for deaf and hard of hearing toddlers and their families: Integrating best practices and future perspectives.* (pp. 297–327). Baltimore: Brookes.

Kagan, J. (2001). The structure of temperament. In R. N. Emde & J. K. Hewitt (Eds.), *Infancy to early childhood: Genetic and environmental influences on developmental change.* New York: Oxford University Press.

Kagan, J., Arcus, D., Snidman, N., Feng, W.Y., Hendler, J., & Greene, S. (1994). Reactivity in infants: A cross-national comparison. *Developmental Psychology, 30,* 342–345.

Kantor, R. (1982). Communicative interaction: Mother modification and child acquisition of American Sign Language. *Sign Language Studies, 36,* 233–282.

Kaye, K., & Fogel, A. (1980). The temporal structure of face-to-face communication between mothers and infants. *Developmental Psychology,* 16, 454–464.

Kelly, C., & Dale, P. (1989). Cognitive skills associated with the onset of multiword utterances. *Journal of Speech and Hearing Research, 32,* 645–656.

Kenworthy, O. (1986). Caregiver–child interaction and language acquisition of hearing-impaired children. *Topics in Language Disorders, 6,* 1–11.

Kochanska, G., Coy, K. C., & Murray, K. T. (2001). The development of self-regulation in the first four years of life. *Child Development, 72,* 1091–1111.

Koester, L. S. (1986, April). *Rhythms and repetitions in infant interactions.* Presentation at the Fifth International Conference on Infant Studies, Los Angeles, CA. (Abstracted in *Infant Behavior and Development, 9,* 203.)

Koester, L. S. (1988). Rhythmicity in parental stimulation of infants. In P. G. Fedor-Freybergh (Ed.), *Prenatal and perinatal psychology and medicine* (pp. 143–152). Lancashire, UK: Parthenon.

Koester, L. S. (1992). Intuitive parenting as a model for understanding variations in parent–infant interactions. *American Annals of the Deaf, 137* (4), 362–369.

Koester, L. S. (1994). Early interactions and the socioemotional development of deaf infants. *Early Development and Parenting* (Special Edition), *3* (1), 51–60.

Koester, L. S. (1995). Characteristics of face-to-face interactions between hearing mothers and their deaf or hearing 9–month-olds. *Infant Behavior and Development, 18* (2), 145–153.

Koester, L. S., & Meadow-Orlans, K. P. (1990). Parenting a deaf child: Stress, strength and support. In D. F. Moores & K. P. Meadow-Orlans (Eds.), *Educational and developmental aspects of deafness* (pp. 299–320). Washington, DC: Gallaudet University Press.

Koester, L. S., Papoušek, H., & Papoušek, M. (1985, July). *Patterns of rhythmic stimulation by mothers with young infants: A comparison of multiple modalities.* Presentation at the Eighth Biennial Meeting of the International Society for the Study of Behavioral Development, Tours, France. (Abstracted in *Cahiers de Psychologie Cognitive, 5,* 270–271.)

Koester, L. S., Papoušek, H., & Smith-Gray, S. (2000). Intuitive parenting, communication, and interaction with deaf infants. In P. E. Spencer, C. J. Erting, & M. Marschark (Eds.), *The deaf child in the family and at school: Essays in honor of Kathryn P. Meadow-Orlans* (pp. 55–72). Mahwah, NJ: Erlbaum.

Koester, L. S., & Trimm, V. (1991 April). *Face-to-face interactions with deaf and hearing infants at 9 months: Do maternal or infant behaviors differ?* Paper presented as part of symposium entitled "Disruptions and Adaptations in Parent–Infant Interactions"; biennial meetings of the Society for Research in Child Development, Seattle, WA.

Kondo-Ikemura, K. (2001). Insufficient evidence. *American Psychologist, 56,* 825–826.

Krause, M. W., & Jacobs, F. (1990). Family assessment: Purposes and techniques. In S. J. Meisels & J. P. Shonkoff (Eds.), *Handbook of early childhood intervention* (pp. 303–325). Cambridge: Cambridge University Press.

Krauss, M. W., Upshur, C. C., Shonkoff, J. P., & Hauser-Cram, P. (1993). The impact of parent groups on mothers of infants with disabilities. *Journal of Early Intervention, 17,* 8–20.

Kusché, C. A., Garfield, T. S., & Greenberg, M. T. (1983). The understanding of emotional and social attributions in deaf adolescents. *Journal of Clinical Child Psychology, 12,* 153–160.

Lamb, M. E., Thompson, R. A., Gardner, W., & Charnov, E. L. (1985). *Infant–mother attachment: The origins and developmental significance of individual differences in strange situation behavior*. Hillsdale, NJ: Erlbaum.

Lang, H. G. (2003). Perspectives on the history of deaf education. In M. Marschark & P. Spencer (Eds.), *Oxford handbook of deaf studies, language, and education* (pp. 9–20). New York: Oxford University Press.

Langhorst, B., & Fogel, A. (March, 1982). *Cross validation of microanalytic approaches to face-to-face play*. Paper presented at the International Conference on Infant Studies, Austin, TX.

Launer, P. (1982, November). *Early signs of motherhood: Motherese in American Sign Language*. Paper presented at the ASHA convention, Toronto, CA.

Lawson, K. R., & Ruff, H. (1984). Infants' visual following: The effects of size and sound. *Developmental Psychology, 20,* 427–434.

Lederberg, A. (2003). Expressing meaning: From communicative intent to building a lexicon. In M. Marschark & P. Spencer (Eds.), *Oxford handbook of deaf studies, education, and language* (pp. 247–260). New York: Oxford University Press.

Lederberg, A., Binz, L., McIntyre, C., & McNorton, M. (1989, April). The impact of child deafness on mother–toddler conversation. Poster presenetd at the biennial meeting of the Society for Research in Child Development, Kansas City, KS.

Lederberg, A., & Everhart, V. (2000). Conversations between deaf children and their hearing mothers: Pragmatic and dialogic characteristics. *Journal of Deaf Studies and Deaf Education, 5,* 303–322.

Lederberg, A. R., & Golbach, T. (2002). Parenting stress and social support in hearing mothers of deaf and hearing children. *Journal of Deaf Studies and Deaf Education, 7*(4), 330–345.

Lederberg, A. R., & Mobley, C. E. (1990). The effect of hearing impairment on the quality of attachment and mother–toddler interaction. *Child Development, 61,* 1596–1604.

Lederberg, A. R., & Prezbindowski, A. K. (2000). Impact of child deafness on mother–toddler interaction: Strengths and weaknesses. In P. E. Spencer, C. J. Erting, & M. Marschark (Eds.), *The deaf child in the family and at school: Essays in honor of Kathryn P. Meadow-Orlans* (pp. 73–92). Mahwah, NJ: Erlbaum.

Lederberg, A., & Spencer, P. (2001). Vocabulary development of deaf and hard of hearing children. In M. Clark, M. Marschark, & M. Karchmer (Eds.), *Context, cognition, and deafness* (pp. 88–112). Washington, DC: Gallaudet University Press.

LeVine, R. A. (1995). Foreword. In R. L. Harwood, J. G. Miller, & N. Lucca Irizarry, *Culture and attachment, Perceptions of the child in context* (pp. ix–xi). New York: Guilford.

Lewis, M., & Feiring, C. (1989). Infant, mother, and mother–infant interaction behavior and subsequent attachment. *Child Development, 60,* 831–837.

Lipsitt, L. (1983). Stress in infancy: Toward understanding the origins of coping behavior. In N. Garmezy & M. Rutter (Eds.), *Stress, coping and development in children.* New York: McGraw-Hill.

Lipsitt, L. P. (1990). Learning and memory in infants. *Merrill-Palmer Quarterly, 36*(1), 53–66.

Loots, G., & Devisé, I., (2003). The use of visual–tactile communication strategies by deaf and hearing fathers and mothers of deaf infants. *Journal of Deaf Studies and Deaf Education, 8,* 31–42.

Lowe, M. (1975). Trends in the development of representational play in infants from one to three years—an observational study. *Journal of Child Psychology and Psychiatry, 16,* 33–47.

Ludwig, J. L. (1999). *An organizational construct approach to the study of mastery motivation in deaf and hearing infants.* Unpublished doctoral dissertation, Purdue University, Lafayette, IN.

Lyons-Ruth, K., & Jacobvitz, D. (1999). Attachment disorganization, unresolved loss, relational violence, and lapses in behavioral and attention strategies. In J. Cassidy & P. R. Shaver (Eds.), *Handbook of attachment: Theory, research, and clinical applications* (pp. 520–554). New York: Guilford.

Mace, A. L., Wallace, K. L., Whan, M. Q., & Stelmachowicz, P. G. (1991). Relevant factors in the identification of hearing loss. *Ear and Hearing, 12,* 287–293.

MacTurk, R. H. (1990). Expression of affect by deaf and hearing infants. In D. F. Moores & K. P. Meadow-Orlans (Eds.), *Research on educational and developmental aspects of deafness* (pp. 339–349). Washington, DC: Gallaudet University Press.

MacTurk, R. H., Day, P. [Spencer], & Meadow-Orlans, K. P. (1986, November). *Coping strategies in a stressful situation: Six-month-old deaf and hearing infants.* Poster session presented at the annual meeting of the International Society for Developmental Psychobiology, Annapolis, MD.

MacTurk, R. H., Hunter, F. T., McCarthy, M. E., Vietze, P. M., & McQuiston, S. (1985). Social mastery motivation in Down syndrome and nondelayed infants. *Topics in Early Childhood Special Education, 4,* 93–109.

MacTurk, R. H., McCarthy, M. E., Vietze, P. M., & Yarrow, L. J. (1987). Sequential analysis of mastery behavior in 6- and 12-month-old infants. *Developmental Psychology, 23,* 199–203.

MacTurk, R. H., & Morgan, G. A. (Eds.). (1995). *Mastery motivation: Origins, conceptualizations, and applications*. Norwood, NJ: Ablex.

MacTurk, R. H., & Trimm, V. M. (1989). Mastery motivation in deaf and hearing infants. *Early Education and Development, 1,* 19–34.

Maestas y Moores, J. (1980). Early linguistic environment: Interactions of deaf parents with their infants. *Sign Language Studies, 26,* 1–13.

Main, M., & Solomon, J. (1986). Discovery of an insecure-disorganized/disoriented attachment pattern: Procedures, findings, and implications for the classification of behavior. In T. B. Brazelton & M. Yogman (Eds.), *Affective development in infancy* (pp. 95–124). Norwood, NJ: Ablex.

Main, M., & Solomon, J. (1990). Procedures for identifying infants as disorganized/disoriented during the Ainsworth Strange Situation. In M. Greenberg, D. Cicchetti, & M. Cummings (Eds.), *Attachment in the preschool years: Theory, research and intervention* (pp. 121–160) Chicago: University of Chicago Press.

Mallory, B. L., Schein, J. O., & Zingle, H. W. (1992). Hearing offspring as visual language mediators in deaf-parented families. *Sign Language Studies, 76,* 193–213.

Mann, L. (1985). Play behaviors of deaf and hearing children. In D. Martin (Ed.), *Cognition, education, and deafness: Directions in research and instruction* (pp. 27–29). Washington, DC: Gallaudet University Press.

Marschark, M. (1993a). Origins and interactions in social, cognitive, and language development of deaf children. In M. Marschark & M. D. Clark (Eds.), *Psychological perspectives on deafness* (pp. 7–26). Hillsdale, NJ: Erlbaum.

Marschark, M. (1993b). *Psychological development of deaf children*. New York: Oxford University Press.

Marschark, M. (1997). *Raising and educating a deaf child.* New York: Oxford University Press.

Marschark, M., Lang, H. G., & Albertini, J. A. (2002). *Educating deaf students: From research to practice.* New York: Oxford University Press.

Marvin, R. S. (1977). An ethological-cognitive model for the attenuation of mother–child attachment behavior. In T. M. Alloway, L. Krames, & P. Pliner (Eds.), *Advances in the study of communication and affect: Vol. 3. Attachment behavior* (pp. 25–60). New York: Plenum.

Marvin, R. S., & Britner, P. A. (1999). Normative development: The ontogeny of attachment. In J. Cassidy & P. R. Shaver (Eds.), *Handbook of attachment: Theory, research, and clinical applications* (pp. 44–67). New York: Guilford.

Masataka, N. (1992). Motherese in a signed language. *Infant Behavior and Development, 15,* 453–460.

Masataka, N. (2000). The role of modality and input in the earliest stage of language acquisition: Studies of Japanese Sign Language. In C. Chamberlain, J. P. Morford, & R. I. Mayberry (Eds.), *Language acquisition by eye* (pp. 3–24). Mahwah, NJ: Erlbaum.

Maslin, C. A., & Morgan, G. A. (1985, April). *Measure of social competence: Toddlers' social and object orientation during mastery tasks.* Paper presented at the biennial meeting of the Society for Research in Child Development, Toronto, Canada.

Maslin-Cole, C., Bretherton, I., & Morgan, G. A. (1993). Toddler mastery motivation and competence: Links with attachment security, maternal scaffolding, and family climate. In D. J. Messer (Ed.), *Mastery motivation in early childhood: Development, measurement, and social processes* (pp. 205–229). London: Routledge.

Maslin-Cole, C., & Spieker, S. J. (1990). Attachment as a basis for independent motivation. In M. T. Greenberg, D. Cicchetti, & E. M. Cummings (Eds.), *Attachment in the preschool years: Theory, research, and intervention* (pp. 245–272). Chicago: University of Chicago Press.

Massie, H. N. (1982). Affective development and the organization of mother–infant behavior from the perspective of psychopathology. In E. Z. Tronick (Ed.), *Social interchange in infancy* (pp. 161–182). Baltimore: University Park Press.

Mavrolas, C. M. (1990). *Attachment behavior of hearing impaired infants and their hearing mothers: Maternal and infant contributions.* Unpublished doctoral dissertation, Northwestern University, Evanston, IL.

Mayer, S., & Musatti, T. (1992). Towards the use of symbol: Play with objects and communication with adults and peers in the second year. *Infant Behavior and Development, 15,* 1–13.

Mayes, L. C., & Carter, A. S. (1990). Emerging social regulatory capacities as seen in the still-face situation. *Child Development, 61,* 754–763.

Mayne, A., Yoshinaga-Itano, C., & Sedey, A. (1999). Receptive vocabulary development of infants and toddlers who are deaf or hard of hearing. *Volta Review, 100*(5), 29–52.

Mayne, A., Yoshinaga-Itano, C., Sedey, A., & Carey, A. (2000). Expressive vocabulary development of infants and toddlers who are deaf or hard of hearing. *The Volta Review, 100*(5), 1–28.

McCall, R. (1974). Exploratory manipulation and play in the human infant. *Monographs of the Society for Research in Child Development, 39* (2, Serial No. 155).

McCall, R. B. (1995). On definitions and measures of mastery motivation. In R. H. MacTurk & G. A. Morgan (Eds.), *Mastery motivation: Origins, conceptualizations, and applications* (pp. 273–292). Norwood, NJ: Ablex.

McCall, R. B., Eichorn, D. H., & Hogarty, P. S. (1977). Transitions in early mental development. *Monographs of the Society for Research in Child Development, 42* (3, Serial No. 171).

McCarthy, M. E., & McQuiston, S. (1983, April). *The relationship of contingent parental behaviors to infant motivation and competence.* Paper presented at the biennial meetings of the Society for Research in Child Development, Detroit, MI.

McCune, L. (1995). A normative study of representational play at the transition to language. *Developmental Psychology, 31,* 198–206.

McCune, L., DiPane, D., Fireoved, R., & Fleck, M. (1994). Play: A context for mutual regulation within mother–child interaction. In A. Slade & D. Wolf (Eds.), *Children at play: Clinical and developmental approaches to meaning and representation* (pp. 148–166). Oxford: Oxford University Press.

McCune-Nicolich, L. (1981). Toward symbolic functioning: Structure of early pretend games and potential parallels with language. *Child Development, 52,* 785–797.

McCune-Nicolich, L. (1983). *A manual for analyzing free play.* Unpublished manuscript.

McLinden, S. E. (1990). Mothers' and fathers' reports of the effects of a young child with special needs on the family. *Journal of Early Intervention, 14,* 249–259.

Meadow, K. P. (1967). *The effect of early manual communication and family climate on the deaf child's development.* Unpublished doctoral dissertation, University of California, Berkeley.

Meadow, K. P. (1968a). Early manual communication in relation to the deaf child's intellectual, social, and communicative functioning. *American Annals of the Deaf, 113,* 29–41.

Meadow, K. P. (1968b). Parental responses to the medical ambiguities of deafness. *Journal of Health and Social Behavior, 9,* 299–399.

Meadow, K. P. (1969). Self-image, family climate, and deafness. *Social Forces, 47,* 428–438.

Meadow, K. P. (1978). The "natural history" of a research project: An illustration of methodological issues with deaf children. In L. S. Liben (Ed.), *Deaf children: Developmental perspectives* (pp. 21–40). New York: Academic Press.

Meadow, K. P. (1980). *Deafness and child development.* Berkeley: University of California Press.

Meadow, K. P. (1984). Social adjustment of preschool children: Deaf and hearing, with and without other handicaps. *Topics in Early Childhood Special Education, 3,* 27–40.

Meadow, K. P., Greenberg, M. T., & Erting, C. (1983). Attachment behavior of deaf children with deaf parents. *Journal of the American Academy of Child Psychiatry, 22,* 23–28.

Meadow, K. P., Greenberg, M. T., Erting, C., & Carmichael, H. (1981). Interactions of deaf mothers and deaf preschool children: Comparisons with three other groups of deaf and hearing dyads. *American Annals of the Deaf, 126,* 454–468.

Meadow-Orlans, K. P. (1987). An analysis of the effectiveness of early intervention programs for hearing-impaired children. In M. J. Guralnick & F. C. Bennett (Eds.), *The effectiveness of early intervention for at-risk and handicapped children* (pp. 325–362). New York: Academic Press.

Meadow-Orlans, K. P. (2001). Social change and conflict: Context for research on deafness. In M. D. Clark, M. Marschark, & M. Karchmer (Eds.), *Context, cognition, and deafness* (pp. 161–178). Washington, DC: Gallaudet University Press.

Meadow-Orlans, K. P. (2002). Parenting with a sensory or physical disability. In M. H. Bornstein (Ed.), *Handbook of parenting* (Vol. 4, 2nd ed., pp. 259–293). Mahwah, NJ: Erlbaum.

Meadow-Orlans, K., & Erting, C. (2000). Deaf people in society. In P. Hindley & N. Kitson (2000). *Mental health and deafness* (pp. 3–24). London: Whurr.

Meadow-Orlans, K. P., Erting, C. J., Bridges-Cline, F., & Prezioso, C. (1985, August). *Deafness and infancy: Research in progress.* Paper presented at the meeting of the International Congress on Education of the Deaf, Manchester, UK.

Meadow-Orlans, K. P., Erting, C., Day, P. [Spencer], MacTurk, R. H., Prezioso, C., & Gianino, A. (1987a, August). *Deaf and hearing mothers of deaf and hearing infants: Interaction in the first year of life.* Paper presented at the meeting of the World Congress of the Deaf, Espoo, Finland.

Meadow-Orlans, K. P., MacTurk, R. H., Prezioso, C., Erting, C., & Day, P. [Spencer]. (1987b, April). Interactions of deaf and hearing mothers with three- and six-month-old infants. In A. Lederberg (Chair), *Relations between communication and social emotional development: Implications from research with deaf children.* Symposium conducted at the biennial meeting of the Society for Research in Child Development, Baltimore, MD.

Meadow-Orlans, K. P., Mertens, D. M., & Sass-Lehrer, M. A. (2003). *Parents and their deaf children: The early years.* Washington, DC: Gallaudet University Press.

Meadow-Orlans, K., & Steinberg, A. (1993). Effects of infant hearing loss and maternal support on mother–infant interactions at eighteen months. *Journal of Applied Developmental Psychology, 14,* 407–426.

Meier, R., & Newport, E. (1990). Out of the hands of babes: On a possible sign advantage in language acquisition. *Language, 66,* 1–23.

Messer, D. J. (1995). Mastery motivation: Past, present, and future. In R. H. MacTurk, & G. A. Morgan (Eds.), *Mastery motivation: Origins, conceptualizations, and applications* (pp. 293–316)). Norwood, NJ: Ablex.

Messer, D. J., McCarthy, M. E., McQuiston, S., MacTurk, R. H., Yarrow, L. J., & Vietze, P. M. (1986). Relation between mastery behavior in infancy and competence in childhood. *Developmental Psychology, 22,* 366–372.

Minde, K., Goldberg, S., Perrotta, M., Washington, J., Lojkasek, M., Corter, C., & Parker, K. (1989). Continuities and discontinuities in the development of 64 very small premature infants to 4 years of age. *Journal of Child Psychology and Child Psychiatry, 30,* 391–404.

Mindel, E. D., & Feldman, V. (1987). The impact of deaf children on their families. In E. D. Mindel & M. Vernon (Eds.), *They grow in silence: Understanding deaf children and adults* (2nd ed., pp. 1–30). Austin, TX: Pro-Ed.

Mitchell, R. E., & Karchmer, M. A. (2004, in press). Chasing the mythical ten percent: Parental hearing status of deaf and hard of hearing students in the United States. *Sign Language Studies.*

Mitchell, T. V., & Quittner, A. L. (1996). Multimethod study of attention and behavior problems in hearing-impaired children. *Journal of Clinical Child Psychology, 25* (1), 83–96.

Miyake, K., Chen, S-J, & Campos, J. (1985). Infant temperament, mother's mode of interaction, and attachment in Japan: An interim report. In I. Bretherton & E. Waters (Eds.), *Growing points of attachment theory and research* (pp. 276–297). *Monographs of the Society for Research in Child Development, 50* (1–2, Serial No. 209).

Moeller, M. (2000). Early intervention and language development in children who are deaf and hard of hearing. *Pediatrics 106*(3), e43.

Mohay, H. (2000). Language in sight: Mothers' strategies for making language visually accessible to children. In P. E. Spencer, C. J. Erting, & M. Marschark (Eds.), *The deaf child in the family and at school: Essays in honor of Kathryn P. Meadow-Orlans* (pp. 151–166). Mahwah, NJ: Erlbaum.

Mohay, H., Hindmarsh, G., & Zhao, S. (1994, June). *Growth patterns of preterm infants from one to nine years of age.* Poster presented at the biennial meetings of the International Conference on Infant Studies, Paris, France.

Moores, D. F. (1967). *Applications of the cloze procedure to the assessment of psycholinguistic functioning of deaf adolescents.* Unpublished doctoral dissertation, University of Illinois, Champagne.

Moores, D. F. (1970). An investigation of the psycholinguistic functioning of deaf adolescents. *Exceptional Children, 36,* 645–652.

Moores, D. F. (1978). Current research and theory with the deaf: Educational implications. In L. S. Liben (Ed.), *Deaf children: Developmental perspectives* (pp. 195–216). New York: Academic Press.

Moores, D. F. (2001). *Educating the deaf: Psychology, principles, and practices* (5th ed.). Boston: Houghton Mifflin.

Moores, D. F., & Oden, C. (1978). Educational needs of black deaf children. *American Annals of the Deaf, 122,* 313–318.

Moores, D. F., Weiss, K. L., & Goodwin, M. W. (1978). Early education programs for hearing-impaired children: Major findings. *American Annals of the Deaf, 123,* 925–936.

Morales, M., Mundy, P., & Rojas, J. (1998). Following the direction of gaze and language development in 6–month-olds. *Infant Behavior and Development, 21*(2), 373–377.

Morford, J. P., & Mayberry, R. I. (2000). A re-examination of "early exposure" and its implications for language acquisition by eye. In C. Chamberlain, J. P. Morford, & R. I. Mayberry (Eds.), *Language acquisition by eye* (pp.111–128). Mahwah, NJ: Erlbaum.

Morgan, G. A., Harmon, R. J., Maslin-Cole, C. A., Busch-Rossnagel, N. A., Jennings, K. A., Hauser-Cram, P., & Brockman, L. (1992). *Assessing perceptions of mastery motivation: The Dimensions of Mastery Questionnaire, its development, psychometrics, and use.* Unpublished manuscript, Colorado State University, Fort Collins, CO.

Morgan, G. A., MacTurk, R. H., & Hrncir, E. J. (1995). Mastery motivation: Overview, definitions, and conceptual issues. In R. H. MacTurk & G. A. Morgan (Eds.), *Mastery motivation: Origins, conceptualizations, and applications* (pp. 1–18). Norwood, NJ: Ablex.

Morgan, G. A., Maslin-Cole, C. A., Biringen, Z., & Harmon, R. J. (1991). Play assessment of mastery motivation in infants and young children. In C. E. Schaefer, K. Gitlin, & A. Sandgrund (Eds.), *Play diagnosis and assessment* (pp. 65–86). New York: Wiley.

Moses, K. L. (1985). Infant deafness and parental grief: Psychosocial early intervention. In F. Powell, T. Finitzo-Hieber, S. Friel-Patti, & D. Henderson (Eds.), *Education of the hearing impaired child* (pp. 86–102). San Diego: College-Hill.

Mundy, P., & Willoughby, J. (1996). Nonverbal communication, joint attention, and early socioemotional development. In M. Lewis & M. W. Sullivan (Eds.), *Emotional development in atypical children* (pp. 65–87). Mahwah, NJ: Erlbaum.

Murray, A. D. (1988). Newborn auditory brainstem-evoked responses (ABRs): Prenatal and contemporary correlates. *Child Development, 59,* 571–588.

Murray, L., & Trevarthen, C. (1985). Emotional regulation of interactions between two-month-olds and their mothers. In T. M. Field & N. A. Fox (Eds.), *Social perception in infants* (pp. 177–197). Norwood, NJ: Ablex.

Musselman, C., & Churchill, A. (1992). The effects of maternal conversational control on the language and social development of deaf children. *Journal of Childhood Communication Disorders, 14,* 99–117.

Musselman, C., & Churchill, A. (1993). Maternal conversational control and the development of deaf children: A test of the stage hypothesis. *First Language, 13,* 271–290.

Neville, H., & Lawson, D. (1987). Attention to central and peripheral visual space in a movement detection task: An event-related potential and behavioral study: II. Congenitally deaf adults. *Brain Research, 405,* 268–283.

Nicholas, J., Geers, A., & Kozak, V. (1994). Development of communicative function in young hearing-impaired and normally hearing children. *The Volta Review, 96,* 113–135.

Nienhuys, T. G., Horsborough, K. M., & Cross, T. G. (1985). Interaction between mothers of deaf or hearing children. *Applied Psycholinguistics, 6,* 121–139.

Nienhuys, T. G., & Tikotin, J. (1983). Pre-speech communication in hearing and hearing-impaired children. *Journal of the British Association of Teachers of the Deaf, 7*(6), 182–194.

Niskar, A. S., Kieszak, S. M., Holmes, A., Esteban, E., Rubin, C., & Brody, D. (1998). Prevalence of hearing loss among children 6 to 19 years of age. The third national health and nutrition examination survey. *JAMA, 279,* 1071–1075.

O'Connell, B., & Bretherton, I. (1984). Toddlers' play, alone and with mother: The role of maternal guidance. In I. Bretherton (Ed.), *Symbolic play: The development of social understanding* (pp. 337–368). Orlando, FL: Academic Press.

Ogura, T. (1991). A longitudinal study of the relationship between early language development and play development. *Journal of Child Language, 18,* 273–294.

Oller, D. (1980). The emergence of the sounds of speech in infancy. In G. Yeni-Komshian, J. Kavanagh, & C. Ferguson (Eds.), *Child phonology: Vol. 1. Production* (pp. 93–112). New York: Academic Press.

Oller, D., & Eilers, R. (1988). The role of audition in infant babbling. *Child Development, 59,* 441–449.

Orlansky, M., & Bonvillian, J. (1985). Sign language acquisition: Language development in children of deaf parents and implications for other populations. *Merrill-Palmer Quarterly, 32,* 127–143.

Orlansky, M. D., & Heward, W. L. (1981). *Voices: Interviews with handicapped people.* Columbus, OH: Merrill.

Padden, C. A. (1996). From the cultural to the bicultural: The modern deaf community. In I. Parasnis (Ed.), *Cultural and language diversity and the deaf experience* (pp. 79–98). New York: Cambridge University Press.

Padden, C., & Humphries, T. (1988). *Deaf in America: Voices from a culture.* Cambridge, MA: Harvard University Press.

Papoušek, H. (1977). Entwicklung der lernfahigkeit im sauglingsalter. In G. Nissen (Ed.), *Intelligenz, lernen und lernstorungen* (pp. 89–107). Berlin: Springer-Verlag.

Papoušek, H., & Papoušek, M. (1983). Biological basis of social interactions: Implications of research for an understanding of behavioral deviance. *Journal of Child Psychology and Psychiatry, 24*(1), 117–129.

Papoušek, H., & Papoušek, M. (1984). Qualitative transitions in integrative processes during the first trimester of human postpartum life. In H. F. R. Prechtl (Ed.), *Continuity of neural functions from prenatal to postnatal life* (pp. 220–244). London: Spastics International Medical Publications.

Papoušek, H., & Papoušek, M. (1987). Intuitive parenting: A dialectic counterpart to the infant's precocity in integrative capacities. In J. D. Osofsky (Ed.), *Handbook of infant development* (2nd ed., pp. 669–720). New York: Wiley.

Papoušek, H., & Papoušek, M. (1997). Fragile aspects of early social integration. In L. Murray & P. J. Cooper (Eds.), *Postpartum depression and child development* (pp. 35–52). New York: Guilford.

Papoušek, M. (1989). Determinants of responsiveness to infant vocal expression of emotional state. *Infant Behavior and Development, 12,* 507–524.

Papoušek, M., Papoušek, H., & Bornstein, M. (1985). The naturalistic vocal environment of young infants: On the significance of homogeneity and variability in parental speech. In T. M. Field & N. Fox (Eds.), *Social perception in infants* (pp. 269–297). Norwood, NJ: Ablex.

Papoušek, H., Papoušek, M., Suomi, S., & Rahn, C. (1991). Preverbal communication and attachment: Comparative views. In J. Gewirtz & W. Kurtines (Eds.), *Intersections with attachment* (pp. 97–122). Hillsdale, NJ: Erlbaum.

Parasnis, I., (1996). On interpreting the deaf experience within the context of cultural and language diversity. In I. Parasnis (Ed.), *Cultural and language diversity and the deaf experience* (pp. 3–19). New York: Cambridge University Press.

Paul, R. (1996). Clinical implications of the natural history of slow expressive language development. *Journal of Speech Language Pathology, 5,* 5–21.

Petitto, L. A. (1986). Language versus gesture: *Why sign languages are not acquired earlier than spoken languages.* Paper presented at the Theoretical Issues in Sign Language Research Conference. Rochester, NY.

Petitto, L. (1988). "Language" in the prelinguistic child. In F. Kessel (Ed.), *The development of language and language researchers* (pp. 187–221). Hillsdale, NJ: Erlbaum.

Petitto, L. A. (2000). The acquisition of natural signed languages: Lessons in the nature of human language and its biological foundations. In C. Chamberlain, J. P. Morford, & R. I. Mayberry (Eds.), *Language acquisition by eye* (pp. 41–50). Mahwah, NJ: Erlbaum.

Petitto, L. A., & Marentette, P. F. (1991). Babbling in the manual mode: Evidence for the ontogeny of language. *Science, 251,* 1493–1496.

Piaget, J. (1952). *The origins of intelligence in children.* New York: International Universities Press (originally published in 1936).

Piaget, J. (1962). *Play, dreams, and imitation in childhood.* New York: Norton.

Pine, J. M. (1994). The language of primary caregivers. In C. Gallaway & B. J. Richards (Eds.), *Input and interaction in language acquisition* (pp. 15–37). New York: Cambridge University Press.

Pipp-Siegel, S., Sedey, A. L., & Yoshinaga-Itano, C. (2002). Predictors of parental stress in mothers of young children. *Journal of Deaf Studies and Deaf Education 7,* 1–17.

Pipp-Siegel, S., Sedey, A. L., VanLeeuwen, A. M., & Yoshinaga-Itano, C. (2003). Mastery motivation and expressive language in young children with hearing loss. *Journal of Deaf Studies and Deaf Education 8,* 133–145.

Pollard, R. Q. (1992). Cross-cultural ethics in the conduct of deafness research. *Rehabilitation Psychology, 37,* 87–101.

Posada, G., & Jacobs, A. (2001). Child–mother attachment relationships and culture. *American Psychologist, 56,* 821–822.

Power, D. J., Wood, D. J., Wood, A., & MacDougall, J. (1990). Maternal control over conversations with hearing and deaf infants and young children. *First Language, 10,* 19–35.

Prendergast, S. G., & McCollum, J. A. (1996). Let's talk: The effect of maternal hearing status on interactions with toddlers who are deaf. *American Annals of the Deaf, 141,* 11–18.

Pressman, L. J., Pipp-Siegel, S., Yoshinaga-Itano, C., & Deas, A. (1999). Maternal sensitivity predicts language gain in preschool children who are deaf and hard of hearing. *Journal of Deaf Studies and Deaf Education, 4,* 294–304.

Pressman, L. J., Pipp-Siegel, S., Yoshinaga-Itano, C., Kubicek, L., & Emde, R. N. (2000). A comparison of the links between emotional availability and language gain in young children with and without hearing loss. In C. Yoshinaga-Itano & A. Sedey (Eds.), Language, speech, and social-emotional development of children who are deaf or hard of hearing: The early years. *Volta Review, 100*(5), 251–277.

Preston, P. (1994). *Mother father deaf: Living between sound and silence.* Cambridge, MA: Harvard University Press.

Prezbindowski, A. K., Adamson, L. B., & Lederberg, A. R. (1998). Joint attention in deaf and hearing 22-month-old children and their hearing mothers. *Journal of Applied Developmental Psychology, 19,* 377–387.

Prinz, P. M., & Prinz, E. A. (1979). Simultaneous acquisition of ASL and spoken English in a hearing child of deaf mother and hearing father: Phase I—Early lexical development. *Sign Language Studies, 25,* 283–296.

Prinz, P. M., & Prinz, E. A. (1981). Acquisition of ASL and spoken English in a hearing child of deaf mother and hearing father: Phase II—Early combinatorial patterns. *Sign Language Studies, 30,* 78–88.

Prior, M. R., Glazner, J., Sanson, A., & Debelle, G. (1988). Research note: Temperament and behavioural adjustment in hearing impaired children. *Journal of Child Psychology and Psychiatry, 29,* 209–216.

Quittner, A. L. (1991). Coping with a hearing-impaired child, A model of adjustment to chronic stress. In J. H. Johnson & S. B. Johnson (Eds.), *Advances in child health psychology* (pp. 206–223). Gainesville: University of Florida Press.

Quittner, A. L., Glueckauf, R. L., & Jackson, D. N. (1990). Chronic parenting stress: Moderating versus mediating effects of social support. *Journal of Personality and Social Psychology, 59,* 1266–1278.

Quittner, A. L., Smith, L. B., Osberger, M. J., Mitchell, T. V., & Katz, D. B. (1994). The impact of audition on the development of visual attention. *Psychological Science,* 5, 347–353.

Rayson, B. (1987). Deaf parents of hearing children. In E. D. Mindel & M. Vernon (Eds.), *They grow in silence: Understanding deaf children and adults* (2nd ed., pp. 103–110). Austin, TX: Pro-Ed.

Rea, C. A., Bonvillian, J. D., & Richards, H. C. (1988). Mother–infant interactive behaviors: Impact of maternal deafness. *American Annals of the Deaf, 133,* 317–324.

Redding, R. E., Harmon, R. J., & Morgan, G. A. (1990). Maternal depression and infants' mastery behaviors. *Infant Behavior and Development, 13,* 391–396.

Reilly, J. S., & Bellugi, U. (1996). Competition on the face: Affect and language in ASL motherese. *Journal of Child Language, 23,* 219–239.

Reis, P. W. (1994). Prevalence and characteristics of persons with hearing trouble: United States, 1990–91. *Vital and Health Statistics,* Series 10, No. 188. U.S. Department of Health and Human Services Publication No. [PHS] 94–1516.

Richards, B. J. (1994). Child-directed speech and influences on language acquisition: Methodology and interpretation. In C. Gallaway & B. J. Richards (Eds.),

Input and interaction in language acquisition (pp. 74–106). New York: Cambridge University Press.

Rienzi, B. M. (1990). Influence and adaptability in families with deaf parents and hearing children. *American Annals of the Deaf, 135,* 402–408.

Riksen-Walraven, J. M. (1978). Effects of caregiver behavior on habituation rate and self-efficacy in infants. *International Journal of Behavioral Development, 1,* 105–130.

Riksen-Walraven, J. M., Meij, H. T., van Roozendaal, J., & Koks, J. (1993). Mastery motivation in toddlers as related to quality of attachment. In D. J. Messer (Ed.), *Mastery motivation in early childhood: Development, measurement, and social processes* (pp. 189–204). New York: Routledge.

Robinson, L. D., & Weathers, O. D. (1974). Family therapy of deaf parents and hearing children: A new dimension in psychotherapeutic intervention. *American Annals of the Deaf, 119,* 325–330.

Robson, (1967). The role of eye-to-eye contact in maternal–infant attachment. *Journal of Child Psychology and Psychiatry, 8,* 13–25.

Rodda, M., & Grove, C. (1987). *Language, cognition, and deafness.* Hillsdale, NJ: Erlbaum.

Roskies, E. (1972). *Abnormality and normality: The mothering of thalidomide children.* Ithaca, NY: Cornell University Press.

Roesser, R. W., & Eccles, J. S. (2000). Schooling and mental health. In A. J. Sameroff & M. Lewis (Eds.), *Handbook of developmental psychopathology* (2nd ed., pp. 135–156). New York: Kluwer Academic/Plenum.

Ross, S., Cohn, J. F., & Campbell, S. B. (1991, April). Infant response in the still-face predicts attachment security. Paper presented at the biennial meetings of the Society for Research in Child Development, Seattle, WA.

Rothbaum, F., Weisz, J., Pott, M., Miyake, K., & Morelli, G. (2000). Attachment and culture: Security in the United States and Japan. *American Psychologist, 55,* 1093–1104.

Rothbaum, F., Weisz, J., Pott, M., Miyake, K., & Morelli, G. (2001). Deeper into attachment and culture. *American Psychologist, 56,* 827–829.

Royster, M. A. (1981). Deaf parents: A personal perspective. *The Deaf American, 34,* 19–22.

Rubin, K., Fein, G., & Vandenburg, B. (1983). Play. In P. Mussen (Series Ed.) & E. M. Hetherington (Vol. Ed.), *Handbook of child psychology: Vol. 4. Socialization, personality, and social development* (pp. 694–774). New York: Wiley.

Ruff, H. A. (1986). Components of attention during infants' manipulative exploration. *Child Development, 57,* 105–114.

Ruff, H. A., & Rothbart, M. K. (1996). *Attention in early development: Themes and variations.* New York: Oxford University Press.

Rutherford, S. D. (1989). Funny in deaf—Not in hearing. In S. Wilcox, (Ed.), *American Deaf culture: An anthology* (pp. 65–82). Burtonsville, MD: Linstok.

Sagi, A., Donnell, F., van IJzendoorn, M. H., Mayseless, O., & Aviezer, O. (1994). Sleeping out of home in a kibbutz communal arrangement: It makes a difference for infant–mother attachment. *Child Development, 65,* 992–1004.

Sagi, A., Koren-Karie, N., Gini, M., Ziv, Y., & Joels, T. (2002). Shedding further light on the effects of various types and quality of early child care on infant–mother attachment relationship: The Haifa Study of Early Child Care. *Child Development, 73,* 1166–1186.

Salisbury, C. L. (1987). Stressors of parents with young handicapped and nonhandicapped children. *Journal of the Division for Early Childhood, 11*, 154–160.

Sameroff, A. J., & Cavanaugh, P J. (1979). Learning in infancy: A developmental perspective. In J. D. Osofsky (Ed.), *Handbook of infant development* (pp. 344–392). New York: Wiley.

Sameroff, A. J., & Fiese, B. H. (1990). Transactional regulation and early intervention. In S. J. Meisels & J. P. Shonkoff (Eds.), *Handbook of early childhood intervention* (pp. 119–149). Cambridge: Cambridge University Press.

Sass-Lehrer, M., & Bodner-Johnson, B. (2003). Early intervention: Current approaches to family-centered programming. In M. Marschark & P. Spencer (Eds.), *Oxford handbook of deaf studies, language, and education* (pp. 65–81). New York: Oxford University Press.

Schaffer, H. R. (1979). Acquiring the concept of the dialogue. In M. H. Bornstein & W. Kessen (Eds.), *Psychological development from infancy: Image to intention* (pp. 279–305). Hillsdale, NJ: Erlbaum.

Schaffer, H. R. (1989). Early social development. In A. Slater & G. Bremner (Eds.), *Infant development* (pp. 189–210). Hillsdale, NJ: Erlbaum.

Schein, J. D. (1996). The demography of deafness. In P. C. Higgins & J. E. Nash (Eds.), *Understanding deafness socially* (pp. 21–43). Springfield, IL: Charles C Thomas.

Schick, B. (2003). The development of American Sign Language and manually-coded English systems. In M. Marschark & P. Spencer (Eds.), *Oxford handbook of deaf studies, education, and language* (pp. 219–231). New York: Oxford University Press.

Schiff, N. B., & Ventry, I. M. (1976). Communication problems in hearing children of deaf parents. *Journal of Speech and Hearing Disorders, 41*, 348–358.

Schiff-Myers, N. (1993). Hearing children of deaf parents. In D. Bishop & K. Mogford (Eds.), *Language development in exceptional circumstances* (pp. 47–61). Hove, East Sussex, UK: Erlbaum.

Schildroth, A. N. (1994) Cytomegalovirus and deafness. *American Journal of Audiology, 3*, 27–38.

Schildroth, A. N., & Hotto, S. A. (1993). Annual survey of hearing-impaired children and youth: 1991–92 school year. *American Annals of the Deaf, 138*, 163–171.

Schirmer, B. (1989). Relationships between imaginative play and language development in hearing-impaired children. *American Annals of the Deaf*, 134, 219–222.

Schlesinger, H. S. (1972). Language acquisition in four deaf children. In H. S. Schlesinger & K. P. Meadow, *Sound and sign: Childhood deafness and mental health* (pp. 45–87). Berkeley: University of California Press.

Schlesinger, H. S. (1985). Deafness, mental health, and language. In F. Powell, T. Finitzo-Hieber, S. Friel-Patti, & D. Henderson (Eds.), *Education of the hearing impaired child* (pp. 103–116). San Diego: College-Hill.

Schlesinger, H. S. (1987). Effects of powerlessness on dialogue and development: Disability, poverty, and the human condition. In B. W. Heller, L. S. Flohr, & L. S. Zegans (Eds.), *Psychosocial interventions with sensorially disabled persons* (pp. 1–27). Orlando, FL: Grune and Stratton.

Schlesinger, H. S. (2000). A developmental model applied to problems of deafness. *Journal of Deaf Studies and Deaf Education, 5*, 349–361.

Schlesinger, H. S., & Meadow, K. P. (1972). *Sound and sign: Childhood deafness and mental health*. Berkeley: University of California Press.

Schoetzau, A., & Papoušek, H. (1977). Maternal behaviors in visually communicating with their newborn [German]. *Zeitschrift fur Entwicklungspsychologie und Padagogische Psychologie, 9,* 231–239.

Seifer, R., & Vaughn, B. E. (1995). Mastery motivation within a general organizational model of competence. In R. H. MacTurk & G. A. Morgan (Eds.), *Mastery motivation: Origins, conceptualizations, and applications* (pp. 95–115). Norwood, NJ: Ablex.

Selmi, A., & Rueda, R. (1998). A naturalistic study of collaborative play transformations of preschoolers with hearing impairments. *Journal of Early Intervention, 21*(4), 299–307.

Shonkoff, J. P., Hauser-Cram, P., Krauss, M. K., & Upshur, C. C. (1992). Development of infants with disabilities and their families. *Monographs of the Society for Research in Child Development, 57* (6, Serial No. 230).

Shore, C., O'Connell, B., & Bates, E. (1984). First sentences in language and symbolic play. *Developmental Psychology, 20,* 872–880.

Sidransky, R. (1990). *In silence: Growing up in a deaf world.* New York: St. Martin's Press.

Singer, D., & Lenahan, M. (1976). Imagination content in dreams of deaf children. *American Annals of the Deaf, 121,* 44–48.

Singleton, J. L., Goldin-Meadow, S., & McNeill, D. (1995). The cataclysmic break between gesticulation and sign: Evidence against a unified continuum of gestural communication. In K. Emmorey & J. S. Reilly (Eds.), *Language, gesture, and space* (pp. 287–312). Hillsdale, NJ: Erlbaum.

Slade, A. (1987a). Quality of attachment and early symbolic play. *Developmental Psychology, 23,* 78–85.

Slade, A. (1987b). A longitudinal study of maternal involvement and symbolic play during the toddler period. *Child Development, 58,* 367–375.

Smith, C., Adamson, L., & Bakeman, R. (1988). Interactional predictors of early language. *First Language, 8,* 143–156.

Smith, L., Quittner, A., Osberger, M., & Miyamoto, R. (1998). Audition and visual attention: The developmental trajectory in deaf and hearing populations. *Developmental Psychology, 34*(5), 840–850.

Snow, C. E. (1984). Parent–child interaction and the development of communicative ability. In R. L. Schiefelbusch & J. Pickar (Eds.), *The development of communicative competence* (pp. 69–107). Baltimore: University Park Press.

Snyder, L., & Yoshinaga-Itano, C. (1999). Specific play behaviors and the development of communication in children with hearing loss. *The Volta Review, 100*(3), 165–185.

Solomon, J., & George, C. (1999). The measurement of attachment security in infancy and childhood. In J. Cassidy & P. R. Shaver (Eds.), *Handbook of attachment: Theory, research, and clinical applications* (pp. 287–316). New York: Guilford.

Spencer, P. (1996). The association between language and play: Evidence from deaf toddlers. *Child Development, 67,* 867–876.

Spencer, P. (1998, July). *Communication, attention, and symbolic development: Mothers and infants as an interactive system.* Symposium poster presented at the International Conference for the Study of Behavioural Development, Berne, Switzerland.

Spencer, P. E. (2000). Every opportunity: A case study of hearing parents and their deaf child. In P. E. Spencer, C. J. Erting, & M. Marschark (Eds.), *The deaf child in the family and at school, Essays in honor of Kathryn P. Meadow-Orlans* (pp. 111–132). Mahwah, NJ: Erlbaum.

Spencer, P. E. (2002). Language development of children with cochlear implants. In J. Christiansen & I. Leigh, *Children with cochlear implants: Ethics and choices* (pp. 222–249). Washington, DC: Gallaudet University Press.

Spencer, P. E. (2003). Mother–child interaction. In B. Bodner-Johnson & M. Sass-Lehrer (Eds.), *Early education for deaf and hard of hearing toddlers and their families: Integrating best practices and future perspectives* (pp. 333–372). Baltimore: Brookes.

Spencer, P. E., Bodner-Johnson, B. A., & Gutfreund, M. K. (1992). Interacting with infants with a hearing loss: What can we learn from mothers who are deaf? *Journal of Early Intervention, 16,* 64–78.

Spencer, P., & Deyo, D. (1993). Cognitive and social aspects of deaf children's play. In M. Marschark & M. D. Clark (Eds.), *Psychological perspectives on deafness* (pp. 65–92). Hillsdale, NJ: Erlbaum.

Spencer, P., Deyo, D., & Grindstaff, N. (1990). Symbolic play behavior of deaf and hearing toddlers. In D. Moores & K. Meadow-Orlans (Eds.), *Educational and developmental aspects of deafness* (pp. 390–406). Washington, DC: Gallaudet University Press.

Spencer, P., Deyo, D., & Grindstaff, N. (1991). Symbolic play behaviors of normally-developing deaf toddlers. In D. Martin (Ed.), *Advances in cognition, education, and deafness: Directions for research and instruction* (pp. 216–222). Washington, DC: Gallaudet University Press.

Spencer, P. E., & Gutfreund, M. (1990). Directiveness in mother–infant interactions. In D. F. Moores & K. P. Meadow-Orlans (Eds.), *Educational and developmental aspects of deafness* (pp. 350–365). Washington, DC: Gallaudet University Press.

Spencer, P., & Hafer, J. (1998). Play as "window" and "room": Assessing and supporting the cognitive and linguistic development of deaf infants and young children. In M. Marschark & D. Clark (Eds.), *Psychological perspectives on deafness* (Vol. 2, pp. 131–152). Mahwah, NJ: Erlbaum.

Spencer, P. E., & Kelly, A. (1993, March). *Deaf infants' coordination of attention to persons and objects.* Presented at the conference of the Society for Research in Child Development. New Orleans, LA.

Spencer, P. E., & Lederberg, A. (1997). Different modes, different models: Communication and language of young deaf children and their mothers. In L. Adamson & M. Romski (Eds.), *Communication and language acquisition: Discoveries from atypical development* (pp. 203–230). Baltimore: Brookes.

Spencer, P. E., & Marschark, M. (2003). Cochlear implants: Issues and implications. In M. Marschark & P. Spencer (Eds.), *Oxford handbook of deaf studies, language, and education* (pp. 434–450). New York: Oxford University Press.

Spencer, P. E., & Meadow-Orlans, K. P. (1996). Play, language, and maternal responsiveness: A longitudinal study of deaf and hearing infants. *Child Development, 67,* 3176–3191.

Sroufe, A., & Waters, E. (1977). Attachment as an organizational construct. *Child Development, 48,* 1184–1199.

Stack, D. M., & Muir, D. W. (1990). Tactile stimulation as a component of social interchange: New interpretations for the still-face effect. *British Journal of Developmental Psychology, 8,* 131–145.

Stern, D. N. (2002). *The first relationship, infant and mother.* Cambridge, MA: Harvard University Press. (Original work published 1977).

Stern, D. N. (1985). *The interpersonal world of the infant: A view from psychoanalysis and developmental psychology.* New York: Basic Books.

Stern, D. N., & Gibbon, J. (1979). Temporal expectancies of social behaviors in mother–infant play. In E. B. Thoman (Ed.), *Origins of the infant's social responsiveness* (pp. 409–430). Hillsdale, NJ: Erlbaum.

Stern, D. N., Hofer, L., Haft, W., & Dore, J. (1985). Affect attunement: The sharing of feeling states between mother and infant by means of inter-modal fluency. In T. M. Field & N. A. Fox (Eds.), *Social perception in infants* (pp. 249–268). Norwood, NJ: Ablex.

Stewart, D. A. (1991). *Deaf sport: The impact of sports within the deaf community.* Washington, DC: Gallaudet University Press.

Stifter, C. A., & Moyer, D. (1991). The regulation of positive affect: Gaze aversion activity during mother–infant interaction. *Infant Behavior and Development, 14,* 111–123.

Stinson, M. S. (1974). Relations between maternal reinforcement and help and the achievement motive in normal-hearing and hearing-impaired sons. *Developmental Psychology, 10,* 348–353.

Stinson, M. S. (1978). Deafness and motivation for achievement: Research with implications for parent counseling. *The Volta Review, 80,* 140–148.

Stuckless, E. R., & Birch, J. W. (1966). The influence of early manual communication on the linguistic development of deaf children. *American Annals of the Deaf, 111,* 452–460; 499–504.

Supalla, S. J. (1992). *The book of name signs. Naming in American Sign Language.* San Diego: DawnSignPress.

Swisher, M. (1984). Signed input of hearing mothers to deaf children. *Language Learning, 34,* 69–85.

Swisher, M. V. (1992). The role of parents in developing visual turn-taking in their young deaf children. *American Annals of the Deaf, 137,* 92–100.

Swisher, M. V. (1993). Perceptual and cognitive aspects of recognition of signs in peripheral vision. In M. Marschark & M. D. Clark (Eds.), *Psychological perspectives on deafness* (pp. 209–227). Hillsdale, NJ: Erlbaum.

Swisher, M. V. (2000). Learning to converse: How deaf mothers support the development of attention and conversational skills in their young deaf children. In P. E. Spencer, C. J. Erting, & M. Marschark (Eds.), *The deaf child in the family and at school: Essays in honor of Kathryn P. Meadow-Orlans* (pp. 21–39). Mahwah, NJ: Erlbaum.

Switzky, H. N., Haywood, H. C., & Isett, R. (1974). Exploration, curiosity, and play in young children: Effects of stimulus complexity. *Developmental Psychology, 10,* 321–329.

Tabachnick, B. G., & Fidell, L. S. (1996). *Using multivariate statistics* (3rd ed.). New York: HarperCollins.

Tamis-LeMonda, C. S., & Bornstein, M. H. (1994). Specificity in mother–toddler language-play relations across the second year. *Developmental Psychology, 30,* 283–292.

Tamis-LeMonda, C. S., Bornstein, M. H., & Baumwell, L. (2001). Maternal responsiveness and children's achievement of language milestones. *Child Development, 72(*3), 748–767.

Thoits, P. A. (1983). Dimensions of life events that influence psychological distress: An evaluation and synthesis of the literature. In H. B. Kaplan (Ed.), *Psychosocial stress, Trends in theory and research* (pp. 33–103). New York: Academic Press.

Thomas, A., & Chess, S. (1977). *Temperament and development.* New York: Brunner/Mazel.

Thompson, R. A. (1990). Vulnerability in research: A developmental perspective on research risk. *Child Development, 61,* 1–16.

Thompson, R. A. (1999). Early attachment and later development. In J. Cassidy & P. R. Shaver (Eds.), *Handbook of attachment: Theory, research, and clinical applications* (pp. 265–286). New York: Guilford.

Toda, S., & Fogel. A. (1993). Infant response to the still-face situation at 3 and 6 months. *Developmental Psychology, 29,* 532–538.

Tolman, E. C. (1932). *Purposive behavior in animals and man.* New York: Appleton-Century.

Tomasello, M. (1988). The role of joint attentional processes in early language development. *Language Sciences, 10,* 69–88.

Tomasello, M., & Farrar, J. (1986). Joint attention and early language. *Child Development, 57,* 1454–1463.

Traci, M., & Koester, L. S. (2003). A transactional approach to understanding the development of deaf infants. In M. Marschark & P. Spencer (Eds.), *Oxford handbook of deaf studies, language, and education* (pp. 190–202). New York: Oxford University Press.

Trevarthen, C. (1979). Instincts for human understanding and for cultural cooperation: Their development in infancy. In M. von Cranach, K. Foppa, W. Lepenics, & D. Ploog (Eds.), *Human ethology: Claims and limits of a new discipline* (pp. 530–594). Cambridge: Cambridge University Press.

Trevarthen, C., & Aitken, K. J. (2001). Infant intersubjectivity: Research, theory, and clinical applications. *Journal of Child Psychology and Psychiatry, and Allied Disciplines, 42*(1), 3–48.

Tronick, E. Z. (1989). Emotions and emotional communication in infants. *American Psychologist, 44,* 112–119.

Tronick, E. Z., Als, H., & Adamson, L. (1979). Structure of early face-to-face communicative interactions. In M. Bullowa (Ed.), *Before speech: The beginnings of human communication* (pp. 349–372). Cambridge: Cambridge University Press.

Tronick, E., Als, H., Adamson, L., Wise, S., & Brazelton, T. (1978). The infant's response to entrapment between contradictory messages in face-to-face interaction. *Journal of the American Academy of Child Psychiatry, 17,* 1–13.

Tronick, E. Z., Als, H., & Brazelton, T. B. (1980). Monadic phases: A structural descriptive analysis of infant–mother face to face interaction. *Merrill-Palmer Quarterly, 26,* 3–24.

Tronick, E. Z., & Field, T. (Eds.). (1986). *Maternal depression and infant disturbance.* San Francisco: Jossey-Bass.

Tronick, E. Z., Ricks, M., & Cohn, J. F. (1982). Maternal and infant affective exchange: Patterns of adaptation. In T. Field & A. Fogel (Eds.), *Emotion and early interaction* (pp. 83–100). Hillsdale, NJ: Erlbaum.

Upshur, C. C. (1991). Mothers' and fathers' ratings of benefits of early intervention services. *Journal of Early Intervention, 15,* 345–357.

Vadasy, P. F., Fewell, R. R., Greenberg, M. T., Dermond, N. L., & Meyer, D. J. (1986). Follow-up evaluation of the effects of involvement in the fathers' program. *Topics in Early Childhood Special Education, 6,* 16–31.

van IJzendoorn, M. H., Goldberg, S., Kroonenberg, P. M., & Frenkel, O. J. (1992). The relative effects of maternal and child problems on the quality of attachment: A meta-analysis of attachment in clinical samples. *Child Development, 63,* 840–858.

van IJzendoorn, M. H., & Sagi, A. (2001). Cultural blindness or selective inattention? *American Psychologist, 56,* 824–825.

Vaughn, B. E. & Waters, E. (1990). Attachment behavior at home and in the laboratory: Q-sort observations and Strange Situation classifications of one-year-olds. *Child Development, 61,* 1965–1973.

Vernon, M., & Koh, S. D. (1970). Early manual communication and deaf children's achievement. *American Annals of the Deaf, 115,* 527–536.

Vibbert, M., & Bornstein, M. (1989). Specific associations between domains of mother–child interaction and toddler referential language and pretense play. *Infant Behavior and Development, 12,* 163–184.

Volterra, V., & Iverson, J. M. (1995). When do modality factors affect the course of language acquisition? In K. Emmorey & J. S. Reilly (Eds.), *Language, gesture, and space* (pp. 371–390). Hillsdale, NJ: Erlbaum.

Vondra, J. I., & Barnett, D. (1999). Atypical attachment in infancy and early childhood among children at developmental risk. *Monographs of the Society for Research in Child Development, 64* (3, Serial No. 258).

Vondra, J. I., & Jennings, K. D. (1990). Infant mastery motivation: The issue of discriminant validity. *Early Education and Development, 1,* 340–353.

Vygotsky, L. (1978). *Mind in society: The development of higher psychological processes.* Cambridge, MA: Harvard University Press.

Wachs, T. D. (1987). Specificity of environmental action as manifest in environmental correlates of infants' mastery motivation. *Developmental Psychology, 23,* 782–790.

Wachs, T. D., & Combs, T. T. (1995). The domains of infant mastery motivation. In R. H. MacTurk & G. A. Morgan (Eds.), *Mastery motivation: Origins, conceptualizations, and applications* (pp. 147–164). Norwood, NJ: Ablex.

Walden, T., & Knieps, L. (1996). Reading and responding to social signals. In M. Lewis & M. W. Sullivan (Eds.), *Emotional development in atypical children* (pp. 29–42). Mahwah, NJ: Erlbaum.

Walker, L. A. (1986). *A loss for words: The story of deafness in a family.* New York: Harper & Row.

Waxman, R. P. (1995). *A longitudinal study of deaf and hearing mothers' use of visual–tactile attentional strategies.* Unpublished doctoral dissertation, The American University, Washington, DC.

Waxman, R. P., & Spencer, P. E. (1997). What mothers do to support infant visual attention: Sensitivities to age and hearing status. *Journal of Deaf Studies and Deaf Education, 2,* 104–114.

Waxman, R., Spencer, P.E., & Poisson, S. S. (1996). Reciprocity, responsiveness, and timing in interactions between mothers and deaf and hearing children. *Journal of Early Intervention, 20* (4), 341–355.

Wedell-Monnig, J., & Lumley, J. (1980). Child deafness and mother–child interaction. *Child Development, 51,* 766–774.

Weinberg, M. K., & Tronick, E. Z. (1991, April). *Stability of infant social and coping behaviors and affective displays between 6 and 15 months: Age-appropriate tasks and stress bring out stability.* Paper presented at the biennial meetings of the Society for Research in Child Development, Seattle, WA.

Weiner, K., Kun, A., & Benesh-Weiner, M. (1980). The development of mastery, emotions, and morality from an attributional perspective. In A. Collings, (Ed.), *Minnesota symposium on child psychology* (Vol. 14), (pp. 235–252). Hillsdale, NJ, Erlbaum.

Weinfield, N. S., Sroufe, L. A., Egeland, B., & Carlson, E. A. (1999). The nature of individual differences in infant–caregiver attachment. In J. Cassidy & P. R. Shaver (Eds.), *Handbook of attachment: Theory, research, and clinical applications* (pp. 68–88). New York: Guilford.

Weinraub, M., & Wolf, B. M. (1987). Stressful life events, social supports, and parent–child interaction: Similarities and differences in single-parent and two-parent families. In C. F. Z. Boukydis (Ed.), *Research on support for parents and infants in the postnatal period* (pp. 114–135). Norwood, NJ: Ablex.

Weisel, A. (1988). Parental hearing status, reading comprehension skills and social-emotional adjustment. *American Annals of the Deaf, 133* (4), 356–359.

Weismer, S., & Evans, J. (2002). The role of processing limitations in early identification of specific language impairment. *Topics in Language Disorders, 22*(3), 15–29.

Wenar, C. (1972). Executive competence and spontaneous social behavior in one-year-old infants. *Child Development, 43,* 256–260.

White, R. W. (1959). Motivation reconsidered: The concept of competence. *Psychological Review, 66,* 297–333.

White, R. W. (1963). Ego and reality in psychoanalytic theory. *Psychological Issues, 3,* 1–40.

Wilcox, S. (Ed.). (1989). *American Deaf culture: An anthology*. Burtonsville, MD: Linstok.

Wilson, S., & Spencer, P. (April, 1997). *Maternal topic responsiveness and child language: A cross-cultural, cross-modality replication*. Poster presented at the biennial meetings of the Society for Research in Child Development, Washington, DC.

Wolff, A. B., & Harkins, J. E. (1986). Multihandicapped students. In A. N. Schildroth & M. A. Karchmer (Eds.), *Deaf children in America* (pp. 55–82). San Diego: College-Hill.

Woll, B., & Kyle, J. G. (1989). Communication and language development in children of deaf parents. In S. von Tetzchner, L. S. Siegel, & L. Smith (Eds.), *The social and cognitive aspects of normal and atypical language development* (pp. 129–144). New York: Springer-Verlag.

Woll, B., & Ladd, P. (2003) Deaf communities. In M. Marschark & P. Spencer (Eds.), *Oxford handbook of deaf studies, language, and education* (pp. 151–163). New York: Oxford University Press.

Wood, D. J. (1982). The linguistic experiences of the prelingually hearing-impaired child. *Journal of the British Association of Teachers of the Deaf, 6,* 86–93.

Wood, D. (1989). Social interaction as tutoring. In M. Bornstein & J. Bruner (Eds.), *Interaction in human development* (pp. 59–80). Hillsdale, NJ: Erlbaum.

Wood, D., Wood, H., Griffiths, A., & Howarth, I. (1986). *Teaching and talking with deaf children*. New York: Wiley.

Yarrow, L. J., MacTurk, R. H., Vietze, P. M., McCarthy, M. E., Klein, R. P., & McQuiston, S. (1984). Developmental course of parental stimulation and its relationship to mastery motivation during infancy. *Developmental Psychology, 20,* 492–503.

Yarrow, L. J., McQuiston, S., MacTurk, R. H., McCarthy, M. E., Klein, R. P., & Vietze, P. M. (1983). Assessment of mastery motivation during the first year of life: Contemporaneous and cross-age relationships. *Developmental Psychology, 19,* 159–171.

Yarrow, L. J., Morgan, G. A., Jennings, K. D., Harmon, R. J., & Gaiter, J. L. (1982). Infants' persistence at tasks: Relationships to cognitive functioning and early experience. *Infant Behavior and Development, 5,* 131–141.

Yarrow, L. J., Rubenstein, J. L., & Pedersen, F. A. (1975). *Infant and environment: Early cognitive and motivational development.* Washington, DC: Hemisphere, Halsted, Wiley.

Yoshinaga-Itano, C. (2003). From screening to early identification and intervention: Discovering predictors to successful outcomes for children with significant hearing losses. *Journal of Deaf Studies and Deaf Education, 8,* 11–30.

Yoshinaga-Itano, C., Sedey, A. L., Coulter, D. K., & Mehl, A. L. (1998). Language of early- and later-identified children with hearing loss. *Pediatrics, 105,* 1161–1171.

Yoshinaga-Itano, C., Snyder, L., & Day, D. (1998). The relationship of language and symbolic play in children with hearing loss. *The Volta Review,* 100(3), 135–164.

Index